Pechalba Down Under

Macedonians in Australia

Nick Anastasovski

Connor Court Publishing

Published in 2021 by Connor Court Publishing Pty Ltd

Connor Court Publishing Pty Ltd.
PO Box 7257
Redland Bay QLD 4165
sales@connorcourt.com
www.connorcourt.com

ISBN: 9781922449474

Cover Design by Maria Giordano

Cover illustration: Risto Turpin (left) and Naume Koiov (right), photographed in the Western Australian bush around Manjimup, approx. 1930. (Permission for use on cover from Annette Turpin and Steve Koios).

Printed in Australia.

This book is dedicated to my late brother

Slobodan 'Peter' Anastasovski

Contents

Foreword by Michael Seraphinoff

Nick Anastasovski has given us a valuable new resource in his comprehensive examination of the history of Macedonian *pechalba* migratory labour to Australia. *Pechalba* labour is associated with both suffering and dream fulfilment. It has often been associated with suffering in the form of difficult and sometimes dangerous and back-breaking labour, far from home and loved ones. It has also been associated with dream fulfilment in the form of a better life as one sent money home to improve life for the family, and then to eventually return home in later life to enjoy the fruits of one's labour. Particularly for those who moved to faraway lands such as Australia, there was establishment of permanent ethnic communities in the new land and far greater assimilation into the new society. Children and grandchildren would grow up in a materially wealthier society with considerable opportunity for advancement, but at the cost of loss of that portion of their Macedonian ethnic cultural heritage not easily maintained far from the homeland.

Few Macedonian families were prosperous enough to avoid *pechalba* labour. My own family is not so unusual in having cousins, aunts and uncles in Germany, Australia and the United States, as well as some who managed to remain at home in Macedonia. Anastasovski's comprehensive historical review of *pechalba* labour reveals how Macedonian workers in Australia, Western Europe, Canada and the US had surprisingly similar experiences. Workers in geographically closer Western Europe, of course, were able to maintain the strongest connection to the homeland. The overall experience of Macedonians in these Western societies, however, as Anastasovski makes quite clear -with their greater economic, social and political freedom and opportunity -has been quite similar. No doubt, organisations with a more right-wing orientation, and even the more left-leaning groups, as they became more disenchanted with Eastern European communism, came to appreciate what they had gained over time by settling in these societies. Much of the suffering they had endured earlier on was eventually rewarded.

Nick Anastasovski offers us a vivid picture of the immigrant experience. He describes men and whole families who came to Australia during and after the terrible struggle for liberation at the end of the nineteenth century and the early twentieth century. He also describes desperately poor people who arrived at the height of the Great Depression and took any work they could find. Many must have done the backbreaking work of clearing woodlands for farming, or working underground in coal and mineral mines. Others managed to turn their Macedonian village farming experience into market gardening enterprises, providing fresh tomatoes and other produce to the city folk.

Anastasovski's detailed accounts of the lives of these people intertwine over time into depictions of vibrant communities in the major cities of Australia. He devotes whole chapters to detailed description of the churches, sports clubs, educational and cultural activities of these Macedonian communities.

The decision to live and work abroad is a defining moment in the life of an individual, and one with consequences for whole families and the society at large. A study such as the present one sheds considerable light on the historical processes that have created the large and thriving Macedonian ethnic communities in Australia today. It provides us with a solid foundation of knowledge upon which to base our understanding of the history of *pechalba* labour in Australia and beyond.

Dr Michael Seraphinoff, Ph.D. Macedonian and South Slavic literature, M.A. Slavic linguistics, B.A. anthropology, author of *The 19th Century Macedonian Awakening*, scholar, teacher and translator, Washington state, USA, February 2021.

Author's Acknowledgements

I acknowledge the Traditional Custodians of the land on which I have lived, worked and which provides the setting for the subject matter of this book. I would like to pay my utmost respect to the Indigenous peoples of this continent and their elders past and present; for this land we now call Australia was never willingly ceded and will always be Aboriginal land. The Macedonians have shared a similar plight to their Indigenous Australian counterparts and they too recognise the experience of having their ancestral homeland torn away by foreign invaders. It is with this mutual understanding that the Macedonians who now find themselves in Australia will forever be indebted to the First Nations peoples and as the author of this book, I extend my deepest gratitude on their behalf.

The completion of this project took longer than what I intended; however, the journey provided me with the opportunity to meet many wonderful and memorable people that have made my life richer for the privilege. There are many people that I would like to thank for different reasons; however, foremost I am grateful to the many interviewees who participated in this important research project and shared their stories of *pechalba*, migration and settlement.

I am extremely grateful to my parents for their sacrifices and inspiration, to my father who undertook his own *pechalba* journey to Australia, and my dearly departed mother for her unfailing love and support.

I express my appreciation to the following people who assisted during this project. John and Kathy Kalcovski for their support of this project and the many interviewees to whom they introduced me. Peter Sarbinov for sharing his large and important photographic collection and always being on hand to follow up the sometimes-obscure matters. Tony and Margaret Menchevski for their hospitality in Sydney and the Pandov/Pandou family for their hospitality in Richmond, New South Wales. John Karajas/Karadzhov deserves special mention, for his valuable assistance in Western Australia, for providing rare and important archival material, arranging interviews with members of the Macedonian community in Perth and assisting with preliminary research. I am deeply indebted to John for his support of this project; the Macedonian community is better when people like John are involved. Victor Damos from Perth for sharing his family story and his tremendous contribution relating to research of the Macedonian community in Geraldton. Furthermore, thanks are also due to the late Ilo Ognenov (Lou Ognenis) from Perth for his valuable contribution regarding the Macedonians of Manjimup, and the many photographs and documents he shared in support of this book.

I also acknowledge and express my gratitude to Jim Balaburov regarding the Shepparton Macedonians, and to Jim Kirko for accompanying me on an interesting visit to Shepparton. Nick Constantinou for coming forward and sharing the wonderful stories of his father Krste and the Macedonians of Sale and Gippsland. Thank you to Done and Cveta Dimov for their hospitality and sharing their family histories. Special mention also needs to be made of Mendo Trajcevski for sharing many historic photographs of Macedonians of the Illawarra and New South Wales. It would be remiss not to mention that Mendo has done a marvellous service to the Macedonian community as editor of *Kompas* magazine. Thanks to Bill Dimovski for generously giving his time, effort, and skill to produce the maps that appear in this book – thank you Bill.

There are a number of people who maintained interest in the progress of the book throughout the lengthy journey. Amongst these Jordan Gruev deserves special mention and I also thank him for his ongoing assistance with any material requiring specialised translation skills. Similarly, I thank Ljupcho Temelkovski for his ongoing support for the project and assistance with the Geelong Macedonian community. Thanks are also due to Victor Bivell, Vangel Paterov (Angelo Pateras), Goran (Sazdo) Kotev, Tony Kitanovski, Bill (Bale) Bozinovski, Borce Dimoski, Phillip Phillipou, Sylvia Stoikos, Fay Constantinou, Con Talidis, Gary Ponzio, Goce Risteski, Victor Georgopoulos, Diana Nolis, Mitch Sideris, Chris Angelkov, the late

Jim Rangelov and Billy (Blagojce) Trajcevski for his important contribution. Thanks also to Pandora Petrovska, Todor Petrov (World Macedonian Congress) and Ordan Andreevski (United Macedonian Diaspora).

Special thanks are due to Robert Pascoe for his ongoing mentoring, friendship, and interest in my research on the Macedonian community. Thanks also to Rosemary Clerehan for the valuable suggestions to improve the text, and to Nik Petrov for his support and providing a welcoming venue for our meetings.

Many people-maintained interest in the project and provided ongoing encouragement; however, without the support of my family, this study would not have been possible – and I express my deepest gratitude to Sophie, Alexandra and Michael.

Dr Nick Anastasovski, Melbourne, Vic, March 2021

List of Maps

All maps designed by Bill Dimovski

List of Tables

List of Photographs

Photo 17 (99): Mitre Veljanovski (on left side) with Ilo Prenzoski in the New South Wales bush, 1940. Mitre spent five years in the bush with other Macedonians producing eucalyptus oil around Khancoban, New South Wales. (Source: Ilija Veljanovski).

Photo 18 (106): Mitre Kotchoff from Konomladi village (Kostur), photographed in Western Australia, circa 1930. Mitre arrived in 1927 and immediately went out to isolated areas in Western Australia to clear bushland. The hut in the background of the photograph was built by Mitre out of gasoline tin cans. (Source: Kosta Kotchoff).

Photo 19 (113): Chris (Risto) Damos on far right, his father Lazo in the middle and a young Paul Popoff on the far left, photographed inspecting the tomato plantation, Geraldton, circa 1938. (Source: Victor Damos).

Photo 20 (115): Turpin family at their Canning Vale dairy farm in Perth, 1936, before moving to Manjimup to be closer to relatives and other Macedonians. (Source: Mary Purcell – nee Turpin)

Photo 21 (116): Londe Kalamarov (left) and Mitre Veliou (right) preparing the tobacco seeding beds for growing during the winter months, Manjimup, circa 1948. The covers were used to keep the frost at bay during the cold nights in Manjimup. Benzol in small tins was used to keep the seedlings warm. (Source: Archives of the Macedonian Community of Western Australia, courtesy of Ilo Ognenov).

Photo 22 (118): Risto Koiov (left) and Tanas Kalamarov inspecting tobacco leaves before placing them in the kiln, circa 1950-60. Macedonian tobacco growers in Manjimup (Western Australia) were the backbone of the tobacco industry in Australia. (Source: Archives of the Macedonian Community of Western Australia, courtesy of Ilo Ognenov).

Photo 23 (119): Macedonian women harvesting apples in Manjimup, circa 1960. For the greater part of the twentieth century Macedonians in Manjimup were major players in the tobacco industry. Following the eventual demise of the industry, tobacco farms were transitioned into orchards and agricultural land. (Source: Archives of the Macedonian Community of Western Australia, courtesy of Ilo Ognenov).

Photo 34 (152): Macedonian refugees from Aegean Macedonia in Tashkent, Uzbekistan, former Soviet Union, circa 1952. (Source: Mary Charlton).

Photo 35 (154): The Anastasovski family reunited in Williamstown, Melbourne, 1966. Note the Hills Hoist clothesline in the background and Australian Rules football at the feet of young Slobodan. (Source: Mihailo Anastasovski).

Photo 36 (172): Macedonian men coming together for a beer and enjoying time away from the steelworks in Port Kembla, 1961. (Source: Robert Stojanovski).

Photo 37 (173): Dushan Stanley from Velushina village (Bitola), circa 1964. Dushan first commenced at the Port Kembla steelworks as a 16-year-old in 1956 and worked across a number of departments in roles such as "Gear Man", "Shearer" and "Striker". Dushan worked at the steelworks for 11 years before establishing a successful travel agency. (Source: Dushan Stanley. Courtesy of Mendo Trajcevski).

Photo 38 (176): Lazo Porkoff (Enoff) seated second from the right with co-workers at Lysaght steelworks in Newcastle, 1929. (Source: Alex Sazdanoff. Courtesy of Mendo Trajcevski).

Photo 39 (177): Aleksandar Stefanoff's cafe in Mayfield, Newcastle, 1941. From left to right: female employee, Aleksandar Stefanoff, George Stefanoff and Eleni Stefanoff. (Source: Margaret Ruhfus – nee Stefanoff).

Photo 40 (183): The Traianos family from Kuchkoveni village (Lerin) during an outing to the Exhibition Gardens (Carlton Gardens), Melbourne, 1958. The Gardens was a popular social meeting place for the Macedonians that lived in Fitzroy and the surrounding suburbs during the 1950s-60s. (Source: Faye Stokes – nee Traianos/Nacov).

Photo 41 (192): Macedonian women at the Gloweave shirt factory in Fitzroy (Melbourne) circa 1985. The textile industry was a major employer of Macedonian women and Gloweave had a workforce overwhelmingly made up of Macedonian employees. (Source: Kathy Kalcovski).

Photo 42 (195): Annual wine making in the backyard of a home in the inner-western suburbs of Melbourne, 1968. (Source: Mihailo Anastasovski).

Conference, Melbourne, 1952. Note the pictures of famous leaders from the Macedonian freedom movement on the wall. (Source: Peter Sarbinov).

Photo 53 (232): Following the July 1963 devastating earthquake in Skopje, Macedonia, the Svetlost Folkloric Dance Group dressed in Macedonian national costumes went into the Melbourne central business district taking up collections for the people of Skopje. Later that day they gathered at the Sveti Giorgi, Macedonian Orthodox Church. (Source: Kathy Karlevski).

Photo 54 (235): Aleksandar Theodorovsky in national costume as the Macedonian flag bearer with the Macedonian contingent at the Melbourne May Day Parade, 1947. (Source: Aleksandar Theodorovsky).

Photo 55 (235): Macedonians at the May Day Parade, Melbourne, 1947. (Source: Aleksandar Theodorovsky).

Photo 56 (237): Macedonian activists, from left to right: Stojan Sarbinov, Dane Trpkov, Jim Filipov and Yani Pandzhari, Melbourne, circa 1940. (Source: Peter Sarbinov).

Photo 57 (242): Lebanese and Macedonians at St Nicholas Church on the occasion of a visit by Bishop Naum from the Macedonian Orthodox Church, 1960. (Source: H92.250/1264. Pictures Collection, State Library of Victoria).

Photo 58 (247): Macedonians gathered for the ground-breaking ceremony, Sveti Kiril and Metodija Church, in Fitzroy, 2 August 1953. (Source: Kosta Kotchoff)

Photo 59 (253): Procession during the consecration of Sveti Giorgi Macedonian Orthodox Church, Fitzroy (Melbourne), 1960. Priests from the Anglican and Lebanese churches participated in the event alongside Macedonian Orthodox clergy. (Source: Image supplied by Yarra Libraries. Photograph created by Allan Studios Collingwood).

Photo 60 (254): Father Gogov (holding large bible) was joined by Metropolitan Metodi (left side) and Bishop Kiril, who travelled from Macedonia for the consecration of the Sveti Ilija Macedonian Orthodox Church in Queanbeyan, New South Wales, 1969. (Source: National Archives of Australia. NAA: A12111, 1/1969/9/7).

marry Vasil Kalcovski from Brajchino, a neighbouring village to her own. (Source: Gele Kalcovski).

Photo 71 (306): Wedding photo of John and Kathy Kalcovski (from Brajchino village, Prespa and Armenoro village, Lerin, respectively) taken at Studio Nicolitch, operated by Pavle Nikolovski from Ohrid, on Gertrude Street, Fitzroy, 1964. (Source: John and Kathy Kalcovski).

Photo 72 (308): Macedonian band performing in Sydney, circa 1960. (Source: Arthur Petrou).

Photo 73 (309): Farewell celebration with musicians in a Port Kembla backyard for Mitre Trajcevski's return to Macedonia, circa 1963. (Source: Mendo Trajcevski. Photograph by Dragan Grozdanovski)

Photo 74 (314): Nikola (Kole) Sazdanoff (on right) took up boxing in Port Kembla NSW, circa 1940. Macedonians were known to enjoy combat sports like wrestling and boxing (Source: Alex Sazdanoff. Courtesy of Mendo Trajcevski).

Photo 75 (318): Lazo Giamov and Aleksandar Theodorovsky proudly representing the Macedonian soccer team in Melbourne, 1948. (Source: Aleksandar Theodorovsky).

Photo 76 (320): Following a triumphant victory over the Melbourne Greek team, the Macedonian team went to Allan photographic studio in Collingwood for a proud photo with the winning trophy, 1949. (Source: Aleksandar Theodorovsky. Photograph by Allan Studio).

Photo 77 (324): Makedonia soccer team photographed at Royal Park in celebration of winning the Victorian second division title, 1961. (Source: Pavle Velov).

Introduction

Migration has been central to the way contemporary Australia has been built, particularly from the twentieth century onwards. A "multicultural" Australia has been shaped and formed by many different groups who have left their mark through permanent settlement in the land down under. When one thinks of prominent migrant groups in Australia they may think of the Irish and the Chinese or perhaps the Italians and the Greeks. The presence of the Macedonians in Australia, however, is far from insignificant, as is the mark they have left – and continue to imprint – on the land and the nation.

As a result of problematic identifiers of ethnicity and heritage in the recording of Australian population statistics, as well as a history of political turbulence, the Macedonians of Australia have been far less visible when compared to their other Southern and Eastern European counterparts. Regardless, 2016 census data from the Australian Bureau of Statistics (ABS) reports that the number of citizens of Macedonian ancestry in Australia was close to one-hundred thousand, with unofficial estimates suggesting that true numbers were actually far greater. Additionally, the Macedonians are by no means a 'more recent' migrant group in Australia, as their presence can be traced back as early as the 1890s.

The arrival of Macedonians in Australia came about through the tradition known as *pechalba,* a Macedonian word which has almost become synonymous with "migration", though its original meaning implied a temporary journey with a promise to return home. The early Macedonian men who arrived on Australian shores reinterpreted *pechalba* by making their home anew in Australia – a process which has spanned over a century and continues to this day.

Geographical patterns of *pechalba* in Australia

In the broad sweep of post-Ottoman societies after the First World War, international migration was much more the pattern of the former Ottoman provinces in Europe than those of the Middle East and

North Africa. With the exception of the Lebanese Christians, the populations of the Ottoman Arab world were far less likely to emigrate abroad than their counterparts in the Balkan Peninsula. This book expands on some of the themes already present in my earlier book, *The Contest for Macedonian Identity 1870-1912.* The topic of this book, Macedonian *pechalba* (later to become migration), was an example of an economic strategy available to families from as early as the sixteenth century. Along with western Europe, Canada and the United States, Australia was an important destination for Macedonian men travelling without women and children during much of the twentieth century.

Economic conditions were difficult when the early *pechalbari* arrived in Australia. There were few jobs available and the men struggled to earn enough money to survive, yet were expected to send money home to their families in the villages. With determination, hard work and perseverance, men such as Con Doikin eventually found success. Doikin from Statica village (Kostur region), established a successful fruit and vegetable business in Canberra where local produce could be sold. Later his son built a motel in the area. These achievements came at a personal cost: Doikin, like many others of his generation, was separated from his family back in Macedonia for 20 years, as a result of the Second World War and the Macedonian struggle for independence in Greece during the Greek Civil War.

In the early twentieth century, the decisions *pechalbari* made about where to work in Australia depended on several factors, including from back home word-of-mouth information about where jobs could be found in the distant continent, as well as chain migration processes whereby new arrivals settled in places where relatives and friends had settled. Knowledge of opportunities in Australia once they arrived was important, as were understandings of work that encompassed skills characteristic of their Macedonian village background.

The broad geographical pattern that provides the framework for the Macedonian story in Australia is quite straightforward but differs in detail from state to state. The *pechalbari*, like other immigrant itinerant males from other backgrounds, arrived by sea at ports such as Fremantle and Melbourne, found their bearings with the help of trusted others, and then set off into the Australian bush for manual labouring jobs. This heroic phase of their lives usually lasted for several years, and often ended with them settling into rural communities, where they continued to work punishing hours and to set themselves up financially. These rural communities quickly developed as strong local economies, with a well-developed social life, sporting organisations and political clubs. In several large cities across Australia, a parallel development of Macedonian neighbourhoods emerged. Having initially relied upon Anglican churches as places of worship, these townships and urban neighbourhoods later established their own Macedonian Orthodox churches.

The heartland of Macedonian Australia was originally Western Australia. There were Macedonian workers in the Kalgoorlie goldfields by the start of the twentieth century, working on the 'woodlines' that ferried timber into the mining towns. This was a hard life, underlined by the death of a Macedonian child in Salmon Gums, near Esperance in 1938. In other parts of this vast state, the Macedonian communities were stronger. In the south-west timber country, tobacco farming at Manjimup was the most successful venture.

Perth, as the state's capital city, offered more opportunities and its Macedonian community grew fast. Macedonian boarding houses offered accommodation for the newly arrived, and their restaurants prospered during the Second World War as American servicemen came to town. In the 1940s, Perth became the centre of Macedonian political life in Australia; but by the 1950s, the Macedonian centre of gravity had shifted eastwards across the continent.

New South Wales, as Australia's most populous state, was (along with Victoria) the regional economy most affected by the nation's industrialisation over the course of the twentieth century. This opened up new employment prospects for Macedonian immigrants in secondary industries, although the first *pechalbari* here, as in Western Australia, were drawn to rural industries, particularly in mining and agriculture. As early as the 1930s there were Macedonians in Captains Flat NSW, working in the copper and silver mines, or as market gardeners. Further north, in the Richmond district, another Macedonian community was forming from the 1920s onwards, based mostly on market gardening, with some employed at the RAAF base. The older families here welcomed newcomers, and the community grew in strength.

Further north, right on the border with Queensland, a remarkable Macedonian community formed at Crabbes Creek. These families learnt how to grow bananas, an entirely new skill unknown in Macedonia, but a sudden drop in the price of bananas in the early 1960s broke their run of luck and they dispersed to other Macedonian localities throughout eastern Australia. It was a salutary lesson in the fragility of farming in Australia and over-dependence on one crop.

The state's main industrial city in its northern part was Newcastle, and the arrival of Macedonians here from 1924 coincided with the development of that city's steelworks. It was a thriving Macedonian community with steady industrial work, though Macedonian children growing up there reported the same kinds of racism that were a common feature of pre-1945 Australia.

Further down the coast, the Sydney Macedonians enjoyed a vigorous cultural life, with picnics, local musical bands and dance groups, and a church to call their own built in 1969. Further south, Wollongong was, in some ways, the archetypal Macedonian rural city in Australia. Here, and at adjacent Port Kembla, were steelworks and other industrial sites offering employment from the 1920s, with numbers increasing post-war as reunited families swelled the population. The Macedonian women of the city became highly politicised and began to demand the same conditions and wages for their factory work as their male relatives were earning.

Victoria, Australia's second-most populated state, was also a strong economy in both rural and urban industries. In country Victoria, the Macedonians worked mostly in the central Goulburn Valley and in the eastern region of Gippsland. The Goulburn Valley is centred on Shepparton, where a dynamic and highly successful Macedonian community emerged among its orchardists and market gardeners.

In Gippsland, to the east, the *pechalbari* followed the well-trodden path of timber work. This eastern half of Victoria had remained relatively undeveloped until the twentieth century, but after 1945 overtook the wealthier western half of the state. Macedonians here were beneficiaries of this growing prosperity.

As in Newcastle and Wollongong, the port city of Geelong proved attractive to Macedonians seeking a combination of factory work and a rural lifestyle. Here the main industrial plant was the Ford motor company, where Macedonians could be found in every aspect of car production.

Melbourne grew into a major Macedonian city, where the inner suburb of Fitzroy was the heart of this immigration – at that time, a run-down suburb ripe for renewal. A gradual move to Preston was part of a larger secondary migration out of Fitzroy into Melbourne's north. On the western side of Melbourne, there had been a Macedonian farming community in Werribee South since the 1920s. These Macedonians welcomed Macedonians from elsewhere to their monthly dance and community picnics; as their families became reunited, their children joined in the farm work. In the inner west of Melbourne, a large Macedonian community formed and had a longstanding connection with meatworks, where Macedonian abattoir workers often made up the majority of employees.

In South Australia, the work of the small population of *pechalbari* included fruit picking in the Riverland district, work on the Trans-continental railway and establishing market gardens in Fulham Gardens. In Queensland, as in South Australia, there was limited opportunity. There was work in the Babinda banana industry, some cotton picking in Biloela and cane-cutting in Tully, alongside the Italians. Some ventured to the Northern Territory and found work in mines and on the Darwin wharves, and finally, the smallest presence of Macedonians could be found in Tasmania, mostly seeking to establish their own businesses there.

Chapter outline

Part One examines the origins and traditions of *pechalba*, providing a historical backdrop for its earlier incarnations. *Pechalba* is examined during the period of late Ottoman Turkish rule and gives an outline of the driving forces behind the decisions to go on *pechalba* to particular destinations, with a particular focus on developments over the course of the disintegrating Ottoman Empire during the nineteenth century and beginning of the twentieth century.

Following more than five centuries of Ottoman Turkish subjugation Macedonia remained one of the last nations in the Balkans seeking freedom and independence. With the help of European powers, Macedonia's neighbors, Greece, Serbia and Bulgaria, from the 1870s, began to plan their territorial expansionism at the expense of Macedonia.

Part Two provides a historical backdrop for the partition of Macedonia in 1913 as a result of the Balkan Wars and the ensuring destructive economic and political consequences faced by the Macedonian people. This section analyses the experience of Macedonians under Greek, Serbian, Bulgarian and Albanian occupation, and the way patterns of *pechalba* and migration developed separately under each regime.

Part Three traces the beginnings of *pechalba* to Australia, the different kinds of work early *pechalbari* engaged in and the difficult challenges faced for those who arrived during tough economic times during the 1920s and 30s. The problem of Australian statistics classifying Macedonians as belonging to the nationality of the passports they carried is considered, as it misrepresented and politicised their identity. The shift towards permanent settlement is explored underpinned by a change in occupation: from bush workers to owning small-scale market gardens and farms, the Macedonians sought to establish themselves financially. Women and children were then brought out from Macedonia and helped to provide labour on the land. Reuniting families was often a slow and expensive process, separated by lengthy distance and times of war, often resulting in the passing of one or two decades before families were reunited. This Part also examines the tragedy of the Macedonian refugee children, the trauma of separation and emotional family reunion in Australia.

The settlement of Macedonians in urban centres of Australia provided significant opportunities for work in industrial sectors as well as their subsequent establishment as homeowners and business operators. Part Four provides an overview of Macedonians in the Australian urban landscape. It includes the history of enterprising Macedonians who established cafés, clubs, and boarding houses. These facilitated waves of migration to Australia as social hubs which supported a range of social services, including the searching for employment and accommodation for new arrivals.

Politics of settlement, from war and religion to political interference in the Macedonian community is considered in Part Five. Considerable attention is paid to the largely unknown presence of Macedonian Ilinden period freedom fighters in Australia, the ways in which Ilinden was commemorated, and the continuity of support for the same ideals of freedom by Macedonians in service of Australia. The establishment of early Macedonian political organisations in Australia, following historical as well as contemporary developments in the homeland is explored. This Part provides a backdrop for the significance of religion in Macedonia history. It traces the rocky road to establishing a place of worship for Macedonians in Australia, with a particular focus on the important developments in Melbourne which saw the establishment of the first Macedonian Orthodox Churches in Australia. This section depicts the interference impacting on the development of Macedonian religious and organisational institutions. In the Balkans, Macedonians endured subjugation on an ethno-national and cultural basis by their Greek, Serbo-Yugoslav and Bulgarian rulers. When they left, they expected to find a safe haven in Australia and other Western countries; instead, Macedonians found that efforts to undermine their identity and control their outward ethnic appearance continued on a transnational level.

Part Six accounts for the development of Macedonian culture and sport in Australia. It explores the development of, and traditions around, large social gatherings in parklands and bush settings which enabled Macedonians to come together in an environment which reminded them of their homeland. The traditional manner in which marriages were organised here in Australia is examined, including the system of finding a marriage partner back in Macedonia, as well as systems of marriage in the conservative Macedonian community of the 1950s and 60s. This Part also describes the development of Macedonian folk musical bands in Australia. Finally, the history of Macedonian sporting organisations throughout Australia is explored, as well as the achievements of individuals in sport. This section also has a focus on the establishment of the Preston Makedonia soccer club in Melbourne, the most famous Macedonian soccer club outside of Macedonia.

A Note on Transliteration

Early Macedonian *pechalbari* in Australia and other Western English-speaking countries such as the United States and Canada were known to Anglicise the spelling of their names. In Macedonian names, the letter j is pronounced like y as in 'you'; however, there are names that appear in this book where y is used rather than j. For example, an Anglicised version of the spelling of Trajan would be Trayan. Many of the early arrivals, used 'off' at the end of their surnames rather than the standard Macedonian 'ov'. The convention for spelling personal names in this book is in line with the manner in which an interviewee has chosen to spell their name, or how the spelling appeared in a document or publication. Where I consider that pronunciation might be confusing, I have included an Anglicised transcription.

A large number of Macedonians from Aegean Macedonia arrived with Greek first names and surnames that were used for official purposes; however, in everyday communication, were known by their Macedonian names. As such, both Macedonian and Greek versions of names appear in the book. Similarly, another group of Macedonians arrived with Serbian surnames due to that part of Macedonia being under Serbian rule. Issues regarding names are explored in further detail in Chapter 6 ('Passports and identity').

Only Macedonian names are used for places such as villages and towns under Greek rule, although I provide a list of original Macedonian names and new Greek names ('Place names'). Whenever a village is mentioned, it is followed by the name of the region that it is found in, for example, Buf village (Lerin) or Graeshnica village (Bitola). For the sake of simplified pronunciation, I have used the Anglicised system of using sh for Macedonian place names, whilst retaining j as y, thus, Krushevo rather than Krusevo or Trcije rather than Trciye.

MAP 1 – Macedonia ethno-geographic borders.

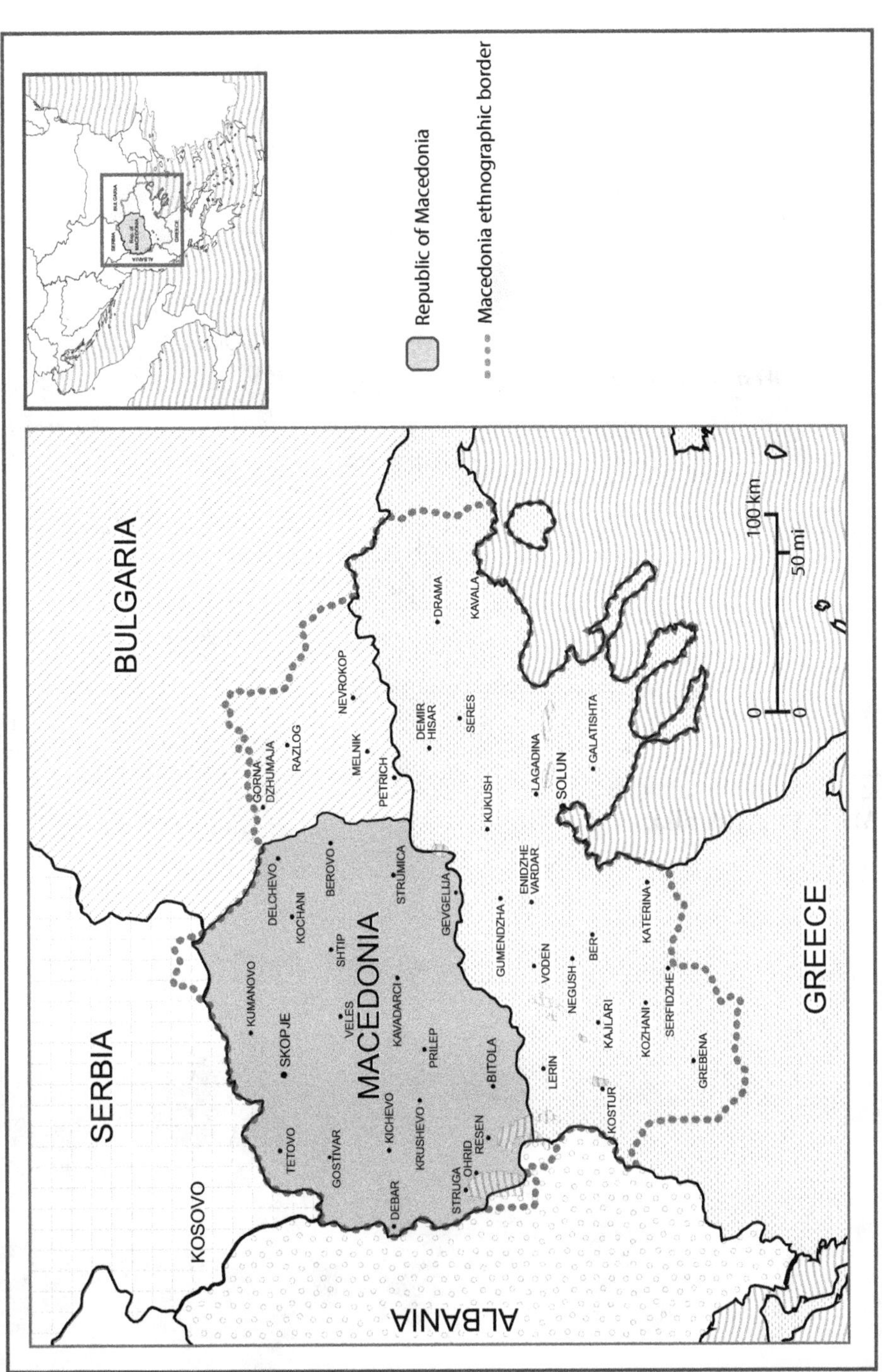

MAP 2 – Republic of Macedonia, 1991.

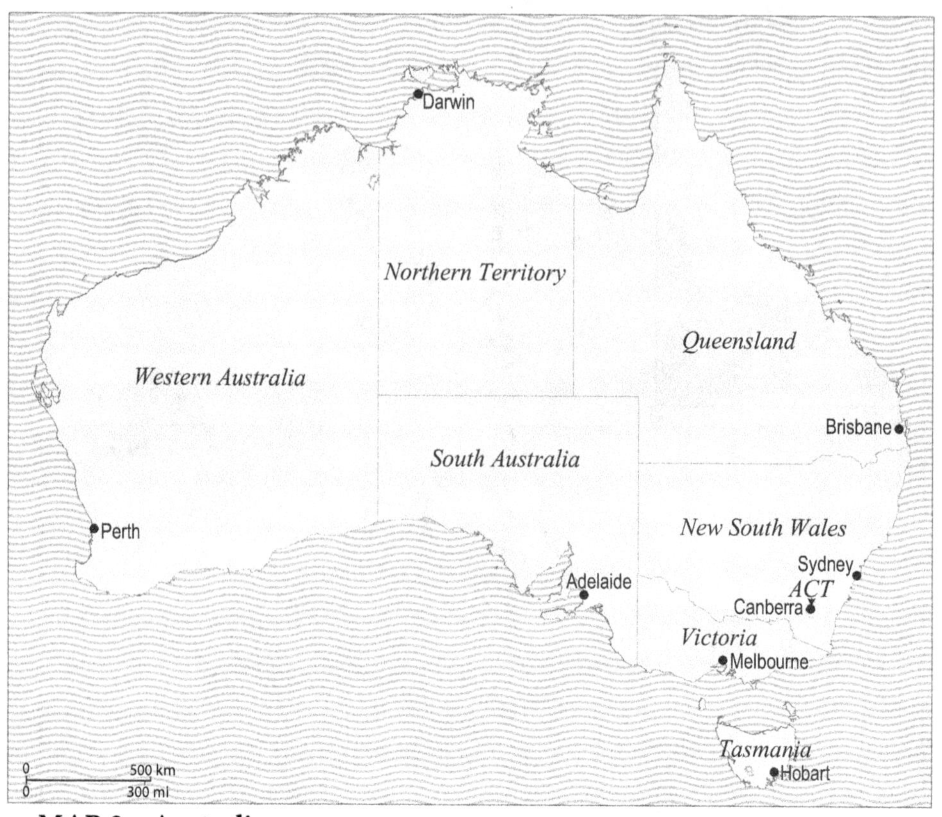

MAP 3 – Australia.

Part One

History of *Pechalba*

1

The Origins and Traditions of *Pechalba*

Temporary migratory labour, or *pechalba* has been a widespread Macedonian custom dating back to early Ottoman Turkish rule.[1] As early as the sixteenth century, men, left their homes to find seasonal or longer-term work in other parts of Macedonia and abroad. The oldest tradition of *pechalba* in Macedonia is said to come from the Reka district in north-western Macedonia. *Pechalba* was to become particularly widespread during the nineteenth century, especially in the western regions of Ohrid, Bitola, Lerin and Kostur.

The origin of the word *pechalba* dates from the old Macedonian words *pechal* and *pekal*, which are defined as grief, sorrow and/or affliction and represent the emotions of the departing *pechalbar's* family knowing that they will not see their father, brother or son often for an extended period of time and anticipating the hardships that lay ahead in their journey.[2]

The principal reason for men undertaking the journey away from their home in search of work was not solely due to economic considerations, but was often forced through political circumstances, particularly from the second half of the nineteenth century whilst still under Ottoman Turkish rule. The underlying cause was the general political insecurity in the country, linked to associated causes such as economic hardship, the taxation burden and the outlawry of Albanian Muslim bandits. Factors of a secondary nature that influenced the rise in *pechalba* include Macedonians buying back *chiflik* land (feudal estates) and the process of chain migration (whereby villagers followed other villagers to work abroad).

The economic problem in late nineteenth-century Macedonia was a consequence of a decaying feudal system that placed a significant portion of fertile land in the ownership of the powerful Turkish *begs* (feudal landlords). Under these circumstances a large portion of the population did not have their own land to work and were forced to work on *chiflik* soil. Even though *chiflik* soil was often in the most fertile districts, the methods employed at working the land were primitive, resulting in a failure to maximise agricultural output, severely affecting the economic potential of the agricultural population. The *chiflik* system was one of exploitation of the peasant population. The average annual earnings of a village household after taxes and other contributions was barely enough to maintain a typical household.

Injustice commonly experienced at the hands of corrupt tax collectors was an annual source of misery that weighed heavily upon the population. In some instances, the excesses of the tax collectors plunged individuals into financial ruin. Consequently, there were those who saw greater potential working abroad, therefore avoiding becoming the victim of Ottoman corruption inside Macedonia. In 1905, the English commentator Henry Noel Brailsford commented that 'the peasantry has abandoned the struggle with the tax collector...and lives by migratory labour'.[3] In addition, aggressive Albanian colonisation along the western Macedonian frontier, welcomed by the Ottoman rulers, and the brigandage of Albanian Muslim bands further contributed towards Macedonians seeking employment outside of their villages and fields. Earlier conversion to Islam guaranteed the Albanians the right to carry weapons, while Christians were forbidden to carry arms, and they exercised a semi-feudal terrorism over the Macedonian Christians. Villages were plundered and the bands stole livestock and looted possessions, resulting in Macedonians leaving to go abroad for work, or moving into the interior of the land to escape Albanian anarchy and oppression. Gjorche Petrov, a prominent leader of the Macedonian revolutionary movement, VMRO (*Vnatreshna Makedonska Revolucionerna Organizacija*), stated in 1909, that the principal motive for *pechalba* in the western regions of Macedonia was the 'cruel burden' brought upon the Macedonians by Albanians bandits crossing into Macedonia and terrorising Macedonian villagers.[4]

At the end of the nineteenth and beginning of the twentieth century, the Ottoman-Turkish element was in a state of decline in

Macedonia. Turkish landowners were selling *chiflik* land back to the local villagers, most often to those who had spent time abroad as *pechalbari*. This appears to have accelerated *pechalba,* as Macedonians were eager to purchase land from *begs*, land which they rightfully considered theirs – which had belonged to their forefathers prior to the arrival of the invading Ottoman Turks.

The rise in *pechalba* from the end of the nineteenth century could also be explained by the news of foreign lands reaching the village through letters. The impact of these missives, describing the conditions and wages in the foreign lands, was a matter of great interest for the *pechalbar*'s family as well as for the entire village. According to the United States Commissioner General for Immigration, such letters were 'read by or to every inhabitant of the village, or perhaps even passed on to neighbouring hamlets'.[5] In the book '*This is my Country*', Stoyan Christowe tells of the pioneering villager from Konomladi, Gurkin, who first went to the United States and when he sent a letter 'it hit the village like a comet' and 'for several days the learned folk of the village kept reading and rereading the letter.'[6]

The most significant change in the lifestyle of the *pechalbar* upon his return to the village was the construction of a new family home and the purchase of more land (*chifliks*) usually from departing *begs*. Upgrading the home to accommodate an extended family was a practical move and a matter of improved lifestyle; however, the purchase of additional land provided the villager with his most essential need. After all, the primary industry in Macedonia was agriculture and by possessing their own land people took greater control over their own lives, would no longer be required to work on the *chiflik* soil, and 'helped to provide a more secure existence for the future'.[7]

Pechalbari often returned to Macedonia having acquired new skills that were utilised in business enterprises. It was not unusual for Macedonians to establish their own businesses whilst abroad, most often cafés and inns. Pande Tantski from Carev Dvor left for the United States in 1901 (at 17 years of age) together with a group of five other men from his village. They travelled by train from Bitola to Solun, and from there embarked on the long voyage by sea. Pande initially worked with other Macedonians constructing railway lines in Detroit, and later found work in a warehouse. With his hard-earned savings he purchased a restaurant in Detroit and operated it for six years before returning to Macedonia. In Macedonia, Pande purchased a substantial amount of *chiflik* land in the Prespa region, as well as a water mill located between the villages of Bela Crkva and Kozjak. He then returned to Detroit to work in the hotel and restaurant industry for close to eight years. Upon his return to Macedonia in approximately 1918, utilising the skills acquired through his experience in the hospitality industry in America, Pande purchased a large hotel in Bitola, in partnership with another *pechalbar,* Paun Spirov (from the village Prostrajne, Kichevo). Pande and Paun paid a Turk (from Kichevo) 600 gold coins (*napoljoni*) for 'Hotel Kichevo'. The partnership operated the business successfully until 1931 when Pande bought Paun's share and continued to operate the business until 1948 when the property was confiscated by the communist Yugoslav regime as part of the nationalisation of private property.[8]

Industrial skills acquired abroad were less likely to be utilised in Macedonia, given that the Ottoman Empire was not an industrialised state and the fact that *pechalbari* principally derived from the rural sector of the population. Just as important as the practical skills that *pechalbar*i acquired, they also returned with a greater sense of self-confidence and a broader view of the world. The contemporary commentator E. Bouchie de Belle stated 'periods spent abroad gave the villager greater experience and courage'.[9] Due to the scale of *pechalba* in western Macedonia, it is likely that returning *pechalbar*i had a positive effect on the general economy in the region.

Pechalbari returning to their villages to tell fabulous stories of distant prosperous lands made a great impression. Such stories were told to an exclusively male audience, often in the village square. They left deep impressions upon the young listeners. Price states that 'semi-literate peasant people's intimate direct conversation and visible signs of success in the form of gold watches or brand-new clothes and shoes have had even more spectacular effects than letters from abroad'.[10] Trifun Hadzianev, from the town of Voden, having left for New York at the end of the Ottoman era, returned to his hometown in 1923 bringing with him a film projector that provided his fellow townsfolk with a rare insight into American life.[11] Young men in Konomladi village (Kostur) dreamed of becoming famous freedom fighters like the VMRO leader Goce Delchev and Boris Sarafov, however, following the return of the first village *pechalbar* from the United States (Gurkin) they would soon be mesmerised by the glamour and spirit of adventure of going to America.[12] Christowe, from Konomladi, stated that he also planned on going to the United States and 'had visions of returning from America twice as glorious as Gurkin and building a new church with an immense cupola and with a new bell brought all the way from Jerusalem'.[13]

Leaving one's village to go abroad on *pechalba* usually saw men leave in groups ranging in size from half a dozen to as many as twenty men. It was a day of celebration and sadness at the same time. Often, one or more men who had previously worked abroad would lead the group and it was not uncommon that they would walk considerable distances. Josif Rendevski together with a group of men from Dragosh village (Bitola) walked for 30 days to Wallachia (Romania) where they found work in the timber industry.[14] Rituals and ceremonies surrounded departing *pechalbari*. In the Drimkol district (Struga) in western Macedonia, when a young man was about to leave for his first trip, the women of his family would fill a jug with water and cover it with a piece of bread. A piece of jewellery belonging to his bride and a twig of dogwood were attached to the jug. The jug was then placed at the entrance of the house and the young *pechalbar* was to kick the jug with his right foot, making sure that he did not completely overturn it. The bread and water symbolised good luck and fortune in the coming *pechalba* journey, the strong and resilient dogwood represents good health for the *pechalbar* and the jewellery to ensure that he thinks of his young fiancée or bride and that he returns to her.[15]

In the Lerin region, departing *pechalbari* would wrap a lump of Macedonian soil and place it close to their heart as they left.[16] Diverse rituals in different regions attest to the rich cultural heritage of the Macedonian people. Renowned for its tradesmen, in the Reka district, exactly when one left for *pechalba* was dependent on the particular type of craft he possessed. Builders would leave in April/May, and others such as woodcarvers, stonemasons and tailors would traditionally leave in October.[17] In Konomladi village, at the beginning of the twentieth century, the men headed for the United States and always started their journey on a Friday, which was considered a lucky day. Tuesday and Saturday were considered unlucky days, especially Tuesday: no one set off for America on these days.[18] In the Struga district, when *pechalbari* left to go abroad, the older men and women from the village would accompany them to the edge of the village to bid them farewell.[19]

Districts – and more specifically villages – developed their own characteristic trades. Particularly famous was the town of Galitchnik in north-western Macedonia, renowned for its builders and woodcarvers, with some of the finest iconostases in the Balkans and beyond, made by the skilled craftsmen of the town. Other villages developed a reputation for market gardening, with carpenters, masons, bakers, dairy farmers, and day labourers. *Pechalbari* from the Debar and Ohrid regions had a reputation as master builders; those from Tetovo, Demir Hisar and Kichevo often found work in Bulgaria, Serbia and Romania as bakers; dairy industry workers were drawn from Kostur and worked in Constantinople and Varna; men from the Prespa region worked as market gardeners in Constantinople; and men from Buf (Lerin) and Gjavato (Bitola) were known as sawyers and coal miners who worked in the mountains in Turkey, Bulgaria and Romania.[20]

Increased opportunities to work abroad were also derived from the numerous shipping companies that established offices in Macedonian urban centres.[21] French, British, Italian and other companies competed with one another, attracting fares for transportation upon their respective vessels.[22] Representatives of shipping companies were found throughout Macedonia and they advertised positive images in newspapers and appointed ticket agents to praise the New World.[23] Intense rivalries developed between shipping agencies with advertisements appearing in newspapers making various claims in order to attract *pechalbari*, such as 'ours is an honourable shipping company' and denying that they exploited men, 'as do other agencies and shipping lines which transport people to America'.[24] In their advertisements, agents advertised for a wide range of workers required in both North and South America – including building and construction workers, tanners, farm workers, factory workers, printers, machinists, blacksmiths, tailors, and so on. To further entice customers, the Agence Maritime Muscombul claimed to provide 'the quickest and cheapest travel to America', as well as offering hotel accommodation and detailing the expected wages one could earn, 'dependent upon skills and experience'.[25] Fares to the one destination varied between shipping agents. Fares ranged between 13 and 27 *napoljoni* (French gold coins) for direct travel from Macedonia to North America, while a fare to South America was as much as 45 Turkish *lira* (Ottoman currency).[26] Fares to America constituted a substantial amount of money, roughly the average annual savings for the ordinary villager, so it was not uncommon for the *pechalbar* to borrow money or sell possessions in order to raise funds to work abroad.[27] When the *pechalbar* commenced earning an income in the new land, he was first obliged to ensure that he repaid his debt. These were the same conditions upon which Macedonians began to arrive in Australia; they paid large sums of money for their shipping fares, money which was invariably borrowed from villagers, relatives or friends, and after arriving and finding work, returning the money was of utmost importance to ensure that the family name and reputation remained intact.

No fewer than eight transatlantic shipping agencies operated in Bitola in 1906. Approximately half of the *pechalbar*i managed to secure their fares and the others relied on loans administered through the agencies at a rate of 2.5–3.0 per cent interest calculated monthly.[28] In the Resen region, villagers commonly borrowed money from a group of ten businessmen situated in Resen town who regularly provided loans to *pechalbar*i and travelled three times a year to Constantinople to collect money owed them.[29] There was no shortage of men willing to go into debt in order to finance their travel abroad.

MAP 4 – Traditional *pechalba* regions in Macedonia.

2

Destinations of *Pechalba* in Late Ottoman Ruled Macedonia

Types of *pechalba*

Common destinations where Macedonian men travelled in search of temporary work can be classified into three categories: those who worked in various regions of Macedonia (internal *pechalba*), those who sought work within the Ottoman Empire, and those who found employment outside the Empire.

Pechalba within Macedonia

Due to limited arable land in the mountainous districts of Macedonia and the tradition of land being divided amongst male heirs, villagers were forced to supplement their earnings by engaging in sheep breeding. Sheep herding was conducted on a seasonal basis, leaving in autumn for greener pastures and returning in spring. Vast distances were travelled by sheep herders who were known to drive a thousand sheep or more from the northern Macedonian regions down to southern Macedonia. In the village of Neret (Lerin), herders left for extended periods, taking their sheep south to Sveta Gora over the winter months.[30] Seasonal work was found in the *chifliks* and large towns of southern Macedonia, and the sheep herding was then handed down to the next eldest male in the family.[31] Seasonal work was performed in *chifliks* in the regions of Drama, Kavala and the Halkidik Peninsula, while others went coke-burning in Katerini.

Large towns in Macedonia such as Skopje and Bitola were popular destinations for internal *pechalbari*. Ottoman tax records for Bitola town during the collection of the Ottoman personal tax (known as *dzize*) for the year 1841-1842 reveal that, of a total of 248 men who were not present to make their tax payment at their usual place of residence, only a small percentage (ten men) were internal *pechalbari* – and these were on *pechalba* in Kozhani, Shtip, Seres, Solun, Skopje and in Sveta Gora.[32]

Prilep town is located on the Pelagonia plain, approximately 35 kilometres north of the central commercial and administrative town of Bitola. Ottoman tax data for Christian males temporarily working in Prilep town in 1845 reveal that there were 238 male *pechalbari* residing in Prilep. They were overwhelmingly drawn from villages in the surrounding Bitola and Ohrid regions, and to a lesser extent from Krushevo. A small number of men were from other regions such as Resen, Veles and Reka (Debar).[33]

The introduction of a railway system in Macedonia in the late nineteenth century provided a modern alternative to traditional forms of *pechalba* transport such as a mule or horse or travelling on foot, and provided greater access to major centres and ports. Funded by Western European industrialists and governments (particularly Austrian), they were established to meet strategic economic needs. In 1873, the first railway in Macedonia was constructed between Solun and Skopje (243 kilometres), and the following year it was extended from Skopje to Mitrovica in Serbia (119 kilometres). It was not until 1894 that Bitola was connected by rail to Solun (218 kilometres) and in 1896, the Solun-Constantinople railway line opened.

Pechalba within the Ottoman Empire

Mid nineteenth-century Ottoman tax records for Bitola town provide an insight into popular destinations within the Ottoman Empire for men from that town. The records represent a list of names and tax categories of individuals who were not residing in their homes during the collection of the Ottoman personal tax (*dzize*) for the year 1841-1842. From a total of 242 registered males who were absent from Bitola, over 50 per cent (128) were in Istanbul, ten persons were working in Anatolia and four in Izmir.[34] The next most popular destination for males from Bitola was Belgrade, Serbia (31 men) followed by Romania (16 men). Others travelled to distant destinations within the Empire, to the east, to places such as Jerusalem and Damascus. There appeared only one instance of a Macedonian travelling to Western Europe: the 21-year-old tailor Giorgi ('son of Atanas'), who left for Germany four years earlier in the 1830s.[35] During the nineteenth century men from Visheni village (Kostur) such as Petre Boskov and his son Vasil travelled to Alexandria in Egypt where they found work in the dairy industry selling milk.[36]

Throughout the nineteenth century Macedonian men from the western regions of Bitola, Ohrid, Lerin and Kostur saw Constantinople as a primary destination for *pechalba*. Principal occupations were market gardening and working in the dairy business. Men from the Resen region were renowned for their market gardening skills. A significant number worked in Constantinople and constituted the bulk of the people in that trade.

Estimates of the number of *pechalbari* in Constantinople vary: in a 1922 publication historian Petar Draganoff stated that, prior to the Ilinden Uprising of 1903, the city hosted 2,500 workers from Lerin and 2,000 from Kostur,[37] whilst drawing on a source from 1890, memoirist Simeon Radev indicates that there were as many as 7,000 people from the Resen region alone.[38] In the mid-nineteenth century Constantinople was the most popular destination for Macedonian *pechalbari* from the Bitola region. By the late nineteenth century, a Macedonian colony had established itself in the cosmopolitan metropolis on the Bosphoros. Numerous Macedonians in Constantinople engaged in market gardening, particularly those from the Resen and wider Prespa region.[39] Eftim Tantski from Carev Dvor (Resen district, Prespa) travelled to Constantinople in 1898 with a group of men from the district and worked there for a period of six years as a market gardener, selling produce door to door.[40]

Pechalba outside the Ottoman Empire

Pechalba outside the Ottoman Empire in the late nineteenth century included states that were previously under Ottoman Rule such as Bulgaria, Serbia and Wallachia (Romania); Western European countries such as Austria-Hungary, Germany and, in particular, France; Argentina, Uruguay and Brazil in South America; and Canada and the United States. Seasonal workers within Macedonia left their homes for periods of months; however, *pechalbari* leaving for foreign lands were normally absent from their homes for much longer periods. It was common for men to be away for at least one or two years; however, they often stayed for five or more years.

Pechalbari were predominantly married men aged between their late teens and 40 years of age, but could also be as young as early teens in which case they would be accompanied by a father, brother or uncle. According to statistics published by the historian Kemal Karpat regarding 'Age characteristics of the Ottoman migrants arriving in the United States in 1889', of a total of 202 men, 21 were under 15 years of age, 162 were between the ages of 15 and 40, and 19 were above 40 years of age.[41] Typically they would spend several years in the one destination; however, *pechalbari* were also known to move around in search of work, from country to country. The unmarried Trifun Kalcovski from the village of Brajchino (Prespa) left for the United States in 1913 at the age of 16, while the married Anasto Kleshtev from Gorno Aglarci (Bitola) spent several years in Romania during the 1870s, having left the village in his thirties. In some instances, *pechalbari* did not spend the entire period in a particular country, but moved around in search of work. Pando Stojkov from Lagen (Lerin) started as a *pechalbar* at the age of 13, initially in Anatolia (Ottoman Empire), then in Romania, Bulgaria, and finally as a sawyer in Austria. Having returned to Macedonia, he set off once more, leaving for America in 1903. After two or three years there he returned to his village but stayed for only a short while and again made the long journey back to the United States where he stayed until 1914. When the Great War was over, he departed for the third time to America, accompanied by his eldest son Dimitar, staying there for a further eight years, and finally returning in 1928 to Macedonia.[42]

Wherever groups of Macedonians worked in common destinations, colonies were formed. In the late nineteenth century, significant colonies were formed in Bulgaria and Romania (Wallachia). It was not unusual for enterprising Macedonians to open restaurants and cafés and these were utilised by newly arrived *pechalbari* as a place where they could obtain valuable information to help them find work and accommodation. Sokole Zhitoshanski (born 1878), from the village of Zhitoshe in the Krushevo district, left his hometownship in his early twenties in search of work in Bulgaria and came to operate his own inn in Sofia. Sokole's establishment was used as a meeting place for Macedonian *pechalbari* in Sofia.[43] Similarly, the famous revolutionary leader Pitu Guli, from Krushevo, also spent a short period in Sofia in 1900 where he operated an inn that operated as a meeting place for Macedonian *pechalbari*, particularly for those from the Krushevo region, as well as for Macedonian political and revolutionary activists.[44]

From Constantinople to North America

Life under the despotic Ottoman Turks had become intolerable: the Ottoman administration was notoriously corrupt; the feudal land system (*chiflik*) was backward and kept the rural population in poverty; and the Macedonian church had been abolished by the Ottoman Sultan in 1767. The Greek, Serbian and Bulgarian governments sought to aggressively expand their territories into Macedonia, utilising churches and educational institutions; and paramilitary bands crossed into Macedonia violently seeking to transform Macedonians into Greeks, Serbians and Bulgarians. The Great Powers of Europe, protecting their own strategic interests, acted as patrons in support of the expansionist designs of Greece, Serbia and Bulgaria. In this chaos, Macedonians aspired for natural justice and sought political freedom through the establishment of a free and independent nation. Under the direction of VMRO, a mass uprising to overthrow Ottoman rule and establish an independent Macedonia was raised on 2 August 1903, on Saint Elijah's day, or 'Ilinden' in Macedonian. As such, the uprising is known as the Ilinden Uprising. Well-organised VMRO *chetas* (military bands) attacked Turkish troops, liberating numerous towns and districts; and the democratic Krushevo Republic was proclaimed in the mountain town of Krushevo under the leadership of the VMRO leader Nikola Karev. The success of the Ilinden Uprising took the Turks by surprise and was impressive in that the fighting ratio was one to thirteen. The uprising was widely reported in the international media at the time. Because the Ottoman military outnumbered the Macedonian fighters one to thirteen, they responded in a brutal manner, massacring and plundering Macedonians towns and villages. In the end, 4,700 people were murdered, 200 villages ruined, and 71,000 people left homeless.[45] The courage and sacrifice of the Macedonians fighting against overwhelming odds was testament to their aspiration for emancipation from tyranny, and is of great historical significance in their centuries long struggle for freedom and a nation state.

Following the Ilinden Uprising the Ottoman government began to discriminate against the sizeable Macedonian colony of *pechalbari* in Constantinople, and many were forced to move elsewhere. Thousands moved to North America.[46] A Macedonian *pechalbar* from the Resen district, working in Constantinople, stated to the contemporary commentator Miss M. Edith Durham, 'the Turks in Constantinople were very frightened of the bands. All Macedonians were ordered to leave at once. I had to go.'[47]

Unlike the Balkan countries that failed to maintain records on immigration, and the Ottoman Empire that did not keep official figures, the United States Government did maintain records, although the country of origin was recorded only as 'European Turkey', a category larger than Macedonia. Nevertheless, these figures do provide an approximation of the extent of emigration from Macedonia, particularly after 1878 and the Berlin Congress, which aimed at defining the territories of the Balkan States following the Russian-Turkish War of 1877-78. At that point, the territory of European Turkey was substantially reduced and was made up of Macedonia, Albania, Kosovo, Thrace and Eastern Rumelia (subsequently joined with Bulgaria in 1885) and *pechalba* took on the form of a mass movement amongst Macedonians.

The American statistical records on emigration from European Turkey enable observations to be drawn from the data.[48] *Pechalba* can be broken down into four distinct periods that correspond to the deteriorating political environment from 1870 to the Balkan Wars of 1912–1913.

During the 1870s, *pechalbari* were commonly working in the neighbouring states of Romania and Bulgaria. The period 1871–1878 is characterised by an insignificant number of people leaving European Turkey for the United States. According to the immigration records for the period 1871 to 1878, 284 people arrived in the United States (Table 2.1).

Year	Number
1871	21
1872	34
1873	78
1874	21
1875	36
1876	46
1877	25
1878	23

Table 2.1 Emigration (*pechalba*) from European Turkey to the United States, 1871–1878.

The statistics for the period 1878 to 1902 reflect the unstable political climate and are characterised by a gradual increase in emigration to the States. From 1880 to 1889, 1,380 people arrived in the United States; during the following ten years, from 1890 to 1899, 2,375 people arrived. The numbers dramatically increased at the beginning of the twentieth century, as 2,475 people arrived in America over a short period of the three years from 1900 to 1902. Increased economic and political instability after the Russo-Turkish wars of 1876–1878 contributed to this increase of Macedonians seeking work abroad from 1878 to 1902. Following the Berlin Congress, there was a general increase in revolutionary activity throughout Macedonia (commencing with the Macedonian Kresna Rebellion in 1878), and the unleashing of religious and educational propaganda by the Balkan States (Greece, Serbia and Bulgaria) in Macedonia. However, the completion of the Bitola-Solun railway connection in 1894 did not appear to have encouraged *pechalba* to the United States, as there was no significant rise in numbers until 1900/1901.

Year	Number	Year	Number
1879	29	1891	265
1880	24	1892	227
1881	72	1893	555
1882	69	1894	278
1883	86	1895	215
1884	150	1896	169
1885	138	1897	152
1886	176	1898	176
1887	206	1899	132
1888	207	1900	393
1889	252	1901	1,044
1890	206	1902	1,038

Table 2.2 Emigration *(pechalba)* from European Turkey to the United States, 1879–1902.

Following the Ilinden Uprising in 1903 against Ottoman Turkish rule and the brutal reprisals the Ottoman army inflicted upon Macedonian villages, there was a large increase in people leaving Macedonia.[49]

Emigration continued during the turbulent years of 1904–1907 when the Macedonian population was subjected to an invasion of Greek, Serbian and Bulgarian paramilitary bands from the neighbouring states. According to the American statistical data from 1903 to 1907, 40,692 people arrived in the United States.[50] The VMRO leader Gjorche Petrov reckoned that over 50,000 Macedonians left for the United States from 1903 to 1906,[51] while there are other estimates that as many as 75,000 people left Macedonia during the period from 1902 to 1907.[52]

Year	Number
1903	1,529
1904	4,344
1905	4,542
1906	9,510
1907	20,767

Table 2.3 Emigration (*pechalba*) from European Turkey to the United States, 1903-1907.

The exodus of men became so great that, in 1909, the Ottoman authorities banned emigration for all men under the age of thirty.[53] However, the ban did not appear to have been effective, as the following year emigration to the USA doubled. In the uncertain climate of the final years leading to the Balkan Wars, *pechalba* continued in large numbers, but most continued to leave with the intention of returning to their homes.[54]

Year	Number
1908	11,290
1909	9,015
1910	18,405
1911	14,438
1912	14,481
1913	14,128

Table 2.4 Emigration (*pechalba*) from European Turkey to the United States, 1908–1913.

Pechalbari were subjected to various perils during their journeys in search of work. In the Balkans, bandits were known to attack and rob *pechalbari*, so for security they would travel in groups with some armed. There were other unforeseen risks for which *pechalbari* could not prepare. *Pechalba* within the Ottoman Empire, particularly in the Balkans, involved overland travel; however, the journey to North and South America involved crossing vast oceans by ship. No one could have predicted the sinking of the greatest passenger ship in the world after the Titanic embarked from Southampton, England, on 10 April 1912, headed for New York. It is uncertain how many Macedonians were on board as not all passengers were recorded on the official passenger list. However, anecdotal evidence suggests that there must have been quite a few, based on both the number of Macedonians known to have perished and others that survived that fateful night of 15 April 1912.

A 104-year-old interviewee, Mitko Bogdanovski, was born in Krivogashtani Macedonia, but resided most of his life in Bela Crkva village (Prilep). He stated that *pechalba*ri from Bela Crkva and the surrounding villages routinely went to the United States from the nineteenth century on. After spending several years working in the United States, the brothers, Atanas and Krste Bogdanovski, from Bela Crkva, returned with a large sum of money. Krste paid for his son Bozhin Bogdanovski to travel to the United States aboard the Titanic where he was one of those who perished. Another villager from Bela Crkva, Bozhin Kukeski and two other *pechalbari* from the nearby village of Vogjani survived the tragic sinking, but all three men never returned to Macedonia, perhaps due to the trauma of the event.[55]

Prior to boarding the *Titanic*, 22-year-old Ace Malinkovski from Shtavica village (Prilep) sent a letter home to his family telling stories of his journey to England and describing Southampton dock. It was the last time his family heard from him.[56] German village in the Lerin region was renowned for sending its young men on *pechalba* to the United States. Alekso Chulakovski and his father both set out for their first journey to the United States on the *Titanic*. They were the only two men from their village on board the ship and neither father nor son survived the sinking.[57] A similar fate befell sixteen-year-old Vangel Chutrevski from Slepche village (Demir Hisar)[58] and the brothers Janko and Mile Smilevski from Tresonche village

(Reka district).[59] Petre Ristevski from Kanino village (Bitola) and the family Yusufi from Debar – also died.[60] A Macedonian from Austria, Dmitri Marinko, appears on the third-class passenger list and is also recorded as having died in the sinking. Amongst the fortunate ones to survive was 16-year-old Stojko Doduloski from Chucher village (Skopje). Stojko jumped into the freezing waters and climbed onto an overturned lifeboat which was towed to safety by Officer Harold Lowe who had returned to pick up survivors. Stojko clambered aboard with another Macedonian, Todor Zazanovski, but Zazanovski did not survive.[61]

A lesser known shipping tragedy involved the *SS Volturno*, which set sail from Rotterdam in the Netherlands headed for New York in October 1913, carrying 651 passengers, mostly emigrants. Whilst crossing the North Atlantic a fire broke out during a heavy storm and quickly began to spread, resulting in the evacuation of all passengers and crew. Approximately 130 people died, mainly women and children who drowned after their lifeboats were launched into the sea and they crashed against the ship in the heavy seas. Five hundred and twenty passengers and crew survived the ordeal, including several Macedonians.[62]

Following the division of Macedonia, the United States remained the principal destination for *pechalbari* until the flow was temporarily disrupted by the Great War, 1914-1918. *Pechalbari* continued to come from the western regions of Macedonia, predominantly from Aegean Macedonia, but also from Macedonia under Serbian occupation. Popular destinations in the United States were large urban centres such as Detroit where Macedonians worked in the automobile industry, in manufacturing industries in the Midwest states of Ohio, Indiana and Illinois, and on the railways.

In the first decades of the twentieth century there were various passages to the United States depending upon established village routes, with many setting off for Marseilles in France or Dover in England from where they boarded ships to the United States. When the United States changed its immigration intake laws through the Immigration Act of 1924, quotas were introduced for the annual number of immigrants, restricting immigration of Southern and

Eastern Europeans and completely prohibiting immigration of certain other ethnic groups. The new laws were discouraging for would-be *pechalbari* and new strategies for entering the United States were quickly found, either by the *pechalbari* or enterprising travel agents to enable them to manoeuvre around the restrictions in place.

Boris Kalcovski from Brajchino village (Prespa) intended to travel to the United States; however, due to entry restrictions he sought an alternative route. He obtained a visa on 22 June 1926, permitting him to migrate to Canada which was intended as a steppingstone into the United States. The journey commenced from his village in a picturesque valley near the shores of Lake Prespa, travelling overland via Jesinice, Slovenia (Yugoslavia), St Louis – Haut-Rhin (France) to Antwerp in Belgium from where he boarded a ship to Dover (England). The ship from Dover took two weeks to arrive in Quebec (Canada) on 31 July 1926, where he immediately headed for Toronto in order to make arrangements through Macedonians living there to cross into the United States. Kalcovski was connected to a people-smuggling operator who used a small boat to take him and other Macedonians over the Saint Lawrence River into the United States.[63]

Photo 1: Boris Kalcovski, circa 1923. In 1926, twenty-two-year-old Boris from Brajchino village (Prespa) travelled to Canada where, with the aid of a people smuggler, he illegally crossed into the United States over the Saint Lawrence River. Later, in the 1970s, Boris migrated to Australia to be with his children. (Source: Gele Kalcovski).

Entering the United States illegally over the Saint Lawrence River may have been a well-travelled route for Macedonians at that time, as a travel agent in Bitola organised for Mitre Lajmanovski from Gjavato village (Bitola) who had arrived in Canada in 1927, to cross the Saint Lawrence River at night to enter the United States.[64] Others entered via more perilous methods such as

Risto Constantinov/Constantinou from Armensko village (Lerin) who entered the United States over a frozen lake during wintertime in the 1920s. Accompanied by a relative from his village, they were guided by an African American who routinely took migrants over the border; however, tragedy struck when the paid guide fell to his death through the ice.[65] The journey to the United States was via an unintended route for Dono Sholdas from Gabresh village (Kostur). In the 1920s Sholdas was conscripted into the Greek army to take part in the attack against Turkey. Not having any reason to kill Turks, Sholdas deliberately shot over the head of an advancing Turkish soldier, and then deserted from the front. He headed for Marseilles, the port from where men from the Kostur region left Europe to head for the United States and Cuba. These had been *pechalba* destinations for men from the Kostur region who worked in the sugar plantation industry there. Sholdas first arrived in Cuba and then attempted to enter the United States, travelling by boat to Florida where he was apprehended by customs authorities and imprisoned for one month before being deported to Marseilles.[66] Immigration restrictions, combined with the difficulties and dangers entering the United States illegally, forced Macedonians to consider other destinations and, from 1924, many began to look towards Australia. It was a land about which they knew very little and which was more distant than any other to which their fathers and grandfathers had travelled previously. These early Macedonian pioneers did not see themselves as permanent settlers but as temporary workers. Their intention, based on the traditional *pechalbar* system, was to work for a few years before returning to Macedonia with enough savings to build a new home, purchase more agricultural land and generally improve their lives.

A negative aspect of the new wealth *pechalbar*i returned with was the unwanted attention they attracted from Ottoman tax gatherers and, more specifically, from Albanian bandits. These bandits were notorious throughout western border regions for pillaging villages, often targeting those who had returned from *pechalba*. Intimidation, coercion and kidnapping were used to extract money. The families of *pechalbari* were singled out in order to extort money. As a result of pressures caused by Albanian banditry, many families were forced to move out of their homes and native villages in search of personal security to urban areas or otherwise further away. A secondary consequence of Albanian lawlessness was the effect on the ethnographic landscape of western Macedonia that saw the Macedonian element gradually decrease and the ethnic Albanian element expand as a colonising element with the support of the Ottoman authorities. Another aspect affecting returning *pechalbari* was the increased price of *chiflik* land. In regions where *pechalba* was widespread, land prices reached artificial heights: for example, a *dolum* (approximately 910 square metres) of good quality agricultural land which had a normal value of 2 silver lira, grew to a value of 5 to 10 silver lira.[67] According to Dr Ranci from the Austrian Consulate in Bitola in 1906, *pechalbari* were willing to pay high prices for land: 'due to the fact that local villagers are proud of their fatherland as well as their own village, whereupon previously he lacked ownership and was a *chiflik* worker, he wishes to acquire his own land. The desire is so great that the value of the land often is paid for twice or three times more'.[68]

Photo 2: Lazo Damovski (Adamos) with wife Tarrpa and son Chris in Labanitsa village (Kostur), circa 1920. Lazo had recently returned from pechalba in Cuba. In 1928, Lazo arrived in Western Australia, and after some travelling back and forth between the homeland and Cuba, he eventually settled in Geraldton, Western Australia in 1935. (Source: Victor Damos).

The level of *pechalba* in a particular village generally affected whether the village as a whole was visibly distinguishable from other villages. In villages that did have a strong tradition of *pechalba,* such as Smerdesh in the Kostur district, there were numerous outward signs differentiating it from other villages. In 1905, Brailsford described Smerdesh as the richest village he had come across, with large and comparatively well-built houses, a thriving school, three or four shops and a large church.[69] Newly constructed homes using funds earned from *pechalba* were known as *pechalbarska kukja* (*pechalbar* house), *majstorska kukja* (craftsman-built home) and *Amerikanska kukja* (American home).[70] Another outward sign of wealth was to wear brand new or Western style clothing.[71]

Endnotes

1 Collectively, migratory labourers were known as *pechalbari*, whilst an individual was known as a *pechalbar*.

2 D. Konstantinov, *Pechalbarstvo* [Pechalba], Nauchno Drustvo Bitola, Bitola, 1964, pp. 14-15.

3 H.N. Brailsford, *Macedonia: Its Races and their Future*, Methuen & Co, London, 1906, p. 50.

4 M. Dimitrijevski, 'Makedonskoto iselenishtvo vo Amerika videno niz analiza na trudot na Gjorche Petrov: Emigrantskoto dvizhenje za Amerika vo Makedonia" [Macedonian Emigres in America as Analysed by Gjorche Petrov], p. 292, *Prv megunaroden nauchen sobir 'iselenishtvoto od Makedonija od pojavata do denes'* [First international academic gathering – the emigration from Macedonia since its beginning], Agencija za Iselenistvo na Republika Makedonija, Skopje, 2001.

5 *Report of the Commissioner General for Immigration*, Washington, 1907, p.60 as cited in C.A. Price, *Southern Europeans in Australia*, Melbourne University Press, Melbourne, 1963, p.108.

6 S. Christowe, *This is my Country*, Carrick and Evans, 1938, pp. 7-8.

7 P. Hill, *The Macedonians in Australia*, Hesperian Press, Perth, 1989, p. 10. H.N. Brailsford also makes the point that the conditions under which agriculture was carried out, particularly the system of land tenure, was 'of the first importance for the happiness of the people'. Op. cit. p. 51.

8 Kole Eftimov interview.

9 E. Bouchie de Belle, *La Macedoine et les Macedoniens* [Macedonia and the Macedonians], Librairie Armand Colin, Paris, 1922, p. 52.

10 C.A. Price, *Southern Europeans in Australia*, Melbourne University Press, Melbourne, 1963, p.108.

11 I. Chapovski, *The Macedonian Orthodox Church of St. George – A Cultural and National History*, York Press, Melbourne, 1992, p. 18.

12 S. Christowe, op. cit., p.15. Goce Delchev (b. 1872 Kukush-d. 1903 Banica, Seres region) and Boris Sarafov (b. 1872 Libjakovo, Nevrokop - d. 1907 Sofia, Bulgaria) were leaders of the Macedonian revolutionary movement seeking freedom for Macedonia from Ottoman rule. Delchev in particular, is one of the most important national figures in Macedonian history.

13 Ibid., p. 16.

14 Cane Rendevski interview. Cane's grandfather, Josif had also travelled to the United States on two occasions as a *pechalbar*, the first-time during Ottoman rule and later returning when the Bitola region fell under Serbian rule.

15 J. Halpern, '*The Pecalba Tradition in Macedonia: A Case Study*', University of Massachusetts, Anthropology Department Faculty Publication Series, Paper 58, Amherst, 1975, p. 2. The original notes, translated by Halpern, were made by a villager from a Struga region village; unfortunately, Halpern does not specify the name of the villager or the name of the village.

16 J. Harper, 'The Pecalbars of Gippsland: Macedonian Farm Workers around Kernot in the 1930s', *Gippsland Heritage Journal,* Number 28, Kapana Press, Briagolong, 2004, pp. 2-9. p. 2.

17 G. Todorovski, *Malorekanskiot Predel* [The Mala Reka District], Institut za Nacionalna Istorija, Skopje 1970, p. 66.

18 S. Christowe, op. cit., p. 3.

19 J. Halpern, op. cit., p. 2.

20 M. Dimitrijevski, op. cit., p. 292.

21 K. Karpat, *The Ottoman Emigration to America 1860-1914*, Vol 17, Cambridge University Press, 1985, p. 188.

22 Shipping companies operating out of Macedonia at the beginning of the twentieth century included Cunard Line, Company General, Transatlantic Hamburg, America Line, Red Star, White Star Line, Lloyd and Royal Company. D. Konstantinov, op. cit., p.18.

23 C.A. Price, op. cit., p. 108.

24 Newspaper advertisement for shipping agency 'Agence Maritime Muscombul' in *Vjesti* newspaper (printed in Constantinople) dated 27 January 1910. Issue Number 61, Year XX, p. 4. (*Vjesti* was a Serb newspaper that was also distributed throughout Macedonia).

25 Ibid., p. 4.

26 D. Konstantinov, op. cit., p. 18.

27 Ibid., p. 18.

28 Diplomatic letter (number 33) by Dr Ranci from the Austrian Consulate in Bitola, dated 11 July 1906. D. Zografski, editor, *Avstriski Dokumenti 1905-1906*

[Austrian Documents 1905-1906], Vol I, Arhiv na Makedonija, Skopje, 1977, p. 158.

29 S. Radev, *Simeon Radev - Rani Spomeni* [Simeon Radev - Early Memoirs], Bulgarski Pisatel, Sofia, 1967, p. 48.

30 Velika Spirova interview.

31 D. Siljanovski, editor, *Makedonia Kako Prirodna i Ekonomska Celina* [Macedonia as a Natural and Economic Unit], Makedonski Nauchen Institut, Sofia, 1945, p. 266.

32 D. Gjorgiev, *Turski Dokumenti za Istorijata na Makedonija, Popisi od XIX vek* (Kniga II), [Turkish Documents regarding the History of Macedonia, Census' in the Nineteenth Century (Book II)], Arhiv na Makedonija – Matica Makedonska, Skopje 1997, pp. 13-46. According to Andon Delov/Foudoulis, men from the village of Armenoro (Lerin) were known to go on *pechalba* to Sveta Gora where they engaged in timber cutting work. Andon Delov/Foudoulis interview.

33 D. Gjorgiev, *Turski Dokumenti za Istorijata na Makedonija, Popisi od XIX vek* (Kniga III), [Turkish Documents regarding the History of Macedonia, Census' in the Nineteenth Century (Book III)], Arhiv na Makedonija – Matica Makedonska, Skopje 1998, pp.197-207.

34 D. Gjorgiev, (1997), op. cit., pp. 13-46.

35 Ibid., p. 24.

36 Petre Boskov and his son Vasil went to Egypt prior to the Ilinden Uprising and stayed there for about 20 years, returning to Visheni village in 1916/17 after Vasil became unwell. Peter Boskov interview.

37 P. Draganoff, *La Macedonie et les Macedoniens* [Macedonia and the Macedonians], Paris, 1922, p. 28.

38 S. Radev, op. cit., p. 47. Radev cites this figure from an 1890 issue of the newspaper, *Zornitsa*.

39 In the memoirs of Simeon Radev, he states that the large colony of men from the Resen region, in Constantinople, predominantly worked as market gardeners, and constituted the bulk of the people in the trade. The market gardens were situated on opposite sides of the city. S. Radev, ibid. pp. 47-48. The revolutionary leader, Slaveyko Arsov also outlined the high rate of *pechalbari* in Constantinople, who were men from the Resen region. The majority worked as market gardeners and only very young men and the elderly remained in the villages. Slaveyko Arsov memoirs from I. Katardzhiev, editor, *Spomeni - S. Arsov, P. Klashev, L. Dzherov, G.P. Hristov, A. Andreev, G. Papanchev, L. Dimitrov* [Memoirs - S. Arsov, P. Klashev, L. Dzherov, G.P. Hristov, A. Andreev, G. Papanchev, L. Dimitrov], Kultura, Skopje, 1997, p. 65.

40 Kole Eftimov interview. Eftim Tantski was Kole's grandfather.

41 K. Karpat, op. cit., p. 197. Similarly, an Austrian diplomatic report from 1906 stated that *pechalbari* were generally made up of men 20 to 40 years of age. Letter by Dr Ranci dated 11 July 1906, D. Zografski, editor, op. cit., p. 158.

42 I. Chapovski, op. cit., pp. 16-17.

43 Dragutin Ristevski notes of interview.

44 K. Topuzoski, *Pitu Guli (1865-1903) Zhivot i Potoa* [Pitu Guli (1865-1903) Life and Beyond], Deset Dena Krushevska Republika, Krushevo, 1995, pp. 23-25.

45 Carnegie Endowment for International Peace, *Report of the International Commission to Inquire into the Causes and Conduct of the Balkan Wars*, Published by the Endowment, Washington, 1914, p. 34.

46 C.A. Price, op. cit., p. 314.

47 M. Durham, *The Burden of the Balkans*, Nelson, London, 1905, p. 120.

48 The American data used here is cited from the historian H. Andonov-Poljanski, *The Attitude of the USA Towards Macedonia,* Skopje, Macedonian Review Editions, 1983, pp. 40–42; and, K. Karpat, op. cit., p. 196.

49 The destroyed villages were exempt from taxation, but in order to make up the expenses of the Ottoman State caused by the uprising, taxes were raised elsewhere. M.E. Durham, op. cit., p. 159.

50 K. Karpat, op. cit., p. 191.

51 Gjorche Petrov gave the following statistics for emigration from Macedonia: 1903 - 7,000-8,000; 1904 - 9,000-10,000; 1905 - 10,000-12,000; and, 1906 - 15,000-16,000. M. Dimitrijevski, op. cit., pp. 294-295.

52 K. Karpat, op. cit., p. 191.

53 Ibid., p. 187.

54 Between 1908 and 1913, 81,752 people left for the United States.

55 Mitko Bogdanovski interview.

56 *Na plovniot dzhin koj potonal so Titanik na 14 April godina imalo i Makedonci,* [There were also Macedonians that drowned with the sailing giant, the Titanic], www.makedonskanacija.mk, 24 May 2017.

57 Sokrat Chulakovski interview.

58 V. Cvetanoski, *Pechalbarstvoto Makedonska Sudbina* [Pechalba a Macedonian Fate], Iris, Struga, 2012, p. 196.

59 *Dvajca Tresoncani zhrtvi na Titanik,* [Two people from Tresonche were sacrificed with the Titanic], from www.makedonskanacija.mk, 8 February 2012.

60 *Galichki kashkaval na trpezata na brodot Titanik,* [Kashkaval from Galitchnik on the ship Titanic], www.makedonskanacija.mk, 27 January 2016.

61 Stojko Dodulovski made it to the United States, and he remained there until 1948 when he returned to Macedonia and lived in Skopje. He eventually went back to the United States as his daughter was there and he lived in Chicago to 80 years of age. *Vo Skopskoto selo Chucher, vo potraga na nesekojdnevna prikazna*, [In the Skopje village Chucher, in search of an unusual story], Ivana Trajkovska. The article was first published in the newspaper Vecer, but has been sourced from www.makedonskanacija.mk.

62 *The Janesville Daily Gazette*, 10 November 1913.

63 Vancho Kalcovski interview. Boris Kalcovski left his Prespa region village soon after being issued the visa for Canada on 22 June 1926. He departed Yugoslavia on 8 July, arrived in St Louis, France, on the same day and at Antwerp, Belgium on 14 July. Boris landed in Dover, England as a transmigrant under bond before reaching his destination in Quebec, Canada, on 31 July 1926.

64 B. Bozinoski and V. Krstevski, *Chetvrta Generacija* [Fourth Generation], Macedonian Australian Association of Culture and Human Rights, Newcastle, 2012, p. 387 (Metodija Lajmanovski interview), The agent arranged for the *pechalbari* to travel to England from where they boarded a ship to Canada.

65 Nick Constantinou interview.

66 John Karajas interview.

67 Diplomatic letter from the Austrian Consulate in Bitola, letter number 33, by Dr Ranci, dated 11 July 1906, D. Zografski, editor, op. cit., p. 160.

68 Ibid., p. 159.

69 H.N. Brailsford, op. cit., pp. 50–51.

70 D. Konstantinov, op. cit., p. 78.

71 *Pechalbari* in the United States and Canada were also known to bring and/or send blue workwear overalls to their families in Macedonia, in particular to the Bitola, Prespa and Ohrid regions. Ibid., p. 78.

Part Two

National Tragedy and Separation

3

Division and Devastation

Ottoman Turkish rule had been firmly entrenched in the Balkans since the fifteenth century. It was a slow and difficult journey to independence for the Balkan lands. The role of the European powers (Russia, England, France and Germany) was instrumental in the establishment of independence for Greece in 1829 (autonomous in 1821), Serbia in 1878 (autonomous in 1817) and Bulgaria in 1908 (autonomous in 1878). Whilst Macedonians continued their struggle for national liberation, the liberated Balkan States entertained their own pretensions of a 'Greater Greece', 'Greater Serbia' and 'Greater Bulgaria' at the expense of the Macedonian people's right to establish their own homeland.

In support of their claims to Macedonia, Greece, Serbia and Bulgaria engaged in a bitter rivalry for the religious adherence of the population that was principally played out between the Greek Patriarchate and Bulgarian Exarchate Churches. These national Churches were used as the primary tool of the young nationalist Balkan States whose expansionist policies saw a fierce competition develop with Greece, Serbia and Bulgaria attempting to prove that the Macedonian land and people were an integral part of their respective states. Historical claims with no factual basis, population statistics and ethnographic data were manufactured to support the respective positions of the Balkan States, and although contradictory to each state's claims, was used to present Macedonia as essentially a Greek, Serbian or Bulgarian land.

The competition commenced as a rivalry between the respective Churches of the Balkan States for the religious adherence of Macedonians. The struggle further developed as an educational competition for Macedonian schoolchildren, and in the last two decades of Ottoman rule – Greek, Serbian and Bulgarian paramilitary bands regularly crossed into Macedonia for the purpose of coercing and intimidating entire villages in the effort to adhere to their particular church or their national state. The main rivalry was between the Bulgarians and Greeks. Harilaos Trikoupis, Greek Prime Minister from 1882 to 1895, declared that 'When the Great War comes, Macedonian will become Greek or Bulgarian according to who wins. If it is taken by the Bulgarians, they will make the population Slavs. If we take it, we will make them all Greeks'.[1] The Balkan Wars of 1912-13 were the climax of Greek, Serbian and Bulgarian competition for Macedonia and a manifestation of the rivalry in the form of open armed conflict for territorial expansion.

In early 1912 the Balkan States commenced entering a series of alliances which aimed to expand their territories to the detriment of the Ottoman Empire; however, they failed to agree on how they would divide Macedonia. On 8 October 1912, an ultimatum was sent to the Ottoman Turks deceptively demanding 'autonomy for Macedonia'. War broke out on 12 October 1912 (the First Balkan War) and, after two months, the Ottoman Turks were driven out of Macedonia. The Bulgarians engaged in most of the fighting, sending the bulk of their troops towards Constantinople to thwart a possible Ottoman offensive. This allowed the old allies, Serbia and Greece, to conquer and divide most of Macedonia against numerically inferior Turkish forces. Bulgaria occupied considerably less territory than she anticipated gaining, and soon realised that Greece and Serbia did not intend to relinquish their larger gains. Peace negotiations began in London on 16 December 1912. The question of territorial settlement created serious tensions, especially as the traditional allies, Serbia and Greece agreed to secure a common frontier in Macedonia. This arrangement would have left the Bulgarians with a small portion of territory in Eastern Macedonia and was bitterly rejected by Bulgaria. The Second Balkan War broke out on 29 June 1913 when Bulgarian troops launched a surprise attack on Greek and Serbian forces in Macedonia. Montenegro and Romania entered the war as allies of Greece and Serbia, and Ottoman forces also re-entered (regaining Eastern Thrace and Edirne), resulting in an overwhelming defeat of Bulgaria.

The Balkan wars brought terrible carnage and destruction to Macedonia. Large towns such as Kukush, Voden, Doiran, Enidzhe Vardar and others were completely destroyed; more than 200 villages were burnt to the ground, with many thousands left homeless or forced to leave as refugees. In strategic regions Macedonians underwent genocidal extermination with evidence of systematic atrocities and war crimes against the civilian population carried out on a massive scale. Confirmation of a co-ordinated attack upon civilians was uncovered in the post baggage of the 19th Greek infantry unit captured by the Bulgarian army near Razlog. The contents of the letters provided frightening graphic detail of the brutalities and cruelties carried out under orders by the Greek army upon the civilian population, comprising the slaughter of non-combatants, including women and children, and the violation of women.[2]

With the signing of the Treaty of Bucharest on 10 August 1913, southern Macedonia was awarded to Greece, north-western Macedonia went to Serbia and eastern Macedonia to Bulgaria. The tragic partitioning of Macedonia was sanctioned by the Versailles Treaty at the Paris Peace Conference on 27 November 1919. At the London Conference in 1920, the recently created Albanian state, which already contained along its eastern regions a sizeable Macedonian Christian and Macedonian Muslim population, was awarded even further Macedonian territory along the Prespa and Ohrid lakes.

Geographically, Macedonia covers a total of 67,741 square kilometres. As a result of the Balkan Wars and treaties that sanctioned the conquest of Macedonia, Greece occupied 34,356 square kilometres of Macedonia, Serbia occupied 25,713 square kilometres, Bulgaria occupied 6,798 square kilometres and Albania occupied 874 square kilometres. The expansion of Serbia and Greece, in particular, saw these two states for the first time in history share a common political border in Macedonia, whereas historically the Greek northern frontier was marked by Mount Olympus before 1913. Macedonia had never in its history been a part of the Greek state.

Since partition, Macedonians refer to the occupied land in the following manner: the Aegean area of Macedonia denoting the territory under Greek rule (Aegean being the Aegean Sea); the Vardar area of Macedonia denoting the territory under Serb rule (Vardar being the principal river that runs through Macedonia); the Pirin area of Macedonia denoting the territory under Bulgarian rule (Pirin being the Pirin Mountain); and the Mala Prespa area denoting the territory under Albanian rule (Prespa relating to Lake Prespa).[3]

Economic impact on Macedonia

Macedonia possessed all the ingredients to independently develop as an economically robust sovereign state, should it have been given the right to self-determination. Blessed with an abundance of natural resources, Macedonia is a largely mountainous country with deep lakes, valleys and fertile plains. There are four main rivers, Vardar, Bistrica, Struma and Mesta. The Vardar is the largest river with a course of 388 kilometres that rises from Shar Mountain (*Shar Planina*) in the north-west of the country and flows south into the Aegean Sea near Solun. The majority of the population lived in villages and engaged primarily in agriculture, with the main produce being cereals, tobacco, red peppers, cotton and opium amongst others. Livestock and animal breeding were popular. Macedonia possessed great potential for economic development through industries that were undeveloped under Ottoman Turkish rule, such as mining natural mineral resources found in many parts of the country: this included copper, chrome, lead, gold, silver, iron, marble and magnesium.

The Balkan Wars brought terrible human suffering to the Macedonian population through forced exodus, with a view to ethnically cleansing Macedonians from their land. Towns and villages were completely destroyed, harvests burned, and properties and livestock destroyed, seized or looted by the armies and individual soldiers of the conquering states. The immense material damage to Macedonia was of vast proportions resulting in immediate economic disruption. The division of Macedonia shattered the territorial unity and natural right of the Macedonians to their own homeland and the imposition of an illegitimate border resulted in Macedonians no longer being able to move freely within their own land. Internal *pechalba* was hit hard as the movement of seasonal workers was disrupted, and those from northern and central Macedonia were unable to continue working in towns located in the southern regions. Families became physically separated from one another in neighbouring states, with relatives divided among the newly created Kingdom of Serbs, Croats and Slovenes (later to become Yugoslavia), the newly established Albanian state (which had never previously been a national state), Bulgaria and the extraordinarily expanded Greek state.

The Great War brought further destruction on Macedonia soon after the end of the Balkan Wars. Dissatisfied with the outcome of the Balkan Wars and the Treaty of Bucharest on 10 August 1913, Bulgaria participated in the Great War on the side of Germany and Austria-Hungary (Central Powers) on the promise that Bulgaria would receive a large share of Macedonian territory. In September 1915, Bulgarian troops attacked the Serbian army in Serb-occupied Macedonia and took control of that territory whilst the dividing line between the (formerly) Serbian and Greek occupied parts of Macedonia became the front line of the Macedonian Front (also known as the Salonica Front). Bulgaria and the Central Powers were positioned on the northern side and Great Britain, France and Russia were to the south. The Bulgarians alone had 550,000 men, and over the course of the war the total combatants on the front numbered 1,300,000 men. Macedonians were mobilised to fight by the opposing sides and were found in the Greek, Serbian and Bulgarian armies. All the fighting was on Macedonian soil and the loss of life and destruction of property brought further hardship and misery to Macedonia.

Economic development in Macedonia under Ottoman Turkish rule grew independently of its neighbours (Serbia, Greece and Bulgaria) which traditionally did not have common commercial relations with Macedonia. Commerce, trade and markets were established within Macedonia and extensive road networks existed which connected key Macedonian economic centres with other areas within the country and in particular, in the direction of Solun and the Aegean Sea, which had been the principal economic centre for Macedonia. Established supply and trade routes, used for commerce since ancient times, suddenly became inaccessible following the division of Macedonia. Trade in general stagnated in towns that became isolated and cut off from their traditional business. Solun, Macedonia's principal city and port, that great prize taken by the Greeks from the clutches of the Bulgarians during the Balkan Wars, after twenty years of Greek rule, 'denied its natural economic background of Eastern and Central Macedonia, [it)] has declined entirely and turned from a principal port of the Aegean Sea into a sad memory of the former wealthy commercial centre'.[4]

After Solun, Bitola was the second most important commercial and administrative centre. After the division of Macedonia, Bitola became an isolated town, situated in the south-westerly corner of the new political borders and its importance quickly declined, as it no longer commanded a strategic trading position and became little more than a far-flung outpost under the new Serbian administration. The same fate also befell Ohrid and many other towns in central and south-west Macedonia which, according to Bistrichki, became isolated from their natural access to the sea via Solun, and have been forced to use the commercial line to Belgrade, unnatural for them. The same applies to Macedonia under the Bulgarian yoke, the economic progress is closely linked to the commercial routes with Seres, Drama, Kavala, Salonika and Strumica, but not with Sofia – Vidin, or Plovdiv – Burgas'.[5]

The division of Macedonia dealt a fatal economic blow to internal seasonal migrations of large-scale sheep herding. It is estimated, prior to the Balkan Wars in 1912-13, that 11 per cent of the Macedonian population was involved in sheep breeding.[6] Macedonian sheep herders traditionally drove hundreds of thousands of sheep on mountain routes along Jablanica, Jama, Bistra, Stogovo, Skopska Crna Gora, Shar, Babuna, Mokra, Baba, Osogovskite, Plachkovica, Vlaina, Bigla, Ograzhden and Pirin, heading towards the Solun plain, the Halkidik and Kasandra peninsulas, the Bistrica river, Seres, Kavala including the mouth of the Struma river and Lake Tahino where they would remain for the winter months.[7] In order to maintain traditional routes, sheepherders had the option of paying customs taxes to take their sheep over the new borders, but to do so meant paying a levy on each individual sheep both times whilst crossing over the border.[8] Macedonian sheep herders from the Gora region were particularly hard hit. Prior to the imposition of the new border which placed a number of the Gora villages in Albania, sheepherding was a significant economic factor in the district with up to 100,000 sheep; however, being cut off from their natural pastures in Serbian-occupied Macedonia, there was a dramatic reduction in the number of sheep in the district and Macedonians commenced leaving on *pechalba*.[9] The economic impact of the division of Macedonia to sheepherders alone was significant. The closure of their natural routes that they had travelled for centuries, if not thousands, of years saw the downfall of large-scale sheepherding and had a negative impact on related industries.

Newly constructed political borders significantly impacted villages close to the border. Villages became separated from their fields, pastures and forests. The village Orgosta (Gora) lost 40 per cent of its agricultural fields positioned over the newly established border, while the number of inhabitants of the village Rbele began to decrease as soon as the border was established.[10] Border areas were seen as sensitive by the occupying states, as Macedonians lived on both sides of the dividing border and there were heightened concerns regarding movement in these areas. Villagers were required to have special permits issued in order to work their land positioned alongside the border. In some instances where village fields were located across the new border, such as in Negochani village and others along the border separating Bitola and Lerin (on the Yugoslav-Greek political border), special arrangements were put in place to enable villagers to work their fields over the border. These arrangements remained in place for several decades until they came to an end, forcibly dispossessing Macedonian families and entire villages of their ancestral lands.

Political impact

Macedonians are not unfamiliar with hardship: for over five centuries they endured Ottoman Turkish rule and for at least a thousand years earlier, if not more, Macedonians were too often under foreign domination. Yet it was the territorial division of Macedonia as a result of the Balkan Wars that brought the greatest tragedy upon Macedonia and the Macedonian people. Macedonia ceased to be a natural ethnographic and economic unit and Macedonians found themselves subjected to the rule of foreign states. For the first time in centuries, *pechalbari* were no longer leaving Macedonia with Ottoman passports, and they were now confronted with differing social, economic and political circumstances.

There is also evidence indicating that their experiences abroad, particularly in the democracies of Western Europe and the USA – but also in the neighbouring liberated Balkan lands – were characterised by a taste of freedom outside of Ottoman subjugation that exposed them to new political ideas. Politicisation of Macedonian *pechalbari* is evident as early as the 1880s. An official diplomatic report by Stojan Novakovic in Constantinople, dated 16 August 1888, refers to '*pechalbari* postal couriers' who maintained a communication link between *pechalba* colonies in Constantinople, Bulgaria, Romania and Serbia with their families and villages. Novakovic states that certain individuals from the Ohrid region engaged in this activity, visited the Macedonian colony in Constantinople, and then travelled to Romania, spreading news that 'others will be heading for the Bitola and Prilep regions to agitate that Macedonia raise a rebellion against the Turks'.[11]

Simjan Simidzhiev (Velmevci village, Ohrid) adopted revolutionary views whilst on *pechalba* in Bulgaria where he mixed with other Macedonian *pechalbari* as well as Macedonian emigrants there who were involved in the Macedonian revolutionary movement, VMRO (*Vnatreshna Makedonska Revolucionerna Organizacija*).[12] In Bulgaria, Simidzhiev came to understand the 'seriousness of my duty towards the liberation of my people'.[13] Similarly, Zhivko Kirov Janevski from the village of Drenoveni (Kostur), left his village due to economic considerations and worked in Burgas (Bulgaria) as a bricklayer. Mixing with members of the Macedonian emigrant community who were active in the VMRO, upon his return to his native village he became an active participant in the revolutionary struggle working with the local commanders Vasil Chakalarov, Mitre Vlahot and Pando Klashev.[14] A report by the Serb Minister for Internal Affairs to the Minister for Foreign Affairs outlines the uncovering of a plan to blow up the Ottoman railway (at the Macedonian village Zibevchu) by five Macedonian *pechalbari* from Bitola (who resided in the Serb city Kragujevac).[15] A group of approximately 100 *pechalbari* from Capari and surrounding villages (Bitola) working in Katerini, returned to their villages at the outbreak of the insurrection in 1903 after having secured arms from over the nearby Greek border.[16] It was not uncommon for *pechalbari* to return home to assist in the revolutionary movement during the Ilinden Rebellion and afterwards, as was the case with Ilija Stojcev Bozhinovski from Armensko (Lerin), who travelled from the United States in 1907 and joined a *cheta* (group of armed Macedonian freedom fighters) under the command of Krsto Londov.[17]

Increased political consciousness appears to have been a consequence of working abroad; widespread *pechalba* in the western regions might have a direct link to the intensity of the 1903 Ilinden Rebellion in the Ohrid, Bitola, Lerin and Kostur regions as Western

MAP 5 – Division of Macedonia, 1913.

Macedonia was a central focus point of the rebellion. The upheaval brought about by the Balkan Wars of 1912-1913 temporarily suspended the movement of *pechalbari* out of Macedonia. While foreign armies engaged in bloody battles, each seeking to carve out a slice of Macedonian territory in order to expand their own states, conditions became far too precarious for *pechalbari* to continue their travels.

Following the division of Macedonia in 1913, the Macedonian people faced differing conditions under their new rulers. The plight of Macedonians under Greek, Serbian, Bulgarian and Albanian rule and the political and economic considerations linked to differing rates of *pechalba* and migration from each respective state will now be considered.

4

Living and Leaving under the new Rulers

Macedonia under Greek rule (Aegean Macedonia)

The arrival of Greek rule in Southern Macedonia represents the most tragic episode in the history of the Macedonian people and provided further stimulus for young Macedonians to be drawn to *pechalba*. The existence of a distinct Macedonian ethnicity was denied, and the Greek government systematically and obsessively attempted to wipe out all traces of indigenous Macedonian ethnic character. Laws were formulated and passed in the Athens Parliament aimed at transforming the newly conquered Macedonian territory to appear as Greek land. The government established a Commission on Toponyms for the purpose of suggesting new names for Macedonian villages and towns, as well as rivers, mountains and other geographic locations. From 1918 to the end of 1928, most places in southern Macedonia had been given new names, and laws were put in place against using the original Macedonian names, punishable by fines of 100 drachma or up to 10 days detention.[18]

Macedonian Christian names and surnames were forcibly changed to appear ethnically Greek to further disguise Southern Macedonia as Greek. Macedonian surnames traditionally end in 'ov/ova', 'ev/eva' and 'ski/ska' and were changed to reflect a Greek character using 'os', 'es', 'opoulos', 'as' and 'iou'. In the Kostur region when Greek officials from the government commission arrived in Konomladi village, new names were prescribed for everyone, with no consultation: the Kotchoff family surname, for instance, was changed to Konstanidou.[19] Often Greek schoolteachers played a role in assigning new names. Velika Spirova from Neret village, born in 1911 (prior to the Greek occupation), recalled that the teacher changed the names of the children in her classroom and that her name was changed from the Macedonian Velika to the Greek Paskaliya.[20] The new 'official' Greek names were alien to the Macedonians who amongst themselves continued to use their own traditional Macedonian names.

Even after surnames were changed to Greek, at times the authorities considered they did not sound sufficiently Greek and would then change their name a second time. For instance, the Domazetov family in Vrbeni village (Lerin), was initially changed to Domazetis; however, after a few weeks the family was notified that the surname 'sounded too Bulgarian' and it was changed to Drosinis.[21] Similarly, the Ashlakoff family in Ofcharani village (Lerin) had their surname changed to Ashlakis, which 'was not considered to be Greek enough' and was later changed to Anastasiadis.[22]

The attack upon all things Macedonian was undertaken with fanatical obsession. Macedonian inscriptions on churches and schools were changed to Greek, books were burned, as were historical and religious documents. Nothing was spared, as even cemeteries were demolished, or tombstones changed to Greek. In 1928, an English journalist, Hild, said that Greeks not only persecute living Macedonians, 'but they even persecute dead ones. They do not leave them in peace even in the graves. They erase the Slavonic inscriptions on the headstones, remove the bones and burn them'.[23]

Since the nineteenth century, the Greek Government maintained the illusion of a vast empire through a doctrine known as the 'Great Idea' ('Megala Idea'). The concept was first coined by a Greek Vlah,[24] Ioannis Kolettis, who erroneously claimed that all the inhabitants of the Kingdom of Greece were exclusively Greek and, further, that those who lived in any land associated with Greek history or the Greek race were Greek.[25] The illusion of the Great Idea sought to establish a greater Greece stretching from the river Menderes in Asia Minor to the city of Edremit and deep into the western regions, including the cities of Izmir, Aydin, and Marmaris; Northern Thrace with Edirne, the Gallipoli Peninsula and including the island Imroz, Western Thrace, southern Macedonia up to Prilep, southern Albania including the Gjirokaster region, nearby islands and the large Mediterranean island of Cyprus. The American journalist and commentator John Reed commented in 1915 that 'Greek ambitions are limitless'.[26] Incredibly, the 'Great Idea' doctrine persists in the mindset of radical Greeks in the twenty-first century and continues to be validated by Greek education and the Greek Orthodox Church.

Following territorial gains in Macedonia (1913) and Western Thrace (1920), both historically and ethnically non-Greek territories, the lust for further expansion in line with the 'Great Idea' led to Greece launching an attack on Turkey to occupy the Anatolian region and parts of its coastline (Greco-Turkish War 1919-1922). Macedonians were forcibly conscripted into the Greek military and routinely placed in the front lines of battle. Initially, Macedonians attempted to avoid conscription by leaving and embarking on *pechalba*, but the Greek state suspended the issuing of passports.

Placed in the front lines of battle as part of the invading Greek force, Macedonians often deserted or surrendered, and were encouraged to do so by the Turkish forces. Macedonians saw first-hand how the Turks distinguished between Macedonians and Greeks, in particular how Macedonian prisoners were treated well by the Turks, in contrast to the harsh treatment of Greek prisoners. The historian, Stavre Dzhikov, states that the Turkish military dropped leaflets on the battlefield calling for Macedonians to desert from the Greek army, that they (Turks and Macedonians) had lived together harmoniously in Macedonia and that the Turks respected Macedonian identity, while the Greeks did not.[27] Vasil Boskov, from Visheni village (Kostur), was involved in the front-line battle in Smyrna, together with many other Macedonians who would gather to rest and eat together. 'Turkish hatred of the Greek was deep. During the retreat when the Turks captured prisoners, they would ask what their nationality was, if they were Greek, they were hanged, whilst Macedonians were told to leave'.[28] Trajko Ailakov from Armenoro village (Lerin) was in the second forward line in the Battle of Sakarya and afterwards told his family how Macedonian prisoners were treated well and the Greek prisoners were treated harshly.[29] Risto Gochev's father, Tanas Gochev, from Maala village (Lerin) and two uncles were conscripted into the Greek army for the attack on Turkey. Although many tried to avoid conscription, it was difficult to do without causing hardship to one's family and village. When individuals failed to report to the barracks in Lerin after the conscription notice arrived, the police or military would arrive to inflict damage to the family in question and the village as a whole would suffer. 'Macedonians were not trusted to be in their own units and were dispersed in amongst Greeks but were most likely to be involved in the front lines of battle. My father (Tanas) was wounded in the leg during a battle at Afyonkarashisar in Turkey. When the Turkish troops found him and realised that he was not Greek, he was saved from certain death.'[30]

When Macedonians returned to their villages after the Greco-Turkish war, even though they had served in the Greek army they continued to experience persecution and discrimination due to their non-Greek identity. This prompted many to leave and seek work abroad. One example relates to the story of Vasil Boskov from Visheni village (Kostur). After returning home he faced constant harassment by the police stationed in the village who would call him a 'Bulgarian bastard' and constantly questioned his presence in the village saying, 'What are you doing here?'. Vasil eventually left for Montenegro where he worked as a timber cutter; however, the pay was low, and he soon returned to Visheni to contemplate his future options. Prior to Greek occupation of Macedonia Vasil had accompanied his father Petre on *pechalba* to Egypt and in 1927 he travelled to Egypt with the intention to continue to the United States. By this stage, the United States travel restrictions had been enforced and the British Consulate suggested that he could travel to Australia. Vasil arrived in Fremantle in 1927.[31]

The Greek military campaign in Turkey failed badly and is known in Greek historiography as the 'Great Disaster'. In 1923, the Lausanne Agreement was signed between triumphant Turkey and defeated Greece. The agreement stipulated a compulsory exchange of populations which resulted in Greece expelling 394,108 Turkish Muslims to Turkey; this figure included over 40,000 Macedonian Muslims uprooted from their homeland. In return Turkey transferred 1,221,849 Christians to Greece from Asia Minor and the Caucasus who were of mixed ethnic background but, as Orthodox Christians, found themselves under the influence of the Greek Orthodox Church. The Greek authorities strategically placed 538,595 of the newly arrived refugees into southern Macedonia as a colonising element to facilitate the modification of the Macedonian character of Aegean Macedonia. During the period 1923 to 1928, over 250,000 colonists were settled in the Solun region alone and over 200,000 in the eastern regions of Seres, Kavala and Drama. Thousands more colonists were settled in central, western and south-western Aegean Macedonia. Macedonians in Aegean Macedonia commonly refer to these people as '*Prosfigi*', denoting foreigners.

Macedonians were excluded from wide-ranging agrarian reforms in the 1920s which benefited only Greek peasants and refugees. Costly government projects to drain swamps and lakes to recover thousands of acres of land were provided to the newly arrived refugees for economic and political reasons.[32] Properties belonging to Macedonians driven out during the Balkan Wars and the expelled Turkish population of Aegean Macedonia were used to accommodate newly arrived colonists. Sometimes there were too many colonists allocated for settlement in a particular village and not enough homes from the expelled population to accommodate them, and in these instances, additional land was forcefully confiscated from Macedonians to construct new homes for colonists. This occurred, for example, in Armenoro village in the Lerin region. Colonists were further supported by the Greek state with gifts of agricultural land forcibly confiscated from Macedonians.[33] An eyewitness during these difficult times, Velika Spirova, stated that 'if the colonist family did not have a barn or shed on the land, the Greek state constructed these for them'.[34] In addition, goods and furniture were appropriated from Macedonians and given to colonists.

Macedonian households could be forced to take in one or two colonising families into their homes. This mostly occurred in the border regions with the aim of making the life of the Macedonians unbearable and speeding up their emigration.[35] New strategically located villages were constructed to accommodate colonists on land confiscated from Macedonians. In the Lerin region, the newly established colonist village of Kafkas, the name designating the non-Greek origins of the colonists, was established near the border (with Macedonia under Serbian rule) on land belonging to Negochani village.

The Greek government did not invest in Macedonian regions to improve economic conditions and although there were a few large scale government projects such as the construction of the Metaxas line of defence, 'they excluded Macedonians unless they joined extreme nationalist, right wing, or fascist organisations'.[36] Discrimination against Macedonians was the norm and they remained neglected and poor, denied employment in favour of colonist refugees.[37]

Extremist ultra-nationalist organisations and armed bands sanctioned by the Greek state were formed and unleashed a bloodthirsty reign of terror on to the Macedonian population, seeking to speed up the process of denationalisation and assimilation, or otherwise make life so difficult that they would migrate to a neighbouring Balkan land. The following is an example of an order issued by a Greek ultranationalist organisation in 1926:[38]

> WE ORDER
>
> 1. Starting today it is forbidden to speak Bulgarian[39] at public places, in the cafés and restaurants, in doing business, at meetings, assemblies, and gatherings, at parties, luncheons, weddings, etc.
>
> 2. We order the above mentioned only to speak in the Greek language.
>
> 3. We recommend to all authorities – the administrative and the military, the civil servants and private employees, neither to accept nor to give information in any other language but Greek.
>
> 4. Parents, teachers, priests and tutors of minors – we call upon you to fulfil your patriotic duties; we shall hold you responsible for the offences[40] of your subordinates.
>
> 5. Whoever violates these orders will be considered a traitor of the fatherland and shall be horribly punished by our organisation which has been created following a lengthy and thorough analysis of the situation and under the slogan 'The Fatherland Above All'. It has the power to punish any who does not carry out its orders.

Photo 3: Stase Kizon, with his wife Anna and mother-in-law, all from the village Neret (Lerin). Stase was in Australia from 1926 to 1930. This photograph was taken in 1936, after Metaxas had taken power and just prior to Stase returning to Australia. (Source: Victor Georgopoulos).

Conditions for Macedonians worsened following the arrival of the fascist dictatorship of Ioannis Metaxas in 1936. Whereas previously the Macedonian language was banned from public use as a criminal offence, with the arrival of Metaxas, it was also banned from use in the home. All Macedonian localities were flooded with posters declaring 'Speak Greek'.[41] Speaking Macedonian became a criminal act under Paragraph 697 of the Greek Penal Code and despite the barbaric nature of the legislation and heavy bondage of Greek occupation, Macedonians continued using their language under extremely difficult conditions. For their perseverance to maintain their identity, thousands were beaten by the Greek police for speaking Macedonian, were brought before the courts and ordered to pay heavy fines, imprisoned and exiled to barren Greek islands, whilst elderly Macedonians in their 70s and 80s were sent to night school, forced to learn Greek. It was no coincidence that during this period, in the 1920s and 1930s, a significant number of Macedonians were leaving to go abroad, particularly from the Lerin, Voden and Kostur regions.[42]

This period was well summarised by the Australian author, Bert Birtles, in his 1938 book, *Exiles in the Aegean* states:

> If Greece has no Jewish problem, she has the Macedonians. In the name of 'Hellenisation' these people are being persecuted continually and arrested for the most fantastic reason.

> Metaxas's way of inculcating the proper nationalist spirit among them has been to change all the native placenames into Greek and to forbid use of the native language. For displaying the slightest resistance to this edict – for this too is a danger to the security of the State – peasants and villagers have been exiled without trial.[43]

The campaign of terror against Macedonians intensified with the outbreak of the Greek-Italian War on 29 October 1940, when 5,000 Macedonians considered as 'dubious elements' and 'dangerous to the security of the state' were expelled to the Greek islands such as Kefallinia, Sifnos, Mikronos and Agios Efstratios. Many innocent Macedonians died of hunger, tuberculosis and torture. Since the 1920s, the international Communist movement, the Comintern, had recognised that Macedonia was an oppressed and occupied nation and a separate ethnicity with a right to their own homeland, and this recognition and support drew many Macedonian activists towards Communist ideology. However, the policy of the Greek Communist Party fluctuated, ranging from 'total independence for Aegean Macedonia' to 'equality for the minorities'. Nevertheless, during the Second World War, Macedonians in Aegean Macedonia followed the example of their brothers in Vardar Macedonia, set up their own resistance organisations and joined the partisan struggle against Nazi German, Bulgarian and Italian occupation. The Macedonians proved themselves to be formidable fighters in their quest for rights and recognition and believed that their rights would be respected in a post-war democratic Greece.

Following the withdrawal of Germany and Italy in 1944, Greek terror against the Macedonian population recommenced with a new intensity by right-wing nationalist elements. Through laws, decrees, and other enactments, the persecution of Macedonians was given a legal basis and their large-scale persecution surpassed even the pre-war Greek regime. Examples of laws enacted which were used as a legal basis to persecute Macedonians include Law Number 453 and Law TOD of July 1945 relating to the 'security of public safety', Law 509/1945 'on public order and banditry' and Law 543/1945 'against organisations and individuals acting in favour of secession from the

Greek territories'. Deportations of Macedonians to the Greek islands recommenced, with 13,529 people interned. Greek Communists were also targeted for persecution during this period and the general tyranny intensified to such an extent that Greece was plunged into a bloody civil war from spring 1946 to autumn 1949. Macedonians played an integral part in the struggle against the Greek government, although their role has been ignored in official Greek historical accounts of the war.

To protect themselves, Macedonians organised armed resistance against the Greek government through their own movement, the National Liberation Front (*Naroden Osloboditelen Front* – NOF) and saw themselves as an ally or partner to the Communist Party of Greece, the *Kommuinstiko Komma tis Elladas* (KKE). Although united by their Marxist-Leninist Communist ideology, the two groups were deeply mistrustful of one another. The KKE sought to take power in Greece and set up a Communist state whilst the struggle for the Macedonians was the national liberation of the Macedonian people in Aegean Macedonia.[44] The Democratic Army of Greece (DAG) was the military arm of the KKE and Macedonian participation in the rebel troops was very significant ranging from a quarter of the fighting force in 1947 to two-thirds in mid-1949.[45] However, the overall participation of Macedonians was much higher when taking into account the roles played by ordinary people behind the battle lines providing support to the partisans with food, shelter and intelligence. In the liberated areas of Aegean Macedonia from 1947 to 1949, Macedonian language schools opened, with thousands of students in attendance, Macedonian newspapers were printed, and literature and culture flourished. However, in areas under Greek government control, Macedonians suffered enormously as thousands of Macedonians were imprisoned, beaten, tortured, their homes or villages burned or looted, and many others resettled by force.[46]

The repercussions of the Greek Civil War were disastrous for the Macedonians. The bulk of the fighting took place on Macedonian territory, particularly in north-western Aegean Macedonia, a large number of Macedonian villages were completely devastated, 30,000 Macedonians were killed, and approximately 50,000 were forced to flee as refugees, including 28,000 children who were to be brought up in orphanages in various Eastern European nations such as Romania, Hungary, Poland, Czechoslovakia and the Republic of Macedonia.

Photo 4: Macedonian refugee children from Lagen village (Lerin) in Bela Crkva, Banat district of Vojvodina, Serbia, former Yugoslavia, 1948. From left to right: Vasilka Pappas, File Gelin, Tsila Pappas and Pandil (Paul) Pappas. (Source: Paul Pappas).

During and immediately after the Civil War, the Greek government implemented several laws and regulations aimed at removing citizenship and confiscating properties belonging to those fighters and families of the Macedonian National Liberation Front and the Greek Democratic Army who left as political refugees. The laws applied to Greeks and Macedonians; however, amendments to these laws have resulted in Greeks being able to reclaim their citizenship and properties, while discrimination against Macedonians continues to this day. There were also many who had arrived as *pechalbari* in Australia and were not in the village during the war years, yet they 'had been wiped off the Greek records as non-existent', could never return to their homeland, and had no alternative but to bring their families to Australia.[47]

In the early 1950s the Greek government introduced a program aimed at removing Macedonians from the border territories between Aegean Macedonia and the Republic of Macedonia and replacing them with Greeks.[48] The Greek state went to extreme measures to close the borders with Albania, Yugoslavia and Bulgaria, bringing in trusted Albanians from Epirus and planting them throughout Macedonian border villages to act as 'eyes and ears for the Greeks'.[49] Ongoing attempts at wiping out the use of the Macedonian language saw the authorities conduct mass ceremonies in villages and towns forcing the inhabitants to declare that they would cease using Macedonian and speak only Greek. A number of these ceremonies were reported in the Greek press, such as the following example from 1959:

> During the last two months, the inhabitants of some villages in North Greece in official mass ceremonies proclaimed that they will cease to use the Slav dialect and that in future they will speak only Greek. The first ceremony took place in the village Trebeno, district of Kojani, which has according to the census of 1952, 692 inhabitants. It was followed by other villages such as Breshcheni, Kostur district (41 inhabitants), Atrapos, Florina district (466 inhabitants), and so forth.[50]

Following its occupation of southern Macedonia, the Greek Government did not restrict Macedonians from leaving, either temporarily as *pechalbari* or permanently as emigrants, and deployed a range of discriminatory practices to encourage their departure in order to facilitate a de facto ethnic cleansing of southern Macedonia. Macedonians were regularly discriminated against, treated as being of a lower culture, undermined and denied employment opportunities. Disillusioned, many left their villages in search of opportunities abroad: for example, in the space of two years from 1950 to 1951, 26 Macedonian families quit Lagen village for Australia.[51]

The period from the end of the Greek Civil War (1949) up until the early 1960s marks the final major phase of emigration of Macedonians from Aegean Macedonia. Conditions for Macedonians deteriorated after the Civil War as the government viewed them as problematic. Discrimination was experienced at all levels of society and, for many, emigration was the only escape as Macedonians were not trusted, were seen as a threat to the security of Greece, and were directly and indirectly encouraged to migrate.

Macedonia under Serb rule (Vardar Macedonia)

In 1913, Serbia immediately undertook to transform its newly conquered Macedonian territory to reflect a Serbian character, renaming the territory as 'Vardarska Banovina' but in everyday language referring to it as 'Southern Serbia' (Juzhna Srbija). The names of some of the larger cities and towns were changed to give them a Serbian character such as Bitola which was modified to Bitolj; however, toponyms generally remained unchanged. The existence of the Macedonian people was denied as they were proclaimed to be Serbs, and Macedonian names were systematically changed to reflect the Serb character: Macedonian surnames were changed from ending in 'ov/ova' and 'ski/ska' to 'ich'.

The Kingdom of Yugoslavia was officially a state belonging to Serbs, Croats and Slovenes. Any expression of Macedonian identity was strictly forbidden and violently opposed by the Serb administration.[52] The Serbianisation of Macedonia was supported by a significant military presence with anywhere between 35,000 to 50,000 armed men from the Yugoslav (Serbian) army, gendarmerie and armed bands from the State Sponsored Association against Bulgarian bandits active in Macedonia. Macedonia was transformed into a police state with 12,000 men out of 17,000 Yugoslav military police stationed there.[53] The police and military stranglehold impacted traditional internal seasonal *pechalba* within Macedonia as special movement authorisations were required from the police and these were difficult to obtain. The imposition of Serb occupation in Macedonia halted *pechalba* and with the onset of the Great War in 1914, young Macedonian men were forcibly conscripted into the Serbian army. For those who managed to avoid conscription, *pechalba* abroad provided a safe haven from the Serbian authorities. Villagers found numerous ways of avoiding conscription and leaving.[54]

The Serbs did nothing to improve the economic situation in Macedonia. Not only did they fail to invest, their discriminatory practices made the plight of the Macedonians worse. Agricultural cultivation methods were primitive and, after The Great War, more land was converted to industrial crops, such as cotton, tobacco and opium poppies. However, cotton declined 'because partition and new boundaries deprived it of its traditional market, the textile industry in Aegean Macedonia.'[55]

From 1918 until 1940, to reinforce their hold on Macedonia, the Serb state had systematically colonised Macedonia with Serbs, especially in the northern regions, but also as far south as the Bitola region.[56] Land belonging to Macedonians and land converted into large estates by Turkish feudal landlords from the Ottoman era – land which Macedonians believed rightfully belonged to them – was confiscated and redistributed to Serb colonists, members of the military veterans from the Solun Front, men from irregular Serbian bands, military police, regular police, frontier guards and government officials. These were all people who had proven their loyalty to the Kingdom of Yugoslavia and aided the colonisation and transformation of Macedonia into a Serbian land.[57] In the Bitola region village of Dedebalci, the head of the Serb colonist family was known to insist on being invited as a guest to all homes in the village for any celebration. He considered that it was mandatory for everyone to invite him to eat and drink at their expense. The villagers feared repercussions from the Serbian authorities if they did not do so.[58]

During the 1920s and 1930s even though Macedonians were treated as second class citizens in their own land, the Serbs did not pursue a strategic policy of forced emigration as was the case for Macedonians under Greek rule. Instead the state placed restrictions on *pechalba* and introduced substantial taxes, including a requirement that state taxes were paid a year in advance prior to the *pechalbar* leaving, which proved a heavy financial burden, in addition to the large sums of money required to finance travel abroad.[59] *Pechalbari* were required to travel to the Serbian capital, Belgrade, to purchase a passport from the government printers; however, to do so one required approval from the authorities to travel to Belgrade. Once the *pechalbar* arrived in Belgrade, unless they were able to make payment to corrupt administrative officials, a *pechalbar* could wait months before obtaining a passport.[60] Men from the renowned *pechalba* village of Graeshnica (Bitola) secured passports by paying corrupt officials to ensure they would be able to work abroad.[61] Enterprising travel agents also found ways to speed up the process for *pechalbari* to obtain a passport, usually by the payment of additional fees. Even with rigid restrictions in place during the period between the two world wars, Macedonians from the upper villages in the Bitola region, and from the Ohrid region who had long established traditions of *pechalba*, continued travelling abroad in search of work.

Macedonians departed, seeking work in Australia, Canada, the United States and South America. Argentina was a popular South American destination and there had been a tradition of Macedonians working there since the end of the nineteenth century. Others went to Brazil (particularly Sao Paolo and the province of Rio Grande do Sul), Bolivia, Uruguay, Paraguay and Peru (Lima). Men from Prespa region villages, including Ezereni, Carev Dvor, Perovo, Podmochani – as well as others from the Bitola region – travelled to Argentina, with many finding work in the construction industry for German companies in Buenos Aires during the 1920s and 1930s. Originally

Photo 5: Mijal Murgev photographed wearing a hat, standing beside the far-right column on a ship departing from England with a long voyage ahead, bound for Australia, 1924. (Source: Kiril Murgev. Courtesy of Mendo Trajcevski).

from Ezereni village, Gogo Kalevski had been born in Argentina in 1930 and worked for many years in the building industry as a welder, a trade he learned during his military service with the Argentinean navy. He worked on building sites in Buenos Aires with other Macedonians before moving to Comodoro Rivadavia, in the Patagonian province of Chubut in Southern Argentina, where he obtained employment working on the construction of a large hospital.[62]

With the outbreak of the Second World War, Serbian-occupied Macedonia was invaded by Bulgaria, Italy and Germany, with the Bulgarians taking control of the bulk of the territory. The Bulgarian military administration sought to make over the Macedonian population into Bulgarians, while parts of the western area of Macedonia were controlled by the Italians until their capitulation in 1943, whereupon their quislings, the Albanian Balli Kombettar organisation, became Nazi collaborators. Macedonians were targeted for persecution and expulsion, whilst Macedonian Muslims were pressured to identify as Albanians. Macedonians responded to the oppression through armed struggle for their national rights and the liberation of their homeland.

In 1944 the Yugoslav Communist Party under the increasingly dictatorial rule of Marshal Tito formed the Federal Peoples Republic of Yugoslavia (Federativna Narodna Republika Jugoslavia - *FNRJ*), forerunner to the Socialist Federal Republic of Yugoslavia (Socialisticka Federativna Republika Jugoalsvia - *SFRJ*), and that part of Macedonia occupied by the Serbs before the war became a constituent Republic within the Yugoslav federation alongside Serbia, Croatia, Bosnia and Herzegovina, Montenegro and Slovenia. Under the leadership of President Metodija Andonov Chento, the Macedonian Republic outlined an independent political vision that included concerns for the welfare and rights of Macedonians living under Greek, Bulgarian and Albanian rule. However, Chento's vision did not correspond with the interests of the Serbian-dominated Yugoslav government which responded by purging the political leadership of the Macedonian government. Trumped up charges were brought against political leaders including terms of imprisonment for the President, the Attorney General, and other leading members of government in notorious Yugoslav political prisons such as Idrizovo (Macedonia) and Goli Otok (Croatia). With the support of Belgrade, pro-Yugoslav elements within the Communist Party of Macedonian took control of the state and, following Tito's split with Stalinist Russia in 1948, there followed a purge against all Russian Stalinist aligned members of the Communist Information Bureau (otherwise known as the Inform Bureau or Cominform) and all other political opponents. Tito's split with the USSR saw Yugoslavia develop friendlier relations with the United States which enabled Tito to obtain financial aid from the United States. Tito's split from the USSR saw the United States and the Western world turn a blind eye to the widespread human rights abuses in Yugoslavia where, from the 1940s to the 1980s, thousands of Macedonians were imprisoned for their membership of organisations advocating Macedonian independence and for expressing anti-Yugoslav sentiments.

At the beginning of the Second World War, in the whole of Yugoslavia, Macedonia ranked last in industrial development,[63] but the economy worsened after the end of the war. Agricultural policies were developed based on the collectivisation policies in the Soviet Union. These policies were backward and fraught with mismanagement and corruption, with a disastrous effect on the rural population in Macedonia. There were various stages in the confiscation of private property which also included forcibly taking villagers' cattle and sheep. Private property was seized, purportedly aimed at establishing social equality for all citizens, but left them economically worse off. The upper class of Macedonian rural and urban society was completely wiped out.

It was common practice for Communist countries to restrict their citizens from migrating to Western societies, as such migration was considered to be a poor reflection on Communist rule. Tito's Yugoslavia was no different and did not tolerate undermining of the regime by leaving what was being touted as the 'perfect society'. However, young Macedonians responded to Serbian domination of Macedonian politics and economically backward policies by escaping over the border into the political boundaries of Greece (they were in fact entering Aegean Macedonia). From the end of the Second World

War in 1945 to approximately 1960, thousands of young Macedonian men, at great risk to themselves, crossed the border seeking passage into the democracies of Western Europe, Australia and Canada.

From Brajchino village in the Prespa region, it was roughly a one hour walk across the border to the Macedonian village of German where they would report to the Greek authorities at the police station in the village. Groups of two to five young men would take cover in the forest above Brajchino and quietly wait for night to slip across the border without attracting the attention of the Yugoslav military who routinely patrolled the mountainous border. Equipped with automatic weapons the soldiers were known to fire upon the departing men. The soldiers were predominantly Serbs, with some Croats and Slovenes included, but never Macedonians – Macedonians were routinely sent to serve in other Yugoslav Republics.[64]

Men were eager to leave all year round, but the most popular period was winter and early spring when they were least likely to be confronted by a military patrol. As early as the 1920s Brajchino village attracted the attention of the Serbian authorities due to that route used by young men to cross the border near Brajchino. Young men from the Prespa villages of Brajchino, Ljubojno, Dolno Dupeni, Nakolec, Shtrbovo, Krani and other villages crossed the mountainous border via Brajchino. From Brajchino village alone, 52 young men aged between 18 and 25 years of age escaped during a two-year period from 1958 to 1959.[65] Escaping to go abroad became so popular that, in the Prespa region, it became a sign of resistance against Yugoslav rule. There was a sense of pride associated with leaving in that fashion, as it was a sign of men wanting to economically advance themselves. However, the Serbo-Yugoslav regime responded to the exodus by rounding up the younger brothers of those who escaped and conscripting them into the army.

In 1958, at 21 years of age, Giorgi Kalcovski embarked, together with Jonche Jovanovski and the brothers Naum and Spase Totevski all from Brajchino village, crossing the border during a snowy winter evening under the cover of the pine forest. Upon their arrival in German village (Giorgi's mother's village in the Lerin region), Giorgi went to visit his uncle, Naum Lelefanov, for the first time (the two villages having been separated since the partition of Macedonia in 1913).[66] Afterwards Giorgi and his friends presented themselves to the Greek police station in the village as so many others from the Prespa region before them had done. They were taken to Lerin for questioning and registration with the Greek authorities before being transferred to the Lavrion detention camp from where they expected to be sent to any number of Western countries. There were many other Macedonians there, as well as Bulgarians, Turks and Albanians. Giorgi spent two years in Lavrion detention camp before departing for a new life in Australia. Some left together with wives and children in tow. Unhappy with the political system which treated Macedonians as second-class citizens, in 1953, 23-year old Vasil Rendev from Dragosh village crossed the border at night with his wife and young child and made it to the Lavrion detention camp. There he found many Macedonians from the Prespa region, particularly from Brajchino village.

The families of the young men left behind in the villages would often have no idea whether their sons successfully arrived in the detention camp, whether they had been caught on the border attempting to escape and been imprisoned or, worse still, killed by the border patrol. Even though individuals would successfully escape, it would take months before they could get word back to their families. Eftim Eftimovski from the Prespa village of Grnchari was 15 years of age when he escaped over the border with his friend Hodo Mehmeti in 1962. He sent letters back to his family from the Greek Lavrion detention camp; however, the authorities intercepted the letters and informed his family that their son had been killed whilst attempting to cross the border.[67] The unnecessary trauma to the families was probably aimed at discouraging others from leaving. After twelve months in Lavrion, Eftim arrived in Australia in 1963.

It was not until the 1960s that the Communist regime commenced relaxing restrictions to leave for abroad. The bureaucracy, however, remained complicated. The Interior Ministry was responsible for the issuing of passports, but unless one had contacts or were capable of bribing the authorities, travel documentation was difficult to obtain. The most difficult aspect involved obtaining approval to

Photo 6: Family gathering in Prilep to farewell Milka Shekeroska, preparing to commence a new life in Melbourne, Australia with Jim (Dime) Merakovsky, 1962. (Source: Jim Merakovsky).

Photo 7: Ilo Dimovski (third adult male from right) from Gorno Lakocerej village, being farewelled by family at the Ohrid bus station before commencing his journey to Australia, April 1969. Ilo settled in the Wollongong suburb of Cringila. (Source: Borce Dimoski).

leave the country from one's employer (all employers were government). Mihailo Anastasovski was an employee in the state-operated cannery on the outskirts of Bitola in 1964 when he planned to leave as a *pechalbar* for Australia. Mihailo made two attempts to obtain a passport, but both times his application was rejected. On the third attempt he made the application via a family contact who worked in the Interior Ministry. The passport application was successful. A visa for Australia was issued soon after, with a letter of guarantee from a relative in Australia. Mihailo was required to travel to Belgrade to the Australian Embassy in order to secure the visa.[68]

In 1970 travel restrictions were removed and the population in traditional *pechalbar* regions such as Ohrid, Prilep and Bitola commenced leaving on a large scale, with Australia as the principal destination. The exodus of Macedonians took on massive proportions in the 1970s. In the Bitola region, hardly any family was left untouched by the scale of the emigration to Australia – many of those leaving did so in the tradition of *pechalba*, intending to work for a few years before returning to Macedonia. Initially, it was only men undertaking the long journey; wives and children would follow later. That lasted up until about 1975.

Economically, Macedonia was still lagging behind the other republics, thanks to insufficient investment in its economy and infrastructure. But there were many other reasons for Macedonians to be dissatisfied with the Tito dictatorship and its rule over Macedonia. For the sake of good neighbourly relations Yugoslavia remained quiet on the plight of the oppressed Macedonians under Greek, Bulgarian and Albanian rule, yet, in the Republic of Macedonia all minorities, in particular, the Albanian minority, enjoyed wide-ranging cultural, educational and language rights. Macedonian historiography was manipulated to accommodate Yugoslav interests and promoted a notion of Macedonians as having a strictly Slavic character and disregarding any connection to ancient Macedonia and Macedonians.

Following the disintegration of the Soviet Union, the viability of Yugoslavia became precarious as it had outlived its strategic importance to the West and, combined with Serbian ultra-nationalism and ethnic tensions, the fate of Yugoslavia was sealed. Croatia and Slovenia declared independence, and Macedonia overwhelmingly voted for independence in a referendum on 8 September 1991, which resulted in the historic establishment of the Republic of Macedonia as an independent and sovereign state. Post- Macedonian independence, another smaller wave of Macedonian migration occurred in the 1990s; however, unlike the earlier migrants these were young, educated professionals seeking economic opportunities in Australia, New Zealand, Canada and the United States.

Macedonia under Bulgarian rule (Pirin Macedonia)

Pirin Macedonia and Bulgaria may have had the largest Macedonian population of the three major occupying Balkan States, yet *pechalba* was not as widespread a tradition there. Approximately ten per cent of Macedonian territory came under the rule of Bulgaria and the population within the Pirin area was overwhelmingly homogeneous; however, there was a significant number of Macedonians living in Bulgaria proper, particularly in the capital, Sofia. Further, unlike the experience of the Macedonians under Greek and Serbian rule, Macedonian nationalism flourished in Pirin Macedonia and in Sofia, where many thousands of Macedonians lived. Although Sofia upheld an ambiguous position in that it maintained paternalism over all Macedonians, including those under Greek and Bulgarian rule, and acted as their patron, while also claiming them as Bulgarians. This approach 'left Pirin Macedonians to do what they wanted. Unlike Athens and Belgrade, Sofia tolerated the free use of the name "Macedonia" and an active Macedonian political and cultural life'.[69] Politically, there were both left and right Macedonian factions. However, the right faction came to dominate, and virtually transformed Pirin Macedonia into a separate state within Bulgaria from where armed struggle was waged against Serbian and Greek rule of Macedonian territories. The leader of the revolutionary movement, from the end of the Great War until his murder in 1924, was Todor Alexandrov.

Vancho (Ivan) Mihailov emerged as the new leader of VMRO after Alexandrov, and under Mihailov the Macedonian movement exerted complete control over all aspects of life in Pirin Macedonia, even introducing an 'autonomy tax' in support of the national cause.

'The VMRO projected a confusing double image – a Macedonian patriotic revolutionary organisation fighting for the national cause, but also an instrument of Bulgarian revisionism pursuing a Great Bulgaria'.[70] Following a split in the Bulgarian government over foreign policy, leaders of the Macedonian movement took opposing sides which saw prolonged infighting, murders and assassinations for a period of six years until the 1934 Bulgarian coup d'état put an end to Macedonian autonomy, banning the Macedonian organisation, with its leaders arrested or expelled. Until the 1934 coup, Pirin Macedonia remained united as a single administrative region made up of five districts. However, the new regime divided the area into two regions, one under Sofia and the other under Plovdid, which brought Pirin Macedonia under greater Bulgarian control.[71] There was little *pechalba* and migration to Australia from Pirin Macedonia during the 1920s and 1930s.

Following the Second World War, Bulgaria came under Communist control and relations between Yugoslavia and Bulgaria improved considerably while the two presidents, Tito and Giorgi Dimitrov, a Macedonian by origin, agreed on a national reunification of the Republic of Macedonia with the Pirin part of Macedonia, and the transfer of territory from Serbia to Bulgaria. The two leaders envisaged a federation of Yugoslavia and Bulgaria. However, the Soviet Union was uneasy with this potential development and the sudden death of Dimitrov whilst in Russia during 1949 ensured that the plan never came to fruition. However, from 1944 to 1948, Macedonians in Pirin Macedonia enjoyed a period of cultural autonomy which saw instruction in the Macedonian language introduced in schools, a Macedonian National Theatre established in Gorna Dzhumaja, newspapers printed, Macedonian bookstores opened, and Macedonian literature thrive.

Macedonians could freely declare their identity and were found to constitute over 70 per cent of the population in Pirin Macedonia during a national census conducted in 1946. Even after the Bulgarian position on Macedonians changed and cultural autonomy ended, the following census conducted in 1956 revealed 187,789 Macedonians living in Bulgaria, with 178,862 in Pirin Macedonia, comprising 63.6

per cent of the total population there. By the 1960s, the Bulgarian government's hard-line anti-Macedonian position was reflected in the 1965 census in that Macedonians had now almost disappeared and comprised only 1,437 people or 0.4 per cent of the population in Pirin Macedonia (8,230 Macedonians in Bulgaria proper). Subsequent census data in Bulgaria reveals that the Macedonians had mysteriously vanished from Bulgaria.[72]

Changed political conditions after 1948 brought oppressive rule upon the Macedonians with individuals active in the Macedonian struggle targeted, people imprisoned on trumped up anti-state and espionage charges, often made anonymously, and large-scale internment of entire families. A complete blockade between the Republic of Macedonia (in Yugoslavia) and the Pirin part of Macedonia (in Bulgaria) was designed to reduce contact between Macedonians from both sides of the border, augmented by a fourfold increase of Bulgarian police in the Pirin region. Many saw the Republic of Macedonia as offering greater freedom and young men regularly sought to escape over the border. The families of those who were imprisoned or had escaped over to the Republic of Macedonia were often interned. In November 1949, the authorities interned 67 entire Macedonian families from the Gorna Dzhumaja region (Blagoevgrad), and over 200 families were interned from across the Pirin region. In an effort to reinforce a closed border, the Bulgarian authorities mobilised villagers from the interior of Pirin Macedonia and sent them to the border areas for periods of five days at a time to maintain security.[73]

Due to Macedonian identity and culture having flourished in Pirin Macedonia from 1944 to 1948, the Macedonian leaders of cultural and educational associations were well-known to the Bulgarian authorities, and this made it easy to identify individuals supporting Macedonian separateness. Hundreds of Macedonians were arrested and imprisoned in 1949 under a range of charges, actual or fabricated, such as having VMRO membership, supporting Tito, aspiring for an independent Macedonia, or engaging in espionage on behalf of Great Britain and the United States. In one example a group of men from the Gorna Dzhumaja villages Lisija, Buchin and Buranovo were arrested and imprisoned for 'intending' to escape to the Republic of Macedonia. Throughout the late 1940s and 1950s, charges were regularly brought against Macedonians and lengthy sentences handed out to those involved in membership of organisations advocating for an independent Macedonia. Macedonian activists and intellectuals were imprisoned and four former partisan fighters for Macedonian independence in Aegean Macedonia (Greek Civil War) were sentenced to death and executed on 28 February 1950.[74] Macedonians were targeted for removal from the Bulgarian Communist Party; in Pirin Macedonia alone, from the end of 1949 to the middle of 1950, 3,000 Macedonians were expelled from the Party.[75]

Bulgarian jails were filled with Macedonians, especially during the rule of the Bulgarian Communist dictator Todor Zhivkov yet, even under these harsh conditions, the yearning for freedom persisted and underground organisations continued to be formed seeking independence for their homeland. From 1965 to 1968, 23 pro-independence groups were uncovered by the Bulgarian security services in Pirin Macedonia and, in 1973, approximately 25 per cent of the Bulgarian security intelligence service capacity was dedicated to the problem of Macedonian nationalism.[76] Economically, the Bulgarian government had made very little investment in Pirin Macedonia, and it was not until 1968, as a response to fears that the region could potentially break away and join with Yugoslavia (Republic of Macedonia), that the government commenced to actively invest in its development.[77]

Emigration was severely restricted by the Bulgarian Communist regime and this diktat applied particularly to Macedonians, who were unable to legally leave Bulgarian rule to work or go abroad. The only opportunity to do so was by escaping over the border. Vasil Tilev, a Macedonian from Kradzhejevo village in the Gorna Dzhumaja region experienced discrimination all too frequently and stated that as 'a Macedonian you are disadvantaged from excelling in Bulgarian society, especially if you question things. However if you stay quiet everything is fine'.[78] With strong views on the injustices Macedonians were experiencing under Bulgarian Communist rule, Vasil's father was afraid that he would be jailed because he was concerned about human rights issues and dared to question the Communist regime.

In the 1970s, the consequences of being caught attempting to leave were severe, with jail sentences ranging from three to ten years. After careful consideration of his future, Vasil decided to leave Bulgarian rule by escaping over the border to the Republic of Macedonia, from where he intended to continue to a Western country, either Australia, Canada or the United States. One spring morning in 1977, Vasil set off for a three-day walk over the Osogovo mountain ranges until he arrived in the town of Kamenica in the Republic of Macedonia, where he surrendered himself to the Macedonian authorities. Initially the authorities looked at him with suspicion, fearing he could be a Bulgarian spy. However, once convinced of his authenticity, he was given the option of remaining in the Republic of Macedonia and was offered employment and an apartment. He was surprised and humbled by the offer and support shown to him as a Macedonian; however, he declined the offer as he intended to continue on to a Western country. From Belgrade, the Yugoslav authorities transferred him to Italy, where he spent five months in an immigration detention facility before securing passage to his first preference destination, Australia, later in the same year.[79]

There had not been any significant waves of migration from Pirin Macedonia to Australia. However, when several Eastern European countries, including Bulgaria, became members of the European Union between 2004 and 2007, free movement within the Union for its citizens resulted in a flow of migration from East to West. There has been an increase in Macedonians from this part migrating to Western European countries. European Union membership has not changed the situation for Macedonians under Bulgarian rule; they continue to have their basic human rights violated; they are refused from registering Macedonian organisations and were prevented from gathering to celebrate the anniversary of the death of the Macedonian revolutionary hero, Jane Sandanski. They are routinely attacked and brutalised by Bulgarian special police forces.

Macedonia under Albanian rule

Although the history of *pechalba* from Macedonia under Albanian rule was limited, it is important to understand why. Unlike Greece,

Serbia and Bulgaria, who each acquired Macedonian land through military invasion, Albania acquired a small portion of Macedonian territory as a result of the London Peace Treaty in 1920. This was followed by an adjustment of the border between Greece and Albania which resulted in a further fourteen villages, entirely Macedonian inhabited, transferred to Albania. Roughly 1,000 square kilometres of Macedonian land came under Albanian rule, although, historically, Macedonians lived in a much wider area within what is now Albania. Although the term, Mala Prespa, is often used to denote Macedonian territory in Albania, the district of Mala Prespa, situated on the western side of Lake Prespa, is only one of several Macedonian regions in Albania. Other Macedonian areas include the western side of Lake Ohrid and the regions of Golo Brdo and Gora (both Christian and Muslim Macedonians), Dolno Pole, Korcha and Bilishta.

Shortly after the start of Albanian occupation, the Macedonians and their culture came under attack, and human rights abuses were rampant. Fanatical Albanian Muslims terrorised Macedonian priests and demanded that the script on church icons be changed to Albanian. Albanian schoolteachers instructed Macedonian children not to speak Macedonian; only the newly introduced Albanian language was accepted. In 1929, civil servants from Tirana accompanied by Albanian police went door to door in Macedonian villages in the Prespa region and tore up all non-Albanian language literature. The Bilishta police interned five villagers from Vrbnik, including Priest Lazor Mushmov, on charges of repeatedly demanding a Macedonian schoolteacher for their village and for acquiring Macedonian literature and newspapers. In 1932, the entire village land holdings were confiscated from Gorna Gorica, a Macedonian village situated beside the Prespa Lake, comprising 62 houses and 560 inhabitants.[80]

From the end of the Balkan Wars to 1944, the Albanian government banned Macedonian language education even though the government had agreed to provide rights to minority groups, and the Albanian constitution guaranteed language rights. From 1925 to 1943, the Bulgarian embassy in Tirana organised for the Mala Prespa villages to receive Bulgarian literature, which included basic readers for children. The Macedonians welcomed these, as they could understand the Cyrillic alphabet due to Bulgarian being much closer to Macedonian, compared to the unfamiliar Greek and Albanian languages. The newspaper of the Macedonian Patriotic Organisation, the *Macedonian Tribune*, regularly arrived from the United States and was read with great interest by the Macedonians.[81]

Communist-ruled Yugoslavia and Albania developed a close relationship from 1944 to 1948 and, during this period, Macedonians were recognised as a national minority in Albania and could freely express their identity and use their language. The Albanian state undertook to establish schools in villages where Macedonians formed the majority of the inhabitants, while teachers and teaching material was supplied from the Republic of Macedonia. However, Macedonian schools were opened in only thirteen villages – a fraction of the number to which the Macedonian population was entitled. In villages where schools were set up, the anticipation was enormous and filled with emotion as entire villages came out to welcome the arrival of the Macedonian teachers. During the day they taught the children, and at night classes were conducted with adults who wanted to attain Macedonian literacy. Educational and cultural life flourished during this period of enlightenment for Macedonians under Albanian rule.

Following the 1948 split between Tito and Stalin, Albania severed its relations with Yugoslavia. This dramatically changed the situation for Macedonians in Albania. It resulted in their rights reduced to a bare minimum: Macedonian schoolteachers were expelled, and schools closed. The closure of the schools caused deep despair to the Macedonians and, when teachers departed for the Republic of Macedonia for the last time, entire village communities accompanied them to the border for an emotional farewell.[82] Instruction in Macedonian was forbidden, all Macedonian textbooks brought from the Republic of Macedonia were burned, and Macedonian schools were replaced with Albanian ones.[83] Newly appointed Albanian teachers discouraged the children from identifying as Macedonian and the teachers took very little interest in performing their role and educating the Macedonian schoolchildren.

With the admission of Albania to the United Nations in 1955,

Macedonian schooling was reintroduced at a minimum level in a limited number of schools, consisting of a separate subject one to two hours per week. However, in several Macedonian villages there was no school building, or the state had allowed the building to fall into disrepair: in these instances, Macedonian villagers came together to construct new schools or renovate existing ones. In Vrbnik village, Macedonian was reduced to a four-year program and further education, only available in Albanian, was continued in the nearby village of Bilishta. In the mid-1970s, the authorities changed the curriculum in Macedonian schools where 50 per cent of the education was in Macedonian and 50 per cent in Albanian.

Under the rule of Enver Xodha, Macedonians and other minorities, as well as the Albanian people, were plunged into a period of darkness. Under a policy of industrialisation of the state, Macedonians were resettled in the interior of the country, a strategic move intended to foster their assimilation. Various laws were introduced which resulted in the changing of names, surnames and place names and, while living in the most isolated state in Europe – possibly the world – the Macedonians became further separated from their relatives in the Republic of Macedonia and in Aegean Macedonia.[84] In the 1970s, the state resettled individuals and families to other areas in Albania and this strategy was used to disperse minority groups, break their independence and reduce their rights.[85] Education in the mother tongue of minority groups was provided up to the fourth grade in villages where the ethnic group was considered of sufficient size. Resettling families from particular villages enabled the authorities to declare that the population of the village no longer met the required number of people and as such 'the minority would lose the status they had and, with this, the Albanian government could decrease minority rights'.[86]

In 1967, religion was banned in Albania under Article 55 of the Albanian Constitution. Officially, there was no religion in Albania under Xodha's dictatorship. Religious holidays were banned, and all places of worship were closed, with many transformed for other secular purposes. In 1967, the Albanian government announced it had closed 2,169 churches, mosques and monasteries, including the destruction of 630 Orthodox churches and the conversion of a similar number of non-religious activities.[87] The authorities confiscated from individuals their personal crosses, icons and bibles and 'religious leaders were accused in public, shaved, deported, imprisoned and killed'.[88] One of the many places of worship closed in 1967 was the Macedonian Orthodox church, Sveti Giorgi, which had stood in the village of Vrbnik since Ottoman times; however, the priest, a Macedonian from the village, continued to christen children secretly inside people's homes for a number of years afterwards.[89]

While the Greek and Serbian states transformed Macedonian names to reflect Greek and Serb nationality early in the twentieth century following the division of Macedonia, the Albanian state initially did not forcibly 'Albanianise' Macedonian names but was reluctant to allow Macedonians to register surnames that ended in traditional 'ov' or 'ski'. Instead, their names were shortened, and modified to end with the letter 'o'.

Village toponyms were changed at different periods throughout the twentieth century. Vrbnik was changed to Vernick during the reign of King Zog before the Second World War, while others such as a group of Macedonian villages in the Prespa region were all changed in 1970. The villages Pustec, Shul'in, Globocheni, Gorna Gorica, Dolna Gorica, Tuminec, L'eska and Zharnosko were officially replaced with the Albanian names Liqenas, Diellas, Gollomboch, Gorica e Madhe, Gorica e Vogel, Kallamas (prior to 1970, Bezmisht), Lajthiza and Zaroshka respectively.[90] Following the renaming of their villages, and like Macedonians under Greek rule, Macedonians in Albania continued to refer to their villages by their traditional Macedonian names.

Following the Second World War, Xodha's newly established dictatorship represented an extreme form of Communist ideology which, until the end of the twentieth century, transformed Albania into the poorest state in all Europe. The backwardness of the Albanian regime is demonstrated in the following example. In 1949, Naum Mano returned to his native village, Vrbnik, to visit his family after 12 years in Western Australia working on his father's market garden in Wanneroo and in Macedonian cafés in Perth. Naum was an Australian citizen and had served in the Australian military in South East Asia during the Second World War. The visit to Vrbnik was intended as a short stay and he did not anticipate the drastic changes of the new regime. Following his arrival, the authorities confiscated his travel documents, preventing him from returning to Australia. He was instructed never to speak about the time he spent in Australia and was threatened with prison if he did (he was told that he must speak about Albania only in positive terms). Naum buried all his Australian documentation and currency as these items were considered anti-state material under the paranoid Albanian Communist regime. Furthermore, to speed up his reinstatement into Albanian life Naum was conscripted into the Albanian army from 1951 to 1953. Mano thought about leaving Albania illegally over the border; however, he did not dare do so as the families of those who left were punished by being relocated to other parts of Albania, put on hard labour and their children removed from school. Naum remained in Vrbnik village where he married Sofia (also from Vrbnik village) and they had nine children. Naum did not return to Australia and died in his village of birth in 1980. Entitled to immigration rights as a result of his military service during the Second World War, seven of his children took the opportunity to reside in Australia, and are amongst the few Macedonians from Albanian rule who have settled in Australia.[91]

At the beginning of the twenty-first century, Macedonians can be found throughout many parts of Albania, including the capital city, Tirana. Officially the Albanian state acknowledges a Macedonian

Photo 8: Naum Mano and Lefter Sotiri in Perth, circa 1940. Mano came from Vrbnik village and Sotiri from Pustec, both Macedonian villages that were under Albanian rule. (Source: Manol Mano).

presence only in the Mala Prespa region; however, this represents a deliberate attempt to downplay and distort the actual number of Macedonians and their geographical distribution. It has been well documented by historians, anthropologists, linguists and human rights groups that the Macedonian presence covers a substantially greater territory within the political boundaries of Albania than the Mala Prespa region alone. Estimates of the number of Macedonians living in Albania vary. The Albanian state has consistently underestimated the number of Macedonians; this is a strategy aimed at reducing claims for minority rights. According to data from the 2011 census there are only 5,870 Macedonians in Albania; however, the Pustec municipality alone has more Macedonians than that. There are serious problems in Albania when it comes to recognising minority rights, with Macedonian, Serbian, Montenegrin, Vlah and Greek minorities routinely intimidated at census time to declare themselves as Albanian. Macedonian organisations in Albania estimate that anywhere between 120,000 and 350,000 Macedonians live in Albania.

Throughout the twentieth century, Macedonians under Albanian rule made up a small number of *pechalbari* to Australia. A limited number arrived prior to the Second World War, some from villages that at the time of their departure were not under Albanian rule, and others left via Greece or Bulgaria.[92] Following the establishment of Communist rule after the Second World War, there was no migration from Albania in the second half of the twentieth century. Post-Communist rule there have been very few arrivals known to have come to Australia. Following the fall of Communist rule in 1990, the most notable movement of Macedonians from Albania has been to the Republic of Macedonia.

Endnotes

1 H. Trikoupis, *History of the Greek People*, Vol 14, Athens Publishing, p. 18, as sourced in J. Shea, *Macedonia and Greece – The Struggle to Define a New Balkan Nation*, McFarland, Jefferson, 1997, p. 101.

2 Carnegie Endowment for International Peace, *Report of the International Commission to Inquire into the Causes and Conduct of the Balkan Wars*, Published by the Endowment, Washington, 1914, p. 105. 'From first to last, in both wars, the fighting was as desperate as though extermination were the end sought', ibid, p. 265.

3 The name Mala Prespa refers only to that part of Macedonian territory that came under Albanian rule as a result of the 1920 London Conference. There are other regions and districts in Albania along the modern border between the Republic of Macedonia and Albania that have been traditionally inhabited by Macedonians such as the Golo Brdo region and a significant part of the Korcha (Goritsa) region. Macedonians in these areas are indigenous inhabitants.

4 Bistrichki, 'Why are we the Macedonians a separate nation', 1934, as cited in *The Historical Truth (Documents, Studies, Resolutions, Appeals and Published Articles) 1896-1956*, editors P. Korobar and O. Ivanovski, Kultura, Skopje 1983, p.76. Solun's traditional markets were to the north, not the south. There was no direct rail line between Solun and Athens (Macedonia and Greece) until a railway was constructed in 1916.

5 Ibid., p. 76.

6 D. Siljanovski, *Makedonija Kako Prirodna i Ekonomska Celina* [Macedonia as a Natural and Economic Unit], Makedonski Nauchen Institut, Sofia, 1945, p. 309.

7 Ibid., pp. 309-311 and D. Konstantinov, *Pechalbarstvo* [Pechalba], Nauchno Drushtvo Bitola, Bitola, 1964, p. 92.

8 D. Konstantinov, op. cit., p. 8.

9 K. Todoroska, *Makedoncite vo Albania (1912-1991)* [Macedonians in Albania (1912-1991)], Menora, Skopje, 2014, p. 149.

10 Ibid., p. 150 and p. 185.

11 Report number 37 dated 16 February 1888, Constantinople. K. Dzhambazovski, editor, *Gradja za istoriju Makedonskog naroda (iz arhiva Srbije)* [Material on the History of the Macedonian people (from the Serbian Archive)], Vol IV, Book III (1888-1889), Prosveta, Belgrade, 1987, pp. 75-76.

12 In English, VMRO is known as the Internal Macedonian Revolutionary Organisation (IMRO).

13 T. Gorgiev, *Po Tragite Na Minatoto* [Tracing the past], Socialen Borec, Skopje, 1967, p. 39. Simjan Simidzhiev memoir.

14 Ibid., p. 48. Zhivko Kirov Janevski memoir.

15 The report was directed to the Foreign Minister in order that the Turkish authorities were notified of the threat. Report number 15.832 dated 3 November 1889, Belgrade, K. Dzhambazovski, op. cit., p. 621.

16 G. Abadzhiev, editor, *Borbite vo Jugozapadna Makedonia po spomenite na Luka Dzherov i Lazar Dimitrov*, [Battles in south-western Macedonia according to the memoirs of Luka Dzherov and Lazar Dimitrov], Drzhavno Knigoizdatelstvo na NR Makedonija, Skopje, 1952, p. 24.

17 T. Gorgiev, op. cit., p. 45. Ilija Stojchev Bozhinovski memoir.

18 T. H. Simovski, *Atlas of the Inhabited Places of Aegean Macedonia*, Turk Tarih Kurumu Basimevi, Ankara, 1999, p. xv. From 1929 to 1940, another 39 places in Aegean Macedonia were renamed. Isolated places which were previously missed were renamed much later. Officially, a total of 1,666 places were renamed from 1918 to 1970. This figure does not include those places which were not announced in the Government Gazette, nor does it include the numerous Macedonian settlements named after saints, the names of which were translated from Macedonian to Greek. Where possible, place names were directly translated, for example the village Vrbeni which in Macedonian means 'birds', was directly translated to the Greek word for birds, 'Itya'.

19 Kosta Kotchoff interview.

20 Velika Spirova interview.

21 Ilija Stojanovski interview. Ilija explained that the Commission members sought to determine whether there was any significance to Macedonian family names in the village before they were changed, and that the village headman (*kmet*) was summoned to provide clarification through an interpreter.

22 Done Ashlakoff interview.

23 R. Stefov, *Short History of the Macedonian People*, National Institution – Library 'Grigor Prlichev', Ohrid, 2007, p. 154.

24 Vlahs are Orthodox Christians who speak a Latin language and can be found scattered throughout South Eastern Europe with a large concentration in Greece, particularly in the regions of Epirus and Thessaly.

25 R. A. Clogg, *A Concise History of Greece*, Cambridge University Press, London, 1992, p. 48.

26 J. Reed, *War in Eastern Europe – Travels through the Balkans in 1915*, Phoenix, London, (1916) 1994, p. 171.

27 S. Dzhikov, *Progoneti* [Persecuted], Studentski Zbor, Skopje, 1991, p. 58.

28 Peter Boskov interview.

29 Peter Ailakis interview.

30 Risto Gochev interview.

31 Peter Boskov interview.

32 A. Rossos, *Macedonia and the Macedonians – A History*, Hoover Institution Press, Stanford, 2008, p. 146. 'Peasants – most of the Aegean Macedonians – became marginal, in subsistence farming. Their plots were too small and infertile, their methods primitive, their yields too low. They barely eked out an existence', p. 146.

33 L. Danforth, *The Macedonian Conflict – Ethnic Nationalism in a Transnational World*, Princeton University Press, Princeton, 1995, p. 71.

34 Velika Spirova interview. '*Ako nemaja plevna ili aur, Grcite mu gradeja takvi raboti*'.

35 T. H. Simovski, op. cit., p. xi.

36 A. Rossos, op. cit., p. 146.

37 Ibid., p. 146.

38 The order was issued on 27 January 1926. H. Andonov-Poljanski, editor. *Documents on the Struggle of the Macedonian People for Independence and a Nation-State*, Vol 11, University of 'Cyril and Methodius', Skopje, 1985, p. 62.

39 An example of the Greek state negating Macedonian ethno-specificity by referring to the Macedonians as 'Bulgarians' and the Macedonian language as 'Bulgarian'.

40 Using the Macedonian language in every day communication was banned from public use as a criminal offence.

41 Association of the Macedonians in Poland, *What Europe Has Forgotten: The Struggle of the Aegean Macedonians*, Pollitecon Publications, Sydney, 1992, p. 8.

42 The historian A. Rossos stated that 'large scale emigration undoubtedly delighted Athens, for it facilitated Hellenization of the area that had the most Macedonians', op. cit., p. 146.

43 B. Birtles, *Exiles in the Aegean, A Personal Narrative of Greek Politics and Travel*, V. Gollancz, London, 1938, p. 388.

44 A. Rossos, 'Incompatible Allies: Greek Communism and Macedonian Nationalism in the Civil War in Greece, 1943-1949', *Journal of Modern History*, Vol 69, No 1, University of Chicago Press, (March 1997), pp. 42-76, p. 42.

45 Ibid., pp. 43-44.

46 J. Shea, *Macedonia and Greece, the struggle to define a new Balkan nation*, McFarland, Jefferson, 1997, p. 116. Greek prison camps where Macedonians were imprisoned, tortured or killed included the island of Ikaria, the Island of Makronis, the Averov jail near Athens, the jail at Larisa near the Volos peninsula and the jail at Salonika. Mass killings were reported on Vicho, Gramos, Kajmakchalan and at Mala Prespa. Ibid., p. 116.

47 M. Allbrook, editor, *Journeys of Hope (Six stories of family migration to Western Australia 1937-1968)*, State Print, Perth, 1994, p.18. Vasilika Markova's husband arrived in Australia in 1937. Her husband's name was wiped off the records along with those of other men from the village. "He would never have been able to return to his home country to live there. So, our life had to be with him and that's why he brought us out here after the war had died down". Ibid., p. 18.

48 On 11 March 1962, it was reported in the Greek journal *Ikonomikos Tahidromos* that the program was a failure with less than 1,000 colonist Greeks moving to the Macedonian border areas.

49 M. Seraphinoff and C. Stefou, *This land we do not give – a history of Macedonian resistance to foreign occupation*, Nettle Hollow with the assistance of Aardvark Global, Shtip, 2008, p.207.

50 *Phoni tis Kastorias*, 4 October 1959. Trebeno/Trbino is in the district of Kaljari.

51 John Nitson interview. The village of Lagen had traditionally sent many of its young men on *pechalba* overseas. Following the Greek Civil War, Macedonians in Lagen village who had experience working in the other countries, particularly in the United States, brought back new systems of farming and irrigation and introduced these to the village to improve agricultural output. Their good intentions were ridiculed by the authorities who could only see the Macedonians as non-Greeks who had fought against the government, and who could not be trusted.

52 The Kingdom of Serbs, Croats and Slovenes was formed in 1918 following the end of World War One. In 1929, the Kingdom of Yugoslavia was officially established, while in 1943, Democratic Federal Yugoslavia was formed (later changed to Socialist Federative Republic of Yugoslavia), which was a federation of six constituent republics; however, Yugoslav politics were characterised by Serbian domination. The final state of Yugoslavia was formed in 1992, comprising Serbia, Montenegro, Kosovo and the province of Vojvodina. This arrangement was short lived however, following the independence of Montenegro in 2003, which finally put to rest the experimental and artificial state of Yugoslavia.

53 A. Rossos, (2008), op. cit., p. 138.

54 In Dragosh village, the Serb authorities gathered a large group of men to process and conscript; however, a local villager, Mitre Temelkovski, a former freedom fighter from the Ilinden battles in 1903, disrupted the gathering which allowed the men the opportunity to escape and head for the nearby Greek border (although Aegean Macedonia was on the other side of the Greek political border). From Greece, Josif Rendevski and a group of village men departed for the USA, a journey many had previously undertaken while under Ottoman Turkish rule. Josif did not return to Macedonia until 1921. Cane Rendevski interview.

55 A. Rossos, (2008), op. cit., p. 139.

56 V. Achkoska, *Agrarno-Sopstvenickite odnoci, promeni i prosesi vo Makedonija 1944-1953* [Agrarian Property Relations, Changes and Trends in Macedonia 1944-1953], Institut za Nacionalna Istorija, Skopje, 1998, pp. 45-46. Bitola was one of the least colonised regions – there were 83 families strategically planted in the Bitola villages up until 1940. Regions such as Skopje, Kumanovo, Ovche Pole and Negotino experienced larger numbers of colonists.

57 'Belgrade gave them the best lands and encouraged them to settle in Macedonia. By 1940, of 381,245 hectares up for distribution, the government had given 142,585 hectares to 17,679 colonists and Serbian volunteers and only 85,511 hectares to 30,582 agricultural tenants and peasants'. A. Rossos, (2008), op. cit. p. 140.

58 Mihailo Anastasovski interview.

59 D. Konstantinov, op. cit., p. 17.

60 Ibid., p. 18.

61 Stojan Spasevski interview.

62 Gogo Kalevski interview. Gogo lived in Comodoro Rivadavia with his wife Lena where they had two children before eventually migrating to Australia in the 1960s.

63 A. Rossos, (2008), op. cit., p. 140.

64 There was a military post along the border at the mountain peak named 'Tsutsa', with approximately 50 soldiers stationed there and they rotated on four-hourly shifts. During the winter months the soldiers were stationed in another barracks situated beside the Sveta Petka monastery immediately above Brajchino village. Vancho Kalcovski interview.

65 Vancho Kalcovski interview.

66 Brajchino and German villages had deep ties and traditionally took marriage partners from one another.

67 Bozinoski, B and Krstevski, V, *Chetvrta Generacija* [Fourth Generation], Macedonian Australian Association of Culture and Human Rights, Newcastle, 2012, pp. 429-432 (interview with Eftim Eftimovski). Eftim managed to contact his parents by writing a letter to a relative in another village (Lera) requesting that he pass a message on that he and Hodo were both safe.

68 Mihailo Anastasovski interview. In the tradition of *pechalba*, Mihailo initially intended on working in Australia for several years and returning to Macedonia with the earnings. Up until Mihailo obtained the visa, he was secretive about his travel plans and did not divulge his intentions to anyone at work. His reluctance to make his intentions known was based on the policy at that time that a government employer could object to an employee leaving the country.

Had the passport been obtained through normal bureaucratic channels, the company would have been contacted for approval of his travel plans. However, in this instance the employer's approval was not sought by the interior ministry.

69 A. Rossos, (2008), op. cit. p.148.

70 Ibid., p. 150.

71 Ibid., pp. 148-150

72 S. Stojkov, 'Makedonskoto Malcinstvo vo Bugaria od priznavajne kon negirajne 1948-1989' [The Macedonian minority in Bulgaria from recognition to negation 1948-1989], pp. 67 – 85, from *Godishen Zbornik 2015/2016* [Annual Anthology 2015/2016], Universitet Goce Delchev, Shtip, Year 6, Volume VI, pages 74 and 77.

73 V. Jotevski, 'Preselbite na Makedoncite od Pirinskiot del na Makedonija 1948-1968' [Migrations of the Macedonians in the Pirin part of Macedonia 1948-1968], pp. 145-153. From *Iselenishtvoto od Makedonija od Pojavata do Denes* [Emigres from Macedonia from Emergence to Today], Agencija za Iselenishtvoto na Republika Makedonija, Skopje 2004, pp. 147-148.

74 Ibid., pp. 149-150.

75 S. Stojkov, op. cit., p. 69.

76 Stojkov states that this figure grew to 50 per cent in 1979 and, in the early 1980s, fluctuated between one-third and one-sixth of the capacity and activity of the Bulgarian security intelligence service. Ibid., p. 81.

77 Ibid., p. 80.

78 The Bulgarian government renamed Gorna Dzhumaja to Blagoevgrad and Kradzhejevo to Balgarchevo.

79 Vasil Tilev interview.

80 B. Minevski, article 'Albanskite Policajci vo Mala Prespa gi kinele site knigi shto ne bile pishani na Albanski jazik' [Albanian police in Mala Prespa destroyed books which were not in Albanian], *Dnevnik*, 6 February 2015.

81 K. Todoroska, op. cit., p. 193

82 Ibid., p. 208.

83 Ibid., p. 208.

84 V. Ortakovski, *Minorities in the Balkans*, Transnational Publishers, New York, 2000, p. 195.

85 Ibid., p. 194. Ortakovski states that forced population resettlements had been taking place since the 1940s.

86 Ibid., p. 194.

87 Amnesty International, 'Albania', *Political Imprisonment and the Law*, 1984, p. 13 as sourced in Ortakovski, ibid, p. 194.

88 Ibid., p. 194.

89 Manol Mano interview.

90 V. Friedman, 'The Macedonian Dialects of Albania', *Slavic and East European Journal*, Vol. 55, n.4, American Association of Teachers of Slavic and East European Languages, 2011, p. 633. The village of Cerje remained unchanged and was not given an Albanian name.

91 Manol Mano interview.

92 A number of Macedonian activists in the Macedonian Peoples League of Australia (MAPL) were from villages under Albanian rule. In 1946, Kristo Kapinkoff served as Vice-President and Sam Manoff and Boris Manoff were committee members. All were from the village Vrbnik. Kristo Kapinkoff (born 1904) and Sam Manoff (born 1900) arrived in Australia together aboard the 'Maria Christina' in 1928. Boris Manoff arrived in 1936 aboard the 'Orford'.

Part Three

Australia: *Pechalba* and Settlement Down Under

5

The Early Pioneers: 'Any Work Will Do'

Although 1924 marks a turning point in Macedonian migration to Australia, Macedonians have been present in Australia since the late nineteenth century. Macedonians working in Solun and Constantinople in the second half of the nineteenth century are reported to have heard about the discovery of gold in Australia. There are stories of Macedonians travelling together with Dalmatian men before the end of the nineteenth century and heading for Kalgoorlie and Broken Hill.[1]

Charles Price states that Macedonians have been present in the mining city of Broken Hill since the 1890s.[2] The historian, Tome Miovski, marks 1891 as the date when Macedonians first arrived in Australia and headed for mining areas.[3] Most of the early Macedonian pioneers to Australia were from the regions of Kostur and Lerin and disembarked at Fremantle port, Western Australia, between 1903, the year of the Ilinden Uprising against the Ottoman Empire, up till 1914 when the Great War broke out.[4] Among those who arrived in Western Australia were Numo Gulio in 1908, who worked for many years on a banana farm in Babinda, Queensland,[5] and Vane Prcul who arrived in 1911 and worked in Broken Hill until 1935 when he returned to Macedonia.[6] Gulio and Prcul were both from the Kosinec village in the Kostur district.

Other early twentieth-century arrivals in Australia included a villager from Dambeni, Kostur district, Stojan Kenkov (Pandov) who worked in Broken Hill from 1914 to 1933, and reportedly died in Kalgoorlie in 1938.[7] There were other arrivals in Western Australia before the First World War, including Boris Shmagranov from Dambeni village and Bill Kolichis from Pozdivishta (Kostur) who worked at Kalgoorlie and the Wiluna gold mine respectively.[8] F. Kadiov (Kadiche) from Dambeni village (Kostur) was one of the earliest Macedonians to arrive in New South Wales.[9] At the end of the First Word War a group of men from the traditional *pechalbar* village of Graeshnica (Bitola) arrived in Western Australia. The group comprised seven men: Karanfil from the Sarievci family, Dzhise from the Saitkikovci family, Cvetko from the Tupchkovci family, Marko and his uncle Stefan from the Ribarovci family, and two other young men.[10]

Overwhelmingly, the early Macedonian *pechalbari* to Australia were from the Kostur and Lerin regions of the Aegean part of Macedonia; however, there was a smaller number of arrivals from Macedonia under Serb rule (Vardar Macedonia) that made up around 20 per cent of the Macedonian population in Australia. They were typically from the Bitola and Prespa regions, with some from the Ohrid region. Those from the Bitola region predominantly came from villages located along the slopes of Pelister Mountain and the Baba ranges that had established traditions of *pechalba* such as Velushina, Graeshnica, Capari, Bukovo, Bistrica, and others.

Most Macedonians had never heard of Australia, and it was an expensive undertaking to purchase a ticket to travel to Australia in the 1920s and 1930s. Few had the money on hand and typically borrowed the funds from family and villagers, particularly from those who had previously spent periods working abroad in places such as the United States. Money lenders also provided funds to *pechalbari* to pay for their shipping fares and shipping agents were located in the main towns, such as Kostur, Lerin, Bitola and Resen. Shipping agents also appointed representatives in villages that had well-developed *pechalba* traditions in an attempt to monopolise ticket sales. The fare to Australia was approximately US$100.

In the late 1920s, quotas for Europeans were introduced and, with the onset of the economic depression, the Australian government further tightened controls on immigration. From 1930, entry permits were only issued to non-British white Europeans (referred to as 'white aliens') and close dependent relatives of Australian residents. An increase to the landing-money requirement to £40 became a hindrance to European immigration and *pechalbari* were required to borrow larger amounts which placed additional pressure on the

Photo 9: Mitre Kotchoff (left) from Konomladi village (Kostur) with Macedonian friends, Perth, circa 1932. (Source: Kosta Kotchoff).

pechalbar to succeed upon arrival in Australia. It was not until the second half of the 1930s when economic conditions improved, that these provisions were eased.

Many of the early *pechalbari* expected there would be an abundance of work in Australia, with high wages on offer, and that they would do well and earn good money like those before them who had succeeded in the United States. It appeared that unscrupulous shipping agents in Macedonia, receiving commissions from steamship companies, promoted Australia as a desirable destination, when in fact there was a depressed economic climate at the time, men struggled to find work and were left with little choice but to travel to the countryside in search of work.[11] During this period Macedonians were typically itinerant workers clearing bushland and scrub for future farms, cutting railway sleepers, gathering eucalypt oil, cutting sugar cane and undertaking any other hard manual work they could obtain. Even employed men were barely making enough to eat and, travelling through remote countryside from farm to farm seeking work as farm hands, they often carried all their possessions on their back. On one particular ship that arrived in Melbourne in 1924, of the twenty Macedonians that arrived, only three remained in Australia. The rest returned to their villages after failing to find employment and believing there were no foreseeable prospects to succeed.[12] Their situation was depressing and even more difficult in that many had borrowed money to pay for their fares to Australia and found themselves unable to repay the money. Neither could they afford the return fare to Macedonia. The situation became so desperate for a group of men, it was reported that eight men left Australia as stowaways aboard the *S.S. Cephee* in February 1925.[13]

Union opposition prevented Macedonians finding work in the cities and they could not find permanent work in country areas. A report demonstrating the plight of these men highlights how difficult the economic climate was at the time. In 1925, a large group of Macedonians became stranded and destitute in Melbourne after being unable to find employment and without the finances to travel out into country areas in search of work. Some walked as far as Healesville unsuccessfully looking for any work available. Their plight came to the attention of the Commonwealth Attorney General's Department Investigation Branch which assessed their position and found that the men did not want to be repatriated to Macedonia as they had sold possessions or borrowed money to come to Australia.[14] It would have been an absolutely last resort of desperation for the men to return to their villages without savings to pay back their money borrowed to fund the *pechalbar* journey. In line with their strong desire to succeed, the men reported that they felt confident that, given an opportunity, they would make good in Australia. Each one was considered to be an 'honest hardworking type'.[15]

Macedonians who had been working temporarily in European and other countries who intended to move on to the United States were left stranded when American immigration restrictions set in. When the United States was no longer a viable destination, many redirected their journey after hearing there were no travel restrictions to Australia, an unintended *pechalba* destination. Others were preyed upon by unscrupulous shipping agents operating in countries where *pechalbari* were living and working. Cousins Lazo and Mitre Porkov from Capari village had been working in France for over twelve months when they were convinced by a French shipping agent of 'guaranteed work, with high daily rates of pay…and other benefits that we could only dream of' awaiting in Australia.[16] The fare was the equivalent of what they had saved from twelve months work. Expecting to travel on a luxury liner with an abundance of food, instead the ship was so old that its departure was delayed by two days due to engine trouble, and then there was barely enough food on the ship for the passengers. The situation deteriorated upon arrival in Sydney in 1924. They expected to be greeted by an associate of the shipping agent who was to set them up with accommodation and employment; however, no such arrangements were in place. As they did not know anyone in Sydney and there were no Macedonian clubs or boarding houses at that time, they found themselves living destitute in a public park for the first two weeks until two Armenians took them in.[17]

The Macedonians were prepared to take on any work that was available and they travelled lengthy distances in search of work, even moving interstate after hearing about work. Quite a few men arrived with familiarity of the English language acquired through previous *pechalba* experience in the United States, but even the ability to communicate was insufficient to secure ongoing employment. Vasil Turpin from Bapchor village (Kostur) arrived in Melbourne in 1924 with a good understanding of English due to having worked for several years in the United States.[18] Even with language skills he was unable to secure employment in Melbourne and travelled to Brisbane looking for work, but was also unsuccessful there and returned to Melbourne. The search for work took him to Port Pirie in South Australia where he found temporary work as a tree grubber for the road works. He then went to Perth after his cousin Risto Stoichkoff wrote to him about work in Western Australia. He worked at East Kirup for one year in the timber cutting industry, together with Tanas Paioff, before finally finding long-term work for the Karri Timber Company at Nannup, log handling with a Wilana machine. The same fate befell many others. Vasil Spirov arrived in Newcastle in 1930, and for ten years could not find permanent work. He travelled on foot from farm to farm, clearing land and earning just enough to buy food and tobacco. In 1930, Boris Giamov was earning three shillings a day clearing farmland in Gippsland, Victoria, barely earning enough to live off, and was unable to send any money back to his family in Trnava village.

The plight of Macedonians and other Southern Europeans in country areas was so dire that it was reported in the media that they 'were working in country districts for no remuneration other than food.' [19] In Northern NSW, Mijal Murgev from Gjavato village (Bitola) worked on a farm for food and board only, in return for looking after a few hundred head of cattle. The farmer had no money to pay him, but in appreciation of the work performed, gave him a suitcase full of old clothes.[20] In Western Australia, prior to the onset of the economic depression, John Christos Vellios (Jovan Risto Numeff) worked with other Macedonians as a sleeper cutter. However, the severe economic downturn meant that they could no longer earn a regular income and the men left their forest campsites to set up canvas tents on the banks of the Blackwood River in Bridgetown. Unemployed, and with little money left, they depended on government welfare for rations of stale bread and potatoes which were delivered to their campsite. In desperate search for work, Vellios and the other Macedonians would walk from farm to farm and, although farmers had work to give them, there was no money to pay them. At times local farmers attended the campsite enquiring whether any of the men would take on a day's work in exchange for a hot, home cooked meal. There was never a shortage of volunteers and at least they knew they would eat well that day.[21]

Local residents, probably due to their own despair, began accusing immigrant labourers of taking their jobs and eating their food rations. Vellios and the other Macedonians had endured unemployment and hardship long enough and, feeling ostracised, decided to return home to their villages. Boarding a ship in Fremantle, Vellios returned to Maala village in late 1930. Pleased to be reunited with his family, he was embarrassed that he had returned with no money and had taken on debt to pay for his voyage home.[22]

Todor Jurukot, the famous Macedonian strongman and wrestler, from Krstoar village (Bitola) arrived in Australia during the depression era with English language skills acquired from previous *pechalba* experiences in the United States. Jurukot described the life of the *pechalbar* as particularly difficult at this time as there was no work available and, at best, they could secure perhaps a couple of days labouring on farms. Newly arrived Macedonians could not even afford to pay for accommodation and instead many went into the bush to work in the eucalyptus oil industry, even though they were poorly paid for the oil they produced. Men wrote home to their families in Macedonia asking them to sell assets in order to pay for their return fares. Instead of improving their economic situation, their situation had worsened.[23]

Photo 10: Group of Macedonians somewhere in central-west New South Wales, 1928. (Source: Koca Sazdanov. Courtesy of Mendo Trajcevski).

Arriving in the cities, foreign citizens faced discrimination as they were unable to find employment and were forced to head out into the countryside. When Mitre Kotchoff arrived in Perth, Western Australia, in 1927 from Konomladi village (Kostur), 'he had no choice but to go out bush for work, there was no work in the city, he could not even get a glass of beer in the city'.[24] Macedonian eucalypt oil gatherers faced discrimination from the local population at Captains Flat each time they came down out of the bush to buy supplies in town. They could not buy a beer at the local hotel as the locals were against their entry and the publican refused to serve them. When the strongman and wrestler Jurukot joined other Macedonians in the eucalyptus industry, the tradition of not serving Macedonians in the pub changed after he stood up and demanded that the discriminatory practice end.[25]

Unfortunately, discrimination was still being experienced decades later and at times even young children were not immune from racism and discriminatory behaviour. During the 1950s, at Queanbeyan Primary School in New South Wales, not far from Canberra, Macedonian children were forced to walk home together in a group for protection to avoid being beaten up. Abused, labelled 'daigoes' and told to go back to their own country, they were frightened and confused as they did not have a free Macedonian homeland to return to. Cveta Dimov stated, 'What country was I to go back to? I did not know any other country, this is where I grew up.'[26]

Forced to take on the lowest paid jobs, Macedonians were often subjected to exploitation and mistreatment and at times not even paid for the work they performed. In Western Australia during the 1930s, Mitre Kotchoff worked on a farm for three years and the promised payment for his labour never eventuated. On another western Australian farm, Vasil Spirov was not paid for the work he completed, and the farmer attempted to deny him clean drinking water, offering him water reserved for farm animals. Many experienced discrimination and mistreatment at the hands of Australian farmers and employers; however, the worst treatment was reserved for Aboriginals. Macedonians saw Aboriginals being treated very badly, much worse than their own experiences.

In the Northern Territory, Macedonian mine workers left their place of employment due to not being paid award rates for working at a depth of more than 20 feet below the surface. The men also reported that they were required to purchase their own water bags and were not permitted to take some breaks. The North Australian

Photo 11: Macedonians proudly photographed with indigenous Australian man in Western Australia, circa 1930. Having their own experiences of oppression and discrimination back in the Balkans, Macedonians felt an affinity with the indigenous peoples of Australia. (Source: Peter Sarbinov).

Workers Union supported the men in their claim.[27] In the late 1920s, Vasil Boskov worked on a farm near Manjimup, Western Australia, cutting trees and clearing farmland but was not paid for the work undertaken. Boskov walked to Manjimup and reported the matter to police who demanded the farmer pay Boskov monies owed through monthly instalments.[28]

(In the United States Macedonian *pechalba* workers were known to participate in industrial action in support of workers' rights. In 1910, a group of Macedonians working on the construction of the railroad in Rock Island, Oklahoma went on strike for increased daily rates of pay. In the same year, in Ohio, Trajche Barbutov from Capari village (Bitola) led 35 Macedonians to strike against the Pennsylvania Railroad Company for increased wages. In 1932, Macedonians actively participated in the infamous Ford Hunger March, where thousands of unemployed workers marched from Detroit to the

Photo 12: Macedonian pioneers of Western Australia in Manjimup, circa 1934. Standing from left: Pejo Donev, Stojan Eftov, and Kosta Eftov. Seated from left: Risto Donev and Kole Angelev. (Source: Archive of the Macedonian Community of Western Australia. Courtesy of Ilo Ognenov).

Ford River Rouge Complex in Dearborn. Here, the police and security guards employed by the Ford Motor Company opened fire on protesters, killing several men and wounding dozens more.[29])

The legacy of the hardship of their experiences in Australia during the depression years lingered for decades in the memories of *pechalbari*. The cousins Giorgija and Risto from the Shokovci family (Brajchino village) arrived during the 1920s, prepared to work hard, repay the fares that they borrowed and send savings back to their families in Macedonia; instead, they experienced hard times, could not find work, and were unable to return to Macedonia for a number of years. In his native village, Giorgija often told his story of hardship in the Australian bush as a warning to the young men who were eager to go abroad and make their fortune.[30]

Mining

Some of the earliest Macedonian arrivals found work in the mining industry and, after disembarking in Fremantle, *pechalbari* travelled vast distances in search of work at mines in Kalgoorlie, Broken Hill, Big Bell, Wiluna and elsewhere. Unlike farm work with which they were familiar, the mining industry was different from what they had previously experienced. However, they possessed all the right qualities to succeed: they were prepared to work long hard hours, in extreme conditions and often without seeing sunlight for long periods.

Twenty-five-year old Stojko Angelkoff left with three other men from Dambeni village (Kostur), travelled on the Italian ship *Miglia di Strasbourg* and arrived in Fremantle in 1924. There was no-one to greet them and they walked to the train station carrying their *valencija* (rugs/blankets) on their backs. Along the way they met a Jew who took them to a Greek café where they were told that in the city they would only find work in restaurants; however, they could make more income if they headed out into the country. On the ship they had met some Dalmatians who told them about Kalgoorlie. Macedonians could communicate with Dalmatian travellers and, due to similarity of language, the two groups got on well together. Angelkoff and the three others made their way to the Perth train station and, together with the Dalmatians, they headed for Kalgoorlie. Along the way, with the help of a stationmaster, they boarded an open wagon train and found the *valenci* useful which they wrapped around themselves for protection from the cold. The men found work on the woodlines – railway lines used to haul timber into Kalgoorlie for the mines and fuel for the industry.[31]

In a typical chain migration pattern, newly arrived *pechalbari* headed for places where friends and relatives were already settled and working. A group of men from Kosinec village, including Naum Bonakey, arrived in Western Australia in 1924 and headed for Broken Hill, NSW, where Bonakey's cousin Vane Prcul had been living for nearly twenty years. Bonakey remained in Broken Hill for six years and brought his family out in 1930. Similarly, when Vasil Boskov arrived in 1927, he immediately set out for Kalgoorlie with other Macedonians to work in the gold and nickel mines after hearing about

Macedonians working there. Boskov earned one shilling per day and worked alongside Macedonians and other foreigners, mainly Dalmatians and Italians. He remained in Kalgoorlie for one year before he set out to go timber cutting in the bush with a group of Macedonians. Others such as Mitre Kotchoff worked on Western Australian farms and in the bush clearing land in the mid-1930s, but payment was irregular and at times not forthcoming at all. When Kotchoff secured employment at a gold mine in Leonora, he was happy to work there as he received regular pay and worked alongside other Macedonians.

Work in the mining industry was mostly around Western Australia and South Australia. However, others found work in the eastern states in places like Woy Woy, New South Wales, where they worked in a basalt mine in the 1930s. Atanas Tomev from Statica village, Kostur, was tall with a solid build and known as 'Big Tom'. He worked in the copper and silver mines at Captains Flat in New South Wales in the 1930s, at a time when few other Macedonians could secure work there.[32] In 1924, Laze Porkov from Capari village worked with a group of men from his village in a quarry at Mudgee New South Wales.[33] Other Macedonians managed to find work on large government projects such as the Snowy Mountains scheme and the construction of dams. Risto Kircos worked on the Sugarloaf Dam in Victoria, built between 1914 and 1928,[34] while in Western Australia, Jovan Mladenov from Krpeshina village and other Macedonians worked on the construction of the Stirling Dam during the early 1940s, working in seven-week cycles before taking one week's leave which Jovan used to visit his family in Perth.[35]

In the 1940s and 1950s chapters of the Macedonian Australian People's League (MAPL) were established in places such as Kalgoorlie, Western Australia, and Broken Hill in outback New South Wales.

Decades later, in the 1960s and 1970s, there was an influx of Macedonians from the Republic of Macedonia headed for the mining industry in Western Australia. Bogdan Pavlevski from Zhelezec village (Demir Hisar) was a stonemason who had the opportunity to work in France but was determined to come to Australia after hearing about the good pay on offer in the mines of Western Australia, seeing it as an opportunity to advance his family's economic position. Bogdan arrived alone in 1968 and lodged with a Macedonian family from the Lerin region, in the area of Perth later named Northbridge, until he could arrange employment. For several weeks, Bogdan worked with other Macedonians for the Perth city council conducting roadworks before travelling by bus to Tom Price in the Pilbara region, where he worked as a contractor in the plumbing section, building workers' accommodation for the Mount Tom Price iron ore mine. For over a decade Bogdan worked in the mining industry in Western Australia at different locations, but always with other Macedonians, particularly from the Lerin and Ohrid regions. Through family connections and Macedonian community contacts, Bogdan secured employment when jobs ended and he worked as a labourer in a number of open pit iron ore mines in the Pilbara region, as a cook at a Port Hedland mine, and on a rail construction project near Dampier in north-west Western Australia.

Clearing bush land

In the first decades of the twentieth century, there were still significant tracts of farming land in Australia yet to be cleared. After arriving in one of the major cities, Macedonians soon found their way into the Australian bush and moved around in small groups of three or four men, clearing bushland in remote areas for future farms. When Mitre Kotchoff arrived in Fremantle, he met up with other Macedonians who took him to a general store to purchase an axe and they immediately headed into the Western Australian bush to clear bushland and cut trees.[36] The work often involved being isolated in the bush for months at a time and living in primitive accommodation made from the most basic materials.

Contractors recruited newly arrived Macedonians from boarding houses to clear bushland in country areas. Done Theodorovsky initially moved into a boarding house in Carlton in Melbourne when he arrived from Buf village (Lerin) in 1924 and soon found work in country Victoria clearing bushland, through a contractor known for picking up workers from boarding houses.[37] When Macedonian boarding houses and cafes were established they would become recruitment centres for contractors looking to hire workers. In Perth during the 1920s and 1930s, a contractor, Jerry Leech, would hire men from Kosta Malco's boarding house to cut railway sleepers in the bush.[38] Contractors also advertised in newspapers for workers, specifying particular ethnic groups. Advertisements in the *West Australian* newspaper sought Macedonians to work as bush clearers (1937) and an unlimited number of Macedonians to work as charcoal burners (1941).[39]

Due to a shortage of petrol during the Second World War, a unique Australian invention saw vehicles fitted with a charcoal burner conversion kit that produced gas from the burning of charcoal. Throughout the 1940s, there was considerable demand for charcoal. The manufacture of charcoal from timber was a lengthy, hot and dirty process and those involved in the work were known as charcoal burners. Macedonians were highly sought after to perform this demanding work. The production of charcoal was well developed in the Zheleznik district villages in the Demir Hisar region of Macedonia, where the craft was well known to the inhabitants and had been a source of economic existence for generations. Villages involved in charcoal production included Suvogrlo, Sopotnica, Zhvan, Dolenci, Zheleznec, Brezevo, Smilevo, Boishte, Leskovo, Cerevo, Virovo, Mrenoga, Sloeshtica, Basernik, Malo Mrenoga, Strugovo and Kutretino.[40] Similarly, Macedonians from the village Shulin in the Dolna Prespa district were renowned charcoal burners and, following the inclusion of Shulin in Albania, the men from the village worked their trade throughout Albania.[41]

The process of clearing land for farming was gruelling work that the hard-working Macedonians were prepared to take on. The historian, Jan Harper, in her account of Macedonian *pechalbari* in Gippsland during the 1930s, explained that Macedonian farm labourers quickly learned the techniques of scrub clearing which involved felling trees and burning the timber, checking the fires throughout the night, man-handling half burnt wood into new piles (a process known as 'picking up') and setting alight the tree stumps, which were covered with earth and allowed to smoulder for days (a process known as 'stoving'). Once land was cleared, native undergrowth presented an ongoing problem in that eradicating it was a never-ending

Photo 13: Stojan Sarbinov (left) visiting a Macedonian bush worker in Western Australia, circa 1938. The Macedonian bush workers made their own tents using timber obtained from the bush and canvas sheets. (Source: Peter Sarbinov).

Photo 14: Macedonian tree cutters gathered for a celebration in the Western Australia bush, 1935. (Source: Archive of the Macedonian Community of Western Australia. Courtesy of Ilo Ognenov).

task with which Australian farmers had traditionally been confronted; however, 'what beat the farmers, the Macedonian workers were prepared to do'; Macedonian workers cut the native undergrowth repeatedly until it completely disappeared.[42]

Timber cutting

Many found work sleeper-cutting in the forests of Western Australia and Victoria where they lived isolated in camps. It was particularly physical and demanding work which was labour intensive in that axes and saws were required to fell large trees which would then be cut into railway sleepers. The men would start each morning 'sharpening and oiling their axes and saws and pouring methylate spirits over their calloused, bruised and blistered hands to clean their wounds and prevent them from becoming infected'.[43] The sleepers would be moved manually or with the use of horses or bullocks and, once they passed inspection, contractors would buy them on behalf of railway companies and the Macedonians would receive payment for sleepers they had carved.[44] In 1925, Kiril Karafilov from Capari village (Bitola) worked as a sleeper cutter in Western Australia and earned two shillings per sleeper.[45]

Photo 15: From left Pavle Vlahov, Petre Vlahov and Done Svetin sleeper cutting near Manjimup, Western Australia, circa 1940. Saws and axes were the main tools required to be a sleeper cutter in the Australian bush. (Source: Archive of Macedonian Community of Western Australia. Courtesy of Ilo Ognenov).

Numerous dangers faced Macedonians working in the Australian bush and, in particular, those in the timber-cutting industry. Felling enormous trees was hazardous work in that at times men were crushed as the trees crashed down and working with sharp saws and axes resulted in serious injuries. Sometime between 1918 and 1920, Karanfil from the Sarievci family (Graeshnica village, Bitola), died in a work accident when a tree fell on him while working in the West Australian bush.[46] A similar tragedy in 1929 saw 'a Macedonian bushman fatally crushed by a tree near Moora (Western Australia)'[47] and around the same time Petre Georgiev Torkoff from German village (Lerin) suffered a similar fate.[48] In 1927, Kosta Malco from Shestevo village (Kostur) broke his arm when a branch fell on him whilst bush clearing at Three Springs in Western Australia, and to pay for his hospital fees he used all the money he earned over the six months working in the bush.[49]

Sugar cane

Macedonians commenced working in the sugar cane industry of North Queensland in the 1920s in areas around Tully, Thangool, South Johnstone and Innisfail where they joined other migrants, in particular, Italians, who were the dominant ethnic group in the industry. Vangel Soklev arrived in Melbourne from Klabuchishta village (Lerin) in 1927 with hopes of earning good income; however, he struggled to find work and, after hearing about the sugar cane industry, set out with other Macedonians for the Tully region. Quite a few Macedonians, after arriving in Sydney and being unable to find work there, also headed out for the sugar cane fields. Others went to places like Newcastle to work in the steelworks and, when work ran out, went north to the Queensland sugar cane fields, while some made the long journey north from Melbourne. It was a hard life: rain or shine the men worked all day throughout the harvesting season from June to December. During the off-season many went to Biloela to pick cotton.[50]

The Macedonians found employment in Feluga in the Tully district, where they lived in three camps that were set up beside a creek. There were approximately 15 men in each of the three barracks which were simple, but poorly constructed buildings, each with six bedrooms and a kitchen. Two or three men were accommodated in each bedroom. Conditions were basic, with the creek being their only source of water for drinking, washing and laundry. Quite a few of the men were from Bitusha and surrounding Lerin region villages, and there were also some from Ohrid. The sugar cane work itself was arduous and conducted out in the open in extreme conditions, intense tropical heat with high humidity and torrential downpours of rain. A hazard was the dreaded Weil's disease, caused by cane field rats in the early 1930s, which resulted in the cutters burning the cane before cutting it to reduce the threat of the disease spreading. Snakes presented another problem for the cane cutters.

Pavle Gulev/Gulevci family/Goulopoulos from Bitusha village (Lerin) arrived in Fremantle but made his way to Innisfail, with his brother Giorgija in the late 1920s.They worked in a gang made up of eight Macedonians. They lived together and worked six days a week, and on the seventh day alternated domestic duties such as food preparation and washing.[51] Similarly, after arriving in Western Australia in 1927, Boshe Gelevski (from Klabuchishta village Lerin) made his way to Queensland where he worked as a sugar cane cutter in Thangool in the 1930s. In 1938, his brother Petre joined him and the enterprising brothers saw an opportunity to improve their earnings by entering into a sharecropping arrangement with the landowner.[52]

Eucalyptus oil

Macedonians worked in the eucalyptus oil industry in New South Wales in various areas but, in particular, the districts around Braidwood and Captains Flat, in close proximity to Queanbeyan and Canberra. Men worked in small groups in remote bush camps along mountain ridges. Eucalyptus trees were either felled or their limps lopped, then the gum leaves were distilled using an iron tank heated by wood fire which required a water supply and length of piping. The Macedonian eucalyptus oil workers lived isolated in the bush for lengthy periods.

When Con Doikin/Doikos from Statica village (Kostur) arrived in Sydney in 1927, he could not find work and headed for Forbes to

Photo 16: Ilo Dimovski (Dimovic) from Bukovo village (Bitola) working as a eucalyptus oil worker filling a distilling tank in Braidwood, New South Wales, circa 1930. Ilo arrived in 1924 and was one of the first Macedonians to settle in the Illawarra region. (Source: Draga Dimovska, Courtesy of Mendo Trajcevski).

Photo 17: Mitre Veljanovski (on left side) with Ilo Prenzoski in the New South Wales bush, 1940. Mitre spent five years in the bush with other Macedonians producing eucalyptus oil around Khancoban, New South Wales. (Source: Ilija Veljanovski).

work in the eucalyptus oil industry where there were others from Statica and more than twenty men from Konomladi village.[53] The men constructed their own rudimentary sleeping huts using wooden poles cut down from trees for a basic frame, corrugated iron for the roof, and hessian from potato bags used for walls to enclose the structure. Palm-like plants were used to create bedding and soften the ground on which they slept. The men found conditions in Australia much worse than what they left behind in their villages.[54]

Dmitri Naumov from Draslajca village (Struga) produced eucalyptus oil in Khancoban, New South Wales, with other Macedonians, including men from his village. In 1938, his co-villager Mitre Veljanovski arrived in Melbourne on the Italian cruise ship *Viminale* and was met at Port Melbourne dock by Dmitri. They immediately left for the bush in Khancoban and remained there for five years. Initially all the work was performed by hand until they saved enough money to buy a horse. They lived in the most rudimentary conditions and relied on setting traps to catch rabbits which they cooked.[55] Small groups of men worked in isolation for years in the bush. The last remaining Macedonian producing eucalyptus oil was Done Romanov who worked in remote bush between Captains Flat and Jerangle until 1970.[56]

6

Passports and Identity

Demographer Charles Price estimated that in 1921 there were 50 Macedonians in Australia.[57] This figure is without doubt, grossly understated, as anecdotal evidence suggests that the number was significantly greater. Accurately determining the number of Macedonians in Australia has been problematic since the first arrivals at the end of the nineteenth century and the issue has persisted into the twenty-first century due to three principal factors. These were: a lack of Macedonian statehood; the psychological impact of systematically demeaning Macedonian identity under oppressive Greek, Serbian, Bulgarian and Albanian rule; and possibly unreliable Australian census data. Throughout the twentieth century, Australian censuses treated birthplace as representing ethnic origin and, as such, Macedonians born in Greece, which constituted the largest number of Macedonians in Australia at the time, were classified as Greeks. It was not until the 2001 and 2006 censuses that changes were introduced that considered a person's ancestry might be different from their country of birth.

When the first Macedonians arrived in Australia prior to the 1912-1913 Balkan Wars, they travelled with Ottoman Turkish passports which did not record the ethnicity of the traveller. Following the Balkan Wars and the division of Macedonia, Macedonians arrived with Greek, Yugoslav, Bulgarian or Albanian passports, although most carried Greek and Yugoslav passports. Arriving with foreign passports resulted in Macedonians being classified as belonging to the nationality according to their passports, and as such they were officially documented as Yugoslavs or Greeks. Further complicating the outward appearance of their ethnic identity was that their names appeared as characteristically Serbian or Greek (due to assimilation policies aimed at Macedonians in those states) which reduced the visibility of the Macedonians while enlarging other ethnic groups. There are also numerous examples in the national archives of Australia where people have recorded Macedonian nationality on Australian immigration registration forms in the 1920s, 30s and 40s, and the designation 'Macedonian' has been crossed out by Australian government officials and replaced with the designation Greek, Yugoslav, Bulgarian or Albanian.

Before the Great War, there were no restrictions on European immigrants arriving in Australia. Between 1916 and 1920 Maltese and Greeks, who were considered 'semi-coloured' were prohibited from entering Australia, and their arrival was seen to be a threat to the jobs of Australian soldiers fighting abroad. After 1920, a strict limit was introduced to the number of Maltese and Greeks, as well as certain other Europeans such as Albanians and Yugoslavs. During this period Macedonians from Greece found a route to Australia via Bulgaria. After crossing into Bulgaria, Macedonians were issued with a Bulgarian passport in place of the Greek one to facilitate access to travel to Australia. Although *pechalbari* came from countryside villages and were not educated, they were practical and were able to competently navigate through bureaucracy and other obstacles in order to successfully achieve their aim of working abroad to economically advance their families. The route via Bulgaria served a practical purpose, but brought unintended consequences for Macedonians in Australia, where they were recorded as Bulgarians, and this caused problems with the Greek authorities when they returned to their villages.

A group of fifteen Macedonians from the Prespa region, under Greek rule, travelled to Bulgaria and remained in Sofia for one month until travel documentation could be prepared to enable passage to Australia. Before they could be issued passports, they were required to take out Bulgarian citizenship, change their names and register a Bulgarian address. Amongst the fifteen men, five were from the village, Orovo, and were all registered to an address in Varna, Bulgaria with the following name changes: Lazo Miovski to Lazar Mihov, Tanas Nelkovski to Atanas Iliov, Vasil Lamevski to Vasil Nikolov, Spiro Dimanovski to Spiro Trajkov and Naum Dzhambazovski to Naum Mitrev.[58]

Boris Giamov from Trnava village (Lerin) sought to come to Australia when migrants from Greece were not being accepted. Like many others, Giamov travelled to Bulgaria and obtained a Bulgarian passport. Even though he was born in Trnava, the new passport recorded him as being born in Sofia, Bulgaria. Giamov arrived in Australia in 1930, and during the Second World War he was classified as an 'enemy alien' due to being considered Bulgarian as, at that time, Bulgaria was fighting on the side of the Axis powers. Giamov went to much effort to prove that he was not Bulgarian.

It was so well known that Macedonians living under Greek rule found their route to Australia through Bulgaria that even the Greek border guards were accustomed to processing Macedonians into Bulgaria, knowing full well that they intended to continue onwards to Australia. Determined to travel to Australia, Vane Ashlakoff from Ofcharani village was issued a Bulgarian passport which recorded his original Macedonian name, Ashlakoff, instead of the imposed Greek name, Anastasiadis. When Ashlakoff arrived in Melbourne in the late 1920s, he headed out to the bush looking for work. However, *pechalba* in Australia did not meet his expectations: working in the bush was hard and isolating, he was making very little money, and economic advancement seemed impossible at that time. He contemplated returning to his village, but a Greek priest in Melbourne warned him not to do so because his Greek name had been discarded when the Bulgarian passport was issued and he faced persecution by the Greek authorities should he return. Ashlakoff remained in Australia, eventually settling in Shepparton where he became a successful market gardener and orchardist.[59]

Regardless of whatever imposed names with which Macedonians arrived, whether Greek, Bulgarian, Serbian, or Albanian, in everyday communication with other Macedonians and in the wider Australian community Macedonians typically used their traditional Macedonian names. Macedonians also have a tendency to use other names in unofficial capacities such as clan/family names, known in Macedonian as *'soi'*, or even nicknames associated with a family. Some Macedonians from Aegean Macedonia became naturalised British citizens as soon as they were eligible to do so in order to formally cut ties with the Greek government, seeing naturalisation as an opportunity to discard their Greek name and either adopting an Anglicised version of their name or reverting to their original Macedonian name. For instance, the Mechkaroff family from Neret village (Lerin) had endured a number of name changes under Greek rule. Firstly, the family name was changed to Mechkaris, to reflect Greek nationality; however, it was found to be 'not Greek enough' as the Macedonian word *mechka* (meaning bear) was still contained in the new surname. A further forced modification to the family name saw it changed to Arkudis, which is a Greek translation of *mechka*. Upon arrival in Australia in 1938, Mechkaroff changed his surname by deed poll back to the original Macedonian name as he did not want to be known by a name imposed upon him by the Greek government which made him appear to be Greek. For those who changed their names to an Anglicised version, this was also perceived as a better way to integrate into Australian society while, at the same time, maintaining pride in one's Macedonian ethnic identity.

Ilija Ilievski from Drenovo village escaped from Greece to Bulgaria with several other young men from the nearby village of Lak in the late 1920s (under Albanian rule – both villages were situated along the shore of Mala Prespa Lake). Following Greek occupation in the district, his surname was changed to Iliopoulous; however, while in Bulgaria he was issued with a Bulgarian passport and entered Fremantle in 1929 with the surname Iliev. He was registered as a Bulgarian arrival. After ten years of working in the bush and on farms in Western Australia, he returned to see his family in his native village. Arriving in Athens, the Greek authorities imprisoned him after becoming enraged that his surname had been changed from the Greek Iliopoulous to the 'Bulgarian' Iliev. With the protection of his Australian citizenship, he appealed to the British Embassy in Athens and was duly released and returned to Australia.

7

Farms and Market Gardens: From Pechalba to Permanent Settlement

Macedonians went from being traditional *pechalbari* to establishing themselves in Australia in a permanent setting. With aspirations of becoming financially independent, there was a change in occupation of the early arrivals, a movement from timber cutting and bush clearing to the setting up of small-scale market gardens and farms, which at first they rented before they managed to acquire sufficient funds to purchase their own farms, usually close to urban centres.[60] This transition was also connected with an increase in the number of women and children that had arrived, providing much needed labour to help work the land. Macedonians established market gardens and farms in places such as Manjimup and Geraldton in Western Australia, and Osborne Park, Balcatta and Wanneroo in Perth; Shepparton and Werribee in Victoria; Fulham Gardens and Findon in Adelaide; Queanbeyan near Canberra; and Crabbes Creek, Wauchope, Forbes, Richmond and the Mona Vale-Warriewood area in New South Wales.

Although familiar with a rural lifestyle from their experiences in Macedonia there were many contrasting features between village life in Macedonia and rural Australia. The Australian climate was much warmer and the landscape often dry. Birds and animals, such as the kookaburra, made strange noises. Homes were constructed of different materials and in rural areas were often spaced much further apart from one another, compared to homes in Macedonian villages, which were closer together and constructed of natural materials that were readily available around them. Construction methods using natural materials had been used for successive generations; for example, in mountainous villages, stone and slate were principal building materials, whilst on the plains, homes were typically constructed from mud brick.

In Macedonia 'villagers had a close affinity with the building materials they used, which were extracted from the earth, stone and forest around the village, … their homes sprang from the very earth they walked upon.'[61] Building materials differed in the Australian countryside. Walls made from hessian bags were sewn together and whitewashed with lime which would set like plaster and every couple of years the whitewash would be reapplied to reinforce the walls. The lime made the walls waterproof, and corrugated iron was used for the roof. In Geraldton, Western Australia, Macedonians built their first basic homes out of metal sheets and hessian bags on rented land used to grow tomatoes.[62] At times the homes were no more than simple huts, particularly when men lived alone before their families arrived. In some areas, they would build their own simple timber homes, and in other places homes were constructed of mud brick like they did in Macedonia. Others, such as Mitre Kotchoff, used novel methods: he built a hut made out of gasoline tins in Western Australia during the 1930s. During this time homes rarely had running water or electricity, as kerosene lamps were used for light, and cooking was conducted over a wood stove. Generally, from the 1940s as families were being reunited, it was common to seek to upgrade to a home built of fibro asbestos sheets, which Macedonians would also build themselves.

Photo 18: Mitre Kotchoff from Konomladi village (Kostur), photographed in Western Australia, circa 1930. Mitre arrived in 1927 and immediately went out to isolated areas in Western Australia to clear bushland. The hut in the background of the photograph was built by Mitre out of gasoline tin cans. (Source: Kosta Kotchoff).

The experiences and recollections of Velika Spirova reflect those of many Macedonians when they arrived in Australia and settled in rural areas. Spirova arrived in 1939 with her twelve-year-old daughter Fania, to be reunited with her husband Vasil at Crossroads near Newcastle in New South Wales.[63] Velika's impressions upon her arrival were vivid: 'I arrived in the bush. The house was made of timber. It had nothing – no curtains, no windows, no rooms, no plaster – it was terrible. It had a dirt floor. It was much worse than what I had left behind. It was a hundred times worse. My daughter cried and cried and wanted to return home. In Macedonia, we had a nicer home, we had our possessions, and we knew people. We had nothing here'.[64]

Adapting to life in rural Australia presented diverse challenges for newly arrived wives and children. However, as the community grew, people became less isolated and aspects of traditional village life were recreated, social interaction improved and regular community events brought them together, usually with music and dancing. Economically, Macedonians pooled their labour resources together when building homes; they helped with work on each other's farms, financially assisted one another to purchase properties, and conducted real estate transactions amongst community members.

In Western Australia, Macedonian market garden communities were established in places close to Perth such as Osborne Park and Wanneroo, the latter being one of the first Macedonian settlements in Western Australia (these places eventually formed part of Perth's northern suburbs). The first to arrive in Wanneroo was Stojko Angelkoff in 1927, who, together with his brother Kiro, and another Macedonian friend Stojko, leased five acres of land for a 30-pound annual fee; in 1930, he brought out his wife and two children.[65] Other Macedonians also arrived in 1927, including Giorgi Zaikov,[66] and Lazo Bonakey (Boshnako) from Kosinec village (Kostur) who arrived with three other Macedonians, and they leased 15 acres of land.[67] Pando Manov from Vrbnik village (Kostur/Korcha) was another early arrival in Wanneroo, operating a market garden in the 1920s; he was later joined by his sons, Naum and Lazo.[68]

The Macedonians settled at Twenty-Two Mile Peg (Lake Neerabup area), renting land from the leaseholder John Pappas. Plots were typically three to five acres, more or less positioned in a straight line alongside swampland. There was no need for irrigation as the soil was moist and, although it could only be worked by hand, was of good quality, ideally suited for market gardening, growing tomatoes, lettuce, cabbages, cauliflower, and cucumbers. They constructed their own homes but had no running water and would carry water from a well at the back of their homes to cook and to bathe. The water was kept clean with lime, which would be dropped into the well, left for a day, and the water would become clean and clear.[69]

Anastas Vosnacos/Vosnacov arrived in Australia in 1924 from Gabresh village (Kostur) and initially settled in Salmon Gums in 1925 before his wife and son joined him in 1931. Two more children were born in Australia. He bought a truck and secured a carting contract with Main Roads and, with his family in tow, followed the work across a number of Western Australian towns before moving to Wanneroo in 1938, where he joined relatives and other Macedonians. Atanas leased a three-acre plot of land to grow vegetables. Neighbouring properties on both sides were Macedonians from the Kostur region – the Plukas family from Pozdivishta and the Milias family from Dzhupanishta. Whilst working with Main Roads, Atanas purchased a 1936 model Chevrolet truck and was only one of three people in Wanneroo with a truck at that time. The vehicle proved to be a valuable asset as he was soon transporting vegetables for other growers to the Metropolitan Fruit and Vegetable Market in West Perth, leaving at 4.00 am three times a week.[70]

There were about 40 Macedonian market gardens at Twenty-Two Mile Peg employing basic agricultural systems with which they were familiar from their homeland. During the war years they made good money, as the market gardens were contracted to provide produce to the Australian army. With a reputation as hard workers and a strong desire to succeed, Macedonians would also contribute innovative methods to cultivation in the market gardening industry. In Osborne Park during the early 1930s market gardeners had been diverting water from the main canal, disrupting water supply to other gardens. Two Macedonians constructed a deep well on their property and connected a motorised pump. During excavation, a permanent spring of fresh water was struck. They then dug a deep ditch from the canal and joined it with the well, thereby securing an everlasting supply of water that, by natural gravitation, flowed down from Osborne Park to the sea. Their irrigation system was so successful that *the West Australian* newspaper reported on their story under the headline 'Ingenious irrigation – gardeners' success'.[71]

At the beginning of the twentieth century, Geraldton was a small coastal town in the wheat belt district in the north of Perth. The town developed into a tomato-growing centre, with Chinese and Japanese market gardeners the first to set up tomato farms; however, it was an Englishman, George Allen, who developed the smooth-skinned Geraldton tomato in the 1920s. He operated substantial land holdings and went on to create a huge business from tomato growing. In their search for work, Macedonians made their way to the district in the 1920s, working as farm labourers and clearing bushland before arriving in Geraldton and finding work on Allen's tomato farms. With aspirations to work for themselves, they started share farming and renting plots before going on to purchase their own properties.

The climate was ideal to grow tomatoes all seasons round, which resulted in high prices for the produce, particularly the early crop. Geraldton tomatoes were sent to Perth, Adelaide and Melbourne and, for many years, shipped to Singapore. Ten-acre lots were sufficient for a man and his family to operate, all the work was performed manually, and this proved attractive to Macedonians who were familiar with agricultural techniques and prepared to work hard. The work involved preparing the seedlings, ploughing the earth, spraying pesticides, setting up stakes, tying the tomato plants, and pruning, weeding, picking and watering the plants, all by hand. For additional income Macedonians would plough the land with horses for other farmers or during the off season would go hay carting.

Among the first Macedonians to arrive in Geraldton from 1924 to 1927 were heads of the families listed in table 7.1.[72]

Family name	Village	Region
Gotsev Lukarov	Breznitsa	Kostur
Donev Kostov Ognenov	Grazhdeno	Kostur
Sekulov	Konomladi	Kostur
Adamaov	Labanitsa	Kostur
Agirov Nedelkov	Orovo	Kostur
Dinev Rajkov	Oschima	Kostur
Angelev Dzatov Filevichin Gotchev Lazov Popov	Pozdivishta	Kostur
Mustakov	Rudari	Kostur
Sotirov	Trnava	Lerin

Table 7.1 Early Macedonians arrive in Geraldton 1924-1927.

Later when they brought out their wives and children in the 1930s, transport between Perth and Geraldton was usually provided by 'Mr Missotto', an Italian who had a small trucking company in Geraldton and, for a fee, would pick up the new arrivals from Fremantle Port and transport them back to Geraldton in one of his trucks. Due to the long drive to Geraldton, they would often have a first night stop-over at a Macedonian boarding house in William Street, Northbridge, or at a Macedonian-owned type of interim boarding house in Eton Street, North Perth.

Ilija Popoff from Konomladi village (Kostur) arrived in Western Australia in 1928 and worked in Narembeen, Carnamah and Three Springs, clearing land for farmers, working agriculture and on the railways before making his way to Geraldton in 1936 where he worked for Allen.[73] He had a share crop arrangement for the first year before he started his own crop at Narra Tarra on land rented from a Mr Rodman, a large property owner in the area. Ilia constructed a shack on the land and brought out his wife, daughter and son from Macedonia in 1939 and, after five years of hard work, bought land in Waggrakine to grow tomatoes. Waggrakine, Narra Tarra and Glenfield were the main places where Macedonians set up tomato farms and these areas lay to the northern edge of the Geraldton township, while Allen's farms were on the south side in Wonthella and Utakarra. Ilija's venture was profitable, and he went on to purchase a large parcel of land on Chapman Road in Bluff Point to build a family home. Once they established themselves, a number of Macedonians moved to Bluff Point which was about 5 kilometres from the tomato plantations in Waggrakine. Such was the concentration of Macedonians living on Chapman Road that, when the community established a Macedonian soccer team in 1946, they named it Chapman Athletic.[74]

As they became established and set up their own farms, it was not uncommon for Macedonian farmers in parts of Western Australia to employ Aboriginal people. In Geraldton, the first Macedonian tomato farmers in the late 1920s did not have family members to help on the farm and were known to employ Aboriginals to help gather the harvest. Later, when the men brought out their wives, they provided additional labour on the farms, but when their wives were giving birth or the children were very young, Aborigines were employed as tomato pickers. As the children became older, the wives would pick up the work again to help their husbands. Generally, work was periodic for the Aborigines; however, some stayed on for much longer, and were regularly called upon to assist during seasonal activities such as planting and harvesting. For example, Risto (Chris) Damos employed an Aboriginal man on his tomato market garden in the mid-1940s, coinciding with Risto's wife Mita giving birth to a son Alex, and then later when their daughter Sophie was born. Risto found the Aboriginal man honest and reliable and by the time Mita was ready to return to work, Risto had planted an additional 30 per cent more tomatoes and, needing extra hands on the farm, he kept the Aboriginal man through all the tomato seasons until the early 1950s.[75]

Snaki Hall, an Anglo-Australian, was a significant Geraldton landowner and entrepreneur with 2,700 acres of good quality tomato-growing land. He was one of the main individuals from whom Macedonians rented land to set up their own tomato-growing businesses. With every rental arrangement, Snaki's son would arrive with a bulldozer to clear a section of the land for the Macedonians to build their homes on. Forty-four Macedonian families rented land from Hall. He got on very well with them and found them to be a hard-working honest lot. As a mark of appreciation for all the years he dealt with the Macedonians without any issues or disagreements, in the late 1940s Snaki donated a five-acre parcel of land in Glenfield (in Geraldton) to the Macedonian community, which was utilised by the Macedonians as a picnic ground.[76] Social events, picnics and sporting activities were organised by the Geraldton Macedonian Community Committee, established in the 1940s. As early as 1946 they had established a local soccer club. Meetings were held in the back sheds of the Committee members' properties and significant effort went towards strengthening and keeping the community together. In the 1940s and 1950s, the Geraldton Macedonian Community Committee included Jani (Yani) Raykos, Jani (Yani) Sotiroff, Risto (Chris) Damos and Con Goches; while John Costopoulos, Jim Costopoulos and Paul Popoff were key individuals behind the soccer team.

The Macedonians eventually constructed a community hall on the site, providing a central place to gather for social activities, and they would take part in group picnics of the sort they recalled from their days back home in the villages.[77] And, as elsewhere they were quick to take up political debates in reaction to the wartime conditions in Macedonia. Macedonians were a very close community in Geraldton: families regularly visited one another, and they enjoyed a rich social life with people celebrating name days and other traditional communal events. Macedonians came to number 300 families

Photo 19: Chris (Risto) Damos on far right, his father Lazo in the middle and a young Paul Popoff on the far left, photographed inspecting the tomato plantation, Geraldton, circa 1938. (Source: Victor Damos).

in Geraldton, with most working in the tomato industry, and they were all members of the Tomato Growers Association. At its peak, the Tomato Growers Association numbered 400 members, so Macedonians made up an overwhelming majority, with Paul Popoff on the board as the Macedonian representative. The industry eventually suffered a downturn in the 1960s when Singapore stopped buying Geraldton tomatoes and Melbourne began sourcing tomatoes from elsewhere. Most Macedonians then left Geraldton and moved to Perth.

The village of Buf (Lerin) had been a traditional *pechalba* village for countless generations when Vasil Sarbinov left for Australia in 1931 and worked in the Western Australia bush before writing back to the village requesting that his 16-year-old son Stojan join him. Accompanied by family friend, Ilo Panov, Stojan arrived at Fremantle dock in January 1937 aboard the English passenger ship, *Orient Line*. Vasil greeted Stojan and Ilo at the dock and the three travelled to Bridgetown, where Macedonians worked clearing farmland and as timber cutters. Stojan worked alongside his father cutting sleepers which were used on the construction of the Asia-Burma railway. In Bridgetown Stojan saw numerous men from Buf village, amongst them Giorgi Nastov, Todorche Valchev and Dime Markovski; and others arrived during the period 1937-38.[78] Most Macedonians in Bridgetown in the late 1930s were from the Lerin region but there were also some from the Bitola region. It is estimated that at that time there were 700 to 800 Macedonians working on farms and in the timber cutting industry in the Bridgetown district.[79]

Kosta Angelkoff arrived in Bridgetown in 1938 and found work clearing farmland on Jace Road for which he received seven shillings per day whilst the contractor was paid two pound five shillings for each acre cleared. The daily rate at the time was ten shillings per day; however, as there was not much work available at the time, Kosta was thankful for the seven shillings.[80] Due to the large number of Macedonians working in the area, a Macedonian boarding house and restaurant was established in Bridgetown in the 1930s and served as a central meeting place. From Bridgetown many went to work in the tobacco industry at Manjimup, south of Perth. When Stojan Sarbinov went to Manjimup from Bridgetown in 1941, he found approximately 1000 Macedonians planting tobacco seed at the time, mainly from the Lerin villages of Babchor, Neret, Turije and Krpeshina, with a few from the Kostur region.[81] Macedonians were first drawn to the area around Manjimup to clear bushland and cut railway sleepers. However, the Macedonian connection to Manjimup would become best known for their involvement in the tobacco industry, an industry they would come to dominate in Western Australia. In 1924, Kole Palashin from Babchor village (Kostur) was one of the first Macedonians to arrive in Manjimup and he along with the Milentises, Lazo Miche (Louis Mitchell) and Jovan Konsolov, all from Babchor village, and Peter Michelides, a Greek entrepreneur from Perth, created a major industry from tobacco growing from the 1930s to the 1950s.[82]

Manjimup's reputation spread to Macedonian communities across Australia with people coming in search of financial rewards through tobacco farming. In the 1930s, Vasil Turpin from Bapchor village operated a 20-acre dairy farm in Canning Vale, south of Perth with his wife and three children; however, there were few other Macedonians in the area. When his cousin John Turpin said, 'Come to Manjimup there are Macedonians here', Vasil sold the Canning Vale property in 1943 and moved in with his cousin for a few months before buying a 110 acre property at Yanmah (Manjimup), where he grew tobacco, potatoes and farmed dairy cattle.[83] Others arrived after hearing that work was available on tobacco plantations. Men such as Jovan Numeff and his son Tanas worked with other Macedonians in a flax mill in Boyup Brook during the 1930s and when they heard that work was available on tobacco plantations they made their way to Manjimup.[84] Work on the plantation was an opportunity to earn income, and for many Macedonian arrivals to Western Australia in the 1950s, the Manjimup tobacco plantations became their first home in Australia. Small homes constructed of white-washed hessian walls and asbestos boards and cladding were available to accommodate families working on large plantations.[85]

Photo 20: Turpin family at their Canning Vale dairy farm in Perth, 1936, before moving to Manjimup to be closer to relatives and other Macedonians. (Source: Mary Purcell – nee Turpin)

Macedonians in Manjimup were involved in other key industries in the area including the timber industry, dairy farming and working in the water supply and roads board. Several large state saw mills operated in the district employing hundreds of men and there were also many spot sawmills throughout the Warren district employing Macedonians.[86] Nikola Ognenov (Ognenis) from Bapchor village arrived in 1951 and made his way to Manjimup where he found work at Dean Mill, a state-run mill. Newly arrived Macedonian men had no trouble finding work at the timber mills

Photo 21: Londe Kalamarov (left) and Mitre Veliou (right) preparing the tobacco seeding beds for growing during the winter months, Manjimup, circa 1948. The covers were used to keep the frost at bay during the cold nights in Manjimup. Benzol in small tins was used to keep the seedlings warm. (Source: Archives of the Macedonian Community of Western Australia, courtesy of Ilo Ognenov).

as they had a reputation as solid workers who helped keep production figures high. Employment at the mills also suited them, as single men's huts, and small dwellings of timber construction, were provided to workers for accommodation. Nikola worked at the mill from Monday to Friday, while on weekends he worked as a labourer on Macedonian-owned tobacco farms to repay the shipping fare that he borrowed and save money to bring out his family from Macedonia.

After three years of hard work, in 1954, Nikola brought out his family (father, wife and two sons) and they moved in with his cousin on Graphite Road for several months before settling into a house obtained through Dean Mill. In 1958, determined to set up his family financially, in partnership with Stojan Mladenov from Turije village, he purchased a block of land with a grading shed and rented paddocks to grow tobacco from another Macedonian, Grozotis, from Bachor village. Their wives worked the tobacco fields whilst Nikola and Stojan continued working at the timber mill on weekdays and at the tobacco plantation on weekends. When the tobacco was picked, stringed and placed in the kilns, their wives monitored the process during the day, and when Nikola and Stojan returned from work at the mill, they would spend the night at the kiln. During this stage of tobacco production, the children would not see their fathers for over a week.

Macedonians lived and worked together. They set up tobacco farms beside one another; for example, all the neighbouring farms around Kosta Ognenov from Neret village (Lerin) belonged to Macedonian families. On one side was the Nolev family and on the other the Vlahov family, while on the opposite side the farms belonged to the Cilemanoff and Saliacos families, all from the village of Neret.[87] They brought their collective labour to help one another and at harvesting time, families and neighbours came together to pick the tobacco by hand, one farm at a time, until all the farms had been harvested. Beginning with crude tin housing thrown up in the early years, these families developed strategies of mutual assistance and built themselves into a viable economic enterprise. The Macedonians also came together in 1942 to set up the Mutual Assistance Association of Manjimup which aimed to help its members when in need of financial support and enable them to draw funds from the Association. Thirty Macedonians attended the inaugural meeting to set up the Association, and 60 signed up as members within days. The enrolment fee was 10 shillings, and two shillings six pence per month thereafter. The majority of the members in the Association also became members of the Manjimup Sloboda (Freedom) organisation which was associated with the Macedonian Australian Peoples League (MAPL).[88] The patriotism of the Mutual Assistance Association was commended at the MAPL national conference in 1947 when it was noted that £50 had been donated towards the Macedonian hospital campaign.[89]

In the 1950s, once a month the Macedonian community held a dance in the Manjimup Town Hall. It was a social event that everyone looked forward to, where young people could meet friends and get to know one another, and the older folk could catch up on news and events from the homeland. The Manjimup band provided music for traditional Macedonian folk dancing and they performed at all social functions for the Macedonian community, including engagements, weddings, and community picnics.[90] Macedonian social events in Manjimup regularly drew Macedonians from Bridgetown, Boyup Brook and Pemberton. Community picnics were enjoyed in the outdoors with Fonty's Pool (near Manjimup), a popular place especially around the Christmas period, and in the 1950s Macedonian tobacco farmers formed the Manjimup Macedonia soccer team.[91]

Photo 22: Risto Koiov (left) and Tanas Kalamarov inspecting tobacco leaves before placing them in the kiln, circa 1950-60. Macedonian tobacco growers in Manjimup (Western Australia) were the backbone of the tobacco industry in Australia. (Source: Archives of the Macedonian Community of Western Australia, courtesy of Ilo Ognenov).

A popular place for families was 'Trpou's Delicatessen', owned by Tanas Trpou from Bapchor village who arrived in Manjimup in the 1930s. Other businesses were established – some as early as the mid-1930s, with one of the first being a tailor shop set up by Mikaili Popov from Bapchor village which was later taken over by his son Kole. In the 1940s and 1950s Macedonians operated businesses including a second tailor store, a clothes shop, a manchester store, a bakery, and others. Macedonian men found a place to gather at the National Café operated by George Milentis from Bapchor, which started as a traditional style Southern European men's café in the 1940s before it underwent a transformation into a restaurant. In the early days, the venue was used for celebrations such as weddings and christenings before the Manjimup Town hall became the main venue for wedding celebrations. As the community grew, they needed their own meeting place. Stojan Stojchev from Turije village (Kostur) donated two and a half acres of prime land for the construction of

Photo 23: Macedonian women harvesting apples in Manjimup, circa 1960. For the greater part of the twentieth century Macedonians in Manjimup were major players in the tobacco industry. Following the eventual demise of the industry, tobacco farms were transitioned into orchards and agricultural land. (Source: Archives of the Macedonian Community of Western Australia, courtesy of Ilo Ognenov).

a Macedonian community centre which was completed with great pride in 1987, and officially opened by Brian Burke, the then Premier of Western Australia.

By the 1960s Macedonians made up nearly half of the overall Manjimup population. However, around this time, the once lucrative tobacco industry took a downward turn and a number of Macedonians eventually moved out and re-established in Perth, whilst others moved to Melbourne and Sydney to be amongst relatives. Some others remained, cleared their land, and turned to growing vegetables, orchards and dairy farming. Transitioning tobacco farms proved very successful for some families, such as the Grozotis family, who turned to cherry farming (Cherry Lane Fields) and are currently the largest producer of cherries in Western Australia. Meanwhile, the Peos family have successfully evolved from farming tobacco in the 1930s, to dairy cattle, beef, mixed horticulture, potatoes, cauliflowers, and beans. In 1996, they established the Peos Estate winery, producing premium Western Australian wines.

The search for a better life saw Macedonians settle in diverse places throughout Western Australia. When they first arrived in Salmon Gums, in the Esperance region, they worked as labourers on wheat and sheep farms. The first Macedonian in the area, Anastas Vosancos/Vosnacov from Gabresh village (Kostur) arrived in Salmon Gums in 1925; he bought cheap land from the government, intending to set up a sheep farm and grow wheat – and he built a mud brick home with his own hands. Soon he was joined by Nick Tolcon, also from Gabresh village, and later that same year, after having been refused entry to the United States due to its immigration restrictions, Dono Sholdov/Sholdas (Gabresh village) headed for Western Australia to join his friend Anastas Vosnacos in Salmon Gums. A fourth Macedonian, also from Gabresh village, arrived sometime later in the 1920s. After setting up wheat and sheep farms, the men were joined by their wives and children from Macedonia. In early 1931, Anastas Vosnacos's wife Cveta and son Tom arrived and, later that year, a daughter, Christine, was born. She was possibly the first Macedonian baby born in Western Australia. In Macedonian villages at that time there were very few doctors available and it was common practice that particular women in the village would act as midwives. The situation was similar in rural areas of Australia where Macedonians settled, and the women continued to help one another when giving birth.

The Macedonians worked hard to succeed in Salmon Gums; however, it was tough going as the land quality was poor and there was very little rainfall. The Vosnacos family were the first Macedonian family to leave Salmon Gums in 1938. That same year, Dono Sholdas's wife, Dana, arrived from Macedonia and, soon after, two sons were born, Sam and Chris. The Sholdas family lived on a farm seven miles east of Salmon Gums and worked hard to set themselves up until a devastating incident changed the family forever and left a deep scar on the entire Salmon Gums community.

Photo 24: Brothers Dono and Vasil Sholdas (on left side), with Macedonian men of Salmon Gums, Western Australia, 1927. (Source: John Karajas).

Photo 25: Macedonian woman Dana Sholdas harvesting wheat in Salmon Gums, circa 1937. (Source: John Karajas).

Three-year-old Chris and his two-year-old younger brother Sam went out looking for their father to arrive from town but wandered away in the wrong direction and became lost. Chris went into virgin bush, while Sam was found the following morning, sitting on the

Photo 26: Lefteria Tolcon and Dana Sholdas, Salmon Gums, Western Australia, 1939. (Source: John Karajas).

edge of a paddock not far from their farm. Police used four Aboriginal trackers and nearly all the residents of Salmon Gums joined the search for young Chris; however, few tracks could be identified through the stony surface of the thick timbered tea tree country. After four days of intensive searching Chris was found by a group of searchers including his father Dono, barely alive 17 miles from the farm. The child had nothing to eat or drink for four days and suffering from exposure, he died in his father's arms minutes after being found. Heartbroken, the Sholdas family left Salmon Gums and moved to Perth and the remaining Macedonians left the area shortly afterwards. The tragedy was reported in the media at the time and the local community erected a memorial at the entry of the Salmon Gums cemetery to commemorate the event. After moving to Perth, Dana Sholdas gave birth to another son whom they named Chris in memory of their lost child.

The first Macedonians in South Australia were itinerant workers and farm labourers who took on any work that was available but in particular, scrub clearing and timber cutting. Macedonians worked in areas along the west coast such as Ceduna and Cungena, in the

Mallee districts, the upper Murray and the Adelaide Hills and plains, as well as fruit picking in Barmera or in the rest of the Riverland, including grape picking in the Barossa Valley and building the East-West Railway.[92] When economic conditions improved, they headed into the city looking for steady work and quite a few ended up settling on open land in places such as Fulham, Lockleys and Ferryden Park where they used their familiar skills to establish market gardens and build their own glasshouses, mainly growing tomatoes which were in short supply at that time.[93] Kotse Tanev (Kotsopoulos), from Kuchkoveni village (Lerin) left his family behind and arrived in Australia in 1937. He worked in the Northern Territory and Western Australia for eleven years before making his way to Adelaide in 1948, where he reunited with his wife Petra and young daughter Traianka. Another daughter, Mary, was born in Australia. They initially lived in Lockleys, however soon after Kotse purchased a market garden in Fulham Gardens which they ran for 30 years. Areas around Fulham and Findon became popular with the Macedonians as market gardens and tomato growing flourished. In 1950, it was reported that land values had soared to £1,000 at an auction of 52 acres into three-acre lots at Fulham Gardens and the principal buyers were Macedonians and Bulgarians.[94]

Adjusting to life in Australia was challenging for young teenagers when they arrived, not speaking any English. When they were enrolled in school, they were often placed in classes with much younger children and this made them feel awkward and embarrassed and not wanting to continue education. Kata Paunovic's experience was similar to many others. She arrived in 1939 as an 11-year-old and was enrolled in the first grade at Feluga Primary School in North Queensland. Her classmates were much younger – around six years of age – and she had very little in common with them. Kata begrudgingly attended school for two years and remembers being 'sad and lonely'.[95]

Many children struggled with education which was further compounded by their parents not speaking any English and having no educational role models. A large number of school-aged children 'were destined to struggle with their education as a result of their poor English literacy skills which clouded their educational experiences and compromised their natural intellectual abilities'.[96] Even when children were born in Australia, their parents could speak very little English and the language of the home was Macedonian, when the children commenced school they could not speak any English. Born in Newcastle in 1941 to parents from Velushina and Egri villages (Bitola), like many others, John Ilich grew up in a home where Macedonian was the principal language and only commenced learning English when he enrolled in primary school. He found it very difficult, and it made him feel as though he had been born in Macedonia and brought out to Australia.[97] Furthermore, in areas where large numbers of Macedonians settled, the local primary school could have a majority of Macedonian school children and it was common that, during breaks, the children would speak to one another in Macedonian.[98]

Children in Macedonian villages were expected to work from a young age, and it was no different on farms and market gardens in Australia. Giorgi Boshev was brought up on a farm in Medowie, Newcastle speaking only Macedonian at home, and described his childhood as similar to growing up in a Macedonian village.[99] Work on farms was never ending, from sunrise to sunset, work was performed manually, and every family member participated. Even the youngest members of the family worked. Growing up on a market garden in Werribee South, Andrew Goulopoulos stated 'we worked after school, weekends and during holidays – we worked all the time'.[100] Expectations were similar for young children whose parents set up businesses in the towns and cities. The Doikin family ran a farm in Queanbeyan, as well as a fruit and vegetable shop in Canberra, and all family members contributed labour, including Tane's nine-year-old daughter Cveta who travelled to the shop by bus every day after school to help restock the fruit and vegetable displays and perform general cleaning work.

New South Wales

Located approximately 60 kilometres north west of Sydney, Richmond came to be a Macedonian market gardening centre with a concentration of people from Dolno Kotori village (Lerin). The first to settle in Richmond was Stevo Pandu and he was likely the first Macedonian from Dolno Kotori to arrive in Australia in the 1920s.[101] The search for work saw Steve Pandu travel to Lithgow in New South Wales where he found employment working on the production of ammunition at the Lithgow Small Arms Factory and, after two years' work, he used the money he had saved to purchase a 25-acre market garden on Old Kurrajohn Road, Agnes Banks, located beside the Nepean/Hawkesbury River, providing direct access to irrigation.[102] Steve grew cauliflower, cabbage, pumpkins, tomatoes, potatoes and lettuce. His wife Dimitra arrived soon after; and in the mid-1930s he brought out his brother Petre to provide additional labour on the farm.[103]

Boshe Chadevich from Orehovo, Bitola region and Ilo Stathis from Dolno Kotori were other early Macedonian settlers in Richmond.[104] Boshe Chadevich arrived in Australia in 1924 and worked as a labourer on farms in New South Wales and Queensland, and in the steelworks in Lithgow, before returning to Macedonia in 1930. He returned to Australia in 1931 and made his way to Richmond working as a farm labourer before leasing a farm with another Macedonian, Kosta Velios from Kotori. Produce was sent to the market in Haymarket in Sydney and, in 1937, Boshe brought out his wife and son from Orehovo.[105] Other Macedonians arrived, mostly from Dolno Kotori, and purchased market gardens concentrated in the Agnes Banks and Castlereagh areas of Richmond. Established farmers were on hand to help newcomers settle in and provided initial employment or otherwise helped them find work. Over time, as families grew, the sons of the original Macedonian settlers purchased their own farms, often beside or close to their parents' farm, which allowed families to remain close to one another, replicating Macedonian village life.

In the 1960s, a new influx of Macedonians from the Bitola region villages arrived, particularly from the villages, Oreovo, Bukovo, Bistrica and elsewhere.[106] Some went on to own market garden farms while others found work in the factories around South Windsor, New South Wales, such as Riverstone Meatworks or the Richmond Royal Australian Air Force base in catering services or as cleaners. Access

Photo 27: Milka Pandov with son George on the farm in Richmond, New South Wales, circa 1965. (Source: Kosta Pandov).

to water via the Nepean/ Hawkesbury River has been an advantage, but also a cause of hardship in times of flood. A major flood in the area in the early 1960s saw many farms devastated and then undergo years of rebuilding. Bad floods helped people bond together, and resilience and hard work saw farms re-established. However, over the years, the Macedonian Richmond market gardeners transitioned their farm produce to enable viability of their business, as a number of farmers, such as Steve Pandu, the original Macedonian settler in Richmond, turned their market gardens into orange orchards. In more recent times, turf farming has become popular in the district. Macedonians in Richmond have also established their own community centre, 'Macedonian Hall – Kotori'.

Located in far north New South Wales, Crabbes Creek was renowned for banana plantations and dairy farming. The story of the Macedonian community in Crabbes Creek is unique because Macedonians had no tradition of banana farming, so it was an entirely new agricultural undertaking. A significant feature of the Crabbes Creek Macedonian community is that the first asset owned by the Macedonian community, a community church hall, was established in the 1940s. Krste Pazov from Statica village (Kostur) was one of the first Macedonians to settle in Crabbes Creek in the 1930s. After having worked for the Anthony and Crannery families in the Tweed area, he purchased property in Crabbes Creek to grow his own banana plantation. Other Macedonians followed, equipped with a strong work ethic and desire to succeed. By the 1940s, the Macedonian population in Crabbes Creek had grown substantially and become prominent in the banana and dairy farming industries.

Crabbes Creek became renowned across Macedonian communities in Australia and newcomers were attracted to the town by stories of economic success and the charismatic personality of Krste Pazov.[107] A successful businessman and leading community figure, he played a prominent role in building the Macedonian community of Crabbes Creek, helping a number of people settle in the area. When Krste met Naum Pavlovich in Brisbane he said to him 'Come with me and we will build a Macedonian village'. Krste offered to help with the purchase of a banana farm, the offer was accepted and, in 1942, Naum and his family moved to Crabbes Creek.[108] Others followed, drawn by family and village ties and the prospect of working their own banana farms.

Renowned as hard-working farmers, Macedonians worked long hours seven days a week. Their children worked on the farms before and after school, and community members helped one another. One day per week, the men would go to one person's banana farm to help with labour and this was done on a rotational basis. The Macedonian community was concentrated in the lower end of Crabbes Creek and, by the 1950s, there were approximately 500 Macedonians, made up of about 100 families.[109] When Macedonians put up their farms for sale, they usually sold to other Macedonians, as there were many who were attracted to the village-like setting which reminded them of life in Macedonia. Advertisements for the sale of farms in Crabbes Creek appeared in *Makedonska Iskra*, such as the sale of a six-acre banana farm in 1948, with the advertisement highlighting the large number of Macedonians in Crabbes Creek stating that 'all around there are Macedonians' *('a nassekade okolu ima naseleni Makedontci').*[110]

In the mid-1940s, a decision was made that a community centre was needed for the Macedonians of Crabbes Creek to celebrate cultural and social activities. Krste Pazov, Naum Pavlovich and Stojan Milenko offered to donate land to the community for the construction of the hall. However, Krste Pazov's offer was accepted, due to the central location of the land.[111] With financial support from the Macedonian community, a community hall was constructed on the site in 1947, and it was built as a church hall as timber was scarce at the end of the Second World War. The hall was used primarily for social activities, with Macedonian traditional dancing a regular feature on Sunday afternoons from 3.00 pm to 8.00 pm. Macedonians from the wider Tweed area attended and musicians came from the local Macedonian community. Whenever a new family arrived to settle in Crabbes Creek, the Macedonian community from Crabbes Creek and the Tweed district in northern New South Wales, gathered at the hall to welcome them.[112]

There were Macedonians throughout the Tweed district growing bananas and working as dairy farmers, and quite a few Macedoni-

Photo 28: Pandora Todevska dressed in traditional Macedonian clothing, Crabbes Creek, New South Wales, circa 1955. (Source: Riste Todevski).

ans consistently took out prizes for their banana-growing in a range of categories at the Tweed Banana Festival and Agricultural show, whilst Chris Pavlovich went on to become a Director on the State Banana Growers Board.[113] Despite their success, in the early 1960s, most Macedonians left the district following a drop in the price of bananas: a number of families from Crabbes Creek moved to Queanbeyan, in the Southern Tablelands of south-eastern New South Wales, close to Canberra, while others relocated to Sydney and Brisbane.

Before the Second World War, Queanbeyan was a small town with its economy linked to primary produce, and it was not until 1972 that it was declared a city. Macedonians arrived in Queanbeyan in the 1920s, with one of the earliest being Giorgi Nano, together with a group of 15 Macedonians all from the village Trcije (Lerin) in 1926. At that time Parliament House was under construction and, as workers were in demand, Giorgi and six other Macedonians managed to secure work until the completion of the project in 1927.[114] Others arrived in the 1920s and 1930s mostly from Trcije and Statica villages and several from Laktinje village (Ohrid). However, they struggled to find work and set off in the surrounding district to provide labour on farms or to Braidwood and Captains Flat where they engaged in eucalyptus distilling, which was a very hard and isolating existence. During the most difficult economic times in the 1930s, unemployed Macedonians such as Aleksandar Stefanoff from Kriveni village (Resen) and others resorted to trapping rabbits in the Yass Valley to survive and were paid just a few pennies for each rabbit; the earnings were barely enough to buy food.[115]

In the late 1930s, many left the life of eucalyptus oil production in the bush and settled in Queanbeyan to establish their own farms and market gardens: of note were the large-scale farms operated by Kosta Pandov and Nace (Natse) Bochkarov.[116] Con Doikin/Doikos from Statica village (Kostur) was one of the early Macedonians to settle in Queanbeyan and his story is one of hard work, determination and success. Con arrived in Sydney in 1927, leaving his wife and three young children in Statica village. Unable to find work in Sydney, he went to the bush, performing labouring work on farms; however, with the onset of difficult economic times, work became harder to come by and Con went to Forbes to work in the eucalyptus industry where there were more than twenty men from Statica's neighbouring village, Konomladi. But times were tough, earnings were low and after twelve months in the bush, he went looking for work on farms in the districts around Canberra and Queanbeyan.[117] Con found work on a farm constructing and maintaining fences but it was a long twenty-mile trip to the farm each day on his bicycle. He also worked as a rabbit bounty hunter in Yass with other Macedonians before finding work on Lloyd's farm, a well-known farming family in the area. The Lloyds gave him work and kept him on when there was no employment available during the height of the economic depression, after Con had rescued their young son when their house caught fire.[118]

Desperate to bring out his wife and three children from Statica, but hindered by the Second World War and the raging conflict in Macedonia during the Greek Civil War, in 1946 Con purchased a large farm in what is now central Queanbeyan. Working alone he ploughed the land, digging trenches late into the evenings under the light of a lantern. He persevered in order to transform the farm into a productive market garden. After 20 years alone in Australia, Con rejoiced when his family arrived in 1947, and the additional help on the farm was a welcome relief. Pumpkins, beans, lettuce, cauliflower, cabbage and various fruit trees were grown on the farm and, in the first few years, Con would load fruit and vegetables in a storage compartment at the back of a three-wheel bicycle and go from house to house selling the produce. Later a horse and cart enabled Con to expand further out to sell produce. In 1953, he purchased an Austin truck and was one of the first farmers in Queanbeyan to invest in a motor vehicle which enabled him to sell produce outside Queanbeyan to nearby towns such as Bungendore.

Con's son, Tane, showed early signs of entrepreneurial business acumen when he started buying large quantities of potatoes in 150-pound hessian bags from a farmer in Crookwell. He sold these to fish and chip shop operators in the district and directly to the public from the back of their Austin truck. The truck became a regular feature on Lingar Street, which was little more than a dirt road at that time (today City Walk, Canberra) and Con and Tane would set up a fruit and vegetable stand from the truck. Later, a block of land was purchased on Lingar Street, which would become the premises for the family fruit shop business but, in the meantime, they parked the truck at the front of the block, from where they continued to sell their produce. Con and Tane dug the foundation trenches by hand and erected a two-storey fruit and vegetable shop, operating as 'Doikos and Son'.

Several large-scale market gardens in Queanbeyan were run by Macedonians in the 1950s. The number of Macedonians grew, with many new arrivals coming from Aegean Macedonia, and the community was further bolstered when 15 families arrived from Crabbes Creek in the early 1960s following the massive drop in the banana industry. The newly-arrived families from Crabbes Creek were connected to Queanbeyan through family and village ties (Statica and Trcije villages) and, at around this time, Macedonians started to move into the motel industry. The first to do so was Done Pazov from Statica village (Kostur) who settled in Queanbeyan with his family from Crabbes Creek and purchased the Kent Hotel, later building the Olympia Motel. Pando Pandov was another Macedonian who entered the motel business at this time.[119] Tane Doikin saw an opportunity to move into the motel business and in 1963 built the largest motel in Queanbeyan at that time, the Central Motel Queanbeyan which he operated with his wife and children.

The increasing number of Macedonians in Queanbeyan saw community activity evolve. *Opshtinska Uprava*, a community council, was formed on 7 July 1957, charged with setting the foundations for purchasing a communal property and establishing a Macedonian Church. Giorgi Nano was elected President, a popular choice for the role.[120] He was one of the first arrivals in Queanbeyan and known to everyone as Dedo Nano *voivodata*, was well-respected and had always been on hand to help newly-arrived Macedonians settle down and find work in Queanbeyan.[121] When the community was searching for premises to establish a Macedonian church and cultural centre, Giorgi Nano was instrumental in organising the acquisition of a hall and the premises was later transformed into the Sveti Ilija Macedonian Orthodox Church.[122] In the sporting sphere, young men had been gathering from the early 1960s playing soccer in Freebody Park, before soccer enthusiasts Vasil Dzhengalov from Statica village (Kostur), Done Dimov and Vangel Hadzheli from Rula village (Kostur) set out to organise a Macedonian soccer team which was established in 1966 as the Macedonian Soccer Club of Queanbeyan. The club remains one of the oldest soccer clubs in the Queanbeyan/Canberra region.[123]

When Macedonians arrived in Queanbeyan and Canberra in the 1960s and 1970s, mostly from the Republic of Macedonia, Canberra was undergoing rapid development, and many found employment in the building and construction industry. Others, in particular Macedonian women, were employed in the cleaning industry with many hired by Dushan Drakalski, a successful Macedonian businessman who established one of the largest cleaning companies in Canberra.[124] One of the attractions that drew Macedonians to Canberra was its climate and landscape which had a resemblance to parts of Macedonia. Aleksandar Stefanoff moved his family to Canberra from Newcastle in 1962, because it reminded him of Macedonia,[125] whilst Done Dimov, who lived in Canberra from 1965, stated that he could successfully grow the same vegetation as in Macedonia.

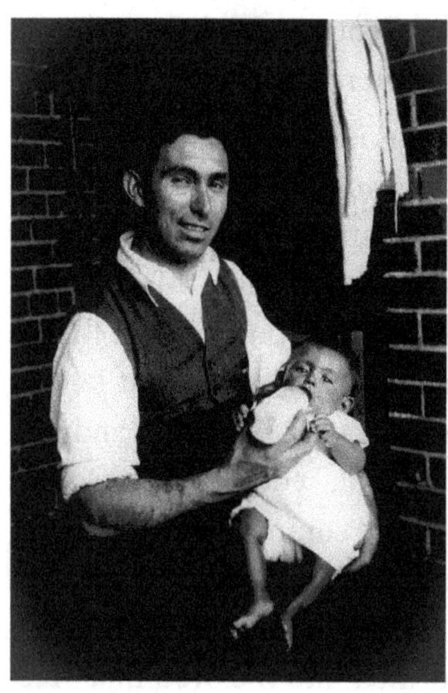

Photo 29: Aleksandar Stefanoff pictured here with baby son George in 1938. Aleksandar established a number of businesses in Newcastle before moving with his family to Canberra in 1962, where the climate there reminded him of Macedonia. (Source: Margaret Ruhfus – nee Stefanoff).

Victoria

Macedonians first arrived in Werribee South, near Melbourne, working as farm labourers in the 1920s before they commenced renting plots of land and eventually purchasing their own farms in the 1930s. The early arrivals in the area were from the Lerin region villages of Kabasnica, Bitusha, Kleshtina, Armensko as well as other places. They made their way to Werribee South after having worked elsewhere. The settlement of the Gulevci/Goulopoulos family in Werribee South in the 1930s is a typical example of the journey Macedonians took before settling down in a more permanent setting. Pavle Goulopoulos, from Bitusha village (Lerin) arrived in Australia in 1927 and first worked as a cane cutter in Queensland before moving to Melbourne where he found work as a truck driver transporting bluestone, much of which was used to build street curbs in Carlton. Pavle went back to Macedonia in 1933 and after a short stay, returned with his wife Sofia and son Con and settled in Hoddle Street, Collingwood. Determined to advance his family, Pavle went into business manufacturing basket shoes,[126] and, although the business did not do well, his unwavering belief that working for himself was the best way forward resulted in him moving to Werribee where he opened a fruit and vegetable shop. A number of Macedonians had set up market gardens in nearby Werribee South and, in the mid-1930s, in partnership with his brother Giorgija, Pavle decided to give market gardening a go and purchased a 36-acre market garden in O'Connor's Road.

Pavle's wife Sofia was the first Macedonian woman to arrive in South Werribee and later in life Pavle would jokingly refer to her as the Macedonian Captain Cook. Sofia gave birth to a daughter, Maria, in 1934, who was the first Macedonian child born in Werribee South. Giorgija's wife and children arrived in 1937 and the two families lived in the one home. They worked the farm together, producing potatoes, cauliflower, cabbages, beans, peas and tomatoes. Horses were commonly used in Werribee South market gardens to plough the land and pull carts to transport produce.[127] At around this time other Macedonians were arriving in Werribee South and their influx into market gardening was reported in the *Argus* newspaper: 'Macedonians continue to buy land for market gardening of the Werribee South irrigation settlement which is becoming a huge market garden supplying Melbourne regularly with vast quantities of vegetables. Recently two holdings changed hands at £100 an acre.'[128] Macedonians, along with the local Italians, became the dominant ethnic group in Werribee South.

In 1944, the brothers Pavle and Giogija amicably agreed to part from their joint market garden venture and divided the property in half, each taking 18 acres. At this time, Pavle purchased his second property in Werribee South, and an eight-acre farm on Duncans Road, where he moved his family. Pavle and his family now operated both farms. The new farm was a market garden, but he also kept poultry for eggs and a number of cows from which he produced feta cheese, a skill he had refined in his native village Bitusha. Pavle sold the eggs and cheese products to a Macedonian grocery store in Brunswick Street, Fitzroy. At times, additional labour was required on the farm, particularly during the picking season when relatives would come from Melbourne to earn extra income, and other workers were drawn from the local Italian community. Even at night, there was additional work to do in the sheds, packing tomatoes and other vegetables which were taken to Victoria market early in the mornings, and sold from the back of a truck to fruit shop operators. There was no time for rest.

Macedonian community life flourished in Werribee South, particularly with the influx of Macedonians following the Greek Civil War after 1949. A monthly dance was held in the Diggers Road municipal hall. A local Macedonian band performed, and the dance was so popular that Macedonians from Melbourne regularly attended. The sense of familial connection, community and support for one another was strongly felt amongst the Macedonians of Werribee South. When new arrivals came to the area aspiring to purchase their own farms, respected community members would go from house to house to help collect a deposit to enable the purchase of a farm.[129] Some elements of running a market garden in Australia were unlike the rural experience back in their Macedonian villages. Occasionally, individuals would have allergic reactions to pesticides and subsequently left farm life for an urban environment. One Macedonian from Rakovo village (Lerin),[130] after developing a skin reaction to pesticides in Werribee South, accepted that farm life did not agree with him and purchased a fish and chip shop in Footscray, operating the business for many years. Some Macedonians expanded their interests outside of market gardening and established businesses that would become household names in the local Werribee area; however, most remained on the land, and although it was hard work, did very well financially.

Photo 30: Naum and Maria Stamkos from Armensko village (Lerin region) with children Fanel, Velika and little Johnny, circa 1940. The Stamkos family settled in Werribee during the 1930s and initially operated a shop before running a poultry farm near Point Cook in an area which has now been overtaken by residential housing estates. (Source: Katrina Tatchell – nee Stoits).

Shepparton is the regional centre of the Goulburn Valley and a major agricultural and irrigation district known for its apple and pear orchards. The Shepparton Macedonian community is one of the oldest and largest Macedonian communities in regional Victoria, with first arrivals in the 1920s and 1930s from the villages, Neret, Lagen, Bitusha, Bapchor and Kabasnica. The men initially worked as labour hands on farms before becoming share farmers and then renting farms for market gardens. Prior to the Second World War, all the Macedonians in Shepparton were from Aegean Macedonia. Few men had their families with them, and they struggled on their own to set themselves up. To supplement their income they travelled in groups by truck to Mildura during the grape-picking season to take on additional work.[131] Market gardens were generally smaller scale farms and, after they established themselves, in the period after the Second World War most went on to purchase farms and orchards on a larger scale. Orchard farming became the principal industry for Macedonians in Shepparton and around this time a number of Macedonians moved to Shepparton from Werribee. They were attracted to the fruit industry as it was more remunerative than market gardening.[132] There were close family and village links between Werribee South and Shepparton.

Vane Ashlakoff from Ofcharani village (Lerin) was one of the earliest arrivals in Shepparton. He arrived in Australia in the 1920s and joined his uncle Krste Ashlakoff (and Krste's son Ilo), clearing bushland for farms around Wagga Wagga, New South Wales, before heading for Shepparton looking for work. Vane noticed that wheat and barley farming techniques in Shepparton were much the same as in Macedonia and he felt confident that he could be a successful farmer in Australia. Back in Ofcharani village, Vane had a reputation as a solid worker, so when he heard about an Australian farmer who could not hold on to workers because the work on his farm was difficult, Vane eagerly followed up and took on all available work.[133] Krste and Vane jointly purchased a market garden growing peas, beans and tomatoes and the produce was transported by horse and cart to Shepparton train station and taken by rail to Melbourne to be sold at Victoria Market. Later in the mid-1950s, Vane purchased a 64-acre apple and pear orchard from a Jewish family.[134]

At around the same time as the first Macedonians arrived in Shepparton during the 1920s, others made their way to nearby towns in the Goulburn Valley such as Stanhope, Kyabram and Tatura. Lazo Mechkaroff, Mitre Novachkoff and Lazo Apostol, all from Neret village were amongst the first Macedonian farmers in Tatura running market gardens and when the Rosella tomato processing factory opened in Tatura in 1947, tomatoes became their dominant produce. One of the earliest Macedonian farming families in Kyabram were the Ristovichki family from Neret village. In the 1950s, these small Macedonian communities moved to Shepparton.[135]

As the reputation of the Shepparton community grew, other Macedonians made their way there, intending to make a livelihood from orchard farming and market gardening. Some Macedonians may not have been motivated so much by a desire to engage in farming, but keen to be amongst their own people in an environment similar to their villages back home. Boris Giamov moved from Melbourne to Shepparton in 1942, attracted by the large number of Macedonians living there from the Lerin region, which reminded him of Trnava village. Boris purchased a 20-acre allotment that was previously a racecourse and he set about transforming it into a farm with a single horse and plough. It was hard work; he harvested tomatoes on seven acres and successfully operated a market garden for two years from which he made some good money. However, he decided not to continue with life on the farm. Even though he was a farmer in Macedonia, he realised that he did not want to be a farmer in Australia. Boris sold the farm and returned to Melbourne with his family where he purchased a fish and chip shop in Carlton.

Family connections run deep in Macedonian culture: these aided chain migration, employment and settlement patterns. In 1957, all seventeen members of the extended Angelovic (Angelovski) family from Dragosh village (Bitola) moved to Shepparton from Geelong so they could be closer to their relatives.[136] Angele Angelovic then arranged for his cousin Cvetko Radevski, also from Dragosh village, to migrate to Australia. Cvetko arrived in 1957 with his parents Bogoja and Blaguna, his wife Nevena, their two sons Pande (Peter) and Ico (Chris), and Cvetko's sister.[137] Employment was secured through a distant relative, Andreja Zurkas (Kabasnica village, Lerin), who owned 600 acres of orchards in Shepparton.[138] The Radevski family were accommodated on the Zurkas property in one of several old timber homes used to house permanent workers and their families. They shared the house with another family and early every morning a truck would collect them and the other workers, taking them to the apple and pear orchards. They worked long hours from sunrise to sunset seven days a week. After two years of hard work the Radevski family purchased a 36-acre farm from their cousins, the Angelovic family, for £15,000, borrowing the deposit from Andreja Zurkas.

Operating their own orchards, the Radevski family initially paid others, including Andreja Zurkas, to transport their produce to the fruit and vegetable market in Melbourne, until they purchased their first utility vehicle and started to carry their own produce. Business grew and they bought a small truck and then a larger one and continued to gradually expand, and today the Radevski family own a substantial fleet of semi-trailer trucks to facilitate transportation of produce and operate one of the largest orchard complex and distribution operations in the southern hemisphere (Radevski Cool Stores).

Cane Rendevski from Dragosh village, was brought out in 1962 by his cousins in Shepparton and they also secured work for his family at the Zurkas farm where they were accommodated in one of the farmhouses. They lived rent-free and made no additional payment for utilities. Many seasonal workers were employed, but there was a permanent workforce of six families, mostly Macedonians, accommodated on the Zurkas farmhouses and each family grew their own vegetable patch for personal use. Cane received £15 weekly payment, whereas factory workers at the Campbell Soup factory were earning £13. The family income was further supplemented through his wife, Trendafilka's employment in the local Clakington textile factory, where a number of Macedonian women worked.

The first Macedonian café was established in Shepparton in 1937. Around the same time that Macedonians arrived in Shepparton, Albanians (from Albania) arrived as well. Macedonians found them to be hard-working people who made good neighbours. Albanians in Shepparton set up their own cafes where men met to drink coffee and play cards. In the 1940s, a café on High Street was run by an Albanian named Kole from the Macedonian part of Albania, and it became the main café where Macedonians attended, Kole could speak Macedonian and was known to get quality tobacco during the war years when no-one else could. The café was eventually taken over in the 1970s by Spase Paskov from Ofcharani village (Lerin) and for the next several years continued to be a popular meeting place for Macedonians. A number of successful Macedonian farming families diversified their business interests to include hotels and pubs and these Macedonian-owned and operated pubs became the new cafes for hard-working Macedonian men. The most popular was the Shepparton Hotel, owned by a well-known Macedonian, John Avram. It was the central meeting place for Macedonians and, in particular, on Friday afternoons, everyone could be found there. Another Macedonian, Peter Copulos, from Bitusha village (Kostur), whose family settled in Shepparton in the 1940s, went on to become a highly successful entrepreneur, building a large fast food and property empire.

Macedonians continued arriving in the 1950s, following the end of the Greek Civil War, seeking to establish new lives in Shepparton after hearing about the opportunity to make good money working in a familiar industry. The community was further reinforced in the 1960s and 1970s with Macedonians arriving from the Republic of Macedonia. There was always work available in Shepparton and when industries in other places slowed down, such as at the Ford factory in Geelong in 1963, a number of Macedonians – many with family ties – headed for Shepparton, with some purchasing their own orchards whilst others gained employment as general labourers. Others travelled to Shepparton as seasonal workers during harvesting periods. In recent times the number of Macedonian orchardists has dwindled, as fewer children have continued with working the land, instead establishing diverse businesses in Shepparton or opting for professional careers in Shepparton and Melbourne.

Gippsland is a large rural region stretching from just east of Melbourne to the far eastern part of Victoria to New South Wales. Macedonians first arrived in Gippsland in the 1920s and 1930s, widely dispersed through the region in small groups performing hard manual work clearing farms and bushland, and sleeper cutting in areas such as the Toora district of South Gippsland, Omeo, Bruthen, Bairnsdale, Maffra, Leongatha, Nowa Nowa, and Wairewa. Many remained in Gippsland after bringing out their families and went on to buy their own cattle and dairy farms, while others set up businesses. Macedonians in Gippsland were generally from the Lerin region and the Lerin villages, Neret and Lagen.

Men set out for Gippsland after being unable to find work in Melbourne. In 1930, Boris Giamov from Trnava village (Lerin) set out for south-east Gippsland looking for work in the bush. He cleared farmland in Yarram for three shillings a day and spent nearly two years working on one farm. Boris remained in the district for six years and developed close friendships with other Macedonian farm workers in the area.[139] In the 1930s and 1940s, a number of Macedonian men worked in the Kernot area, a farming district in the Bass Valley, near Western Port Bay. They travelled there on foot from Melbourne and although there was no shortage of work in the area, the work was hard and repetitive; however, the Macedonians were equipped to do it and gained a reputation for being capable workers. As farm labourers they carried out the most difficult work, and they soon learnt the techniques of scrub clearing, followed by the tortuous task of clearing the undergrowth.[140] Due to wide river flats around Kernot, after clearing the land, it became waterlogged in winter. The land required draining to become productive, and this was done either by hand or with the assistance of a bullock team. 'Either way, the Macedonians were prepared to carry out this arduous work and many a farm on the flat owes its current productivity to their labour'.[141] There were particular jobs that Macedonian farm workers liked to do and enjoyed, such as harvesting and building haystacks as they had become skilled at that type of work in Macedonia and they took to the task in Kernot eagerly.[142]

Photo 31: Petre Christoff from Lagen village (Lerin), circa 1933. Petre arrived as a twenty-year-old in 1924 and eventually made his way to Gippsland where he bought a farm in Wairewa with another Macedonian with their primary crop being beans. Eventually they parted ways and Petre set up a dairy farm which he worked for many years. In 1953 he was joined in Australia by his wife Lena and daughter Christina. (Source: Ellyn Harpantidis).

In the 1940s and 1950s, contractors attended the Macedonian Club in Gertrude Street, Fitzroy, seeking to employ Macedonians, as they had a reputation as good workers, taking them to country Victoria to perform timber-cutting work. Most ended up in Gippsland, particularly around Noojee, Thomson River, Matlock and

Walhalla. Krste Constantinov/Constantinou from Armensko village (Lerin) was one of the many men hired by a contractor through the Macedonian Club. Krste arrived in Australia in 1952 and worked in the Reece plumbing factory in Fitzroy trying to save money to bring out his wife and children from the village. Earnings were low and he was concerned about the length of time it would take to save the money required to bring his family to Australia so when he heard about a contractor expected at the Macedonian Club in Fitzroy, he went along and waited together with a dozen other men. When the contractor arrived, a Jew named Jim Hall, he asked to see their hands and then hired the men with the most toughened hands.

Trees in the bush around Noojee, typically of the Mountain Ash variety, grew to staggering heights and could be hundreds of years old. Timber cutting was conducted by hand using axes, cross-saws and wedges. Not everyone was suited to such hard manual and dangerous work, and the hours were long, 12 hours a day, seven days a week. Although the men were paid well, living conditions were rudimentary, camps were set up in the forest and these were basic timber huts or tents. Some lived in these conditions for years. Father and son, Todor and Tanas Velov from Kotori village (Lerin), spent two years living in makeshift huts,[143] whilst Krste Constantinou lived for four years in a camp with approximately 40 men, mostly Macedonians, in tents accommodating between four to six men and sleeping in stretchers made of hessian bags.

Photo 32: Krste Constantinou lived in a camp and worked as a timber cutter in the Noojee district of Gippsland during the 1950s, before settling in Sale in 1955. (Source: Nick Constantinou).

Men earned good money working as timber cutters and, although it took a physical toll on their bodies, they endured years isolated in the bush. Eventually most returned to

Melbourne after bringing out their families and purchasing homes. However, a number remained in Gippsland where they found general labouring work in agricultural industries and settled in towns where they established businesses or set up their own farms. For example, two brothers from the Pappas family (Lagen village) worked in the Bairnsdale region in the 1930s and, after trying their hand at farming, felt that the earnings were not sufficient and they each respectively opened a fish and chip and hamburger shop in Bairnsdale. They were later joined by another brother who set up a cattle farm on the outskirts of town.

Macedonians first settled in the central Gippsland town of Sale in the 1940s. The first was Stoiche Bivolche from Neret village, who arrived after working in Gippsland clearing farmland and cutting trees. Others followed, initially arriving as single men and brought out their families afterwards. When Krste Constantinou moved to Sale in 1955 he purchased a house in Raglan Street close to other Macedonians. He wrote to his wife in Armensko village describing his experiences and impressions of Australia, and when he told her that milk and bread were delivered to the front door, she wrote back saying that she was amazed at the thought of such a thing and that it sounded like heaven.

Macedonians resided exclusively in Sale township and did not operate farms in the outlying area. They found employment as cooks and cleaners at the Royal Australian Air Force base and the Gippsland Base Hospital, some worked in the Victorian Railways, and others established their own businesses. Giorgi Kircos/Kircov from Neret village worked for many years as an assistant cook at the air force base during the 1940s and 50s. His son, Mitre, together with his wife Lena and their two children, were amongst the last Macedonians to settle in Sale in the mid-1960s. Mitre obtained employment as an assistant cook at the air force base and worked there for 22 years before taking on a similar role at the Gippsland Base Hospital where he remained until his retirement.

Self-employed Macedonians operated take-away food businesses such as fish and chip shops, hamburger shops and general grocery stores. Stoiche Bivolche from Neret opened the first fish and chip shop in Sale in the 1940s on Raymond Street. Later Stase (Stan) Stoikos from Neret village also opened a fish and chip shop on Raymond Street while Krste Constantinou ran a number of businesses, including a café on Foster Street and later a hamburger shop in Raglan Street.[144] For those who operated businesses their wives worked alongside them; otherwise there were few employment opportunities available for the Macedonian women except for seasonal work tomato picking on local farms.

A Sale chapter of the Macedonian Australian Peoples League was formed in the 1940s, Ljubo Makedonija undertaking fundraising activities for the hospital campaign. Although it was not a large community, it was close-knit; families regularly visited one another and came together for celebrations. During the warmer months, Macedonians enjoyed family outings at Seaspray on the Ninety Mile Beach and the Sale Hotel was a popular meeting place for the Macedonian men. The hotel owner, a Macedonian, Chris Doulopoulos, allowed the Macedonians to use a room upstairs in the hotel where they could play cards privately. In the 1960s and 1970s, there was few employment opportunities for the children of the Macedonians and, around this time, families commenced leaving Sale for Melbourne, with a number moving to the northern suburbs where they could live closer to relatives and amongst the large concentration of Macedonians in that area.

8

Reuniting Families

In the nineteenth century and first half of the twentieth, *pechalbari* traditionally would return to the village every few years, father more children and leave again. Children grew up only knowing stories about their fathers, about the hard work they were doing abroad and the sacrifices they were making for their families. *Pechalbari* left their wives behind with responsibility for raising the children, working the land, living with, and looking after, in-laws. It was difficult for the women, waiting for their husbands to return home. It was never precisely clear how long they would be gone on *pechalba* as they always left having purchased a one-way ticket, so the wait could be far longer than expected. Living with in-laws must have been challenging in that the young bride was expected to be completely subservient to them. As extended families lived together in the one home, a young bride whose husband was on *pechalba* would likely be unofficially allocated a low position in the status system of the family home. Unlike the female head of a household whose position of authority and status becomes 'complementary and comparable to that of her husband',[145] a young bride would be referred to as *nevesto* ('young bride') and never by her own name. In time she would take on a modified form of her husband's name which would signify that she had been elevated in the family status system. For example, the wife of Trajche would be Trajchejtsa, Mishe's wife would be Mishejtsa, Ilo's wife would become Ilojtsa. However, that could take a number of years. A young bride whose husband was away on *pechalba* would be subordinate to everyone in the home, her father and mother in-laws, brothers-in-law and sisters-in-law. She would work the fields and tend to the animals and would have no say in the house. It was a heavy responsibility. Every so often, a letter would arrive, and money would be sent to the family to help them get by. Money received made a significant difference to the families left behind in the villages. Giorgi Todorovski from Bitola first arrived in Australia in 1924 and, over the years until he brought his family to Australia in 1955, sent all his earnings back to his wife and children in Macedonia. Giorgi maintained detailed records of the monies he sent, which in total amounted to £2,188, while £300 were spent on postage during the period 1946-1952.[146]

Photographs were rare but prized possessions as they enabled family members, particularly fathers and their children, to see what they looked like. Most Macedonian men arrived in Australia without their families and intended to return; however, unforeseen circumstances such as the onset of the economic depression, the Second World War and the Greek Civil War (1946-1949), saw the men become stranded in Australia, separated from their families. With conditions under Greek rule deteriorating for the Macedonian population, few returned to their villages, and sought to bring out their wives and children to Australia. Many years passed before they could reunite with their loved ones.

In the 1920s, the Macedonian population in Australia was overwhelmingly made up of single men. A few brought out their families shortly after arrival; this process became more prevalent during the 1930s after they had the opportunity to establish themselves. One of the early arrivals to bring out his family was Vasil Borshoff from Bapchor village (Lerin). Vasil arrived in 1924 and, after two and a half years in Australia, applied to bring out his wife Vasilitsa and children Stefka and Nickolas.[147] It is interesting to note that, when the application was lodged, unlike most Macedonians at that time who were working in country areas, Vasil was likely earning a regular income through his employment at a kitchen appliance manufacturing company (Metters Ltd), in the perth suburb of Subiaco.

For young children, the journey on the ship to Australia was one of excitement and adventure, but the most anticipated event was to be reunited with their fathers, with whom they would have to reacquaint themselves. There were questions such as, would father remember them and what would he be like? Often children were too young even to remember their fathers, such as Aleksandar Theodorovsky from Buf village, who arrived in Melbourne in September 1937, and saw his father Done for the first time since he left the village to come to Australia in 1924 when Aleksandar was only 11 months old. The anticipation of fathers waiting to see their wives and children was intensely emotional. Giorgi Mechkaroff left his family in 1938, intending to return after three or four years; instead, ten years passed before they were reunited. When the ship carrying his wife and two children sailed into Port Phillip Bay, headed for Melbourne on 28 November 1948, Giorgi and a group of Macedonian men whose families were aboard the ship, hired a small boat and sailed alongside the ship waving to their families as it approached North Wharf.

A range of factors delayed the reuniting of families. During the difficult economic times of the 1920s and 1930s, men struggled to earn an income and were unable to afford the fares to bring out their families or return to Macedonia. During the Second World War, movement between Macedonia and Australia came to a halt and communication through letters was rare. From 1946 to 1949, the Macedonian war for liberation (as part of the Greek Civil War) further disrupted communication and movement from Aegean Macedonia. Complicating an already difficult situation was the exodus of 28,000 children evacuated in 1948, the majority Macedonian. The struggle for liberation and human rights in Greece brought enormous hardship and trauma to the Macedonian population. The plight of Macedonian refugee children and the separation from their parents (even though the intention was to place the children in a safe environment), caused deep emotional trauma to thousands of Macedonian children and their parents as families were torn apart, siblings separated and sent to various Eastern European countries to be raised in orphanages. Mothers were left behind in the village and fathers, some of whom had arrived years earlier in Australia as *pechalbari*, were unable to return during the war years.

Family reunions resulting from the war were regularly reported in the *Makedonska Iskra* newspaper and in the mainstream Australian press, describing the torment and pain the families had experienced. The *West Australian* newspaper reported that relatives eagerly gathered at Perth's Guildford airport waiting for loved ones to arrive and 'When the doors were opened the migrants streamed out and many touching reunions took place'. Mr. N. Borgios, who worked at a Bridgetown timber mill, saw his wife, his daughters aged 16 and 17, and 14-year-old son for the first time in 14 years. Mr. L. Bourjios, a Wanneroo market gardener who resided in Western Australia for 23 years, in 1950 was reunited with his wife whom he saw last when he went to Macedonia for a holiday in 1937. Mr L. Raykos of Geraldton, greeted his wife, mother and brother, whom he last saw 12 years ago.[148] Vasil Delianov from Bapchor village was four years old when his father left for Australia as a *pechalbar* in 1937. Separated by the Second World War, then the Greek Civil War, in 1948 Vasil was evacuated as a child refugee and spent the following eight years in Romania until 1956 when, through the help of the Red Cross, he arrived in Australia. Vasil was 23 years of age when he met a father whom he did not remember.[149]

The emotional turmoil of Lefa Ognenova-Michova, a refugee child reuniting with her father in Australia in 1955 after a long period of separation, is described in an extract from the book *A Girl from Neret*:

> Our ship arrived in Australian waters late in the evening and waited till morning before docking at Fremantle. We all went on deck to look out. The pier was full of people waiting to greet new arrivals. I knew that father was waiting for us and hoped that he looked a lot like the photo he had sent us. I searched the people waiting at the quayside but could not recognise him. I looked for a family resemblance, some common Macedonian feature or dress. I spotted a gentleman with a blue hand knitted pullover and it reminded me of my mother's knitting. I immediately thought this must be my father. I waved to the man in the blue pullover and as we disembarked, my brother and I began to walk towards him. As we got closer, we realised it was not our father. Next to him stood a very well-dressed man, the epitome of an Australian gentleman with a hat. We recognised him from the photo. This was my father. We embraced and he cried. I was not sure how I should feel or how I should act. I had never had a father. [150]

The voyage to Australia in the late 1940s and 1950s presented its own challenges. The journey took over 30 days to reach Australia and travel experiences varied: some enjoyed the journey immensely, seeing vast oceans, engaging in various pastimes and usually having an abundance of food available. Many were leaving their villages for the first time and were in wonder at the adventure before them. However, for some the journey was a difficult one. They had never been at sea before and they experienced lengthy delays particularly around the time of the Second World War. Others simply found conditions on the ship difficult to endure.

Giorgi Mechkaroff left his family behind in Kuchkoveni village (Lerin) to travel to Australia in 1938 intending to work for three or four years, save some money and return home; however, the Second World War and the Macedonian war in Greece interrupted his plans. To protect his family, Giorgi applied to bring them out to Australia. His wife and two young children left their home in June 1948 on a journey that would take six months. The travel agent had not booked them a berth and sent them to Solun in the hope that a ship would be available to take them. The Mechkaroff family left the village in the back of a five-tonne truck half loaded with strawberries, headed for Solun. With a military conflict raging around them, the truck avoided main roads, instead travelling on mountain routes until they finally arrived in Solun where they stayed overnight in a hotel and boarded a ship the following day.

The ship took them to Athens where they were introduced to a travel agent who arranged hotel accommodation until shipping tickets were obtained to enable the journey to Australia. Remaining in Athens for almost two months, every second day they contacted the travel agent to enquire about the ship's departure. The delay caused a significant financial burden as food was very expensive and they were alone in a foreign city where people spoke a different language. Eventually, they boarded a small aeroplane and were taken to Cairo, Egypt and from there continued a further 200 kilometres overland to Port Said, where they remained for two months in a cheap hotel before a ship was available to take passengers to Australia. It was a very small ship, perhaps no more than 2000 tonnes, with a capacity for 250 passengers; however, about 500 passengers were crammed onboard.

Passengers and supplies for the ship were conveyed on small boats, as the shipping company had not paid docking fees in Port Said. There was not enough room for all the passengers to be accommodated in the cabins, and many people were provided with old mattresses and slept on deck most of the trip, including 14-year-old Pandil whose mother and sister were able to be accommodated in a cabin. The ship arrived in Melbourne on 28 November 1948. Bringing his family to Australia put Giorgi in debt for £1,000, being for travel fares for the lengthy journey, hotels, and food.[151]

Krste Constantinou from Armensko village (Lerin) travelled to Australia on board an Italian ship in 1952. It was a thirty-day journey and the vast majority of passengers were Italian. Passengers were served the same pasta meal three times a day and this caused uproar on the ship until the captain agreed that kitchen staff would make variations of the pasta dish.[152] In time the journey improved with modern ships and improved conditions. In 1965, Done Dimov boarded the *Marconi*, an Italian ship in Genoa. It was a brand-new ship, and left a positive impression on Done, who saw it as a grand floating hotel.[153]

The emotional pain of long-term separation, feelings of helplessness and the longing to reunite families was further burdened by the heavy financial commitment to pay for the passage of family members to Australia. Kole Lazorov from Turije village (Lerin) was one of many whose family members were separated as refugees due to the war in Aegean Macedonia. He had a daughter in Poland (Tina), a daughter in Serbia (Mara) and a son (Risto) who had been a partisan in Aegean Macedonia and spent a considerable period as a prisoner on the Greek island of Leros. Kole had been living in Western Australia since 1937 and it was not until 1949 that he succeeded in bringing his son to Australia after borrowing £400 to pay for his passage. The average wage at that time was £5-6 per week. Nearly a year later, Kole managed to bring out his daughter Mara from Serbia and he had to borrow £225 from the International Services to pay for her passage to Sydney, followed by a further £90 for the passage from Sydney to Guilford Airport, Perth.[154]

In 1951, Kole borrowed another £400 from his friends to bring out his wife, Olga, who had suffered war-related trauma. By this stage Kole had amassed significant debt and taken on a heavy financial burden to reunite his family. He was prepared to go to any length to bring his family together. However, it seemed unfair to him that at the same time migrants were arriving from the United Kingdom for £10 and refugees from the Second World War were arriving for practically no payment, while Kole's family, refugees from the Greek Civil War, were required to pay full fare passage to Australia. Kole repeatedly tried to bring out his daughter, Tina, to Australia; however, Poland's strict Communist regime prevented her from leaving. Tina married a Macedonian refugee in Poland, and they had two children. In 1957, they successfully migrated to Canada where her husband Mito's parents lived.[155]

Con Doikin/Doikos arrived in 1927, but almost twenty years passed before he could get his family out to join him in Queanbeyan after borrowing a large sum of money to pay the travel expenses for eight family members: his wife Ana, son Tane with his wife Olga and their baby daughter Cveta; his pregnant daughter Stasa, with her husband Nase and children Risto and Donka. Their departure in 1947 from Statica village was difficult as they were in the middle of a war and, due to the urgency surrounding their departure, Con was only able to organise for a ship to take them as far as Port Said, Egypt. A connecting ship to Australia could not be organised for another six months. The family lived in a hotel in Port Said during this period. They found Egypt culturally challenging. The women were frightened of the dark-skinned Egyptians and the inability to communicate made matters worse. During a family outing one afternoon after Stasa had given birth to a daughter, Gira, a kidnapper snatched baby Gira out of her mother's arms and ran off with her. Fortunately, a police officer was nearby and apprehended the kidnapper and beat him severely with a baton; Olga was traumatised by the incident and barely left the hotel again until they secured tickets on a passenger ship to Australia.

The emotional ramifications of divided families could leave deep scars for decades. Some families would never be reunited. Mitre Kircos's/Kircov's story is one of lifelong separation. Mitre was born in Neret village in 1926 and at the age of two, in 1928, his father Giorgi

Photo 33: Almost twenty years passed before Con Doikin was reunited with his family in Queanbeyan during the late 1940s. (Source: Done and Cveta Dimov).

left for Australia with a group of *pechalbari* from their village. Giorgi made his way to the Gippsland region of Victoria, eventually settling in Sale where he worked for many years at the Royal Australian Air Force base. All communication with his family ceased during the Second World War and Greek Civil War. In 1947, along with countless other young men in the Lerin region, Mitre, at twenty-one years of age, volunteered and joined the partisan forces fighting for a free Macedonian homeland. In 1949, as defeat of the democratic forces was imminent, and the Yugoslav dictator Tito closed the border into the Republic of Macedonia, Mitre and other fighters were forced to cross into Albania, seeking refugee from advancing government forces. The fighters were subsequently given refuge by the Russian government which transported thousands of men, mainly Macedonians, but also Greek communist fighters, to Tashkent, in the Soviet Republic of Uzbekistan. In Tashkent, Mitre met Lena, a Macedonian partisan fighter from Mokreni village (Kostur), and they married in 1952 and had two children, Giorgi and Mary.

Former Greek partisans living in Tashkent returned to Greece; however, Macedonians were not welcome by the Greek government to return to their homes.[156] Mitre appealed to, and was supported by, the Russian authorities with repatriation to his village. This serves as a rare example of a former Macedonian freedom fighter permitted by the Greek government to return to their home. After sixteen years in Tashkent, Mitre and his family returned to Neret village in 1965; however, he found that he was not welcomed as the authorities brought him before the courts for fighting against the Greek government. Subjected to several appearances in the distant Kozhani court, which involved costly legal representation, eventually Mitre was found guilty and given a significantly large fine. Realising that he would never be allowed to live in peace under Greek rule, Mitre commenced preparing documentation to migrate to Australia to be reunited with his father Giorgi, and mother Jana.[157] Mitre's plans to go to Australia were disrupted as the Greek authorities would not issue him with a passport unless he publicly renounced and signed a declaration that he would not participate in any anti-Greek activities in Australia which Mitre understood to mean that he would not openly express or promote Macedonian identity abroad. This racist

Photo 34: Macedonian refugees from Aegean Macedonia in Tashkent, Uzbekistan, former Soviet Union, circa 1952. (Source: Mary Charlton).

request further delayed Mitre's migration, and when he eventually succeeded in obtaining a passport and travelling to Australia, his father Giorgi had passed away two months earlier. As such, Mitre lived his entire life separated from his father and was unable to reflect on any shared memories with him.

Reunions continued for years into the 1960s and 70s and, sadly, some families never reunited and were lost forever. Due to a range of circumstances that emerge in times of conflict, some children believed that their fathers had been killed during the war and years later as adults discovered that they were still alive. Along with 154 children from Statica village, six-year-old Done Dimov was evacuated in 1948 and sent to Poland where he lived for seven years in Londek Zdruy, Zgorzelets, Klush and Police, until with the help of the Red Cross he reunited with his mother in Skopje, Republic of Macedonia, in 1955. His mother did not recognise him when they met. Done and his mother remained in Macedonia until 1965 when they migrated to Australia for a better life. Done's experiences and losses would have a profound effect on him: dispossessed of his homeland, he was a man without a country. Believing that his father had been killed in the war, he was shocked to discover that he was still alive and living in Perth. Done was 36 years of age when he met his father.

Some men left their wives behind, disappeared in Australia, never to be heard of again; however, it was well known that they remarried and set up new lives for themselves. Perhaps they were ashamed of what they had done and the embarrassment they had caused their families. In contrast, young brides left behind lived under difficult circumstances with their in-laws patiently waiting for their husbands to return. An unusual example involved Vane Prcul, one of the early Macedonian pioneers making his way to Australia at the turn of the twentieth century. His young wife remained in Kosinec village (Kostur) living with Vane's mother but, having not heard from her husband for many years over the course of the Balkan Wars and the First World War, her brothers believing Vane had abandoned their sister brought her to live with them in Sofia, Bulgaria, but Vane heard that his wife had remarried and moved to Sofia. When Vane's cousin, Nume Bonakey arrived in Australia, he informed Vane, who was running a fish and chip shop in Broken Hill that his wife had not remarried but was taken to Sofia by her brothers where she continued to wait for news of him. Bonakey also brought an address in Sofia for Vane to write to his wife. Vane contacted her, sold the fish and chip business and other assets and travelled to Sofia with a large sum of money where he reunited with his wife; they subsequently had two children.[158]

The process of men arriving first and bringing out families later was replicated in the 1960s and 70s during the massive migration of Macedonians from the Republic of Macedonia. In contrast to the men who arrived earlier in the century who were hindered in reuniting with their families due to tough economic times and periods of war, the new arrivals were able to reunite their families in much shorter time frames. In the 1960s and 70s there was an abundance of work available in factories; they were able to establish themselves quickly, purchase a home, and within two to three years brought out fiancés, wives and children. A typical example is that of Mihailo Anastasovski from Gorno Aglarci village (Bitola) who arrived in Australia in December 1965, immediately found work in the manufacturing industry, brought out his wife and two young children in May 1966 and, in August 1966, purchased a home in Williamstown, Melbourne.

Photo 35: The Anastasovski family reunited in Williamstown, Melbourne, 1966. Note the Hills Hoist clothesline in the background and Australian Rules football at the feet of young Slobodan. (Source: Mihailo Anastasovski).

Endnotes

1 P. Hill, *The Macedonians in Australia*, Hesperian Press, Perth, 1989, p. 12.

2 C.A. Price, *Southern Europeans in Australia*, Melbourne University Press, Melbourne, 1963, p. 172.

3 T. Miovski, *Avstralija i Makedonskite Doselenici* [Australia and the Macedonian immigrants], Misla, Skopje, 1971, p. 31.

4 I. Chapovski, *The Macedonian Orthodox Church of St George*, York Press, Melbourne, 1992, p. 16.

5 T. Miovski, *Makedoncite vo Zapadna Avstralija* [The Macedonians in Western Australia], Zdruzhenie na decata begalci od Egejskiot del na Makedonija, Skopje, 1999, p. 20.

6 Lazo Bonakey (Boshnako) interview conducted by Connie Sideris, 1981. Vane Prcul was Lazo Bonakey's cousin. See also T. Miovski, 1999, op. cit., pp. 19-20.

7 P. Hill, op. cit., p. 12.

8 John Karajas interview.

9 P. Hill, op. cit., p.12.

10 The group from Graeshnica village arrived in Australia with the intention of returning to their homes after a few years. However only Stefan from the Ribarovci family returned to Macedonia, Karanfil from the Sarievci family died in a work accident when a tree fell on him whilst clearing land in Western Australia. The other five men remained in Australia. Stojan Spasevski interview.

11 Commonwealth Attorney General, Investigations Branch, Melbourne, 21 March 1925, National Archives of Australia.

12 Aleksandar Theodorovsky interview.

13 Attorney General's Department, Investigation Branch, document dated 27 February 1925, National Archives of Australia.

14 Commonwealth Attorney General, Investigations Branch, Melbourne, 21 March 1925, National Archives of Australia. The majority of the men from the stranded group in Melbourne were from Aegean Macedonia, while a smaller number were from under Yugoslav rule. As there were few Macedonians in Melbourne in 1925, they found themselves without friends and it was reported that 'there has been a lack of sympathy and help extended to them by the Greek community in Melbourne'; however, the Attorney General's Department made arrangements through the Greek Honorary Consul in Brisbane for 40 men to find work in Queensland.

15 Ibid.

16 B. Bozinoski and V, Krstevski, *Chetvrta Generacija* [Fourth Generation], Macedonian Australia Association of Culture and Human Rights, Newcastle, 2012, p. 401.

17 Ibid., pp. 402-03. Other Macedonians on board the ship included Lambo Shtatev, Mirche Grozdanov with his father Apostol, Milcho Ljakov, and others.

18 Vasil Turpin arrived in the United States in 1914 as a 16-year-old.

19 'Working for food only', *Argus* (Melbourne), 15 October 1927, p. 36.

20 M. Trajcevski, editor, *Kompas*, Spring 2006, p. 13. Mijal Murgev initially went to the United States and returned to Macedonia at the end of the Great War (1918). He planned to return to the United States; however, following the new immigration laws of 1924, Mijal came to Australia that year and he remained for three years before going back to Macedonia in 1927. In late 1928 or early 1929 he returned to Australia. Ibid., p. 12.

21 J. Vellios, *Faded Memories – Life and Times of a Macedonian Villager*, unpublished, 2014, p. 137.

22 Ibid., p. 138.

23 V. Trajceski, *Najsilniot Makedonec – Todor Jurukot* [The Strongest Macedonian – Todor Jurukot], Self-published, Melbourne 1995, p. 60.

24 Kosta Kotchoff interview.

25 Viktor Bogdanovski interview. The story was told to Viktor by Giorgi Nano, one of the men working in the eucalyptus industry with Todor Jurukot at the time.

26 Cveta Dimov (nee Doikin/Doikos) interview.

27 *Northern Standard* (Darwin), Friday 21 June 1940, p. 12.

28 Vasil Boskov stopped working on the farm after reporting the matter to the police. Afterwards, each month he walked to the farm to collect money that he was owed, however the farmer failed to pay him the full amount. Peter Boskov interview.

29 D. Konstantinov, *Pechalbarstvo* [Pechalba], Nauchno Drushtvo Bitola, Bitola, 1964, pp. 43-44.

30 In the early 1960s when 18-year-old Vancho Kalcovski was preparing to leave for Australia, Giorgija discouraged him from doing so. Vancho Kalcovski interview.

31 Connie Sideris interview with Stojko Angelkoff.

32 Big Tom had also worked in the eucalyptus industry and was renowned for his ability to carry 44- gallon drums of eucalyptus oil on his own. Done Dimov interview.

33 B. Bozinoski and V. Krstevski, op. cit., p. 399. Laze arrived in Sydney in Janu-

ary 1924 along with Lamo Shtatev, Mirche Grozdanov, and his father Apostol, Micho Ljakov and others, all from the village Capari (Bitola). Laze worked in the quarry in Mudgee, New South Wales, alongside the group of men with whom he arrived in Australia.

34 J. Harper, 'The Pecalbars of Gippsland: Macedonian Farm Workers around Kernot in the 1930s', *Gippsland Heritage Journal*, No. 28, Kapana Press, Briagolong, 2004, p.4. The Sugarloaf Dam was repaired in 1929 and then swamped by the Eildon Reservoir in 1952.

35 Connie Sideris interview with Jovan Mladenov. Bogdan Pavlevski interview.

36 Years later Mitre Kotchoff would tell stories how when the timber stumps were burned, even though they worked in a hot dry climate, he would dress in thick clothing for protection from the heat. Kosta Kotchoff interview.

37 According to Aleksandar Theodorovsky there were no Macedonian boarding houses in Melbourne established at that time. Other Macedonians from Buf (Lerin) that were in Victoria prior to the arrival of Done Theodorovsky in 1924, included Atanas Theodorovsky (Done's brother), Petre Todorovski, Todorche Gagachov and others. Aleksandar Theodorovsky interview.

38 Connie Sideris interview transcript.

39 *The West Australian*, 5 August 1937, p. 22; 18 August 1941.

40 B. Nedelkovski, 'Kumurdzhilnici vo seloto Virovo-Zheleznik' [Coal gatherers in the village Virovo-Zheleznik], pp.169-176, *Etnolog* (Broj 4-5), Skopje 1994. (Review of the Ethnological Association of Macedonia).

41 K. Todoroska, *Makedoncite vo Albania (1912-1991)* [Macedonians in Albania 1912-1991], Menora, Skopje, 2014, p. 140.

42 J. Harper, op. cit., pp. 2-9.

43 J. Vellios, op. cit., p. 127.

44 Vasil Vellios from Kotori village (Lerin) worked sleeper cutting in Western Australia in the 1920s and noted that rejected sleepers were not paid for 'but often cynically carried out of the forest by contractors and sold to local farmers as fence posts or as firewood to the residents of nearby townships'. J. Vellios, op. cit., p. 137.

45 B. Bozinoski and V. Krstevski, op. cit., p. 236.

46 Stojan Spasevski interview.

47 *Mercury* (Hobart), Tuesday 10 September 1929, p. 6.

48 *Makedonska Iskra*, May/June 1956, p. 2.

49 Interview with Connie Sideris conducted in 2007 for the Northbridge History Project.

50 Kata Paunovic (nee Soklev) interview.

51 Andrew Goulopoulos interview.

52 Riste Todevski interview.

53 Konomladi is the neighbouring village to Statica. A number of the Konomladi men eventually returned to their village due to a lack of work in Australia. Done Dimov interview. Macedonians from Trcije village (Kostur) worked in the eucalyptus oil industry in Braidwood at around the same time, one of the early arrivals from Trcije was Giorgi Nano, he arrived in 1926 and spent a period of time in the bush producing eucalyptus oil. Viktor Bogdanovski interview

Amongst the first men to arrive from Statica village between 1925 and 1936 were Nese Patrikov-Dzhakata, Fimio and Vane Klefanov, Mitre Ilov, Giorgi Ralev, Stefo Maznikov, Risto Dimov, Yorge Vasilov, Stoyan Bogoyov, Vane Gakev, Stoyan Dudev, Gavre Kalayanov, Tsilo Zunzurov, Yorge Zunzurov, Sotir Klunov, Ilo Bilkov, Kosta Pandov, Dine Doikin, Ilo Sudzhov, Stojan Dzhengalov and Krste Pazov. Data compiled by Done Dimov

54 Cveta Dimov interview. Cveta recalled the stories told by her grandfather Con Doikin/Doikos about the miserable conditions he and other Macedonians endured in the bush.

55 Ilija Veljanovski interview. When Mitre Veljanovski arrived in 1938 his surname was recorded as Veljanovtich, due to the Struga region being under Serbian rule. Dimitri Naumov was from the Danchevci *soi* (family).

56 Done Dimov interview.

57 C.A. Price, op. cit. p. 11, 1963.

58 T. Miovski, (1999), op. cit., pp. 20-21.

59 Done Ashlakoff interview. V. Cvetanovski, *Pechalbarstvoto Makedonska Sudbina* [Pechalba a Macedonian Fate], Iris, Struga 2012, pp. 36–39.

60 C.A. Price, op. cit., pp. 180-81.

61 A. Glafchev, *The Migrant Experience: From Village to Suburb*, unpublished paper, p. 3. http://www.pollitecon.com

62 Victor Damos interview.

63 In 1939, at the beginning of the Second World War, Velika Spirova and her daughter Fania boarded the last ship to leave for Australia from the port of Piraeus. Velika's husband Vasil had arrived in 1930 and after a number of years working as an itinerant labourer, he purchased a small farm at Crossroads near Newcastle.

64 Velika Spirova interview.

65 Stojko Angelkoff interview by Connie Sideris, 1981.

66 P. Hill, op. cit., p. 38.

67 Lazo Bonakey (Boshnako) interview by Connie Sideris, 1981.

68 Manol Mano interview

69 Steve and Nick Jambanis, from B. Marwick, *The Times of Wanneroo - As told to Bill Marwick*, Wanneroo and Districts Historical Society, Perth, 2005, p. 197.

70 Christine Stergiou (nee Vosnacos/Vosnacov) interview and B. Marwick, *Stories of Old Wanneroo - As told to Bill Marwick*, Ultra Printing Services, Perth, 2002, pp. 193-200.

71 *West Australian* (Perth) 23 February 1931, p. 13. Giorgi Mechkaroff from Kuchkoveni village (Lerin) brought out his family from Macedonia in 1948 which resulted in his amassing considerable debt of £1,000. Operating a market garden in Shepparton, Victoria, Giorgi's agricultural ingenuity saw him quickly pay off his debt. At that time fruit and vegetables were seasonal. Giorgi had an idea to plant early tomatoes after noticing thousands of tops from 10-gallon tins discarded in the local tip. Together with his 14-year-old son Peter (Pandil), they would ride their bicycles and load as many of the tins as they could carry back to their farm. After many trips, they hauled about 2,000 tins and then planted 2,000 tomato plants. The tins were curved and placed around each tomato plant from the south side as that would protect them from frost. Giorgi's strategy worked; they had tomatoes three weeks before anyone else in Shepparton and sold them at a higher price and combined with a good season, he managed to wipe out his debt completely. Peter (Pandil) Mechkaroff interview and autobiographical notes.

72 Article 'Makedoncite vo Geraldton' [Macedonians in Geraldton] by A. Ognenovski, in *Vesnik na Makedonskite Opshtini vo Avstralija*, Perth, August 1982.

73 Ilija arrived in Australia with the surname Papadopoulos but changed it to Popoff in Geraldton.

74 *Vesnik na Makedonskite Opshtini vo Avstralija*, Perth, August 1983, p.8. In the 1960s a second Macedonian team, named Skopje, was established in Geraldton.

75 Victor Damos interview.

76 Alex Damos and Stan Milenko interview.

77 The Macedonians of Geraldton have left their mark in the area, streets near the community hall have been named Macedonia Drive, Alexander Drive and Dulchev Way (Goce Delchev).

78 Others who arrived from Buf during the period 1937-1938 include Giorgi Klashovski, German Alabakov, Kosta Angelevski, Risto Shapardanov, Sime Angelevski, Pande Vlchev and Goche Markovski. Stojan Sarbinov autobiographical notes.

79 Stojan Sarbinov autobiographical notes.

80 Kosta Angelkoff, *Deinosta na eden emigrant* [Activities of an emigrant]. Archives of the Macedonian Community of Western Australia.

81 Stojan Sarbinov autobiographical notes, op. cit.

82 P. Hill, op. cit., p. 24.

83 Mary Purcell (nee Turpin) interview and Vasil Turpin biographical notes.

84 J. Vellios, op. cit., p. 183

85 L. Ognenova-Michova and K. Mitsou-Lazaridis, *A Girl from Neret*, Pollitecon Publications, Sydney, 2006, p. 94.

86 Kosta Angelkoff, *Deinosta na Eden Emigrant*, op. cit.

87 L. Ognenova-Michova and K. Mitsou-Lazaridis, op. cit., p. 95.

88 Ilo Ognenov (Lou Ognenis) interview and Kosta Angelkoff, *Deinosta na edin emigrant,* op. cit.

89 *Doklad od vtorata konferencija na MANS za WA* [Report from the second conference of MAPL in WA], 31 August 1947, Archive of the Macedonian Community of Western Australia. When the Mutual Benefit Association eventually ceased to exist, the remaining funds were donated to the Warren District Hospital as stipulated in Clause 17 of the constitution which stated that 'if the Association is left with only seven members it is considered as wound up and in that case all its financial assets are to be left to the district hospital, Manjimup, Western Australia'.

90 L. Ognenova-Michova and K. Mitsou-Lazaridis, op. cit., p. 89.

91 Although there was no organised league in the Warren district (Western Australia) at that time, the team played friendly games with local teams in the area – Manjimup Rovers, Bridgetown, Boyup Brook, Pemberton and Donnelly Mill. In the late 1950s, team members included Risto Silemanov, Georgi Stojkov, Georgi Temov, Stase Ristovski, Naume Bogdanovski, Naume Gegov, Naume Temov, Tome Kotev, Georgi Belchurov, Pando Greshkov, Jovan Andriov and Christos Ailakis. http://manjimuprovers.com

92 B. Kris, *A Study of the Slav-Macedonian Community in Adelaide*, South Australia, University of Adelaide, unpublished thesis, 1970, p. 9; A. Glafchev, op. cit. p. 4; P. Hill, op. cit., p. 20.

93 A. Glafchev, ibid, pp. 5-6. Glafchev states that in Fulham, Lockleys and Feryden Park 'they found large unused tracts of broad acres, which at that time was used primarily for agistment', p. 6.

94 *Advertiser* (Adelaide), 19 December 1950, p. 4.

95 Kata Paunovic (nee Soklev) interview.

96 J. Vellios, op. cit. p. 185.

97 B. Bozinoski and V. Krstevski, op. cit., p, 304, (interview with John Ilich).

98 For instance, this occurred in places such as Pappinbarra, New South Wales, in the 1930s and 40s or in Meadowie, Newcastle in the 1950s. See B. Bozinoski

and V. Krstevski, ibid, interviews with Risto Iliev, pp. 291-292 and Giorgi Boshev, p. 308.

99 *'Iako ne sum roden vo Makedonija, veruvajte detsvoto go imam pominato kako selanche od Makedonija'*. Ibid., interview with Giorgi Boshev, p. 308.

100 Andrew Goulopoulos interview.

101 Men from Dolno Kotori were known to travel to the United States to work. Steve Pandu's father, Kole and grandfather Miti worked for 14 years on the construction of the railway line from New York to Syracuse.

102 During the Great War the Lithgow Small Arms factory mass-produced Short Magazine Lee-Enfield rifles; however, between the two world wars, armament production was limited to converting rifle barrels to the new Mk VII ammunition.

103 Kosta Pandov interview.

104 Ibid.

105 P. Hill, op. cit., p. 15.

106 These villages were mainly located under the slopes of the Baba Mountain ranges and are known as upper villages *(gornite sela)*.

107 Krste Pazov was also known by his Anglicised name Peter Steve. However, with the Macedonians he was known by the nickname 'begot'. Begot/beg was a common term for a feudal landlord in Macedonia during the period of Ottoman rule, however the term can also denote a distinguished or wealthy person.

108 M. Trajcevski, editor, article *'Crabbes Creek Macedonian village', Kompas,* Macedonian Welfare Association, Vol 2, Issue 4, pp. 26-31.

109 Shirley Donelly interview and autobiographical notes. Shirley Donelly was the Pazov family neighbour.

110 *Makedonska Iskra,* July 1948, p. 4.

111 M. Trajcevski, editor, *Kompas,* Vol 2, Issue 4, op. cit. p. 28.

112 Shirley Donelly interview and autobiographical notes.

113 M. Trajcevski, editor, *Kompas,* Vol 2, Issue 4, op. cit., pp. 29-30. In nearby Upper Burringbar, Macedonians were mainly from the village Klabuchishta (Lerin). Boshe Gelevski from Klabuchishta purchased a banana plantation in Upper Burringbar in 1941 after having cleared bushland in Western Australia in the 1920s and then worked on sugar cane plantations in Queensland in the 1930s. A well-known and respected farmer, the road where he lived and operated his banana farm was named after him, Geles Road. Riste Todevski interview.

114 Martin Trenevski, *Nepoznata Juzhna Zemja* [Unknown Southern Land], Matica Makedonska, 1992, p. 204.

115 Viktor Bogdanovski interview; and George Stefanoff and Margaret Ruhfus (nee Stefanoff) interview.

116 Done Dimov, *Staticheni vo Avstralija* [People from Statica in Australia], unpublished.

117 Due to a lack of work in Australia, a number of the Konomladi men eventually returned to their village. Of the remaining men, quite a few settled in the Forbes district and established market gardens and dairy farms.

118 Cveta Dimov interview.

119 Done Dimov, *Staticheni vo Avstralija,* op. cit.

120 The following individuals were elected to positions on the *Opshtinska Uprava,* Nikola Nichov Secretary, Giorgi Ralev Treasurer, and committee members Ilo Durov, Stanko Zangalov, Dimitar Sarov, Ivan Pandov, Trpo Nanov, Krsto Lagov and Phillip Rukov. V. Bogdanovski, *Kratka Istorija za Prvite Makedonci doselenici vo Kvinbeyan* [A short history of the first Macedonian immigrants in Queanbeyan], unpublished.

121 Viktor Bogdanovski interview.

122 Giorgi Nano gathered the following group of men – Krste Pazov 'Begot', Jane Manushi, Tsile Manigano, Done Pazov, Jordan Golev, Trpo Nano, Pando Panov, Vlado Jancheski, Vane Mangov, Dushan Drakalski and other interested Macedonians to purchase the Buffalo Club, V. Bogdanovski, *Kratka Istorija za Prvite Makedonci vo Kvinbeyan,* op. cit.

123 Done Dimov, *Staticheni vo Avstralija,* op. cit.

After only a few months playing in the second division, the club was asked by the Australian Capital Territory soccer federation to compete in the first division following the withdrawal of another team (Kingston). Club president Tony Steve (formerly of Crabbes Creek) provided capable leadership and solid foundations for the future. *Canberra Times*, 27 April 1966.

124 Viktor Bogdanovski interview.

125 Aleksandar Stefanoff was already a successful businessman before his arrival in Canberra. Strongly committed to contribute positively to help advance the Macedonian community, he played an active part in the establishment of the Macedonian Orthodox Church, Sveti Kliment Ohridski in 1987, the first Macedonian Church in the national capital.

126 Basket shoes were similar to sandals and made from strips of leather in a plaited or woven style.

127 Pavle Goulopoulos had two Clydesdale working horses on his Werribee South farm named 'Bibi' and 'Pancho'. Macedonians traditionally name their animals with animal specific names.

128 *Argus* (Melbourne), 22 October 1941, p. 3.

129 Pavle Goulopoulos often assisted in this task. Andrew Goulopoulos interview.

130 Name unknown.

131 Cane Rendevski interview.

132 J. Mapstone, *The Greek Macedonians of Shepparton: A study of immigrant assimilation in a rural area of Australia*, Australian National University, 1966, p. 110

133 Done Ashlakoff interview.

134 The Jewish family that sold the orchard to Vane Ashlakoff went on to establish the Alexander's clothing stores in Melbourne which was a household name in the 1970s. The Jewish settlement in Shepparton was centred on Orrvale and Shepparton East, with the first families arriving in 1913. Between the 1930s and 1960s over sixty Jewish families lived in Shepparton. For an account of the Jewish community in Shepparton see S. Randles, *No Locked Doors – Jewish Life in Shepparton*, Makor Jewish Community Library, Melbourne, 2004.

135 Peter Mechkaroff interview.

136 After five years of life on the land the Angelovic family decided that farming was not the livelihood they sought in Australia and subsequently returned to Geelong. Jim Angelovic interview. There were strong family networks between Geelong and Shepparton, evidenced by an annual friendly soccer match played over many years by the Macedonian teams from Geelong and Shepparton.

137 A third son, Tome (Tom) was born in Australia.

138 Cvetko Radevski interview.

139 Lazo Giamov interview.

140 J. Harper, op. cit., p. 3.

141 Ibid., p. 3.

142 Ibid., p. 3.

143 Todor Velov from Kotori village (Lerin) arrived in Australia in 1952. Not long after his arrival Todor, together with his son Tanas, and other Macedonians, were hired by a contractor through the Macedonian Social Club in Gertrude Street, Fitzroy. Todor and Tanas worked in the Gippsland region for two years, living in a camp in Noojee and cutting trees around Walhalla and the Thompson River. The work was hard but well paid. Pavle Velov interview.

144 Krste Constantinou's decision to buy a business in Sale was influenced by the timber cutting contractor, Jim Hall. Whilst working as a timber cutter in Noojee, Krste sustained an injury when a branch fell on him and while Krste was contemplating his future, Jim Hall encouraged him to buy a business in Sale. Krste subsequently purchased the café in Sale in 1955. Nick Constantinou interview. Macedonians set up businesses in a number of towns throughout the Gippsland area. Peter Stoitse from Neret village (Lerin) is a notable example of a successful trucking entrepreneur who built a large-scale transport busi-

ness. In the early 1960s, Peter purchased his first truck and transported loads of wood from Binginwarri for boilers at an old butter factory at Toora. From that single truck, he went on to establish Peter Stoitse Transport, which would eventually come to have several depots across regional Victoria with a large fleet of trucks prepared to haul virtually any product that required carting. A proud Macedonian, Peter was described as 'fearless, strong- minded and able to relate well to everyone he met. As an honourable man, deals were simply made with a handshake'. *Transpec Digest*, Footscray, Spring 2012, p. 42.

145 J. Obrebski, *Ritual and Social Structure in a Macedonian Village*, Research Report No 16, Department of Anthropology, University of Massachusetts, Amherst, 1977, p. 7.

146 B. Bozinoski and V. Krstevski, op. cit. p,195 (Interview with Mile Todorovski regarding his father Giorgi Todorovski, 'Chevlarot').

147 'Application for Admission of relatives or friends into Australia', 11 April 1927, National Archives of Australia.

148 *The West Australian*, 4 November 1950, p. 3.

149 Macedonian Welfare Workers Network of Victoria, *From War to Whittlesea – Oral Histories of Macedonian Child Refugees*, 1999, p. 28.

150 L. Ognenova-Michova and K. Mitsou-Lazaridis, op. cit., p. 84.

151 Peter (Pandil) Mechkaroff interview and autobiographical notes.

152 Nick Constantinou interview.

153 D. Dimov autobiographical notes, p. 2.

154 *Life History of Kole Nedelkov Lazorov and his family*, compiled by M. Lazorov, Perth, Western Australia.

155 Ibid.

156 Many of the Macedonian partisans that were living in Tashkent eventually settled in the Republic of Macedonia.

157 Jana Kircov/Kircos arrived in Australia in 1954, joining her husband Giorgi in Sale.

158 Interview with Vanka Bonakey conducted by Connie Sideris.

Part Four

Urban Settlement

9

Smoke and Steel: Work and Settlement in the Urban Landscape

Due to a lack of opportunities in the cities, Macedonians typically made their way into country areas soon after their arrival in Australia; however, those who remained in the cities generally found work in ethnic-operated businesses, such as cafés and restaurants or in hotels. In the early twentieth century, up until 1924, when the United States closed its doors to migrants, a number of these men had worked in the United States (some in Canada), and arrived in Australia speaking English with a North American accent. Some were amongst the few Macedonian *pechalbari* who did not go into debt to pay for their travel to Australia. They were able quickly to set up businesses such as cafés, boarding houses, take-away food shops and bakeries in working-class areas that developed into ethnic centres, such as North Perth (Northbridge), Fitzroy in Melbourne and Rockdale in Sydney.

Macedonian-operated boarding houses, cafés and other businesses sprang up in the 1920s in North Perth, on and around William Street and James Street. An urban presence developed more rapidly in Perth than in other places because many of the earliest arrivals first disembarked at Fremantle. By the 1930s, there were several bakeries, take-away food shops, a butcher shop and other businesses operating in what became the Northbridge area. The brothers Kole and Risto Peoff ran a fish and chip shop in Como Beach and were amongst the first Macedonians in Perth to operate their own business.[1] With the onset of the Second World War and the large presence of American servicemen, Macedonians who had set up businesses in the cities prospered, as the servicemen, mostly sailors, spent abundantly whilst stationed in Australian ports. Dono Sholdas' hamburger shop in Hay Street Perth, Vasil Turpin and partners in 'The Little Arcadia' café in Hay Street and a restaurant owned by Vasil Peoff and partners in central Perth were a few of the Macedonian-operated businesses that thrived through dealings with Americans stationed in Fremantle. Similarly, in New South Wales, American servicemen stationed at the Port Stevens Naval Base regularly frequented Aleksandar Stefanoff's café restaurant in Mayfield (Newcastle).[2] In 1941, Risto Altin bought a restaurant from a Macedonian family in South Melbourne for £400, and, due to the large patronage of American servicemen, in the first two months of operation Risto earned the equivalent of what he had earned in his last five years in Australia.[3]

In contrast to Macedonian arrivals to Perth and Melbourne that were mostly from Aegean Macedonia, the earliest Macedonian migrants to Sydney were predominantly from Serbian-occupied Macedonia. They arrived in small groups expecting to find work, but few managed to do so as there was a lack of work available during the onset of the global depression which was further compounded due to discrimination against non-English speaking migrants. Most left Sydney to search for work in country areas, as itinerant farm labourers, eucalyptus gatherers or at the steelworks in Lithgow, Port Kembla or Newcastle in New South Wales for those fortunate enough to secure employment there. One early arrival in Sydney was Aleksandar Stefanoff from Kriveni village (Resen district). He arrived in 1924 with a group of men that included his close friend Eftin Naumov (also from Kriveni). In their early twenties, they were eager to perform any work available and send money back to their families in Macedonia; however, work was hard to come by and Aleksandar could only find employment in a hotel in Cronulla working as a rouseabout for food and board only. Job prospects were limited, and he left Sydney after hearing about the Newcastle steelworks.

In the 1940s, Macedonians commenced settling in inner city areas south of the Sydney central business district around Rockdale, Newtown, Bexley, Arncliffe and Erskineville, operating small businesses such as milk bars, fish and chip shops, bakeries and grocery stores. In Sydney, the Macedonian epicentre was Rockdale. Risto Belcheff from Capari village (Bitola) arrived in Australia in 1938 and, after six years working in the steelworks at Port Kembla, in 1944 moved to Rockdale in Sydney where he purchased a fish and chip shop on Princess Highway.[4] Another early arrival in Rockdale was Kiril Karafiloff from Capari village (Bitola), who came from Newcastle together with his family. Around this time, Riste Sazdanoff, also from Capari village, operated a fruit and vegetable business. He would drive in his truck selling produce from the northern suburbs of Sydney down to Liverpool, visiting all the Macedonian homes along the way.[5] The early settlers in Rockdale and the surrounding suburbs between the 1920s and 1940s were from the Bitola region villages Capari, Gjavato, Dolenci, and other nearby villages. Macedonians from other regions arrived later and, after the Civil War in Greece, Macedonians arrived from Aegean Macedonia while others came from under Bulgarian rule.[6] Rockdale would become closely associated with the Macedonian community and, with the influx of large numbers in the 1960s and 70s, a rich community life developed which saw the establishment of churches, sporting clubs, and a range of other community facilities and resources. In 1983, Rockdale and Bitola, a large source of Macedonian migrants in Rockdale, became sister cities.

In South Australia, Macedonians working in country areas headed back towards Adelaide in search of stable employment when the economy began to recover from the Great Depression in the 1930s. They found work performing manual labour in factories, whilst others found employment in shops, cafés and businesses operated by migrants. Accommodation was found in lodgings in inner-city Adelaide located close to their workplaces. As the men were being joined by their families, they rented houses towards the outer-urban edge of Adelaide in places such as Kilkenny, Challa Gardens and Croyden.[7]

Searching for work, Macedonians ventured north to Queensland's sugar cane fields. A few managed to find work in Brisbane during the 1920s. Their number gradually increased and in the 1930s a Macedonian café was established which became a focal point for new arrivals in the city and for men continuing through to the sugar cane fields or looking for work at the Biloela cotton fields. In the 1950s and 60s, a number of Macedonians from Crabbes Creek and the surrounding banana-farming areas moved to Brisbane in search of retirement and greater opportunities for their children, or as a consequence of the drop in the price of bananas and the decline of the industry.

When worked dried up in one place the Macedonian men went searching elsewhere. From Western Australia and Queensland, some headed to the Northern Territory where they found work in the mining industry or on the wharves in Darwin. Kotse Tanev (Kotsopoulos) from Kuchkoveni village (Lerin) arrived in Western Australia in 1937, and like many other Macedonians worked as an itinerant labourer and cleared bushland; however, the search for on-going work led him to Darwin where he found a wharf job loading ships. Fortuitously, Kotse left Darwin on 18 February 1942, the day before the Japanese bombing of Darwin during the Second World War, and headed back to Western Australia to clear bush for farms. Tasmania was the least travelled destination for Macedonian *pechalbari*, although there are reports of a small number of individuals known to have made their way to work in the Tasmanian logging industry in the 1940s whilst others set out for Tasmania in search of business opportunities. One example is Risto Kapetanovski, the father of the highly decorated and distinguished Victoria Police detective John Kapetanovski, who operated a bakery in Bitola before migrating to Australia in the 1950s. Risto initially lived in Melbourne and leased a bakery in Prahran before opening another in Brunswick. After hearing that there were no ethnic bakeries in Tasmania, the entrepreneurial Risto travelled to Hobart where he opened a bakery café in the suburb of Newtown, later establishing two other bakeries along the west coast of Tasmania, in the small mining town of Roseberry and in picturesque Strahan.[8]

Steel towns: Wollongong and Newcastle

Wollongong is a seaside city 82 kilometres south of Sydney in the Illawarra region of New South Wales. Macedonians have been present in the Illawarra region since the 1920s and their presence has been directly linked to the steelworks industry. Port Kembla, a suburb of Wollongong, has been synonymous with the steelworks industry since the early twentieth century. A copper smelter and refinery company (the Electrolyte Refinery and Smelting Company of Australia) operated in Port Kembla from 1908, and Metal Manufacturers set up in 1917. Macedonian employment in the industry can be marked with the arrival of Hoskins Iron and Steel Works from Lithgow in 1927, as Macedonians first worked in the steel industry in Lithgow in Central NSW. When the industry relocated to Port Kembla, they moved with it to continue employment.[9]

One of the earliest to arrive in Port Kembla was Riste Sazdanoff (Capari village, Bitola) who was involved in the relocation of the steelworks, transporting goods from Lithgow to Port Kembla with his truck. Many of the early arrivals were men from Velushina and Bukovo villages in the Bitola region such as Ilo Dimovski (Dimovic) and Todor Kasovski (Kasovich). Todor Kasovski arrived in Australia in 1927 and, within a few days of arriving in Sydney, went with a group of Macedonians to Lithgow seeking work at Hoskins Iron and Steel Works. 'There was no employment office then, you just lined up, and if you were lucky to be picked you were instantly employed, at least for that day… and if there wasn't work at the factory we did anything that we could find'. When the steel works relocated to Port Kembla, Todor followed and secured work there.[10] As there were not many Macedonians in the area at the time, the men boarded together and later on when one of them bought a house, the rest of the group became his boarders.[11]

Work in the steel industry was not constant and could be sporadic at times. When the work slowed down, they had to find alternative employment such as timber cutting, extracting eucalyptus oil in the bush and manual labouring jobs in Sydney; when the steel industry recommenced, the Macedonians would return. In 1935, Australian Iron and Steel merged with Broken Hill Pty Co Ltd (BHP); however, Macedonians referred to the company as 'Port Kembla Steelworks' or simply, the 'steelworks'. Men arrived from afar to work at the steelworks with some travelling from interstate such as Risto Belcheff who came from Perth, Western Australia in 1938, and Angele Brglevski from Velushina village, who worked in rural Victoria in the 1930s and moved to Port Kembla in 1941.[12] At the beginning of the Second World War there were at least 145 Macedonian men living in Port Kembla/Wollongong, with the majority working in the steelworks. The figure only represents the number of men and does not include the wives and children of the small number of men who had their families with them in Australia at that time. [13]

After the Second World War, the Port Kembla steelworks underwent massive expansion on such a scale that the surrounding area could not meet the workforce demand. In 1949, there were 4,000 employees and by 1961, the number of employees grew to 15,000. Large waves of migration, which included Macedonians, saw the population of Wollongong increase from 63,000 in 1947 to 171,000 in 1976.[14] The steelworks became the economic mainstay of Wollongong and Port Kembla and Macedonian men were drawn to the area and the high wages on offer. Renowned as hard workers, Macedonians made up the largest numbers in the toughest areas of the steelworks, often in crews made up entirely of Macedonians. They worked in the coke ovens, blast furnace, slab mill, sinter plant, strip mill, and other areas. In the slab yard they worked as scarfers, a process that involved manually scarfing the surface for defects in the steel, where the men

Photo 36: Macedonian men coming together for a beer and enjoying time away from the steelworks in Port Kembla, 1961. (Source: Robert Stojanovski).

Photo 37: Dushan Stanley from Velushina village (Bitola), circa 1964. Dushan first commenced at the Port Kembla steelworks as a 16-year-old in 1956 and worked across a number of departments in roles such as "Gear Man", "Shearer" and "Striker". Dushan worked at the steelworks for 11 years before establishing a successful travel agency. (Source: Dushan Stanley. Courtesy of Mendo Trajcevski).

were required to wear thick heavy leather aprons and face shields to protect them from the intense heat. The men used Macedonian names for the roles they performed; for example, scarfers referred to themselves as *kosachi* as the scarfing process reminded them of reaping crops with a scythe which they performed back in their villages.

At its height in the 1980s, the Port Kembla steelworks employed 30,000 people. Following the arrival of large numbers of Macedonians to Wollongong in the 1960s and 1970s, mostly from the Bitola region, thousands found employment at the steelworks and settled in the nearby suburbs of Cringila, Port Kembla, Warrawong and Coniston. The Macedonian workforce at the Port Kembla steelworks was almost entirely from the Republic of Macedonia and, in particular, from the Bitola region's upper villages and from the Ohrid region. Wollongong became renowned as a Macedonian centre with the highest concentration of Macedonians in Australia. As the community grew, some moved out to the hinterland suburb of Figtree.

There was ample work for men in the steelworks; however, employment opportunities for women were limited, resulting in high levels of female unemployment and, in particular, migrant women in Wollongong. The most common source of employment for migrant women was clothing factories. Most of these clothing factories moved to Wollongong due to financial assistance received from the government specifically to deal with the problem of female unemployment and were required to have a female workforce of at least 75 per cent. Data from 1977 revealed that 68 per cent of female workers in textile industries were migrant women.[15] Macedonian women were eager to secure employment in the clothing factories to help support their families but found the industry non-unionised and exploitative. A lack of available work to meet the demand for female employment resulted in female unemployment in Wollongong reaching nearly 40 per cent in 1980.

The steelworks employed tens of thousands, but less than one per cent were women. This was a point of contention to women of Wollongong and, in response, in 1980 a 'Jobs for Women Action Group' was established to lobby for their rights. Macedonian women were fervent activists and participated in the setting up of a tent embassy (modelled on the Aboriginal tent embassy in Canberra in 1972), picketed the steelworks and took part in street marches.[16] Discrimination against women at the steelworks resulted in a series of complaints and legal challenges because women were being treated less favourably than men. One of the first legal challenges against the company brought before the New South Wales Anti-Discrimination Board was the matter of Donka Najdovska and 33 others against Australian Iron and Steel in 1980. In response, the company hired women. However, a downturn in the industry saw most of these women, who were the last employees to be hired, become the first to be retrenched.

The lack of employment opportunities for women at the steelworks and in Wollongong generally brought financial and other pressures on families. Macedonian women in Australia have a tradition of contributing financially to the household which made them feel useful and enhanced their self-esteem. Alexandra Trajcevska provides an example of the sacrifice Macedonian women made to support their families. Her husband, Trendo Trajcevski, worked in the steelworks from his arrival in Port Kembla in 1958. Unable to find work in Wollongong, Alexandra travelled by bus to Sydney each day to work in a chicken-processing factory. The distance and excessive travel time was a sacrifice which took its toll on the family and following protests from her husband and children, Alexandra left her employment in Sydney.[17] Some families moved to Sydney where both husband and wife could find work; however, most Macedonians remained in the Illawarra region where employment at the steelworks provided them with the financial means to build homes and raise their families.

Newcastle is located approximately 150 kilometres north of Sydney and has also been known for its steelworks industry since the early twentieth century. The prospect of finding work in the steelworks also drew Macedonians to the area. Laze Porkov from Capari village (Bitola) was most likely the first Macedonian in Newcastle, arriving in 1924. Other early arrivals in 1924 were men such as Boris Gulabov from Gjavato village (Bitola), Pasko Ilinkovski from Capari village, Kiril Karafilov from Capari village, Nestor Trpovski from Pokreveni village (Prespa), Andon Lajmanov from Gjavato village (Bitola), and Aleksandar Stefanoff from Kriveni village (Resen).[18] All the early Macedonian arrivals worked in the steelworks. Aleksandar Stefanoff first arrived in Sydney in 1924 but soon made his way to Newcastle after hearing about the steelworks. He arrived in the middle of winter with virtually no money but determined to do whatever he could to get a job. Every morning men lined up at the front gate in the hope they would be employed and to ensure he would be first in line, Aleksandar slept under a railway bridge close to the steelworks. The strategy paid off and although the work was difficult and dirty, he was grateful to have a job.[19]

The steelworks was the principal place of employment for Macedonians in Newcastle, and most laboured in the open furnace section which was the toughest area in which to work. Others found employment on the shipping docks and a few went on to set up their own businesses. The steelworks industry did not operate continuously and, during periods of downtime, working men would leave and

Photo 38: Lazo Porkov (Enoff) seated second from the right with co-workers at Lysaght steelworks in Newcastle, 1929. (Source: Alex Sazdanoff. Courtesy of Mendo Trajcevski).

work in the eucalyptus industry, perform sleeper-cutting in Grafton or any other work they could find. Quite a few of the Macedonians set up their own businesses as early as the 1920s. Naume Simonov from Rotino village (Bitola) sold fruit and vegetables throughout Newcastle from the back of a horse-drawn cart, whilst Spire Kukulov from Capari village operated a similar business before opening a fruit shop in Mayfield.[20] Aleksandar Stefanoff left the steelworks in 1929 and opened a café restaurant in Hunter Street, in the main shopping district of Newcastle. A few years later he set up another café restaurant in nearby Mayfield. Kiril Karafilov set up a fruit shop business on Union Street in Cooks Hill before establishing a number of other businesses in Hunter Street.

From the end of the Great War to the mid-1930s, there were 60 to 70 single men and fewer than 20 families living in Newcastle. These Newcastle Macedonians were mostly from the Bitola, Resen and Lerin regions. At this time, the Macedonian men were mostly working in the steelworks and living in the Cooks Hill area of Newcastle.

Photo 39: Aleksandar Stefanoff's café in Mayfield, Newcastle, 1941. From left to right: female employee, Aleksandar Stefanoff, George Stefanoff and Eleni Stefanoff. (Source: Margaret Ruhfus – nee Stefanoff).

Between 1935 and 1939, single men and families continued arriving in Newcastle and by 1939, the Macedonian community was made up of approximately 200 people.[21] The community came together for picnics on farms belonging to Macedonians and the first community dances were held at the Medowie Primary School hall,[22] while the population grew with the local economic stimulus of the Second World War. The number of Macedonians settling in Newcastle was at its height between 1950 and 1970, with over 4,000 arriving and settling in the suburbs in close proximity to their workplace at the steelworks, in particular Mayfield, Tighes Hill and Hamilton where over 400 families had settled.[23] Macedonians made up the largest ethnic group employed at the steelworks, but these were mostly men. Macedonian women typically worked in the textile industry and as dressmakers and in tailor shops, although some found work in the steelworks. With each downturn in the industry, the women were always the first to go.[24] When the steelworks ceased operation in 1999 it was a massive industrial shutdown with 2,000 workers and 1,000 contractors out of work.

Geelong is Victoria's second largest city, located 75 kilometres south-west of Melbourne on Port Phillip Bay. The first Macedonian in Geelong was probably an individual from Negochani village (Lerin) who arrived in the 1930s. Others arrived soon after, in the late 1930s and 1940s, including Dimko Vergov from Gradeshnica village (Bitola), a villager from Sveta Petka (Lerin), Angele Radevski, the brothers Angele and Ilo Angelovic/Angelovski and Krste Tasich (from the Dungovci family), all from the village of Dragosh, Bitola region. The Macedonian community in Geelong was characterised by the district from where they migrated – mostly from the villages under the slopes of the Baba mountain ranges situated south of Bitola, such as Dragosh, Graeshnica, Velushina, Lazhec, Bareshani, Oleveni, and others. A high proportion of people from the district settled in Geelong as a result of chain migration. A particularly large number were from Dragosh village; theirs was the first village association to form in Geelong in 1964 and they became a prominent part of the local Macedonian community.

Angele Angelovic, a well-known member of the Geelong Dragosh community, had previously worked as a cook in France and North America in restaurants in Detroit and Toronto prior to arriving in Australia in 1937. When Angele arrived in Geelong in 1941, he set up a restaurant in Ryrie Street, close to the Geelong Theatre and went on to operate several restaurants in Geelong over the years. Angele assisted a number of Macedonians to migrate from Dragosh, helped them find work and, at one time in the late 1950s, six newly arrived families lived with Angele, his wife and children. By the early 1960s, the number of Macedonians in Geelong grew, and the community became concentrated around Pakington Street in West Geelong. It was not unusual for family members, including brothers, uncles and aunties, to live in the same street, and this made visiting one another easier. Dances were regularly held in the Geelong West town hall, the Slavkovci brothers from Bareshani village (Bitola) provided traditional Macedonian music and the Pakington Street shopping strip was a meeting place for the older folk. In the 1970s, about a decade after their arrival en masse, Macedonians commenced moving to Bell Post Hill where they built new brick homes on large blocks of land.

Macedonian women worked in the textile industry and in scallop and footwear factories while men generally worked at one of two principal employers, Ford Motor Company and International Harvester.[25] Hundreds of Macedonians have worked at the Ford Motor plant across a range of areas including the engine plant, machine shop, press shop and assembly line. Cane Rendevski from Dragosh village (Bitola) arrived in Geelong in 1967 after having worked in Shepparton for five years. He went to the Ford factory, drawn by the large number of Macedonians there. At that time there were over 5,000 employees working three shifts, 24 hours a day. Cane was hired immediately and given the option as to which area he preferred to work in. He asked to work as a forklift driver because, when he lived in Shepparton, he had operated a forklift loading fruit boxes onto trucks. Cane spent the rest of his working life at Ford, 32 years in all, before retiring in 1998.

It seemed as if every Macedonian in Geelong drove a Ford vehicle because, as employees, they were entitled to a discount when purchasing a new vehicle. Driving a brand-new Ford that one had helped build became a symbol of acceptance into this working-class community. Employment at the Ford Motor Company was also used to entice young men to play soccer for the Geelong Makedonia soccer club after its establishment in 1959. One of the founders and administrators of the club, Jim Angelovic, in an effort to strengthen the team, attended Port Melbourne dock looking to recruit new arrivals from Dragosh and the surrounding villages with assurances that he would find them work and accommodation in Geelong. Many of these young men went on to work in the Ford factory.[26]

The Geelong Macedonian community regularly came together for social events, and one of the most popular gatherings was the annual Australia Day picnic held at Lake Burrumbeet near Ballarat. However, it was the 'Geelong picnic' held on 25 December each year at Eastern Beach since at least the 1940s that attracted thousands of Macedonians from Melbourne and the Geelong Macedonian community. It was one of the biggest events on the Melbourne Macedonian social calendar and provided an opportunity after the picnic to visit relatives and friends in Geelong.

Small business: Melbourne

Fitzroy was Melbourne's first suburb and located two kilometres from the Melbourne central business district. It was a run-down working-class area with a tough reputation. For many of the first Macedonian arrivals, Fitzroy was the base from which they left Melbourne to go work in the Victorian bush and the place to which they returned. Fitzroy and the surrounding suburbs contained numerous factories and industrial facilities; however, newly arrived ethnics could only obtain work as dishwashers and kitchen hands in hotels and restaurants and ethnic-operated businesses. The brothers Atanas and Done Theodorovsky from Buf village arrived in Melbourne in 1924. Done's first job was working as a dishwasher in an ethnic-operated hotel, before gaining employment as a kitchen hand at the Victoria Hotel in Little Collins Street where the chefs were Russians. Done left dishwashing in Melbourne to cut railway sleepers in Gippsland and in Eden (New South Wales), seeking to earn more money before his wife Lenka and son Alex arrived in 1937.[27] Angele Angelovic from Dragosh village (Bitola) worked for two years, from 1937 to 1939, in a restaurant in Swanston Street, opposite the Melbourne Town Hall, and, in the 1940s, Mitre Veljanovski, when not in the bush producing eucalyptus oil, worked in hotels and restaurants in Melbourne including a period working as a cook at the Victoria Hotel in the city.[28]

Ethnic-operated small businesses were often small manufacturing businesses, and could also be, at times, a source of labour exploitation of newly arrived migrants. In 1933, *The Argus* newspaper reported that five Macedonian employees of a Bulgarian-owned shoe manufacturing company operating in Fitzroy complained of being paid below the award wage and working excessive hours. The employees stated that their hours of employment were 15 hours per day on weekdays and twelve hours on Saturdays. The matter was initially heard at the Fitzroy Magistrates Court which ruled against the shoe manufacturer, Anghel Petroff. Petroff appealed the decision and the matter went to the County Court, where the finding was made in favour of the five Macedonian employees.[29] Similarly, on the outskirts of Melbourne in the market garden industry of South Werribee a Macedonian farmer that routinely hired Macedonian workers maintained unrealistic expectations of the amount of work that they should do and denied his workers reasonable rest breaks.

Macedonians established their own businesses in Fitzroy, many centred on Gertrude Street, as well as surrounding suburbs. One of the earliest businesses was a fish and chip shop opened in 1926 in Gertrude Street by a Macedonian from Velushina village (Bitola).[30] In and around Gertrude Street, hairdressers, restaurants, cafés, fish and chip shops, bakeries, grocery stores, mechanical workshops and other businesses were established. As Macedonians continued arriving, businesses flourished as they met the needs of the community. In the 1950s, a number of Macedonian-owned real estate businesses operated in the Fitzroy area, assisting members of the Macedonian community to purchase homes and investment properties. A well-known real estate business was Jim Sapurmas Real Estate (Gorno Kleshtina village, Lerin), situated at 120 Gertrude Street, which advertised in *Makedonska Iskra*, declaring that it was located 'right in the heart of the Macedonian community and social centre'.[31] One of the longest running Macedonian-owned businesses in Gertrude Street was the Medal Boot and Shoe Repair, operated for over half a century by Tony Carroll from Buf village (Lerin) and his wife Mary. Renowned for manufacturing the best quality motorcycle boots, they supplied riding boots to Victoria Police for many years.[32]

Macedonians would come to have a strong presence in the fish and chip shop industry in Melbourne and other large urban centres across Australia. Interestingly, the perception of the Greek connection to the fish and chip shop industry in Australia is overstated and confused due to a large number of Macedonian fish and chip shop operators coming from under Greek rule. In Jim Vellios's *Faded Memories– Life and Times of a Macedonian Villager*, he explains that 'at one time, it was commonly said that every fish and chip shop seemed to be owned and operated by "Nick the Greek". This was partly true but, in reality, many *Nicks* were in fact Macedonians'.[33] From at least the 1940s, fish and chip shop businesses have been popular with Macedonians. For instance, in 1944, after selling his farm in Shepparton, Boris Giamov from Trnava village (Lerin) returned to Melbourne and purchased a fish and chip shop in Queensberry Street Carlton, from another Macedonian named Jovan from Kladorabi village (Lerin). Boris moved his family into the residence above the shop and operated the business for two years. At around the same time Kole, from Kotori village (Lerin), operated a fish and chip shop in Brunswick Street, Fitzroy, whilst Done Opashinov from Buf village (Lerin) operated a fish and chip shop in North Melbourne. Aleksandar Theodorovsky left Fitzroy in 1947 and purchased a fish and chip shop in Bentleigh.

Macedonian migration increased considerably after the end of the Civil War in 1949, with many settling in Fitzroy and surrounding suburbs. Pavle Velov was seventeen years old when he arrived in Melbourne in 1956. Together with his younger brother and mother, they moved into a home in Young Street, Fitzroy, that his father had purchased earlier. As Pavle recalled, at that time there were so many Macedonians arriving every day, 'it seemed as though every second house in Fitzroy and Collingwood was Macedonian'. Kosta Kotchoff lived in Charles Street, Fitzroy, in the 1950s and noted that 'Fitzroy was like a second Lerin region' and that in many respects 'it did not feel that we were in a foreign land – that we were still in Macedonia'. Fitzroy became 'the social centre for the Macedonian community',[34] with the Fitzroy town hall a regular venue for community dances, fundraisers and gala events, including 'Miss Macedonia' competitions. The first Macedonian soccer team in Melbourne was based in the area in the 1940s and the first Macedonian church in Australia was established there.

The utilisation of public open spaces for everyday community socialising was replicated in the suburbs of large urban centres where concentrations of Macedonians resided. The Exhibition Gardens in Melbourne, near Fitzroy, was a popular meeting place for Macedonians in the 1950s and 1960s. People walked to the gardens, others travelled by public transport, and those who owned motor vehicles drove there. Single young men would meet up in the gardens before going out to Macedonian community functions and clubs in the city. Many refer to it as being like the famous central promenade in Bitola, the *korzo*; however, it also resembled the outdoor social space of a traditional village square. Interviewees fondly reflected back to that time stating 'it was a meeting place for our people' (John Nitson), 'every Saturday all roads led there...and there were hundreds, possibly a thousand, Macedonians there every weekend' ('*Sekoja sabota site patoj odeja tamu*', Pavle Velov), 'you would find whoever you wanted there' ('*ke go naideshe kogo sakash tamu*', Vancho Kalcovski) and another stated 'everyone from Lerin was there' ('*Lerinsko beshe tamu*', Kosta Kotchoff).

Photo 40: The Traianos family from Kuchkoveni village (Lerin) during an outing to the Exhibition Gardens (Carlton Gardens), Melbourne, 1958. The Gardens was a popular social meeting place for the Macedonians that lived in Fitzroy and the surrounding suburbs during the 1950s-60s. (Source: Faye Stokes – nee Traianos/Nacov).

One of the smallest suburbs in Melbourne, Fitzroy had an extraordinarily high number of pubs and a reputation as a rough working-class area. After their economic consolidation, in the 1970s Macedonians commenced moving out of the area yet maintained a warm and fond connection with their time in Fitzroy. Kosta Kotchoff lived in Fitzroy in the 1950s and at one time rented a room in the backyard of the notorious Mahoneys, well-known Irish ruffians. Kosta recalled, 'People were scared of Fitzroy – they thought it was not a good place, but I found it to be the best place in Melbourne'. Similarly, Tony Kotsopoulos lived in Fitzroy as a young man in the 1950s and remembered it as a 'beautiful' place and that it was safe to walk anywhere at any time of night.[35]

Powerful connections were formed with the suburbs Macedonians lived in and it is no coincidence many became supporters of Australian Rules football clubs Fitzroy and adjacent Collingwood. The connection would transcend generations within families. Andon Delov arrived from Armenoro village (Lerin) in 1957 and, after initially staying in North Fitzroy, he soon bought a home in Collingwood opposite Victoria Park, then the home ground of Collingwood Football Club. Andon and his children became supporters of the club, and his grandchildren and great grandchildren continued this tradition into the twenty-first century.

'It was their home': the Builders Arms and the Aboriginal community in Fitzroy

In 1950, Chris Soklev arrived in Australia as a six-year-old from Klabuchishta village (Lerin). The family first lived in Shepparton for a short time before moving to Melbourne, initially settling in Hawthorn, but wishing to be closer to other Macedonians they made their way to the Croxton locality of Northcote. As a young man, no older than 16 years, Chris and his friends were drawn to Gertrude Street and would travel by tram to visit the Macedonian Social Club and then on to a snooker hall just a few doors down which was operated by a Macedonian from Kotori village.

Chris left school early and secured a job working in the postal service, which was known at that time as the Postmaster-Generals Department (PMG). During his employment there he was given the nickname 'PMG', and Chris has carried the name Chris 'PMG' ever since.

Tall, strong and with a solid build, in 1965, his friend and bouncer at the Builders Arms hotel in Gertrude Street, Boshko (Josif) Ognenovski (from the Bitola region), offered Chris a night-time job working with him as bouncer. The Builders Arms had a reputation as one of the roughest pubs in Melbourne. For the next two years Boshko and Chris had their hands full keeping the patrons in order and at times the pub licensee, an ex-Olympic weightlifter from Latvia, would get involved in the fracas.

A part of Fitzroy's character was its toughness and over time Chris had worked at several pubs including the Rob Roy and the Renown Hotel, both also on Gertrude Street. At one time the owners of a pub in Carlton hired him to 'clean it up' and after six months, which included a shooting incident in the bar, the pub quietened down to enable Chris PMG to return to the Builders Arms.

A few years later in 1977, Chris 'PMG' bought the license for the Builders Arms together with another Macedonian John Zikos from Banica village (Lerin). There was always a large number of Aboriginals who attended the Builders Arms, and some could be difficult at times when intoxicated. Chris always tried to amicably resolve issues as best he could, but also relied upon respected Aboriginal leaders such as Sonny Booth, who was a 'straight shooter' in the community and could sort out problems between his people. Aboriginals were always welcome at the Builders Arms, and the nearby Royal Hotel, which was also owned by a Macedonian, but there were other hotels where they were not so welcome. Chris knew that Aboriginals had suffered under White Australia, and as a Macedonian he felt a connection to their plight as a dispossessed people. He knew Australia was the lucky country for some but not for the Aboriginals. Chris was grateful that, in Australia he was able to economically advance, become a business owner and could freely remove the shackles of Greek subjugation. When Chris arrived, he came with a Greek imposed surname, Sotiriadis; however, in democratic Australia he was able to legally change this back to his original Macedonian name, Soklev.

There was a large presence of Aboriginal people in Fitzroy in the 1970s and they obtained their medical needs from the dedicated staff at the Aboriginal Health Service which was located across the road from the Builders Arms. The Fitzroy Stars Boxing Gym was just a few doors further down. About 80 per cent of all patrons at the Builders Arms were Aboriginal people; other patrons included Macedonians, who had their own separate section and they were always well looked after by Chris, who would take their car keys from them if they had drunk too much or would lend them money when they needed help; Serbs also frequented the pub, at times paying for their drinks with opals they had mined at Coober Pedy; there were a group of tough union men the Painters and Dockers; and quite a few well-known criminals including the infamous Mark 'Chopper' Read. Although the dominant cultural group was Aboriginal, multicultural harmony prevailed in the Builders Arms, and Chris 'PMG' noted that the Aboriginals considered that Southern and Mediterranean Europeans, especially if they were olive skinned, had also experienced racism from White Australia.

Every Thursday to Saturday night the pub was bustling with people, mostly local Aboriginal people. Newly arrived Aboriginals to Fitzroy quickly learned that the Builders Arms was the place to gather to find friends and relatives and meet others. Chris 'PMG' recounted how one Aboriginal family regularly came from Silvan, 50 kilometres away; they would quietly sit together, not drink any alcohol, but 'came so they could be with their own people'. The Aboriginals had a sense of ownership of the pub; Chris 'PMG' stated, 'it was their home … they liked to share with others, they liked to be together'. 'They were the first ones waiting for the doors to open and the last ones to leave'. One time, they started a fire on the floor in the lounge area as part of an Aboriginal ceremony, and although it was quickly extinguished by hotel staff, the burn mark that remained on the floor was a constant reminder that it was a place of importance to the Aboriginal community. Culturally, the Builders Arms may have been significant, but it was not for the faint-hearted; over the five years that Chris PMG ran the business, there were four murders associated with the place – two at the bar – which included a shooting and a stabbing.

Chris would meet many colourful personalities at the Builders Arms, and sometimes the most unlikely people would arrive. The Aboriginal former World Champion boxer Lionel Rose was a regular and was particularly well-loved by the Aboriginal community. After a chance meeting with William Cheung, a world-renowned grandmaster of Wing Chun kung fu, William would come every Tuesday morning to teach Chris how to use nun chukkas while

Chris's mates would show up just to watch the master at work. Following some dedicated training, Chris became quite skilled at the art of nun chukka and always kept a pair under the bar just in case. When Muhammad Ali visited Melbourne in March 1979, as a renowned activist for Black Power and a voice for oppressed peoples, he went to Gertrude Street and visited the Aboriginal Health Service. Word quickly spread amongst the Aboriginal community that the world champion boxer was in Gertrude Street, and Aboriginal people arrived in their hundreds. The gathering spilled over the road and Ali was brought inside the Builders Arms where Chris 'PMG' proudly shook hands with him. Macedonians, Italians, Turks, Greeks, Serbs – everyone tried to get into the pub that afternoon for a glimpse of Ali.

While Chris was busy running the Builders Arms, his wife Pauline (from Lagen village, Lerin) had established a successful hairdressing salon in Lalor, where the family had already moved, to be among the large Macedonian population in that area. Chris enjoyed life in Lalor, he had many friends there and it was close to his beloved Preston Makedonia soccer club. After five years operating one of the roughest pubs in Melbourne, Chris 'PMG' left the Builders Arms, for a much quieter life working for VicRail.

Factory work: Melbourne

Macedonians missed the fresh air and green fields, and the valleys and hills surrounding their villages. In contrast, they came to work in noisy factories and worked long hours, seeing little sunlight and seeking as much overtime as they could get in order to accelerate their economic advancement. This involved firstly paying off the loan they had borrowed for the fare to Australia, saving for a home or intending to pay off their home sooner. Economic growth in the 1950s and 1960s saw an increasing demand for workers in the manufacturing sector. Employers of Macedonian immigrants during this period included: Elastic Webbing in Victoria Parade, Collingwood; Leggett Rubber Industries in Doonside Street Richmond; Rosella Factory in Richmond; Carlton and United Breweries in Victoria Parade, Abbotsford; and Goodchild Shoes in Cromwell

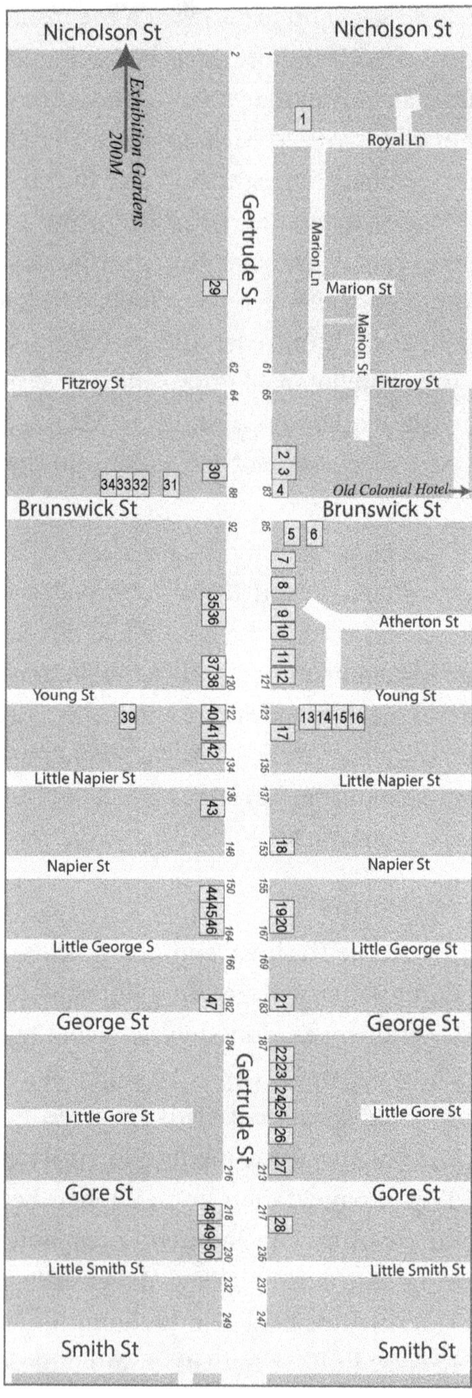

MAP 6 – Gertrude Street Fitzroy – Macedonian commercial presence 1940-1980.

Legend – Gertrude Street Map

No.	Macedonian church or business	No.	Macedonian church or business
1	Macedonian café - established 1930s. Royal Lane	26	Makedonia United Club 203 Gertrude St
2	Boarding House 81 Gertrude St	27	Builders Arms Hotel 211 Gertrude St
3	Boarding House 83 Gertrude St	28	Restaurant/café 229 Gertrude St
4	Rob Roy Hotel 51 Brunswick St (Cnr Gertrude St)	29	Restaurant/café Approx. 40 Gertrude St
5	Boarding House 58 Brunswick St	30	Fish and chip shop Approx. 80 Gertrude St
6	Hamburger shop 64 Brunswick St	31	Boarding House 35 Brunswick St
7	Balkan Café 91 Gertrude St	32	Boarding House 29 Brunswick St
8	Adelaide Club 99-101 Gertrude St	33	Boarding House 27 Brunswick St
9	Billiard hall/Pool room 107/109 Gertrude St	34	Boarding House 25 Brunswick Street
10	Macedonian Social Club (Lagen club) Original location. 111 Gertrude St	35	P. Nicolitch Photographer 108 Gertrude St
11	Macedonian Club 115-117 Gertrude St	36	Card joint (upstairs) 110 Gertrude St
12	Milk Bar 119 Gertrude St	37	Barber (Sime) 118 Gertrude St
13	Boarding House 76 Young St	38	Jim Sapurmas Real Estate 120 Gertrude St
14	Boarding House 78 Young St	39	Sveti Giorgi, Macedonian Orthodox Church, 52-54 Young St
15	Boarding House 80 Young St	40	Macedonian club (upstairs) 122 Gertrude St
16	Sveti Kiril i Metodi, Independent Macedonian Orthodox Church, 82-92 Young St	41	Delicatessen/Grocery 126 Gertrude St
17	Card joint (upstairs) Approx. 127 Gertrude S	42	Fish and Chip shop 130 Gertrude St
18	Card joint 153 Gertrude St	43	Restaurant/cafe 140 Gertrude St
19	Vardar Restaurant 161 Gertrude St	44	Auction House 156 Gertrude St
20	Continental tailor 163 Gertrude St	45	Record shop Approx. 158 Gertrude St
21	Auction House 183 Gertrude St	46	Medal boot and shoe repair 160 Gertrude St
22	Barber 191 Gertrude St	47	Petrol Station 182 Gertrude St (Cnr George St)
23	Restaurant 193 Gertrude St	48	Macedonian Social Club (Lagen club) 218 Gertrude St
24	Restaurant 197 Gertrude St	49	Vardar Club 222 Gertrude St
25	Restaurant/café 199 Gertrude St	50	Shoe manufacturer 226-228 Gertrude St

Street, Collinwood, amongst others. Twenty-three-year-old Kosta Kotchoff arrived in Melbourne in 1950 from the mountainous village Konomladi in the Kostur region of western Macedonia. Prior to Kosta's arrival his father arranged a job for him at Elastic Webbing in Collingwood through Jani Pandzhari, from Nevoljani village (Lerin), who was a foreman there. In contrast to the outdoor work Kosta performed in his village in Macedonia, at Elastic Webbing he was indoors, working a twelve-hour shift, one week on day shift commencing from 7.00 am and the following week on night shift from 7.00 pm. He found it difficult adjusting to the rotating weekly shifts; however, the biggest challenge was coping with the unbearable industrial noise from the large machines in his particular work area and, even after finishing his shift, he could still hear the buzzing sound in his head. After three months, he left Elastic Webbing for the Victorian Railways where he remained until he retired from the workforce.

Elastic Webbing was a popular workplace throughout the 1950s and 1960s, with a majority of the 700 employees Macedonians. In 1962, 18-year-old Vancho Kalcovski arrived from the mountainous village of Brajchino in the Prespa region and initially moved in with his brother Giorgi in Clifton Hill. Giorgi also organised a job for him at Elastic Webbing where he worked for 15 years. Vancho found the pay was good and overtime routinely available, which helped him advance economically. There was an abundance of work available in the manufacturing industry during the 1960s and Vancho regularly worked long hours, taking all the overtime he could get. Recently married, he was committed to working hard and his work ethic was noted by the factory owner who asked him to bring other hard-working Macedonians to the factory and he was paid an extra week's wage for each new person hired.

Macedonian women traditionally worked in the village, looking after livestock, working the fields and performing domestic duties. In Australia, Macedonian women maintained their customary role of actively supporting the household through employment and were rarely stay-at-home mothers. They would become most prevalent in the textile industry where many worked on a 'piece work' arrangement which saw them paid on the amount of work completed, instead of payment on an hourly rate. Amongst the textile factories that Macedonian women worked in from the 1950s included Yarra Falls Mills (Abbotsford), Prasby Knitting Mills (Collingwood), Sterling (Fitzroy), Pelaco (Richmond), Gloweave (Fitzroy), and numerous other smaller companies. During the 1950s and 1960s, many found work at the Foy and Gibson factory complex in Collingwood which had operated since the late nineteenth century, was a major employer in the area providing goods for the company's department stores, and produced men and women's clothing as well as furniture, hardware and bedding.

One of many Macedonian women who spent her entire working life in the textile industry was Kathy Kalcovski (Delov/Foudoulis). Kathy arrived in Australia as a 15-year-old from the village Armenoro (Lerin) in 1960. Three days after arriving in Australia, her father, Andon, arranged employment for her at Gloweave, a shirt manufacturing company in Fitzroy. Kathy worked at Gloweave for thirty years, across all sections of the factory before moving into a managerial role. In 1960, 220 were employed at Gloweave and Kathy was one of only 20 Macedonians; however, within the space of a decade, more than half the workforce was made up of Macedonian women.

Macedonians worked in the meatworks industry of Melbourne's inner west from at least the 1950s, travelling from Fitzroy and surrounding areas, attracted to the higher wages that the industry offered. From the 1970s, Macedonians came to dominate the meatworks industry, following their mass arrival from the Republic of Macedonia and settlement in the inner western suburbs. Most Macedonians had come to Australia from rural villages, where all households maintained livestock, essential for the family's sustenance. Meat in the villagers' diet came from the farm animals on the family farm, and these were slaughtered by male members of the household (however women would kill chickens). Macedonians were used to slaughtering farm animals and familiar with the processes of meat prepa-

Photo 41: Macedonian women at the Gloweave shirt factory in Fitzroy (Melbourne) circa 1985. The textile industry was a major employer of Macedonian women and Gloweave had a workforce overwhelmingly made up of Macedonian employees. (Source: Kathy Kalcovski).

ration and preservation. Men worked as slaughtermen, boners and butchers, whilst women worked as meat cleaners and packers.[36] Varying numbers of Macedonians worked across the meatworks of the inner western suburbs at Gilbertson's Meatworks (later Greenham's), Angliss, Borthwick's and Smorgons. As many as 70 per cent of the 3000 employees at Smorgons during the 1970s were Macedonian men and women. Entire sections of the workforce were almost exclusively made up of Macedonians. For example, 80 per cent of the workers on the mutton chains, beef chains and the boning rooms were Macedonians.[37]

Housing

As Macedonians became more affluent, in the 1970s many began to leave Fitzroy and the surrounding areas, moving predominantly towards the northern suburbs, with others settling in eastern suburbs such as Doncaster, Balwyn and Kew. The initial movement north was to the Northcote/Thornbury area, then to Preston/Reservoir and

Thomastown/Lalor where they acquired new brick homes on large blocks of land, furnished them well and paid them off quickly. Home ownership was always important to Macedonians, as in their villages they owned their own homes, and ownership represented an integral sign of successful permanent settlement in their new home – Australia.

From the late 1960s and particularly in the early to mid-1970s, large waves of Macedonians arrived from the Republic of Macedonia. Similar to the bulk of Macedonians that had arrived before them, whether from under Greek or Yugoslav rule, the average Macedonian came from rural villages and typically lacked formal education beyond primary school level. Between 1965 and 1970, 22,000 emigrated from the Republic of Macedonia, with almost all coming to Australia.[38] Significantly greater numbers migrated during the 1970s. In Melbourne, many settled alongside established Macedonian communities in the inner northern suburbs whilst a large group moved to the inner western working class suburbs of Melbourne, particularly Yarraville, Seddon and Footscray, due to the availability of inexpensive accommodation and an abundance of employment opportunities, in particular, the meatworks and textile industries. In the 1980s, a similar process occurred in the inner western suburbs, as occurred earlier around Fitzroy, in that, as they became established, there was a movement into newer outer suburbs. The movement of Macedonians out of inner areas to outer suburbs has been replicated in other Australian urban centres, such as Sydney and Perth.

The passenger list from the Italian passenger ship *Achille Lauro*, which docked in Melbourne on 7 May 1966, provides an insight into the suburbs where Macedonians first settled, as the intended address for the new arrivals was recorded on the manifest. Seventy-four Macedonians were identified as disembarking in Melbourne. Of those that settled in Melbourne, the majority (over half) went to Fitzroy and the surrounding suburbs (inner northern suburbs), followed by the inner west, whilst another group went to Geelong, primarily to Geelong West (Table 9.1).

Place of residence	Number of Macedonians	Percentage of total
Fitzroy	20	27
Inner North (Carlton, Clifton Hill, Alphington, Thornbury, Northcote)	21	28
Outer North (Reservoir, Thomastown)	3	4
Inner West (Footscray, Yarraville, Spotswood, Newport, Altona North)	17	23
Geelong (Geelong, Geelong West, Bell Park)	13	17

Table 9.1: Destinations in Melbourne and Geelong for Macedonians arriving in May 1996 (source: *Achille Lauro* passenger list).

The movement to outer areas was driven by a desire to improve themselves, much in the same sense that traditionally the *pechalbar* went abroad and earned income with which he returned to the village, constructed a new and larger home and purchased more agricultural land. This was the sign of his success; of the sacrifice he had made abroad. In Australia, the original homes they lived in were typically of timber construction, Victorian- style single-fronted workers' cottages or double-fronted period style homes, usually on small blocks of land; the new homes to which they moved were of brick construction with three, four or more bedrooms, multiple bathrooms, a driveway and garage for two vehicles on a large block of land. Many built large houses believing that their children would marry, and they would live together, and the grandparents would help raise the grandchildren as had been the norm back in Macedonia.

The size of the land on their new home was important as it provided the space to set up a *bafcha*, the prized vegetable patch. Often a large portion of the available space would be dedicated to the *bafcha*. Chillies, tomatoes, cucumbers, garlic, onion and other vegetables were grown, with chillies, in particular, being popular due to their being a staple food source in Macedonian cuisine. The vegetable patch connected people to their traditional agricultural way of life in the village. The *bafcha* would be carefully tended with special manure obtained to fertilise the soil, often directly from farms, and the produce gave them a sense of pride. The backyard became a place where people could carry on traditions from their homeland and maintain cultural identity.[39]

In *Australian Backyard Gardens and the Journeys of Migration*, the authors found that for many migrants, 'the production of food in their backyard in Australia continued the pattern of life from their homeland'.[40] A Macedonian participant, Gore from Figtree (Wollongong, New South Wales) talking about bringing traditions and plant varieties stated: 'And every tradition from there we brought it here, so that's why we are making gardens and trying to produce chillies and tomatoes or something little, in a way to remind us of there, but somehow to have the taste from there brought here, and to continue the tradition of making produce and something from the soil.'[41] The study found that the Macedonians spoke of the backyard 'as a place that made them happy.'[42]

Photo 42: Annual wine making in the backyard of a home in the inner-western suburbs of Melbourne, 1968. (Source: Mihailo Anastasovski).

Another important tradition carried over from the homeland, and maintained by Macedonians in Australia, was the annual making of wine. Grapes would be purchased from a designated place where trucks would bring the grapes from country areas specifically for wine making. There you would find Macedonians, Italians and perhaps some Serbs and Croatians with trailers and utes buying boxes of white or black grapes, or a mixture of both in their endeavour to produce the best wine they could, as the finished product was a source of pride for each family. Many also used the leftover from the winemaking (skin, pulp and seeds) to produce *rakia*, a popular type of Macedonian grappa.

In addition to caring for a *bafcha* and making wine and *rakia*, Macedonians also signalled their connection to their homeland through decorating their homes with nameplates. Historically, nameplates on Australian homes are usually connected to the history of the area or have a geographical basis or some other significance. However, for Macedonians, nameplates erected on their homes usually carried the name of their village or region, depicting an expression of pride in their Macedonian identity and place of origin. Name plates such as 'Lerin', 'This is a Buf house', 'Makedonija', and 'Kostur' appeared and can still be found on some homes in Fitzroy and Clifton Hill. The placing of nameplates can be simultaneously interpreted as evidence of permanency- of Macedonians making Australia their home, as well as their ongoing, powerful connection to their homeland.

10

Urban Social Hubs: Cafés, Clubs and Boarding Houses

Enterprising Macedonians established cafés and boarding houses in foreign lands where *pechalbari* communities formed during the nineteenth century in places like Romania, Serbia and Bulgaria, while at the beginning of the twentieth century they catered for the ever-increasing *pechalbar* population in Canada and the United States. Cafés served as a centre for newcomers, as places where they could get a warm-cooked Macedonian meal, where their unofficial social service needs could be met, and as a place of socialising, whilst boarding houses, often part of the same building as the café, provided budget accommodation for newly arrived single men. Macedonian cafés and boarding houses opened across Australian urban centres where Macedonians arrived, seeking information and temporary accommodation before heading out to the bush or upon their return to the city. The earliest cafés and boarding houses were established in Perth, Western Australia in the early 1920s. The first Macedonian café/boarding house in Australia was the *Makedonski Dom* (Macedonian House) at 180 William Street, Perth, operated by Mikaili Peikov, Niko Borshoff and Tanas Borshoff from the village of Babchor (Kostur).[43] Ownership of *Makedonski Dom* changed hands a number of times as new partners bought into the business. In 1927, Kosta Malco from Shestevo village (Kostur) became a partner for a short period, Vasil Turpin from Bapchor village also bought into the business in 1927 and remained a partner until 1929, and during this period Tanas Vishin also had a share in the business.[44]

Makedonski Dom was the place where many new arrivals spent their first night in Australia. One of the owners, Mikaili Peikov, was known to attend Fremantle port looking out for new arrivals from Macedonia. When Lazo Bonakey from Kosinec village arrived at

Fremantle port in 1927 with several men from his village, to their surprise they could hear someone (Mikaili Peikov) calling out *'koi e Makedonec?'* ('Who is Macedonian?'), and quickly made their way to him. Approximately twenty Macedonians from the ship climbed into Mihaili's wood truck and were taken to Macedonian House where they were given information about economic conditions in Australia, where they might find work and what they might expect to earn. Each of the men had brought £40 as required to enter Australia; Mihaili warned them not to send the money back to their families as the Macedonians often did, as they would need the money to survive.[45]

After selling his share of *Makedonski Dom*, in 1927, Kosta Malco established a café and boarding house at 242 William Street, Perth, known as 'Macedonian House'.[46] It was the first stop for many new arrivals from Macedonia and people attended for a wide variety of unofficial social services such as immigration, employment, medical and other matters. Kosta helped Macedonians find work bush clearing, sleeper cutting, on the woodlines in Kalgoorlie and at the goldmines in Cue and Wiluna, and took the men to purchase supplies such as clothes, boots and other equipment from Luisini's store. Purchases were usually on credit with Kosta as guarantee. Kosta also arranged for newly-arrived Macedonians with no experience of sleeper cutting, to partner with an experienced worker and out of every ten sleepers cut, the experienced sleeper cutter would take one sleeper; this would be his commission for training the new worker.[47] Kosta's boarders ranged from young men in their teens to men in their 50s. Kosta's wife prepared meals for the boarders which typically consisted of eggs, bacon, tomatoes, sausages and toast for breakfast, soup and a casserole or stew (the boarders were given two choices) with lots of bread for lunch and dinner. Sometimes when the boarders got homesick, Kosta's wife would bake traditional Macedonian pastries (*maznik* and *zelnik*), as many as ten of them, with leek and feta cheese, eggs, or with pumpkin and other fillings.[48]

Another notable Macedonian café and boarding house was the 'Macedonian and Slavonic Club' at 82 James Street, Perth. Ownership of the club changed hands several times as partners sold their share. In the 1940s, Risto Angelkov from Dambeni village (Kostur) bought into the business in partnership with two other Macedonians, Krumo from Vrbnik village (Kostur/Korcha) and Jonche from the Republic of Macedonia. The café was a popular meeting place for Macedonians and other Slavonic speaking peoples such as Dalmatians and Bulgarians. It was a place for people to meet and get things done. Steve Bonakey from Kosinec village would complete forms for people and many used it as a mailing address to collect mail when they returned from the bush. Farmers and market gardeners from places like Wanneroo and Osborne Park would visit the café when they came to Perth to meet up with people and hear news about Macedonia.[49]

Photo 43: Macedonians gathered at Bridgetown, Western Australia, 1937. Time for rest from the hard work of cutting timber in the bush (Source: Peter Sarbinov).

Bridgetown is located approximately 250 kilometres south of Perth. In 1937 Naum Keremelic from Capari village (Bitola) transformed a large house into the 'Macedonia Restaurant and Boarding House', but it was generally known as 'Macedonia House'. Full board was provided for up to 30 men, and at times there were so many people that tenants would sleep on the veranda. During weekends, at Macedonian Orthodox Easter and Christmas, New Year and other celebrations, hundreds of Macedonians gathered there and were entertained by Macedonian musicians. Macedonia House was a meeting point for Macedonians who lived and worked on farms and in the bush.[50] For others scattered in remote bush areas where there were no Macedonian cafés to attend, they created their own meeting places where they gathered to meet, play cards, smoke tobacco and drink. *Pechalbari* working on farms in the south Gippsland region of Victoria in the 1930s and 1940s would have Sunday get-togethers at the town store in Kernot. One of the men, Chris Kircos, 'would walk the three miles there, cross country, all seasons all weathers, to share gossip with his fellow *pechalbari*'.[51] Spending time with other fellow Macedonians was an important way for the men to share their experiences and maintain a connection with the homeland they left behind.

David Paparusis from Banica village (Lerin) operated a Macedonian café in Fremantle in 1938.[52] From the early 1930s, Macedonians in Adelaide operated several cafés; one of the earliest was the 'Makedonija' café which operated in Hindley Street; other émigré cafés included the 'Macedonian Balkan Club' at 133 Hindley Street operated by Steve Lazenkas in the 1930s and 40s. [53] This became an important meeting point where messages could be left for people and the community notified of events such as film nights and picnics. In New South Wales, cafés and boarding houses operated in Sydney, Wollongong and Newcastle. Nume (Norm) Bonakey from Kosinec village (Kostur), together with a partner, successfully operated a large boarding house in central Sydney until the depression of 1929 hit.[54] In Queensland, a Macedonian café operated in Brisbane in 1938.[55] Riste Sazdanoff from the village of Capari (Bitola) arrived in 1924 and is believed to be the first Macedonian to settle in the Illawara region. He built his own house in Flinders Street, Port Kembla, 'which served as a boarding house, café and gambling joint for the Macedonian men at the steelworks'.[56]

Boarding houses offered cheap accommodation for Macedonians following their arrival in urban centres whilst organising employment in the bush or until they could set themselves up in the city. Boarding houses could be attached to cafés or could operate exclusively as boarding houses. In Melbourne, several Macedonian boarding houses operated in Fitzroy in the 1940s and 1950s. A well-known boarding house operated at 66 King William Street Fitzroy by Stase Kizon (Anastas Ristos Kizos) from Neret village (Lerin). Stase purchased the boarding house in 1950 for the sum of £1,500. The property consisted of seven bedrooms and two bungalows and at the time of purchase was earning £10 a week rent. Newly arrived single Macedonian men sought accommodation at Stase's boarding house, and Stase was on hand to assist when Macedonians were fleeing persecution of the Greek government post-1949. A well-known identity in the Macedonian community, Stase was a people's man, ready to provide assistance with welfare and social service issues to all who needed a hand. Stase operated the boarding house and assisted a great number of Macedonians up until his death in the early 1980s.[57]

Photo 44: At Stase Kizon's boarding house in King William Street Fitzroy, 1962. Kata Biltsouris (Stase's niece, in centre of photograph) with Macedonian boarders. Later when Kata married, she and her husband bought the house next door. (Source: Victor Georgopoulos).

One of the earliest Macedonian cafés in Melbourne was established in Royal Lane, off Gertrude Street, Fitzroy in the 1930s by Atanas Naumov from Neret village.[58] However, the most famous Macedonian café in Melbourne was established in Gertrude Street by Risto Popov from Lagen (Lerin/Kostur) and Petre Popov (no relation), from Neret (Lerin), operating for more than four decades and known as the Macedonian Social Club.[59] Prior to his arrival in Australia, Risto

Popov was convicted by a Greek court for assaulting a military sergeant who had harassed him because of his Macedonian ethnicity. The judge convicted Risto of the assault and fined him 40 drachmas, a significant sum of money. At the time, Risto operated a café in his native village (Lagen) but realised there was no future living under Greek rule and in 1938 he departed for Australia. The first few years were spent working as a timber cutter, clearing farms in the Orbost and Sale districts in Victoria. However, he had no intention of remaining in the bush for long, as he aspired to operate his own business in Melbourne. Using money he had saved from timber cutting, and together with Petre Popov, in 1940 leased a commercial premises at 111 Gertrude Street Fitzroy in the growing Macedonian community in that area.[60] The Macedonian Social Club remains of historical importance to the Macedonian community of Melbourne. It served as a central meeting point and was the place where politics and history were debated, community affairs discussed, ideas born, and many early community meetings held.

Photo 45: Risto Popov operated a café in his native village of Lagen (Lerin) before he migrated to Australia in 1938. Together with Petre Popov, they established the famous Macedonian Social Club in Gertrude Street, Fitzroy (Melbourne). (Source: Risto Gochev).

Patrons were overwhelmingly young, single Macedonian men and for many it was their first stop after arriving from the old country. There they could organise accommodation and employment and socialise with other Macedonians. Others would visit after returning from work in country Victoria and enquire about work in Melbourne. Men arrived from as far as Sydney and Perth as it was the place where they could find a friend or relative or leave a message for them. Melbourne taxi drivers became familiar with the club and new arrivals often with very limited English language skills only needed to mention the 'Macedonian Club' and they would find their way there. The Macedonian Club was well known to contractors who regularly attended seeking to employ Macedonians, who had a reputation as hard workers, and to take them to country Victoria to perform timber cutting and clearing farmland. The upper level of the Macedonian Social Club was used as a boarding house and in the first few years the four upstairs bedrooms provided accommodation for five to six men in each room.[61] This kept costs down for the boarders: to pay board for an entire room would have been an unnecessary luxury. Sleeping arrangements were on a rotational basis, depending on the shifts worked, with some sleeping during the day and others at night. Young, single Macedonian men, mostly from the Lerin region and living in the Fitzroy area, frequented the club in the evenings for traditional Macedonian meals. Mitre Veljanovski, a qualified cook from Draslajca village (Struga), prepared meals at the club from 1950 until 1958, and was a boarder upstairs whilst working there.[62]

The club was a focal point for men in the Macedonian community. It was a meeting place for community activists and many of the early community meetings in the 1940s and 1950s were held there. In the 1960s, villagers from Velushina village (Bitola), who had settled in the inner western suburbs of Melbourne, in Yarraville and Footscray, conducted their initial village committee meetings at the club. Men travelled to the club from considerable distances. Mihailo Anastasovski from Gorno Aglarci village (Bitola) arrived in Australia in 1964. He was one of the first Macedonians to settle in Williamstown and often went to Fitzroy with friends to visit the Macedonian Social Club where he found others with similar political ideals, Macedonian language newspapers were available, and he felt at home there.[63] The Macedonian Club was of great significance to many people: many saw it as 'a kind of embassy'.[64] A large map of united Macedonia was proudly displayed and Risto Gochev recalled newly arrived Macedonians from Aegean Macedonia with tears in their eyes when they saw the map, as maps of Macedonia were forbidden under Greek rule.

The club was also a meeting place for young men before they went out on the town. John Nitson, from Lagen village, was a young man in his late teens at the end of the 1950s. With a group of 20 similar aged young men, all from the village of Lagen living in Fitzroy, Collingwood and Clifton Hill they gathered at the Macedonian Club on weekends before going out to city bars and clubs. John Nitson described the club as 'a place where we could gather and discuss politics, sport and exchange ideas. We heard news regarding Macedonian affairs, and we gathered there pre and post matches played by the Macedonian soccer team. It was our meeting place'.[65] In the 1950s, Australian media portrayed ethnic clubs in negative terms as places of vice where men gambled and partook in other undesirable activities. However, this was in contrast to their true significance which 'constituted a bridge between the old world back home and the new world in Australia'.[66] A 1996 study by Zoran Jovanovski regarding the cultural significance of the Macedonian Social Club to Macedonian immigrants tells how patrons swapped the open fresh countryside of Macedonia and replaced it with surroundings of concrete and smoke; and how monotonous hours of factory work accounted for a large part of their lives so the Macedonian Social Club provided a retreat for the men as they adjusted to their new life in the city. The café was 'a small humble place where men could talk to each other, play cards, and escape the rigours of the real world. It could almost be viewed as having a church-like status among the Macedonian community, where the traditions and cultures are guarded against foreign externalities'.[67] Risto Popov was always there to help people with a range of social service matters, and he was well known for completing immigration documentation to help men bring out their families. For newcomers who found themselves in difficult circumstances Risto would co-ordinate welfare collections and those who were longer established were always on hand to assist.[68] When men with no family in Australia had passed away and there was no one to organise and pay for their funeral, Risto organised for donations to be gathered at the club to ensure a respectable burial.[69] In 1959, Risto Popov brought out his sister's son, Risto Gochev from Maala village to join him in Australia. Arriving at Port Melbourne on the Italian cruise ship *Aurelia*, Risto had not seen his nephew since he was six years old. Risto moved in with his uncle above the club and was given the prized bedroom at the front of the building, overlooking Gertrude Street. Risto worked at the Club where he assisted in the general day-to-day running of the business which included making Macedonian-style Turkish coffee for patrons, serving tables, helping in the kitchen and organising supplies.

Photo 46: The 'Macedonian Embassy' in Melbourne, the Macedonian Social Club, corner of Gertrude and Gore Streets, Fitzroy (Melbourne), 1970. (Source: H2010.105/518d. Pictures Collection, State Library of Victoria. Series – Alan K. Jordan collection).

In 1967, the state government compulsorily acquired the Macedonian Club and a swathe of properties in the area for public housing projects.[70] Risto Popov retired from the business at this time; however, his nephew, Risto Gochev, secured a lease on nearby premises at 218 Gertrude Street, Fitzroy, and continued operating the business from that location in May 1967. With the gradual movement out of the area by the early 1980s significantly fewer Macedonians lived in Fitzroy and the neighbouring suburbs; however, men continued to be drawn to the café travelling from places such as Preston, Thomastown and Lalor in the northern suburbs, and from Doncaster, Bulleen and Balwyn in the eastern suburbs, even though by this time a number of other cafés operated, particularly in the northern suburbs. After 43 years serving the Macedonian community, the club finally closed its doors in 1983 when the building was sold. Other Macedonian cafés operated in Melbourne during the 1950s and 1960s. Of note was a café in Russell Street operated by a villager from Bapchor, and two other cafés in Fitzroy operated by villagers from Neret and Kotori respectively and the Balkan Club in Exhibition Street. Several other Macedonian cafés in Fitzroy and surrounding area were gambling joints for card players. Around 1970, Janko Malinov from Banica village (Lerin) established the Vardar Club at 222 Gertrude Street, Fitzroy, and it became a central meeting place for right-wing Macedonian activists and those connected with the DOOM organisation (*Dvizhenje za Oslobuduvajne i Obidinuvajne na Makedonija*) which advocated for Macedonian freedom and independence.

Photo 47: Young men from Lagen village playing pool in one of the several Macedonian cafés that operated in Fitzroy during the 1950s. (Source: Paul Pappas).

Endnotes

1 J. Vellios, *Faded Memories – Life and Times of a Macedonian Villager*, unpublished, 2014, p. 221.

2 The area in Mayfield where Aleksandar Stefanoff owned the café restaurant was known as 'Pommy town'. It was the first suburb that American servicemen would go to when they left the naval base. George Stefanoff and Margaret Ruhfus (nee Stefanoff) interview.

3 Following the Japanese attack on Australia, Risto Altin was conscripted into the army and sold the restaurant for £1,000. I. Chapovski, *The Macedonian Orthodox Church of St George*, York Press, Melbourne, 1992, p. 28.

4 M. Trajcevski editor, *Kompas*, Spring 2006, pp. 21-22.

5 B. Bozinoski, and V. Krstevski, *Chetvrta Generacija* [Fourth Generation], 2012, pp. 177 and 239.

6 L. Mitreska, *The Macedonians in Rockdale – A Vivid Life*, unpublished, Sydney, 2015, p. 1.

7 A. Glafchev, *The Migrant Experience: From Village to Suburb*, unpublished, http://www.pollitecon.com, pp. 5-6.

8 Risto eventually returned to Melbourne with his family. Autobiographical notes of John (Nake) Kapetanovski, dated November 2011.

9 Hoskins Iron and Steel Works became Australian Iron and Steel from 1928.

10 'The First Pioneers', article by M. Trajcevski in *Informativen Vesnik* [Informative Newsletter], Macedonian Welfare Association of Port Kembla, 2 December 1989, p. 10

11 Ibid., p. 10.

12 M. Trajcevski editor, *Kompas*, spring 2006, op. cit., p. 21.

13 Data compiled by Ilo Kasovich (Kasovski). Each individual Macedonian was recorded by name and approximately 70% of the data also includes their village of origin. Kasovich was from Bukovo village (Bitola) and arrived in Australia in 1927. Eklund states that there were over a hundred Macedonians in the area at that time. E. Eklund. *Steel Town: The Making and Breaking of Port Kembla*, Melbourne University Press, Melbourne, 2002, p. 161.

14 L. Thom, *The Places Migrant Women Found Work in Wollongong 1943-1990*, Migration Heritage Project, Wollongong's Migration Heritage Thematic Study, 'Places Project', p. 2.

15 Ibid., p. 11.

16 'Jobs for women: how BHP was made to change its tune', *Green Left Weekly*, 9 March 1994.

17 Mendo Trajcevski interview.

18 See B. Bozinoski and V. Krstevski, op. cit.

19 George Stefanoff and Margaret Ruhfus (nee Stefanoff) interview.

20 B. Bozinoski and V. Krstevski, op. cit., pp. 444 and 448.

21 Ibid., p. 26.

22 Ibid., p. 45.

23 Ibid., p. 52.

24 Ibid., p. 53.

25 Both Ford and International Harvester have a long association with Geelong. Ford opened its Australian Headquarters there in 1925 whilst International Harvester commenced production of agricultural equipment in 1939.

26 Angele Angelovic's son, Jim, was a bright and energetic eighteen-year-old when he arrived from Dragosh in 1955. Jim attended night school to learn English, worked in his father's restaurants in Geelong, spent periods employed at International Harvester and Ford, worked as a real estate salesman, and eventually went on to become a successful businessman establishing a thriving furniture business with his brothers. Well known in the community, he was always on hand to help newly arrived Macedonians in finding work, accommodation, and organising bank loans to finance the purchase of their first homes.

27 When Done Theodorovsky's family arrived they initially moved in with another family in Fitzroy (also from Buf village), before they rented a home on George Street, Fitzroy. Aleksandar Theodorovsky interview.

28 Ilija Veljanovski interview. A number of Macedonians worked in the Victoria Hotel between the 1920s and 1940s. It is a large and historic hotel and established in 1880 making it one of the original hotels in Melbourne. At one stage it was advertised as the largest hotel in the Commonwealth.

29 *Argus*, (Melbourne) 2 August 1933, p. 9. See also *Argus*, 4 August 1933, p. 6.

30 P. Hill, *The Macedonians in Australia*, Hesperian Press, Perth, 1989, p. 21.

31 *Makedonska Iskra*, October/November 1955, p. 4. Other Macedonian-operated real estate agencies at that time were George Samargis Real Estate, 131 Gertrude Street, Fitzroy, and Dines Estate Agency, 700 Nicholson Street, North Fitzroy.

32 Other notable businesses still operating in the 1980s and 1990s include the Vardar Restaurant, operated by a family from Tetovo, and Skopje Burek, owned and operated by George and Slavica Zileski. Both businesses developed a loyal customer base from locals and Macedonians across Melbourne.

33 J. Vellios, op. cit., p. 221.

34 L. O'Brien, 'The Macedonian Community', in *Fitzroy, Melbourne's First Suburb*, Hyland House, Melbourne, 1989, p. 249.

35 Ibid., p. 251. Like Kosta Kotchoff, Tony Kotsopoulous also commented on the Mahoney's stating, 'They wouldn't touch you if you left them alone'.

36 N. Anastasovski, 'The Arrival and Settlement of Macedonians in the Inner Western Suburbs of Melbourne', *Victorian Historical Journal*, Volume 82, No. 1, Royal Historical Society of Victoria, June 2011, pp. 39-40.

37 Ibid., pp. 40-41

38 S. Karoski, *The Macedonian Community Profile*, Macedonian Australian Welfare Association of NSW, 1983, p.30, quoted from *Australia Government Commission of Inquiry into Poverty, Welfare of Migrants*, 1975, p.56.

39 L. Head, P. Muir and E. Hampel, 'Australian Backyard Gardens and the Journey of Migration', *Geographical Review*, 2004, p. 327.

40 Ibid., p. 338.

41 Ibid., p. 338.

42 Ibid., p. 343.

43 P. Hill, op. cit., p. 50.

44 Connie Sideris interview transcript, op. cit. Mary Turpin interview and Vasil Turpin biographical notes.

45 Lazo Bonakey interview conducted by Connie Sideris in 1982. It is interesting to note that Mikaili Peikov had previously been a *pechalbar* in the United States and spoke English with an American accent as a result.

46 Kosta Malco initially went into this business with another Macedonian, Kole Jufkoff from Bapchor village; however, he soon after bought out Kole's half share.

47 Connie Sideris interview transcript, op. cit., pp. 17-18.

48 Ibid. Kosta Malco would buy food supplies from the markets in West Perth whilst some of the Macedonian market gardeners from Wanneroo would deliver vegetables direct to Malco's boarding house, p. 43.

49 Kosta Angelkov autobiography (unpublished), p. 92.

50 S. Sarbinov, *Makedoncite vo Avstralija, 1940-1988* [The Macedonians in Australia 1940-1988], unpublished, p. 1. Macedonia House operated until the 1950s.

51 J. Harper, 'The Pecalbars of Gippsland: Macedonian Farm Workers around Kernot in the 1930s', *Gippsland Heritage Journal*, No. 28, Kapana Press, Briagolong, 2004, p. 28.

52 L. O'Brien, op. cit., p. 248.

53 A. Glafchev, op. cit., p. 6.

54 Vanka Bonakey (wife of Nume) interview conducted by Connie Sideris, 1982.

55 M. Trajcevski, editor, *Kompas*, Vol 2, issue 4, p. 14.

56 M. Trajcevski, *Macedonian Migration to the Illawarra*, from *Ties with Tradition - Macedonian Apron Designs*, Powerhouse Museum, Sydney, 2009, p. 7.

57 Victor Georgopoulos interview. Details regarding the purchase price of the boarding house and rental income (produced at the time of purchase) derived from property settlement documentation. At the time Stase purchased the boarding house, he was living at 39 Palmer Street Fitzroy.

58 P. Hill, op. cit., p. 59.

59 The name Macedonian Social Club was displayed on the front window of the café.

60 Risto Gochev interview. The partnership with Petre Popov lasted until 1945 when Petre sold his share to File Deluchin from Lagen village. File Deluchin later sold his interest in the business to his first cousin, Vasil Deluchin, who remained a partner for many years.

61 Ibid.

62 Mitre Veljanovski was one of few Macedonians at that time in Melbourne from the Republic of Macedonia. In 1956, Mitre brought out his son Metodija and they initially shared a room above the café before Mitre purchased a house in West Preston. Metodija moved into the house whilst Mitre returned to Macedonia in 1958, where he remained for two years before returning to Australia in 1960. Upon his return, Mitre obtained employment as a cook at the Preston and Northcote Community Hospital (PANCH) where he worked for several years. Ilija Veljanovski interview.

63 Mihailo Anastasovski interview.

64 L. O'Brien, op. cit., p. 251.

65 John Nitson interview.

66 Allan Lovell & Associates Pty Ltd, *Fitzroy Urban Conservation Study Review (Report, Planning Guidelines and Thematic History)* prepared for The City of Fitzroy, 1992, p. 30.

67 Z. Jovanovski. *The importance of cafés in Carlton and Fitzroy to settling migrants during the 1950s and 1960s was striking; in particular, the cultural significance of the Macedonian Social Club in Gertrude Street, Fitzroy, to Macedonian immigrants*, p. 6. (unpublished), www.unimelb.edu.au/infoserv/lee/htm/carlton_cafés.htm

68 Risto Gochev interview.

69 Vancho Kalcovski interview.

70 Risto Popov sold 111 Gertrude Street, as well as two other adjoining properties at 113 and 115, to the Victorian Government.

Part Five

Inescapable Politics: From War and Religion to Interference and Intimidation

11

Commemorating the Old, Defending the New (*Ilindenci* and Diggers)

Ilinden

Macedonians regard the 1903 Ilinden Uprising as a powerful symbol of their centuries long struggle for freedom and an independent homeland. Outside of major religious celebrations such as Christmas and Easter, Ilinden is the principal community event celebrated by Macedonians in Australia, dating back to the arrival of the earliest pioneers.

Ilinden was celebrated in every Macedonian community, large and small, in urban and regional areas. Gatherings were organised in scout, council and trades halls, and, in rural areas with a warmer mid-year climate, such as Crabbes Creek and Geraldton, Macedonians celebrated Ilinden with a community picnic. In the early 1940s, Macedonians in Newcastle came together to celebrate Ilinden in the Merewether scout hall, while in the early 1950s in New South Wales, Macedonians came from Warriewood, Richmond, Newcastle and Port Kembla to celebrate Ilinden in Sydney. At around the same time, the Melbourne organising committee would hire large town halls in central Melbourne, such as Fitzroy or Richmond, as these venues could hold over a thousand guests. Venue walls would be adorned with pictures of Macedonian revolutionary heroes of the Ilinden Uprising, such as Goce Delchev, Dame Gruev, Jane Sandanski, and heroes from the Second World War, such as Metodija Andonov Chento, and Captain Goche from the Macedonian struggle for independence from Greece.

Passionate speeches were made regarding the significance of Ilinden and a band played traditional Macedonian music. Owing to the special status of the Ilinden celebration as a Macedonian national commemoration, there is a tradition in Australia that musical bands perform gratis for this important event. At the 1950 Ilinden celebration in Sydney the performance was by a band made up of Lazo Zhavela, Vangel and Boris Petkov, Alek Chadevich, Jim Delioff and the singers Giorgi Stefanoff and J. Pizhroff.[1]

It is normal practice for an Ilinden celebration to have a priest from the Macedonian Orthodox Church conduct a service (*panahida*) in memory of fallen fighters for the liberation of Macedonia; however, prior to the establishment of the Macedonian Orthodox Church in Australia, this was not possible. In the 1950s, Father Elliott from St Luke's Anglican Church in North Fitzroy conducted services for Ilinden celebrations in Melbourne. Major events in the Macedonian community have traditionally coincided with Ilinden, such as the opening of churches and community centres. For example, when the first Macedonian church was established in Australia, the Sveti Giorgi church in Fitzroy, milestone events corresponded with Ilinden anniversaries, such as setting the foundation stone, the official opening of the church and the first liturgy conducted, dedicated to the fallen fighters of Ilinden.

Special radio programs were organised by MAPL branches in the 1940s and 1950s for Ilinden celebrations where the significance of Ilinden was discussed, recitations of the heroic stories of the freedom fighters retold, and traditional Macedonian music broadcast. These events were of great significance for the Macedonian community at the time, and were seen as an ideal way to promote Macedonian identity and educate Australian society about the history of the Macedonian people and their struggle for freedom. Film nights, conferences and other cultural manifestations were organised such as the '*Eden noyk pred Ilinden*' ('One night before Ilinden') theatre production held at St Luke's hall in North Fitzroy.[2]

Observance of the Ilinden anniversary continues to this day in Macedonian communities across Australia. Commemorative services and ceremonies are held in Macedonian churches and community centres, dinner dances, and a commemoration ceremony at the Shrine of Remembrance in Melbourne each year. Ilinden is a rallying point, uniting Macedonians to remember the sacrifices made for the ideal of independence and statehood and towards the future goal of human rights and freedom for Macedonians who remain subjugated and oppressed.[3] Former freedom fighters from the Ilinden rebellion are known as *Ilindenci* and are revered by Macedonians as they fought against overwhelming odds to remove Ottoman Turkish rule from Macedonia and simultaneously battle Greek, Serbian and Bulgarian paramilitary forces sent into Macedonia to wreak havoc and prepare the ground for its eventual partition.

Photo 48: Stojan Sarbinov (standing) making a speech during an Ilinden celebration in Sydney, 1948. (Source: Peter Sarbinov).

Former Ilinden freedom fighters living in Australia were special guests of honour at Ilinden celebrations. At the 1948 Ilinden celebration in Queanbeyan, NSW, organised by the MANS branch Mladi Goche, guests arrived from as far afield as Captains Flat. Two former freedom fighters (*komiti*) were present, Kosta Pandov and Vasil Anastasov, from Trcije village (Lerin). At the 50-year Ilinden anniversary celebration in Adelaide held at Trades Hall in 1953, Stefo Kalkov from Visheni village (Kostur), a 70-year-old former freedom fighter who participated in the Ilinden rebellion gave a '45-minute fiery speech' about his participation in the Ilinden rebellion and the significance of Ilinden to the Macedonian people.[4]

Atanas Vaslieff (Milankov), from Statica village (Kostur), was born in 1882 and, as an 18-year-old in 1900, took the VMRO oath of allegiance before *voivoda* (military commander) Pando Chulakov and worked as a courier before joining the *cheta* (armed band of men) of Tsilo Konomlatski. Atanas actively participated in the Ilinden battles in the Kostur region; however, following the division of Macedonia, life under Greek rule was difficult, so he left for the United States in 1920 where he worked in Detroit. In the late 1950s, Atanas arrived in Australia to join his family in Queanbeyan, New South Wales, and lived there until 91 years of age.[5] In 1950, the 80-year old former Ilinden freedom fighter Giorgi Kuleov arrived in Sydney, Australia,[6] while Petre Maleganov, from Trcije village (Lerin) arrived in Australia to be with his daughter Jana and her family in Queanbeyan in late 1950, at 90 years of age. He passed away in April 1951 and the funeral service was held in the Anglican Church.[7] Trpo Martinovski, born in 1883, Pozdivishta village (Kostur) fought in the Ilinden rebellion in the *cheta* of the famous *voivoda* Lazar Pop Trajkov from Dambeni village (Kostur) and came to live in Perth, Western Australia. Veljan Ilich lived in New South Wales during the 1940s and was a member of the Sydney MAPL branch, Vesela Makedonija, where he was actively involved in the hospital campaign. Veljan was born in Velmevci village (Demir Hisar) and had taken part in the Ilinden rebellion as a *komita* in the *cheta* led by the famous Bitola region *voivoda* Giorgi Sugarev.[8]

Born in 1881 in Asanovo (Lerin), Krsto Malikov joined the ranks of VMRO in 1901 and, during the Ilinden rebellion, fought to liberate the Lerin region. Post Ilinden Krsto was appointed as a district *voivoda* for the Lerin plain, maintaining the struggle against Ottoman rule and incursions by Greek paramilitary bandits who worked in collaboration with Ottoman forces and brought hardship to the Macedonian population in the region. Krsto's determination, leadership and fighting spirit saw him elevated to regional *voivoda* in 1908. During the First Balkan War in 1912, Krsto was involved in diversion actions in the rear of Ottoman forces in the Bitola/Lerin region, which included blowing up the train line between Bitola and Kremenica. In 1913, Krsto migrated to Australia and made his way to Queensland, but returned to Macedonia in 1914, prior to the commencement of the First World War. At the end of the war he left Asanovo and moved to Bitola where he had earlier married (in 1909); however, life was impossible under Serbian rule and he was forced to escape, leaving his wife Katarina and five children behind. He made his way back to Australia, settling in Deniliquin, New South Wales, where he lived until his death in 1952.[9] The number of Macedonian freedom fighters who participated in the Ilinden Uprising and lived in Australia has not been documented; however, anecdotal evidence suggests that there may have been as many as 50 *Ilindenci* residing in Australia.

Photo 49: Krsto Malikov, fought for the freedom and independence of Macedonia and participated in the Ilinden rebellion of 1903. Later he would make his way to Australia and lived on a farm at Deniliquin, New South Wales. (Source: Dusko Apostoloski and Tale Gogovchevski).

Wartime links between Macedonia and Australia

In the late nineteenth and early twentieth centuries, people in Western countries became familiar with Macedonia, reading stories about the oppression of the Macedonians by the Ottomans, the general state of anarchy in the land and the Ilinden Uprising. After hearing about the Macedonian struggle for freedom from Ottoman rule and the exploits of the Macedonian freedom fighters, brave men from Europe and America seeking adventure and a worthy cause travelled to Macedonia to join the Macedonian *chetas* and partake in the just struggle for liberty. In 1903, Arthur Greenwood Hales, an Australian writer, novelist, and war correspondent, travelled to Macedonia and took part in the fighting against the Turks during the Ilinden Uprising. Hales became familiar with the Macedonians, their struggle, and ethnic characteristics. In the first decade of the twentieth century, there was significant political debate in Australia concerning immigration issues.

Hales considered Macedonians as an ideal people to develop the northern territory of South Australia as they were a hardworking people adaptable to the harsh Australian bush. In 1905, Hales wrote that the agriculturally focused Macedonians are 'wonderfully industrious, frugal, honest and hospitable ... the very type of people that I would like to see settled in the Northern Territory' (the Northern Territory was a part of South Australia until 1911). Hales remarked that the government of South Australia could get '100,000 families of Macedonians to come into the Northern Territory, and a finer race of people to help us to build up a nation could not be found in any portion of the globe'.[10] It is interesting to note that in 1955, the *Makedonska Iskra* newspaper acknowledged Hales's participation as a volunteer in the Ilinden Uprising and honoured him as a fighter for liberty and humanity against tyranny and barbarism.[11]

The destruction and terrible human carnage during war can also connect and bring people together in unlikely circumstances. During the First World War, Australian soldiers participated in military operations alongside British forces in Europe including the Macedonian front. J. J. Elliot, manager of the Smyrna Fig Company in Barmera, South Australia, was so impressed with Macedonians he met whilst serving in the Australian army in Macedonia during the First World War that he induced them to come to Australia to engage in fruit growing. Macedonians helped transform 70 acres of what was useless land into a fine garden on the banks of Lake Bonney. In 1930, the Smyrna Fig Company principally grew tomatoes, but also other fruit and vegetables, and all the workers were Macedonians.[12]

Costa Kapinkoff from Capari village (Bitola) had completed a mechanic's trade in Bitola and, in the early 1940s, was looking for work in Perth in line with his motor mechanic skills. Costa heard from another Macedonian, Naum Sharin that Ford motor company had opened a new car division at Leighton near Fremantle, and he was keen to get a job there. A number of foreigners, however, had obtained jobs at the plant and there were concerns that, if any more foreigners were employed, it might lead to trouble with the Australian workers. When Costa handed the hiring manager, Knight, a copy of his Bitola mechanic's qualification certificate, Knight immediately recognised Bitola as the city close to Kajmakshalan Mountain, where he fought during the First World War as an Australian soldier together with the British against the Germans and Bulgarians. Knight immediately gave Costa a job and he started work the next day.[13]

When Australia joined in the conflict of the Second World War, Macedonians proudly contributed towards the war effort as they were grateful to live in a democracy where they could express their identity without fear of persecution. Committed to the Allied fight against Fascism, Macedonians voluntarily enlisted with the regular army, conducted important support work in the employment companies and invested in Commonwealth government security and war loans.

Mick Veloskey and Ilo Malco became close friends after arriving in Australia in 1935, on board the same ship, to join their fathers who had been living in Western Australia since the 1920s. In 1943, they enlisted for the armed services in Perth, Western Australia, to help defend Australia and fight Fascism. Most enlisted Macedonians were serving in the army or the employment companies. Ilo and Mick, however, were determined to join the Royal Australian Air Force (RAAF) and they believed that changing their names by deed poll to appear Anglo-Australian would guarantee success. Coming from Macedonia under Greek rule, they arrived with Greek names and were pleased to discard them. Ilo Malco's Greek name was Elias Konstantine Malco-Elias, which he changed to Laurie Malcolm, and Mick Veloskey's name was Mihails Iliopolous, which he changed to Michael Elliott. They both succeeded in their aspiration to join the air force and were probably the first Macedonians to do so.[14]

Mick Veloskey's journey in the air force commenced with three months' basic training in Busselton (Western Australia), and then, following a short course in Perth, Mick went to Sydney to complete an electronics course at the Ultimo Technical College before being sent to Melbourne for a course on high frequency radio while stationed at the Melbourne Exhibition Buildings. Following short stints in Darwin and then at the Batchelor air base (Northern Territory), which was an important base for allied air operations throughout the war, Mick was posted to Dutch East Timor at the Panfooi Air Strip in the radio transmission section until the end of the war. Ilo Malco served two years and eight months in the Australian Military Forces and one year as a volunteer in the Second Australian Imperial Force before serving as a Sergeant Air Gunner in the RAAF for 17 months to the end of the war.

A deteriorating shortage of labour in Australia during the Second World War resulted in the establishment of employment companies to undertake construction projects in support of Australian military forces. The Civil Construction Corps established for those with British citizenship and the Civil Aliens Corps was established in May 1943. Alien classification was according to nationality, classifying people as Allied, Neutral, Indeterminate, Refugee or Enemy. Allied Aliens were considered 'friendly aliens'; however, the distinction between classifications was not always clear and depending on their alien category, serving in the Civil Alien Corps was based on conscription for some and voluntary service for others. Alien classification signs were placed on the front of business premises during this period. Aleksandar Stefanoff operated a café restaurant in Maitland Road, Mayfield (Newcastle), and a sign stating 'Friendly Alien' was placed on the front window around 1943, remaining there until the end of the war.[15]

Men supplied labour to construct infrastructure works such as roads and airstrips, they worked on telecommunications projects, or at the wharves, or drove trucks carrying military equipment. They also worked on the trains, loading and unloading military supplies. Although the alien companies were not armed, they engaged in important work and they themselves considered the work to be a valuable contribution to the war effort.[16] Done Theodorovsky from Buf village (Lerin) served with other Macedonians performing military transport and warehousing work in Tocumwal, Albury and Cairns, and maintained a sense of pride throughout his life that he made a positive contribution to the Australian war effort. It is interesting to note that, following the war, those who served in the Alien Civil Corps were not accepted as members in the Returned Services League because they had not been on active service outside Australia. The employment companies, made up of more than 15,000 men, have been almost forgotten from standard histories of Australia and the Second World War.[17]

Citizen Military Forces remained in Australia to ensure home defence – this included the defence of Australian territories in Papua and New Guinea. Later, this was extended to include other areas which fell under the South-West Pacific Zone. Macedonians provided support to those in the front lines and they saw their involvement as important. Men such as Naum Mano from Vrbnik village (Kostur/Korcha) served in Indonesia where he worked as a supply truck driver. Leo Tallas from Pilkati village (Kostur) joined the army in 1942 and was posted to the Australian army base in Lae, Papua New Guinea where he worked in the catering unit.[18] Similarly, Giorgi Mechkaroff from Neret village (Lerin) served in New Guinea as a cook in a mobile kitchen. In 1942, Nume Karajas from Dambeni village (Kostur), and resident of Perth, was conscripted and sent to Northam Army Camp military training base in Western Australia before being posted to the catering corps near Brisbane with other Macedonians, including Trpo Tsalev, also from Dambeni village, where he remained until the end of the war.

Photo 50: Nume Karajas with wife Fana and baby daughter Diana, North Perth, 1943. Nume served in the catering corps in Queensland with other Macedonians during the Second World War. (Source: John Karajas).

Macedonians proudly supported the Australia war effort. They continued, however, to maintain a strong interest in events back in Macedonia. Conscripted in the Citizen Military Forces, Nick Karadzhov had hoped to take a more active and direct part in the war against Fascism, especially as his brother Panajoti was a partisan in Aegean Macedonia initially during the Second World War, and then during the civil war fighting for Macedonian freedom against Greek government forces. In aid of the Macedonian struggle, Nick sent his Australian army uniform to his brother who wore it during the fight for Macedonian human rights and national emancipation. Nick Karadzhov's cousin, Vasko Karadzhov, who was also a partisan fighting for Macedonian rights in Aegean Macedonia during this period, stated after the war that he was envious he did not have a uniform of the same quality.[19]

In addition to supporting the war effort through direct service either in the regular army or the employment companies, Macedonians demonstrated their support for Australia by purchasing war loans and security loans which were issued by the Australian government to generate capital to raise revenue for the war effort. Citizens were encouraged to invest their savings in these loans that promised better rates of interest than the banks. Macedonians wholeheartedly gave their support to the program and community leaders from the MAPL spoke at meetings to raise awareness of the benefit of investing in Commonwealth loans, and how their support would assist the war effort in the fight against Fascism and tyranny. In Manjimup, Western Australia, 56 Macedonians subscribed over £5,000. The achievement was reported in the Sunday Times newspaper under the title 'Tribute to Macedonians'.[20] The Macedonian community undertook a range of activities in support of the war effort. In Perth, community dances were held three times a year, with all proceeds going towards the war effort and Macedonian women in Wanneroo knitted socks to send to Australian soldiers through the Red Cross.[21]

In 1947, the Australian Macedonian Ex-Servicemen's League was founded in Perth, Western Australia, through the Macedonian Australian Peoples League. The initiators of its formation were Mick Veloskey and Ilo Malco. The organisation brought together Macedonians who defended Australia during the Second World War in all capacities, regardless of whether they served in the employment companies or were regular soldiers. The men gathered for meetings, regular reunions and general fellowship in a spirit of pride of service to their adopted homeland, being good role models for younger Macedonians in Australia and, looking towards the future, aspiring for the establishment of an independent and democratic Macedonian homeland.

Photo 51: Macedonian War Memorial commemorating Macedonians who sacrificed their lives for the independence of Macedonian and Australia. Sveti Nikola, Macedonian Orthodox Church, North Perth. (Source: Monument Australia [Bryan Hardy]).

12

MACEDONIAN POLITICS DOWN UNDER

Struggle

For the past few centuries Macedonians have been ruled by others. Macedonians have struggled to have their voice heard as, in much of history everywhere, the rulers have been the ones to tell the stories. During the Ottoman rule (to 1912), Macedonian organisations were formed in countries such as France, Russia and Switzerland, aiming at informing European public opinion of the internal political situation in Macedonia. This was as a reaction to the manipulations presented by the hostile Balkan States who were strategically preparing Macedonia for territorial partition. The widely disseminated narrative from the Balkan States was inspired by the irredentist policies of the governments of Greece, Serbia and Bulgaria. In contrast, the Macedonian position was drowned out by their propaganda. Following the end of Ottoman rule and the 1912-1913 conquest and division of Macedonia, the Macedonian struggle focused on ending persecution and oppression of Macedonians and the reunification of their homeland. Wherever Macedonian diaspora communities formed, associations were established to bring Macedonians together, support the struggle for independence, and inform people in the host country of the Macedonian yearning for freedom and democracy.

In the early twentieth century, the largest Macedonian organisation amongst Macedonian émigré communities in the Western world was the Macedonian Political Organisation (MPO) founded in the United States in 1922.[22] The MPO newspaper, the *Macedonian Tribune* commenced publication in 1924 and, from 1930, it began to arrive in Australia and was distributed through Macedonian cafés. Macedonians who had previously worked in the United States were familiar with the *Macedonian Tribune*, its vehement anti-Greek position in relation to the brutal Greek occupation of Macedonia, and its advocacy of an independent Macedonian nation.[23]

Macedonian Australian People's League

Application was first made in Melbourne to register a Macedonian Political Organisation (MPO club) with Victoria Police in 1934. The applicants submitted a copy of the constitution and by-laws of the union of the Macedonian Political Organisations of the United States and Canada and stipulated that the proposed club would adopt a similar Constitution. It was noted that 'the principal points within the Constitution referred to the freedom of Macedonia and the formation of a Macedonian republic'.[24] The Melbourne MPO chapter, 'Todor Alexandrov', would become the first Macedonian organisation to form in Australia and established its club headquarters at 22 Market Lane, Melbourne, in the mid-1930s. The Todor Alexandrov branch organised some of the first Melbourne Macedonian community events in the 1930s, such as the first MPO picnic in 1936. Risto Avramov from Neret village (Lerin), a Macedonian community activist in Victoria, initiated the formation of the Melbourne chapter.[25] Other MPO chapters were also set up in Shepparton and Adelaide in the 1930s.

Macedonians became disillusioned with the MPO when, in 1941, Germany and Bulgaria occupied Macedonia, and the *Macedonian Tribune* declared that Macedonia had become free. That same year, in September 1941, a group of young men in Perth, who had been coming together socially and engaging in sporting activities (Ilo Malco, Mick Veloskey, Jovan Pizarkoff, Andrea Nikoloff, Todor Todoroff and others), formed one of the earliest Macedonian organisations, Edinstvo (Unity).[26] Edinstvo's slogan was 'free, independent, united Macedonia – a Macedonia for the Macedonians'; similar to the 1897 declaration of William Gladstone, former Prime Minister of the United Kingdom, who famously declared 'Macedonia for the Macedonians'. The first public meeting was held at Kosta Malco's café/boarding house at 242 William Street, Perth. Message was sent out, through word of mouth that a meeting would be held to discuss the establishment of a Macedonian organisation. The organisers expected twenty or thirty people to attend; however, the response exceeded all expectations as there was standing room only. Macedonians came from as far away as Fremantle, Perth and Wanneroo.[27]

Soon after Edinstvo was established, during the Second World War, the young men leading the organisation were mobilised into the Australian armed forces and the leadership of Edinstvo was transferred to and actively managed by three middle-aged men closely connected to the organisation – Naum Sharin (President), Sabko Todoroff (Treasurer) and Pavle Bozhinov (Secretary). Sharin, Todoroff and Bozhinov worked tirelessly for the Macedonian cause and soon had 150 regular financial members.[28] A women's committee was formed and played a key role organising social activities including dances and community picnics throughout the war years. There were no Macedonian newspapers published in Australia or radio programmes at that time, and notification of functions was by word of mouth. Those who operated businesses helped spread the news. Mitcho Pappas from Dambeni village (Kostur), known as Mitcho Furnadzhijata (Mitcho the baker) was a respected community activist who operated a bakery in North Perth and travelled as far as Wanneroo delivering bread to Macedonians during the 1930s and 1940s. He played an important role informing Macedonians of news and events organised by Edinstvo.[29]

Public meetings, radio announcements and telegrams were sent by Edinstvo to foreign governments and international organisations informing them of the plight of Macedonians and, in particular, the terror to which Macedonians were subjected by the Greek government. An example is the cablegram sent to the Council of Foreign Ministers in London in 1945:

> Representing the Macedonian immigrants of Western Australia we appeal on an international level to you in the name of democracy and freedom established at the San Francisco Conference to investigate the brutal terror carried out by the Greek Fascist reaction over the Macedonian people under Greece and to grant independence, with every democratic right, to those Macedonians on the lines already given in Yugoslavia, so that they can, as free Macedonian people, contribute to a peaceful solution of the Balkan problems.[30]

During a public meeting held by the Edinstvo organisation on 24

February 1946, at the Victory Club in James Street, Perth, committee members spoke about the need to have a well -organised community association as, without one, the community would be at a loss and could even disappear ('*zaguba i izchezvane*'). In addition, it was stated that not being well organised would negatively impact on their ability to help oppressed Macedonians in the homeland which they were obligated to do.[31]

There were several Macedonian organisations in Australia by the mid-1940s, mostly concentrated in Western Australia – Edinstvo (Unity) based in Perth, Nova Makedonia (New Macedonia) in Geraldton and Sloboda (Freedom) in Manjimup. Macedonian organisations were also being formed in the eastern states. At that time 120 Macedonians from Aegean Macedonia and 20 Bulgarians were members of the Yugoslav Immigrants Association of Australia and New Zealand, which had 1,800 members in total, overwhelmingly Yugoslav nationals, made up of Croatians and Slovenians who were supportive of Macedonian ambitions for their rights in the Balkans and the formation of an independent Macedonian state.[32] Through its affiliation with the Yugoslav Immigrants Association, Edinstvo received assistance to establish a Macedonian national umbrella body along the same lines as the Yugoslav Association, and the Macedonians in North America who had prior to the Second World War formed an umbrella organisation the Macedonian American People's League *(Makedonsko Amerikansko Naroden Soyuz)* to bring together and co-ordinate the community. Macedonians in Canada had also followed suit and set up the Macedonian Canadian People's League *(Makedonsko Kanadsko Naroden Soyuz)* along the same lines. Inspired by their North American cousins, Macedonians in Australia planned to set up a similar body.

The first national conference of Macedonian organisations was held in Perth on 24 and 25 August 1946 and was attended by representatives from the Western Australian-based branches Edinstvo, Nova Makedonia and Sloboda. Edinstvo was the organiser and host of the conference, with the Edinstvo Women's Committee playing a large part in organising the conference. In support of the Macedonians, delegates from the Yugoslav Association, the Bulgarian progressive group 'Hristo Botev', the 'all Slavic Congress', and representatives from the Australian Labor Party and trade unions from Perth also attended.[33] It was agreed that a national umbrella body would be established, *Makedonsko Avstralijanski Naroden Soyuz* - MANS (Macedonian Australian Peoples League – MAPL) to represent Macedonians and their interests in Australia; that a newspaper, *Makedonska Iskra* (*Macedonian Spark*), would be published on a monthly basis; that an organiser was to be appointed to promote the establishment of branches in other parts of Australia; and a campaign undertaken to raise £10,000 to support the construction of a hospital in the Republic of Macedonia.

Kiro Angelkov was appointed the first President of the Central Committee, a tireless worker for the Macedonian cause, Angelkov departed Perth by train, travelling thousands of kilometres to promote the formation of branches in the eastern states of Australia in areas where Macedonians lived and worked. Ceremoniously farewelled from the Perth train station with great hopes that the undertaking would be successful, Macedonians took heed of the messages delivered by Angelkov and within six months of the inaugural conference in Perth, fifteen new branches were formed across Australia, attesting to the enthusiasm of Macedonians to promote their identity and continue the struggle for freedom and independence. The branches took different names: in Sydney – *Vesela Makedonija* (Joyful Macedonia), Newcastle – *Balkan* (Balkan), Adelaide – *Aleksandar Makedonski* (Alexander the Great), Crabbes Creek –*Sloboda* (Freedom) and Queanbeyan *Mladi Goche* (Young Goche), after the Macedonian partisan leader in Aegean Macedonia who fought for Macedonian independence during the Greek Civil War. Those in regional Victoria included Shepparton – *Vardar* (Vardar) and Sale – *Ljubo Makedonija* (Love Macedonia), while others were established in Richmond, Forbes, and Braidwood in NSW and Kalgoorlie in Western Australia. Numerous unofficial branches provided financial support and were founded in regional areas where Macedonians worked, such as Broken Hill, Katoomba, Mildura and elsewhere. Branches were established in every state in Australia, except Tasmania, where there were probably too few Macedonians and they were geographically too dispersed to set up a branch.

The MANS branches had a significant impact on the lives of the Macedonian community, people rallied around the branches as they became a focal point in the community and forged the community closer together through social activities and gave real hope that the Macedonian aspiration for freedom and independence would be achieved across all subjugated Macedonia and, in particular, Aegean Macedonia where it was optimistically expected to replicate the accomplishments already seen with the establishment of the Republic of Macedonia. The 1947 MANS Conference was held in Melbourne and attended by delegates from communities across Australia, with the newly elected Central Committee reflecting a national organisation. The 12 committee members were made up of Spiro Chloakoff from Geraldton, Ilo Malco from Perth, Kiro Angelkov from Perth, V. Velevich from Sydney, Angel Ristich from Port Kembla, Kiril Murgev from Newcastle, Done Pazov from Crabbes Creek, Tanas Rachkoff from Melbourne, Dane Trpkov from Melbourne, Rade Voinovich from Shepparton, Spiro Ordanin from Melbourne and Mito Saroff from Forbes.

Photo 52: Macedonian Australian People's League National Conference, Melbourne, 1952. Note the pictures of famous leaders from the Macedonian freedom movement on the wall. (Source: Peter Sarbinov).

Community and humanitarian campaigns

The Edinstvo branch pioneered the first Macedonian radio broadcasting program in Australia when, in 1945, a weekly radio program was aired every Wednesday from 7.15 pm to 7.30 pm on radio station 6KY (an Australian Labor Party station). Presented by Mick Veloskey in English, key topics related to the plight of the Macedonians in the Balkans and information about their activities in Australia. To assist the integration of newly-arrived Macedonians to Australia, in 1950 English language classes were organised by the Edinstvo branch. Classes were conducted by Steve Bonakey and held on a weekly basis at the Edinstvo club premises on the corner of James and Williams Streets, Perth.[34]

At the inaugural National Conference in Perth and, following the example of the Macedonians in North America, a Macedonian Hospital Committee was formed *(Makedonski Bolnichki Komitet)* to co-ordinate the campaign to raise funds for the construction of a modern hospital in the Republic of Macedonia. It was the first national fundraising campaign organised by Macedonians in Australia, with a target to collect £10,000, a staggering amount of money at the time. Hospital committees were established across Australia and the campaign, referred to as being for the 'Australian Hospital', produced remarkable success. In the first nine months, 53 committees formed and by August, 1947, twelve months from the commencement of the campaign, £7,357 had been raised.[35] Even though most Macedonians in Australia at the time were from Aegean Macedonia, the success of the campaign demonstrated a close spiritual connection to the newly established Republic of Macedonia.

Community picnics, dinner dances, baby competitions and other social functions were organised with the ladies' section playing a significant part in the campaign which exceeded the set goal and collected £11,024. It is not surprising that the largest amount was achieved in Western Australia where Macedonians had been settled longest (£5,563); in NSW £3,791; Victoria £1,350; and South Australia, £320.[36] £10,000, being the target amount set, was sent to Macedonia for the construction of the hospital and the remaining £1,000 was distributed to a number of hospitals in Australia. In Canada and the

United States, Macedonian communities donated $154,000 towards the hospital campaign.[37] Macedonians in Australia expected that they might have some influence in the decision as to where the new hospital would be built. At the 1947 MAPL conference held in Melbourne it was reported that voting had been conducted across branches in Australia, with the city of Gevgelija selected as the preferred location for the hospital with 2,014 votes out of a total of 4,606.[38] Ultimately the government of the Republic of Macedonia selected the capital, Skopje as the location for the new hospital.

Humanitarian campaigns coordinated through *Makedonska Iskra* were a common activity undertaken by MAPL. While large numbers of Macedonian refugees were fleeing from the pogroms of the Greek Government during the Civil War a committee was established to co-ordinate the collection of clothing for the refugees, to be sent to the Republic of Macedonia aboard the Yugoslav ships *Partizanka* and *Radnik*, which were arriving in Australia to repatriate citizens of Yugoslavia.[39] With great passion and enthusiasm, 57 Macedonians boarded *Partizanka* in December 1947 to assist the Republic of Macedonia to help in its post-war reconstruction and progress. Fifty Macedonians were from Aegean Macedonia and seven from the Republic of Macedonia. Mick Veloskey went 'to help Macedonia get on its feet' utilising technical skills in radio transmissions in which he had been trained while in the Australian Air Force during the Second World War. Mick's younger sister also volunteered to return to Macedonia, working as a stenographer.[40]

With experiences of war, trauma, poverty and oppression in their memory and recent history following uprisings against the Ottoman Turks, devastation caused by the Balkan Wars, the widespread fighting on Macedonia soil during the First World War, as well as the destruction caused by the Greek government in the late 1940s, Macedonian communities in Australia organised fundraising activities in support of humanitarian appeals and projects. There were numerous such examples: in 1940, Macedonians from South Werribee contributed funds to the Werribee branch of the Red Cross Society, while in 1948, Macedonians supported Queensland railway strikers. In 1952, the Macedonian community donated £100 in support of the Lord

Mayor's Hospital Appeal in Melbourne, after having already donated £700 to aid tuberculosis sufferers. In March 1955, proceeds from fundraising events at St Luke's Church Hall in North Fitzroy and from the Macedonian Queanbeyan community went towards flood victims in New South Wales. This tradition of community spirit continues in the twenty-first century; for example, the Village of Bitusha Macedonian Community of Shepparton made a $20,000 donation to Goulburn Valley Hospital in 2014. Other campaigns were conducted, some going back to the 1920s, to aid Macedonians in Australia who had sustained serious injuries through work-related and other accidents, and during times of natural disasters and other tragedies in Macedonia, Macedonians in Australia came together to support their fellow Macedonians.[41]

Photo 53: Following the July 1963 devastating earthquake in Skopje, Macedonia, the Svetlost Folkloric Dance Group dressed in Macedonian national costumes went into the Melbourne central business district taking up collections for the people of Skopje. Later that day they gathered at the Sveti Giorgi, Macedonian Orthodox Church. (Source: Kathy Karlevski).

Traditionally, Macedonian society has been male-dominated and the important role played by women in community organisational activities has been underrated. When the Edinstvo organisation formed in Perth in the early 1940s, a separate women's section was established, as noted, and their valuable contribution towards supporting the goals of Edinstvo, as well as their tremendous fundraising activity towards the hospital campaign, deserved particular recognition. Inspired by the formation of the Macedonian Australian People's League, a reorganised temporary women's committee was set up, until a general meeting was called on 25 July 1948 at the Oreski Club at 82 James Street, Perth, and a formal committee was elected.[42] With great energy and commitment, the Committee went about organising social, cultural and sporting activities. A women's basketball team was established in October 1948 and a theatre group formed to perform the Macedonian classic, *Krvava Svadba*, for its inaugural production. Dances and picnics were regularly organised and, in the late 1940s, dances were held at Trades Hall (Beaufort Street, Perth), and picnics were often held on farms belonging to Macedonians, such as the picnic held on George Geneff's property in Osborne Park in October 1948. Buses to convey people to the picnic were organised to leave from the Macedonian Club in James Street, Perth.[43]

The Women's Committee provided leadership for the purchase of a Macedonian community hall. In September 1948, the Committee set a task to purchase a property for use as a Macedonian community hall to serve the needs of the community. It established a Community Committee (*Naroden Komitet*) comprising nine members, made up of three representatives from the Women's Committee, three from Edinstvo, and three from the Macedonian soccer team whose role would be to locate a hall to be purchased.[44] There is no doubt that, without the support and organised activity of the Women's Committee, the Macedonian community of Western Australia would not have progressed to the high level of achievement attained in all spheres of community life, including social, cultural, educational and sporting accomplishments.

May Day and Russia Day parades

Macedonian political activity in Australia in the 1940s and 1950s was characterised by its left-leaning political affiliations; however, the political left was not exclusive to all Macedonians and many were prepared to support any movement that advocated the setting up of an independent Macedonian state.

Macedonians proudly participated in annual May Day (Labour Day) and Russian Day parades held at that time. Labour Day Parades were massive events across Australian capital cities with thousands of participants representing trade unions, political parties, ideologies, and workers, while thousands more lined the streets in support of those marching. Macedonian participation in Labour Day marches commenced in Melbourne from 1943, and involvement in the march was a matter of great pride and excitement for the participants and community as a whole. It was reported that, in 1943, 5,000 people marched in Melbourne and 'for the first time there were Russian, Greek, Italian, Jewish and Macedonian groups'.[45] Well-organised floats and banners proudly conveyed messages affirming Macedonian identity, promoting the formation of a united and independent Macedonia and expressing gratitude to Australia for allowing Macedonians to freely express their identity.

The number of Macedonians participating in the 1946 Perth May Day march was the largest of all the ethnic groups and its success was due to the well-organised activities of the Edinstvo organisation.[46] In the 1947 Perth parade, girls dressed in Macedonian traditional costume and a band accompanied the Macedonian float playing the national anthem of the Republic of Macedonia while, at the Melbourne march, players from the recently established Macedonian soccer club participated, and Aleksandar Theodorovsky, one of the young players from the team, attended in Macedonian national costume. *Makedonska Iska* reported that, in Perth, 83 Macedonians marched, and in Melbourne there were over 40 participants. In both cities, Macedonians carried the flag of the People's Republic of Macedonia and banners supporting the Macedonian war effort in Greece. At the 1949 May Day march in Melbourne, Macedonians carried a large photograph of Lazo Trpovski (1900-1943), a prominent political and revolutionary activist for Macedonian rights in Aegean Macedonia. Macedonian participation in May Day marches continued into the 1960s.

Photo 54: Aleksandar Theodorovsky in national costume as the Macedonian flag bearer with the Macedonian contingent at the Melbourne May Day Parade, 1947. (Source: Aleksandar Theodorovsky).

A newspaper of one's own

Following the decision at the inaugural national conference to publish a Macedonian language newspaper, within the short space of two months, the first edition of *Makedonska Iskra* was released on 11 October 1946, a symbolic date being the anniversary of the Macedonian uprising against the 1941 Nazi German/Bulgarian occupation. Published in Perth on a monthly basis, *Makedonska Iskra* was a bi-lingual newspaper

Photo 55: Macedonians at the May Day Parade, Melbourne, 1947. (Source: Aleksandar Theodorovsky).

printed in English and Macedonian using the Latin script, as most Macedonians at the time were from Aegean Macedonia and had been denied education in their mother tongue by the Greek government, so that few were able to read Macedonian Cyrillic. In support of the publication, community members generously donated funds to assist with printing and distribution costs.

The aim of *Makedonska Iskra* was to inform and educate Macedonians and the wider Australian community about the situation of the Macedonians in the Balkans, about Macedonians in Australia and to unite Macedonians around MAPL.[47] *Makedonska Iskra* was the principal source of information for Macedonians in Australia regarding events in the Republic of Macedonia, Macedonia under Bulgarian rule, the war for independence in Aegean Macedonia (Greek Civil War) and community news in Australia. Macedonians perceived the newspaper as a great achievement and it gave them a strong sense of pride in their identity as, back in Macedonia, particularly those from Aegean Macedonia, were still struggling for the recognition of their basic human rights. Reflecting on the success of the newspaper in the ten-year anniversary edition in 1956, Laurie Malco noted that the newspaper also played an important role in helping Macedonians integrate into Australian society.[48] Subscriptions to *Makedonska Iskra* were received from across Australia and from as far away as the United States and Canada.

The newspaper connected people across the vast Australian continent in a time when there were no modern forms of communication. Announcements of engagements, weddings and the birth of children were regular features, as were death notices. Monetary collections were arranged to aid individuals who had suffered serious work-related injuries or those who were gravely ill, as well as support for widows. Individuals seeking to find loved ones placed notices in the paper: for example, in May 1948, Hristo Deloff of Young Street, Fitzroy, informed readers that he was searching for his relative, Atanas Naumoff, from Chetirok village (Kostur). Letters arrived from as far as Macedonia and other countries in search for news of loved ones. In December 1948, a letter arrived from Sofia, Bulgaria, from a young student searching for his uncle Anastas Hristov Dineff from Nevoljani village (Lerin) who was last known to be living on a farm near Canberra in 1937. Others announced their contact details to family and friends such as the Stefania family from Asanovo village (Lerin) after moving to Griffith NSW in 1947.[49]

Initially, 600 copies were printed when the first edition appeared in October, 1946; however, within two years to October 1948, 1,200 copies were being printed.[50] Publication of the newspaper was initially managed in Perth before transferring to Sydney in 1948 and later to Melbourne in 1952, due to a greater number of Macedonians settling in the eastern states.[51] The move to Sydney was reported in the *West Australian* newspaper under the title 'Macedonian paper to leave Western Australia', attesting to the profile of *Makedonska Iskra* at that time.[52] The first editor of the newspaper was Ilo Malco from

Photo 56: Macedonian activists, from left to right: Stojan Sarbinov, Dane Trpkov, Jim Filipov and Jani Pandzhari, Melbourne, circa 1940. (Source: Peter Sarbinov).

Shestovo village (Kostur) followed by Dane Trpkov from Nevoljani village (Lerin), Vasil Boskov from Visheni village (Kostur) and Stojan Sarbinov from Buf village (Lerin).

13

A Church of Our Own

Historical background

Macedonia was the first European land to receive the Christian faith through the arrival of Paul the Apostle, and Macedonia became a Christian centre from where Christianity spread throughout the Balkan Peninsula and later to western Europe. The first Christian bishopric was established in Macedonia in the early fourth century and in the sixth century the independent Archbishopric of Justiniana Prima was founded. Eventually the town of Ohrid would become the Christian centre of Macedonia and the Archbishopric of Ohrid, restored upon the ruins of Justiniana Prima by the Emperor Samuel in the tenth century, became a large and important Christian institution in the Balkans, operating as a centre of arts, letters and learning. The church played a significant role in 'defining and in defending' a uniquely Macedonian culture.[53] For over eight centuries the church maintained its autocephalous status through Serbian, Bulgarian and Byzantine rule, and for the first three and a half centuries of Ottoman Turkish rule. As the sole religious institution of the Macedonian people, the Archbishopric of Ohrid assisted, and at times led, the struggle to liberate Macedonia from Ottoman rule. In 1767, following a prolonged campaign of the Constantinople Patriarchate to dominate the Orthodox Christian Balkans under Ottoman rule, the Patriarchate succeeded in its intrigues against the Archbishopric when the Archbishopric of Ohrid was abolished under a decree of the Ottoman Turkish Sultan.[54]

Following the abolition of the Archbishopric of Ohrid, the Macedonian church was annexed to the Patriarchate of Constantinople which took ecclesiastical control over Macedonia and sent Greek bishops and other senior clerics whose aim was to Hellenise the Macedonians through the church and the schools attached to the church (these were transformed into Greek schools). Macedonian manuscripts, records, books and religious texts were destroyed in an attempt to wipe out all traces of the Macedonian character of the Archbishopric of Ohrid, while pro-Greek propaganda was given an unobstructed monopoly in Macedonia through the Patriarchate of Constantinople (known as the Patriarchate), with the support of the Ottoman authorities.

In 1870, with the aid of Russian influence, the Bulgarian Exarchate Church (known as the Exarchate) was established, and its jurisdiction included non-Bulgarian Ottoman territories. This enabled the Exarchate to expand its churches and schools into Macedonia. Macedonians resented the Patriarchate as an oppressive and exploitative organisation whose official Greek language was incomprehensible to the Macedonians. In contrast, Macedonians favoured the Exarchate due to similarity of language. However, they became exposed to the influence of the Bulgarian government. Later, at the end of the nineteenth century the Ottomans also permitted the Serbian church to expand into Macedonia. Allowing opposing churches to operate in Macedonia was seen by the Ottomans as a way of creating division and preventing any single foreign propaganda from dominating Macedonia on its own. This resulted in an intense rivalry between Greece, Serbia and Bulgaria as religious jurisdiction became the primary instrument to support their territorial claims to Macedonia. Further, the Macedonian population was also subjected to violence and terror by foreign paramilitary bands sent into Macedonia to pressure the population to adhere to the respective churches as, to do so, registered the village as belonging to that particular 'nationality'.

Later, following the division of Macedonia, the national churches of Greece, Serbia and Bulgaria annexed all the Macedonian churches and eparchies in their respective occupied Macedonian territories and the newly transformed churches became important instruments in the attempted assimilation of Macedonians into Greeks, Serbs and Bulgarians. In 1944, following the establishment of the People's Republic of Macedonia, a board was established seeking the organisation of the Macedonian Orthodox Church. The Macedonian government, led by Metodija Andonov Chento, supported the calls for the restoration of the Archbishopric of Ohrid as the national church of Macedonia; however, even though Tito's Yugoslavia promoted the slogan of 'brotherhood and unity', the Serbian Orthodox Church refused to release its colonial religious control over the Macedonian Republic. It was not until 1958 that the Macedonian Church proclaimed autonomy from the Serbian Church, and in the following year, the Macedonian Church formally gained autonomous status.

A further eight years would pass before the Macedonian Orthodox Church Ohrid Archbishopric announced its autocephaly and independence from the Serbian Church, during the bicentenary of the abolition of the Archbishopric of Ohrid. According to the historian Peter Hill, 'full autocephaly did not prove possible until the downfall in 1966 of Aleksandar Rankovich, Yugoslavian Interior Minister, head of the state security police, and champion of Serbian nationalism, which was still opposed to the idea of Macedonian autonomy'.[55] Prior to 1967, and without the support of a mother church, Macedonians in Australia and other diasporas struggled to set up their own Church as they did not have the backing of a mother church and were fiercely opposed by the Greek, Serbian and Bulgarian Churches which all had a mutual interest in averting the establishment of a Macedonian Church, as it would affirm the existence of Macedonian identity.

Utilising other churches

Prior to the establishment of a Church of their own, Macedonians in Australia attended a range of churches for their religious needs which included Greek and Serbian churches; in particular, many attended the Greek church out of fear of being labelled as anti-Greek. Others refused to attend Greek and Serbian churches because of their political roles in the historical persecution of Macedonians. Alternatively, Macedonians attended Anglican and Methodist churches, as well as other Orthodox Churches such as the Russian, Lebanese, and Syrian churches. Macedonians attending the Greek church reported discrimination when they were subjected to racial taunts, such as '*Vulgaros*' (Bulgarians), when heard speaking Macedonian. Similarly, in Newcastle (Wickham), prior to the establishment of a Macedonian

Church, many used the Serbian Orthodox Church for their religious needs until they were addressed during a church service as '*Juzhni Srbi*' (Southern Serbians), from which point they all deserted that church.[56]

In Melbourne, Victoria, the Lebanese St Nicholas Antiochian Orthodox Church on the corner of Victoria Parade and Simpson Street, East Melbourne, provided a spiritual home for many Macedonians from the time of its establishment in 1932. A lasting bond formed between the Macedonian and Lebanese Orthodox communities and in a sign of friendship Father George Haydar, St Nicholas parish priest, was also given the honour of blessing the foundation stone at the Macedonian Sveti Giorgi church.[57] In Adelaide, the Macedonian and Bulgarian communities were too small to establish their own separate churches, so they joined to support the Russian Orthodox Church. It was a temporary arrangement that produced no lasting contact between the Macedonian and Bulgarian ethnic groups.[58] Macedonians in Newcastle regularly used Anglican and Methodist churches and considered them closely related to the Orthodox Church and were welcomed there.[59]

Photo 57: Lebanese and Macedonians at St Nicholas Church on the occasion of a visit by Bishop Naum from the Macedonian Orthodox Church, 1960. (Source: H92.250/1264. Pictures Collection, State Library of Victoria).

In Melbourne, arrangements were made during the 1950s for church services to be conducted in Anglican churches for the Macedonians, while they waited to establish their own Church. Following the progress of the community in Melbourne the Sydney Macedonian community was eager to make similar arrangements. A church committee was elected, with Mick Veloskey appointed President, initially given the task of organising church services to be held for the Macedonian community in existing churches prior to establishing their own church. Arrangements were agreed to with St Mary's Catholic Church in Swanson Street, Erskineville, and the Anglican Christ Church St Lawrence in George Street, Sydney,[60] while in central Perth, St Hilda's Anglican Church in View Street was utilised by the community.

In regional areas, Macedonian communities used non-Orthodox Christian churches for their religious needs, which were typically Methodist, Protestant or Anglican and had a tradition of respect for their Macedonian parishioners as a separate and unique ethnic group. Over many years, Macedonians formed a close bond and a sense of belonging to these churches. For example, in Sale, Victoria, Macedonians used St Paul's (Anglican) Cathedral; in Richmond, New South Wales, where they used St Peter's Anglican Church; while in Manjimup, St Martin's Anglican church served as a place of worship for Macedonians with all weddings, christenings and funerals held there. The Macedonian community connection to these churches predates the establishment of the Macedonian Orthodox Church in Australia. Following the founding of the Macedonian Church in Australia and the arrival of Macedonian Orthodox priests, it was common for priests to attend these churches to conduct services for the Macedonian congregation. For example, in the 1960s the Macedonian priest from the Sveti Nikola Macedonian Orthodox Church in Perth would make the three-hour journey to Manjimup to conduct services at St Martin's Anglican Church which was met with much joy by the Manjimup Macedonians.

St Augustine's Anglican Church in Shepparton, Victoria, is a church with which the Macedonian community formed close links and adopted as their own. The relationship with the Church commenced from around the end of the Second World War when Macedonians started purchasing farms and settling permanently in Shepparton, when the men were bringing out their families from Macedonia and found they were welcomed at St Augustine's. Reverend Donald Gibson officiated at the church for many years and established a close working relationship with the community based on respect of Macedonian identity and Orthodox traditions. Reverend Gibson familiarised himself with the customs and traditions of the Macedonian Orthodox Church and incorporated these into wedding, christening and funeral ceremonies. He further refined his understanding and practices after travelling to the Republic of Macedonia and meeting with leaders of the Macedonian Orthodox Church. To ensure that respect for the Macedonian Orthodox traditions continued into the future, when Reverend Gibson's tenure ended, he prepared detailed written instructions on the religious rituals and customs required to meet the needs of the Macedonian parishioners which have been handed down from priest to priest.

When Bishop Naum of the Macedonian Orthodox Church came to Melbourne for the historic blessing of the Sveti Giorgi Macedonian Church in Fitzroy in 1960, he conducted a liturgy in St Augustine's church in Shepparton and acknowledged the bond between the two churches. Following the establishment of the Macedonian Orthodox Church in Melbourne, Macedonian Orthodox priests were regularly invited by the Shepparton community to conduct ceremonies at St Augustine's church. A local community activist, Vasil Rendev, organised for Macedonian priests from Melbourne to officiate at wedding ceremonies at a number of Macedonian weddings at St Augustine's. When plans were made to expand St Augustine's church, which included a new facade and entry, the Macedonian community unreservedly contributed funds towards the project including the construction of a dedicated space within the church for prayer and reflection known as the 'Macedonian section' which is adorned with icons depicting Macedonian saints such as St Kliment of Ohrid.[61] Macedonians funded the construction of a fountain and small pool within the church grounds where the *vodici* (Epiphany), the annual throwing of the cross ceremony is held, further reinforcing the unique connection that the Orthodox Christian Macedonians had with St Augustine's Methodist Church.

Orthodox Christians celebrate Epiphany to recall the baptism of Jesus in the Jordan River and mark the day with a symbolic throwing of a cross into a body of water whilst young men vie to retrieve the cross. It is said that the successful one is blessed for the year ahead. Epiphany in Macedonian is known as *Vodici* and celebrated according to the Julian calendar together with other major Eastern Orthodox Churches such as the Russian Orthodox. A calendar reform, that was controversially made in 1924 by the Pan-Orthodox Congress of Constantinople and driven by Patriarch Meletius, who was likely motivated by political considerations, sought to coincide the Orthodox Church calendar (Julian calendar) with the Western calendar and the Catholic Church (Gregorian calendar). Although a few of the Eastern Orthodox Churches have since changed their traditional ecclesiastical calendar in line with the revised calendar of 1924, most Orthodox Churches have maintained the traditional Julian calendar. The Greek Orthodox Church adopted the new calendar and subsequently celebrates Christmas on 25 December along with the Catholic Church; however, and confusingly, it celebrates Easter according to the Eastern Orthodox calendar. In Australia, Orthodox Easter is often erroneously promoted by Greeks as 'Greek Easter': this is a point of contention for all non-Greek Orthodox Christians. Furthermore, Greek Orthodox Christians make up only a very small percentage – approximately 3 per cent – of the 260 million Orthodox Christians worldwide.

A false start: the Saint Cyril and Methodius's Church in Melbourne

The first initiative to establish a Macedonian church in Australia was taken in Melbourne in 1950 when a committee was formed made up of men from fourteen villages, predominantly from the Lerin region, but also from the Kostur region. This group of immigrants identified as Macedonians and were opposed to communism.[62] The Committee set out to raise funds for setting up a church and to find a Priest. Petre Phillipoff, a Macedonian from Dolno Kotori village (Lerin), was living in Adelaide and had completed priesthood training in Istanbul;

however, he had not yet been ordained. The Committee were fiercely opposed to having any ties with the Greek Orthodox Church and at that time the Macedonian Orthodox Church had not yet established its independence from the Serbian Orthodox Church in the Republic of Macedonia. In their search for a Bishop to ordain Petre Phillipoff, the committee approached the Russian Bishop in Sydney and he directed them towards the Bulgarian anti-Communist Bishop Velichky in the United States, who had previously broken ties with the Bulgarian Orthodox Church.

Bishop Velichky ordained priest Phillipoff and arrangements were put in place for regular services to be held in St Mark's Anglican Church in George Street, Fitzroy, whilst the Committee searched for an appropriate site to establish their own church. In April 1952, land was purchased at 82-92 Young Street, Fitzroy, in the Macedonian neighbourhood, for the construction of a church where the priest would conduct services in Macedonian. Several individuals, all from the Lerin region, registered as proprietors.[63] On Ilinden, 2 August 1953, Macedonians gathered at the ground-breaking ceremony for the building of their church. Stirred by the advances they were making to have their own church, a fundraising campaign saw Macedonians subscribing £8,000 towards the £10,200 required for building a new brick church.[64] Within approximately 18 months of purchasing the property the new church was completed. Bishop Velichky made the journey from the United States and on 5 January 1954, consecrated the new Macedonian church 'Saints Cyril and Methodius' (*Sv Kiril i Metodi*).

On the advice and guidance of Bishop Velichky, the church would fall under the jurisdiction of the Bulgarian Eastern Orthodox Diocese of America, Canada and Australia, an independent Orthodox Church through which some Macedonian communities in the United States and Canada had established their own churches. The trustees believed that as registered proprietors of the church its Macedonian character was guaranteed, and the bishop was only a symbolic figure whose role was to provide ordained priests. Kosta Kotchoff, a former committee member of the church explains, 'Our people thought that, if they were the trustees, that gave them direct ownership... We all

Photo 58: Macedonians gathered for the ground-breaking ceremony, Sveti Kiril and Metodija Church, in Fitzroy, 2 August 1953. (Source: Kosta Kotchoff).

thought that the church was ours – exclusively Macedonian and that no one else could take it over'.[65]

A large crowd gathered for the historic opening of the church. It was a day of great pride for Macedonians, almost exclusively from Aegean Macedonia. The church symbolised their rejection of the Greek Church, a church that represented the oppression of Macedonians back in their occupied villages and homeland. Australian daily newspapers reported on the opening of the church describing it as the 'first Macedonian church in Australia' and that hundreds of 'Macedonian men, women and children' attended the event.[66]

Macedonians embraced the church and regularly attended Sunday services, other religious celebrations, weddings and christenings and church social functions. The church was a central point of Macedonian community life; however, questions were soon raised about the need for any Bulgarian reference in the name of the church. This issue simmered for some time until 1958, when the first steps were taken towards discarding the Bulgarian reference when the committee and members voted to change the name of the church to 'Macedonian Independent Orthodox Church'; however, Bishop Velichky did not accept the Committee's decision.[67] Following the death of Priest Phillipoff in 1960, Russian and Ukrainian Orthodox priests conducted services until 1963 when priest, Kliment Dimitrov, a Macedonian with origins from the Tetovo region, arrived from Bulgaria where he had moved with his family when he was four years of age. During the 1960s, community dances were held inside the church on Sunday nights, as there was no separate church hall. Canvas sheets covered the icons and altar and the church was transformed into a function centre which was filled to capacity with families and young people. The band exclusively played Macedonian music and the people danced the Macedonian *oro*.[68]

Lazo Giamov from Trnava village (Lerin), was elected Secretary of the church in 1963, and remained in the role until 1969. He described that period as one in which change was sought from the way some things had been in the past, that he was part of the younger generation of Macedonians raised in Australia who could only identify 'as Macedonians and with Australia' and who had no connection to living under the rule of Greeks, Bulgarians or Serbs. In an attempt to distance the church from the Balkan States, Archbishop Woods from the Anglican Church was approached to place the church under Anglican jurisdiction, whilst allowing the church to continue operating in a uniquely Macedonian manner. Lazo Giamov stated 'We did not want to have anything to do with Bulgarians, Greeks or anyone else'. Archbishop Woods understood that Macedonians desired independent church life and, although prepared to support their aspirations, he could not interfere unless Bishop Velichky approved the transfer of church jurisdiction. Not surprisingly, Bishop Velichky was opposed to any such move.[69]

Priest Dimitrov was requested by the Committee and parishioners to refer to the church only as a Macedonian church, to provide all christening certificates in the Macedonian language and that any reference to Bulgarian be removed from the church and replaced with the name 'Macedonian Independent Church'. Priest Dimitrov agreed to the requests and, after seeking legal advice the church Committee registered the church under the name 'Macedonian Independent Orthodox Church'.[70] These were alarming developments for Bishop Velichky and, in 1967, Priest Dimitrov announced that Bulgaria sought to control the church and guide Macedonians towards a Bulgarian orientation.[71] Bishop Velichky soon arrived from the United States and expressed concern that the church was describing itself as a Macedonian Independent Church, 'insisting that it should be known as the "Macedono-Bulgarian Church" or a name similar to that, including a reference to Bulgarian'.[72] Bishop Velichky subsequently relieved Priest Dimitrov of his duties as he had failed to fulfil the task set for him. Alarmed at the Bulgarian influence exerted upon the church by Bishop Velichky, the congregation was thrown into disarray with many deserting the church for the Macedonian Orthodox Church of Sveti Giorgi in Fitzroy.[73]

The subsequent priest to arrive from Bulgaria was Priest Stefanov, a Macedonian originally from Kalenik village (Lerin) and, as with Macedonian priests before him, he was acceptable to the parishioners and freely communicated with them in Macedonian. In 1968, the church was forced to relocate when the State Government compulsorily acquired the Sveti Kiril i Metodi Church along with a swathe of neighbouring properties to construct high-rise government housing. The Church Committee then purchased the Church of the Epiphany (an Anglican Church) in the nearby suburb of Northcote and relocated the Sveti Kiril i Metodi Church to the new site.[74]

When Priest Stefanov retired in 1973, he was replaced by Priest Alexandar Popov, the first Bulgarian priest appointed to the church. The appointment coincided with the formal reconciliation of Bishop Velichky with the Bulgarian Orthodox Church, placing the Bulgarian Eastern Orthodox Diocese of America, Canada and Australia under the direct control and jurisdiction of the Bulgarian Orthodox Church and the anti-Macedonian Communist regime in Sofia. Priest Popov was a controversial figure who had no respect for the Macedonian identity of the church and its adherents and openly declared that he 'did not recognise the existence of Macedonia or Macedonians – that there were only Bulgarians'.[75] Macedonians soon began to question whether Bishop Velichky had ever genuinely been estranged from the Bulgarian Orthodox Church and whether they had been manipulated all along. Former Committee members and parishioners of the church believed that the men who set up the church were innocent and naive, that they were fooled by Bishop Velichky, that he was never genuinely anti-Communist, but that he was a Communist agent from the beginning, working with the regime in Sofia.

In 1984, matters between the Committee and the priest came to a head when the Committee terminated Priest Popov, evicting him from the manse, and the Church Committee and parishioners requested that the church enter union with the Macedonian Orthodox Church. Priest Popov responded by instigating legal action. The matter went before the courts and in 1986, Justice Murray of the Supreme Court of Victoria declared that, although sympathetic to the wishes of the Macedonian parishioners, he was forced to accept that the church came under the legal jurisdiction of the Bulgarian Orthodox Church. Of significant historical importance as the first Macedonian place of worship in Australia and a valuable community asset, the loss of the Sveti Kiril i Metodi church was a painful blow to the Macedonian community.

Establishment of the Macedonian Orthodox Church, 'Sveti Giorgi'

The Sveti Kiril i Metodi Church attracted considerable support from the Macedonian community and addressed their religious needs as separate from the Greek Church. However, Macedonians linked to the Macedonian Australian People's League (MAPL) were uneasy with the perceived pro-Bulgarian link the church had through Bishop Velichky, the success of the church attracting large numbers of Macedonians and the ideological positioning of the Committee to the right, which was in conflict with the Communist-influenced MAPL.[76] Activists from the former Melbourne MAPL branch reacted by calling a community meeting in Fitzroy with the intention of seeking support for the establishment of a Macedonian Orthodox Church in Fitzroy, independent of the Greek, Bulgarian and Serbian church. At this meeting, a steering committee was elected, made up of people from the Lerin and Kostur regions of Macedonia, and tasked with finding a suitable church to purchase.[77] As a temporary measure the steering committee approached the Anglican Church and it was agreed that all services would be held at St Luke's Anglican Church in North Fitzroy. Throughout the 1950s, until the establishment of the Macedonian Orthodox Church Saint George, numerous Macedonian marriages and baptisms were held at St Luke's.[78]

On 18 May 1956, a community meeting held at St Luke's Anglican Church Hall announced that a site for the new church was located on the premises of the Dalmatian Club at 52-54 Young Street, Fitzroy. £4,700 was donated at that meeting in support of establishing a Macedonian church. Macedonians rejoiced at the prospect of having their own place to worship, free from the influence of those that denied their identity and had a history of persecuting Macedonians. Opposition to the establishment of the Macedonian Orthodox Church came from the Greek, Bulgarian and Serbian Orthodox Churches and, in a coordinated strategy, the three Balkan Church organisations protested the construction of the Macedonian church to Fitzroy City Council, on the grounds that no such Church organisation existed. Fitzroy Council responded by revoking the initial proposal for construction of the church. The Church Committee then took the matter to the Supreme Court of Victoria which recognised the right for the Macedonian church to be established.[79] In 1958, the Church Committee invited the Macedonian community to attend the Ilinden celebration at the Fitzroy Town Hall for the purpose of supporting the construction of the church. The response was overwhelming, with the community donating £6,000 that one evening.[80] The Church Committee sought financial support from Macedonians throughout Australia and, in an expression of solidarity with the Melbourne community in its aspirations to build a church, funds were collected in Macedonian communities across Australia, at times from house to house.

The original building which housed the Dalmatian Club was subsequently demolished and, on 2 August 1959, on the anniversary of the Ilinden uprising, the foundation stone was laid and blessed by a group of four Orthodox priests led by Father George Haydar of the Lebanese St Nicholas Antiochian Orthodox Church. At the blessing ceremony the Macedonian community donated a further £5,000 and one year later, again coinciding with Ilinden, on 7 August 1960, the church officially opened and was blessed by Bishop Naum who had travelled from Macedonia for the historic ceremony. During the service, which was conducted in their mother tongue, Macedonians from Aegean Macedonia visibly shed tears. The event was of tremendous significance, seeing that Macedonians had systematically been denied the right to worship in their own language under Greek rule since 1913; and it was also the first time a bishop of the Macedonian Orthodox Church had opened a church outside Macedonia. It was a monumental occasion for all Macedonians across the world. In recognition of the support and friendship given to Macedonians to establish their own church, Father George Haydar from the Lebanese Orthodox Church and Father Elliott from the Anglican Church participated in the historic blessing ceremony. A large crowd attending the blessing of the church and on that day, the Macedonian community donated a further £10,000. Although a large number of volunteers assisted with the construction which helped keep costs down, by the time the church was completed over £40,000 was spent on the construction.

Regardless of how strictly Macedonians observed their religion, the connection to their church represents a powerful bond to their identity. The church was a spiritual and national cultural centre for all Macedonians in Australia and a monument for all the heroes that had fought for the freedom of the Macedonian homeland.[81] The establishment of the Sveti Giorgi Church became a rallying point for all Macedonians around Australia and a matter of status, particularly for the Melbourne Macedonian community. This church paved the way for the establishment of other Macedonian churches in Australia. Motivated by the success in Melbourne, other Macedonian communities led by activists formerly linked to the MAPL, aspired to set up their own churches.[82] Following in succession over the next few years, churches were established in Adelaide (1968); Queanbeyan, Perth and Sydney (1969); Newcastle (1970); and Wollongong (1972). A Macedonian religious and cultural renaissance was taking place in Australia. Macedonian churches reinforced Macedonian identity and became vehicles through which Macedonians could express their ethnic individuality. A rich community life developed around

Photo 59: Procession during the consecration of Sveti Giorgi Macedonian Orthodox Church, Fitzroy (Melbourne), 1960. Priests from the Anglican and Lebanese churches participated in the event alongside Macedonian Orthodox clergy. (Source: Image supplied by Yarra Libraries).

the church. The newly established churches were not all legally under the jurisdiction of the Macedonian Orthodox Church, as they were established as incorporated associations following the lead of the St George Church in Fitzroy. They maintained a spiritual connection to the mother church, however and, unlike the Sveti Kiril i Metodi Church in Melbourne which was tied to Bishop Velichky, they were not linked to any other religious jurisdiction in the Balkans which had a history of persecuting Macedonians.

The success with which Macedonians were able to establish their own churches was due to the tireless efforts of community activists and the generous support of the Macedonian community. Encouraged by the accomplishment in Melbourne, Macedonians in Perth purchased a parcel of land in North Perth intending to construct a

Photo 60: Father Gogov (holding large bible) was joined by Metropolitan Metodi (left side) and Bishop Kiril, who travelled from Macedonia for the consecration of the Sveti Ilija Macedonian Orthodox Church in Queanbeyan, New South Wales, 1969. (Source: National Archives of Australia. NAA: A12111, 1/1969/9/7).

large church and an imposing community centre. In 1965, teams were formed which voluntarily door knocked Macedonian homes in Perth, and as far afield as Bridgetown and Manjimup, seeking donations. Such was the enthusiasm and support for the project that, wherever they went, 'All the Macedonians welcomed the door knockers with happiness and open hearts' ('*celiot narod so radosti so otvoreno srce ne precekuvaa*').[83] A delegation from the committee made up of Kosta Angelkov, Vane Ciglev, Tome Mijovski, Trpche Pajov, Vane Borshoff, Jane Delianov and Manoli Stanisev attended a Macedonian community picnic at the Wanneroo Showgrounds and, following a fiery speech by Kosta Angelkov from the platform of a truck, over $7,000 was donated within one hour.[84] In an attempt to keep construction costs down, the Committee in Perth, made up of 37 people, purchased tools and worked voluntarily on weekends preparing moulds for the concrete frame, and were joined by a large number of volunteers who came to provide their labour. Even with an extraordinary number of unpaid hours and numerous functions held, funds were insufficient to complete the project and raising additional funds from banks proved difficult until 25 individuals offered their homes as security to enable further loans to be accessed.[85]

It was a matter of enormous pride for every Macedonian that similar efforts were undertaken in other Macedonian centres in support of setting up Macedonian churches. In Newcastle, $9,000 was donated at a Macedonian community fundraising event in 1969 which enabled construction to commence of the Macedonian Orthodox Church Sveti Bogorodica.[86] The Sveta Petka Macedonian Church in Rockdale, Sydney, benefited from at least 597 voluntary work days, in addition to contracted work, during four months of construction in 1977.[87] Others provided interest free loans to assist with building churches and these could involve substantial sums of money; for example, in 1967, in addition to generous donations already given, Giorgi Nano and John Antanakis, respectively, gave interest free loans of $3,200 and $2,000 towards the establishment of the Macedonian Church in Queanbeyan, which was purchased for $12,000.[88]

When the first Macedonian churches were being formed in Australia, there was nominal involvement from the Church in Skopje, as during the 1950s and 60s, the Macedonian Orthodox Church, the Archbishopric of Ohrid, was itself in the process of formally re-establishing its independence from control of the Serbian Church (in the Republic of Macedonia). In Australia, when the first churches were being established matters were generally administered through the committee with the backing of the community. For example, normally a bishop would play a role in determining the name a church was given; however, decisions of this nature were usually left for the community in Australia to resolve. When the Macedonian church parish was established in Queanbeyan in 1958, Macedonians from Trcije and Statica made up a large proportion of the Macedonian community in Queanbeyan and, due to the village churches in Trcije and Statica both named Sveti Prorok Ilija (St Prophet Elijah), that name was accepted as the patron saint of the church in Queanbeyan.[89] Similarly, several options were put forward when names were being considered for the first Macedonian church in Newcastle; however, when the issue was put to a community vote, the overwhelming number of Macedonians in Newcastle being from the village of Gjavato (Gyavato), they voted for the name, Sveta Bogorodica, which is the name of the church in Gjavato village.[90]

When the early Macedonian arrivals came together to celebrate, they gathered in homes, on farms and rented halls. However, as the community continued to grow, so did the need for their own halls, to accommodate large social and cultural events. In the early 1950s, over 500 people would gather at the Oddfellows Hall in La Trobe Street, Melbourne for the annual Christmas dance.[91] However, the first community centre was established in an unlikely place, by Macedonian banana farmers in Crabbes Creek in 1947. By no means did Crabbes Creek have a large Macedonian community, but they were making good money from banana farming, and no doubt their affluence contributed towards the establishment of the hall immediately after the war, when timber and other building materials were scarce. Built as both a community hall and a church hall, at its opening it was dedicated by a Russian priest from Brisbane.[92]

Although the hall was primarily used for social functions, it was also intended that it would be used as a place of religious worship. A 1950 newspaper report stated that 'the hall was erected for members to meet for religious exercises and social functions'.[93] Reverend Canon Charles Rowe of St Martin's Anglican Church in Mullumbimby officiated at the Easter communion in the hall in 1950.[94] Built as a hall and although not formally established as a church, it had been utilised for religious services. The Crabbes Creek hall is of important social and religious significance to the Macedonians of Australia. Later when the first churches were established in Melbourne, the Sveti Kiril i Metodi Church and the Sveti Giorgi Church, although built as churches, were also utilised as social venues. Covers were placed over the altar and the icons and the church was temporarily transformed into a church hall for social and cultural functions. Over time, Macedonian Orthodox Churches built their own church halls and community centres, and these gave Macedonians the opportunity to further preserve and develop their culture and traditions.

Sveti Giorgi Church: cultural, artistic, and educational life

Wherever Macedonian churches were established, they played a pivotal role promoting Macedonian identity through cultural, artistic, and educational activities. In Melbourne, the St George church was a beacon for the Macedonian community in that it drew people together to worship their faith and celebrate Macedonian identity and culture. Many contributed to activities associated with Macedonian cultural advancement. Two people, Ana and Risto Vasilev, deserve special mention for their tireless effort in preserving and advancing Macedonian culture through the Sveti Giorgi church community. With a background in music and the arts they were instrumental in setting up a children's and adult's choir, a folkloric dance group and Macedonian language classes. The Church became a bastion of Macedonian culture.[95] The children's choir was established in 1961 by Ana Vaslieva, and they performed at Sunday morning church services Amongst the children was the Collingwood Australian Rules footballer, Peter Daicos, 'The Macedonian Marvel', and Nadia Tass, a famous Australian film director, producer and actor. An adult church choir followed, as did the first Macedonian folkloric dancing group in Victoria, Svetlost, which provided young Macedonians with the opportunity to learn traditional Macedonian dancing at a semi-professional level, performing at community functions, cultural events and Moomba parades. Risto provided musical support whilst Ana choreographed the dancing and singing. Their experience in the field of music and the arts resulted in the promotion of Macedonian national identity through cultural expression and fostered healthy and positive community life for young Macedonians.

A Macedonian language school, the first in Victoria, was established and drew Macedonian children from Fitzroy, Collingwood, Clifton Hill, and the surrounding areas. Children studied Macedonian language, reading, writing and grammar as well as Macedonian history and culture. The school was of great significance to the com-

Photo 61: Svetlost Folkloric Dance Group, displaying traditional Macedonian dance skills, circa 1960. (Source: Pavle Velov).

Photo 62: Svetlost Macedonian folkloric dance group marching in the Moomba Parade, Melbourne, 1966. Participation in the Moomba Parade is a long-held tradition for the Macedonian community in Melbourne which continues into the twenty-first century. (Source: Ana Vasileva).

munity and a source of enormous pride, as most parishioners previously lived under oppressive Greek rule where Macedonians were denied education in their mother tongue. Over time, hundreds of children enrolled in the classes. Macedonian language classes, dancing groups and other cultural activities helped to perpetuate the national heritage and provide the children with a connection to their cultural background in Australia.

Ana Vasileva took on the role as teacher with passion and enthusiasm. Word quickly spread and the number of children attending Saturday morning Macedonian classes rapidly grew, with the large second storey church classroom barely able to contain all the children. Enrolment in Macedonian school required the children attend an extra day's schooling on weekends and to ensure they enjoyed the experience and to encourage their return the following week, Ana routinely handed out lollies to the children. She capably and voluntarily ran the classes from 1961 until 1965. With the success of the Macedonian classes, in the mid-1960s the Sveti Giorgi church established a second Macedonian language school which operated out of a State Primary School in Highett Street, Richmond, to service a growing demand in that area. Classes were taught by Lena Krushoradi from Buf village (Lerin).

The growth of the community across Australia in the 1960s and 1970s resulted in Macedonian language schools established in all major urban centres where Macedonians settled and established churches. The schools were very popular as parents saw them as important for their children to learn the language of their culture, perpetuate its use and give them a greater awareness of their Macedonian identity. From the mid-1970s the Macedonian Orthodox Church St Prophet Elijah in Seddon, Melbourne, operated with junior, intermediate, and senior levels for three decades in the 'Goce Delchev Macedonian Saturday School'. Church-administered Macedonian language schools have generally experienced a slow decline since Saturday morning Macedonian language classes were introduced within the Victorian State Education system, whereby Macedonian is taught up to Year 12 High School level. A number of churches continued to run classes for children, and these were usually administered by the priest, providing instruction in Macedonian language, culture and religion.

Other Macedonian Christian denominations and religious groups

Overwhelmingly Macedonians belong to the Macedonian Orthodox Christian faith. In the nineteenth century, during Ottoman rule,

Photo 63: Lena Krushoradi, Macedonian language teacher with students, Richmond (Melbourne), 1960s. (Source: Peter Sarbinov).

Protestant, Methodist and Catholic missionaries had been sent into Macedonia from Western countries and experienced limited success converting Macedonians to their respective denominations. These were mostly in the central Macedonian regions of Strumica, Gevgelija and Kukush. Small numbers of Macedonian Protestants and Methodists arrived from the Republic of Macedonia in the 1960s and 1970s, principally settling in Melbourne and, to a lesser degree, in Sydney. In 1973 a Macedonian Methodist community used the Fitzroy North Presbyterian Church (in Melbourne) for regular worship in Macedonian on Sunday mornings and other times as arranged. In 1978, the congregation brought out the Reverend Boris Doncev from Macedonia and that same year, the congregation moved to its own venue in East Preston. The core of this community is from the Strumica area in Macedonia. Since the departure of that group, another Macedonian congregation used the Fitzroy North church for a number of years. There is also a very small number of Macedonian Catholics in the Republic of Macedonia; however, there is no organised Macedonian Catholic community in Australia.

The second largest Macedonian religious group is the Macedonian Muslims who were converted to Islam following the Ottoman invasion of Macedonia in the fourteenth century. The colonising nature of Ottoman rule created conditions favourable for the new ruler to 'Islamicise' elements of the indigenous Macedonian Christian population. Islamisation to varying degrees was a process that lasted to the end of Ottoman rule. Following the division of Macedonia, under direct Serbian rule, the Macedonian Muslims did not fare well and underwent discrimination and forced Serbianisation. Under Greek rule, over 40,000 Macedonian Muslims were forcibly expelled to Turkey in the 1920s as part of the infamous population exchange between Greece and Turkey.

Following the establishment of the Republic of Macedonia in 1944, the Yugoslav-Macedonian communist authorities unfortunately did not view the Macedonian Muslims as part of the Macedonian nation. State policies encouraged Macedonian Muslims to declare themselves as belonging to other ethnic groups, primarily Turkish, but also Albanian. Consequently, there was an exodus of Macedonian Muslims to Turkey during the period from 1954 to 1962. Thousands of Macedonian Muslims migrated to various Turkish cities, establishing concentrations in Istanbul, Izmir, Adana, Izmit and Karshiyaka. Although there is a very small number of Macedonian Muslims in Australia, a few have arrived from the Republic of Macedonia and others from Turkey, who have typically maintained their Macedonian mother tongue.

14

Interference and Intimidation

After migrating to the free democracies of the Western world such as the United States, Canada, Western Europe and Australia, Macedonians initially believed they were safe from the oppressive Yugoslav, Greek and Bulgarian regimes. In Australia, being the most distant land from the Balkans, Macedonians believed they could live peacefully, free of intimidation and harassment, and express their identity without reservation; however, this would not be the case. The Balkan States, in particular the Greek government, and the Tito regime in Yugoslavia sought, through their diplomatic missions, to maintain influence over diasporic Macedonian communities, and control their outward appearance so that Macedonians from Aegean Macedonia presented as 'Greeks', with those from the Republic of Macedonia as 'Yugoslavs'. This strategy fostered division and fragmentation and sought to separate Macedonians into two categories. This was not a new approach, as attempts to influence the outward appearance of Macedonians had been a central feature of Greek, Serbian and Bulgarian expansionist policy in Macedonia dating back to the nineteenth century when all three states attempted to demonstrate to Europe that there were no Macedonians but only Greeks, Serbs and Bulgarians in Macedonia.

Greece and Serbia traditionally maintained friendly relations with each other, and had a common understanding towards Macedonia and the Macedonians. During Ottoman rule, the two countries negotiated and agreed as to where they would divide Macedonia to share a common border, even though they had never in history shared a joint frontier. The Greek, Bulgarian and Serbian Orthodox Churches were key players supporting the territorial aspirations of their respective states and shared a common objective to deny Macedonians the re-establishment of their own church. Co-operation between the Balkan Orthodox Churches resurfaced in Australia in the second half of the twentieth century in an alliance to try to hinder Macedonian independent church life.

Macedonians who arrived in Australia prior to the Second World War experienced a new-found sense of freedom, particularly those who arrived from under Greek rule. Dispersed throughout the countryside in small rural and market gardening communities, initially there was little direct outside political influence upon them from the states from which they migrated. Velika Spirova lived on a small farm at Crossroads, outside Newcastle, New South Wales, in the 1930s, and her experience of life in a free democracy is telling. An immediate impression Velika had of Australia concerned the sense of freedom she felt that, for the first time, she could speak Macedonian freely without fear of discrimination as she had experienced on a daily basis from the Greek authorities back in Macedonia.[96] When Gona Fotev-Murgev from Drenoveni village (Kostur) arrived in 1948 to be reunited with her father Lazo, after hearing her whisper to her brother in Greek, her father said 'We are now free and from now on we can speak Macedonian'.[97]

After the tragic division of their homeland, Macedonians continued to consider themselves as belonging to a single national identity while retaining the language of their forefathers, their culture and traditions. The freedom Macedonians experienced after their arrival in Australia in the 1920s and 1930s is a common theme; and it was the first time, since prior to the division of Macedonia in 1913, that Macedonians from all four divided parts of Macedonia were able to freely congregate as one community. In Bridgetown (Western Australia) during the 1930s, Macedonians from Greek and Serbian-occupied Macedonia gathered to celebrate important Macedonian religious days at the 'Macedonian Restaurant and Boarding House'; Stojan Sarbinov, a participant at the gatherings, stated, 'We gathered with our brothers from both sides of the border, which was natural, as they and we felt as one'.[98]

Macedonians received increased attention from the Balkan regimes as they became more visible as a group when their population increased and they came together to form communities, becoming established in larger cities, and organising themselves into associations and political organisations. When the Edinstvo organisation in Perth established a weekly radio program in 1945 to discuss the plight of Macedonians in the Balkans, the Greek community in Perth, overwhelmingly from the island of Castelorizo, was in shock that Macedonians were publicly voicing their grievances against Greece, and protested to the radio station management 'that Macedonians should not be allowed to broadcast false information', and threatened the presenter and organisers of the radio program.[99] The reaction by the Greek community, highly likely under the direction of official Greece, was to set the scene in Australia thereafter for a pattern of continued harassment, intimidation and protest against the Macedonian community and its activities, be they educational, cultural, artistic or otherwise.

Greek influence

Since the end of the Second World War the Greek government's 'anti-Macedonian' campaign has been orchestrated by the Greek embassy and consulates, with a strategic partner in the Greek Orthodox Church and other organisations, some specifically established and funded by the Greek government to promote the notion of the 'Greekness' of Macedonia. A 'Macedonian section' within the Greek embassy in Canberra was specifically tasked with the role of promoting the Greekness of Macedonia. The Greek ethnic media unconditionally supported the Greek government's discriminatory position and the Greek community was easily stirred by the disseminated propaganda. Greek consuls sought to recruit Macedonians to inform on the activities of other Macedonians and advocate the Greek position with promises of personal benefits and employment for family members back in their villages. These individuals promoted the notion of a pseudo-'Greek Macedonian' identity.

Concern developed amongst Macedonians who had migrated from under Greek rule that to openly self-identify as Macedonian and engage in everyday community activities including attendance at Macedonian churches, would be construed as anti-Greek. They felt intimidated and threatened and, fearing repercussions upon family members still living back in the villages, some in Australia began to publicly present as 'Greek' or the pseudo-'Greek Macedonian'. An individual or family could be regarded as behaving in an anti-Greek manner depending on which church they frequented, or which community social functions they attended. Some became concerned about being seen as openly pro-Macedonian and withdrew from attending Macedonian community functions. During an Ilinden picnic in Murwillumbah, New South Wales, in 1956, half of the picnic goers moved away to avoid being photographed for the *Makedonska Iskra* newspaper fearing they would be publicly identified as being involved in anti-Greek activity, specifically their attendance at the picnic.[100] Discouraging Macedonians from associating with Macedonian community activities could involve subtle suggestions or overt threats. Some were pre-warned even before they arrived in Australia. Mitre Kircos/Kircov from Neret village (Lerin) a former freedom fighter for Macedonian independence during the 1940s, was prevented from leaving Greece by the authorities who would not issue him with a passport during the 1960s unless he signed an oath that he would not partake in anti-Greek activity in Australia, meaning that he should not openly identify as Macedonian in Australia or express anti-Greek political views.[101]

Makedonska Iskra routinely published the names of individuals that donated money for various humanitarian and other appeals for Macedonian projects such as the fund for the construction of a hospital in the Republic of Macedonia. The reluctance of some donors to be publicly identified is evident through their choosing to declare themselves anonymously as *Makedonec* (Macedonian). Similarly, when a property was purchased by the Macedonian community in Melbourne to establish the Sveti Giorgi church in Fitzroy in the 1950s, Committee members involved in fundraising routinely reported that some from Aegean Macedonia were apprehensive about their names being recorded as donors. They feared being publicly identified as supporters of the Macedonian Church; they would be branded anti-Greek; and their families would suffer in Aegean Macedonia. Interestingly, during fundraising for the Sveti Giorgi Church, families who had taken on a pro-Greek public identity and therefore were unlikely to attend the Macedonian church, made generous donations anonymously. It was considered they were motivated out of a sense of guilt for adopting a public pro-Greek stance and obscuring their Macedonian identity.

Those who openly identified as Macedonian, or advocated Macedonian separateness and political independence, were viewed as hostile enemies of Greece and their families in Aegean Macedonia were harassed and denied job opportunities, particularly in government employment. Macedonians were often denied entry to their place of birth if they refused to openly identify as Greek. This may even apply to second- or third-generation Macedonians. Passports issued in Australia and other Western countries stating the original Macedonian name of the birthplace of the passport holder rather than the Greek replacement (introduced in the 1920s), have been, and continue to be, denied entry to Greece.

The aim of the Greek anti-Macedonian campaign in Australia was for Macedonians from under Greek rule to identify as Greek and attend Greek churches, as this was seen as confirmation of their 'Greekness'. Significant resources were invested towards this goal particularly after the first Macedonian churches were established in Australia, a development that alarmed the Greek anti-Macedonian movement. After failing to hinder the establishment of the Macedonian Orthodox Church in Australia, the Greek lobby attempted to prevent the church from acquiring a priest. When the committee of the Sveti Giorgi Church made application for a Macedonian Orthodox priest to be granted a visa to Australia, Archbishop Ezekiel of the Greek Orthodox Church opposed the application, protesting to the Department of Immigration on the erroneous grounds that the 'Macedonian people of Melbourne are in reality Greek Orthodox people' because they come from Greece and as such they come under the jurisdiction of the Greek Orthodox Church.[102]

Greek clergy played a central role in the anti-Macedonian campaign. During the construction of the first Macedonian Orthodox Church in Perth in 1969, the Church President and Committee members, all from Macedonia under Greek rule, were threatened by the bishop of the Greek Orthodox Church (Western Australia) not to establish the church separately from the Greek Church, otherwise their families living in Greece would suffer.[103] When Bishop Naum of the Macedonian Orthodox Church arrived in Australia in 1960 to officiate the blessing of the Sveti Giorgi Church in Melbourne, Macedonians were elated that a senior cleric from the Church was in Australia for the first time and they flocked to see him. A grand function was held in the Shepparton town hall in Bishop Naum's honour which drew an immediate reaction from the Greek Orthodox Church protesting his presence, concerned at the warm welcome he received, and alarmed at the prospect that Macedonians might worship in their own church. The following week, the Greek Orthodox bishop announced a public meeting in Shepparton demanding that everyone born in Greece attend 'because you are all Greeks'; he reminded them of their obligation of loyalty to Greece, that they had families still living there and he spoke of the Macedonian bishop as 'a devil sent to cause mayhem'.[104] Macedonians perceived the Greek bishop as a political figure representing the Greek government rather than a pious religious cleric, and the link between government and church should not come as a surprise as the Greek Government paid the salaries of all Greek Orthodox priests.

Provocative and threatening statements by Greek bishops and other anti-Macedonian elements have had an effect on sections of the Macedonian community who gradually withdrew from Macedonian community activities, replacing the Macedonian church for the Greek church and adopting a 'Greek/Greek-Macedonian' pseudo-identity. The eminent Australian historian Charles Price described Macedonians (from under Greek rule) choosing to join in with Greek Orthodox communities and 'Greek Macedonian' social organisations, because the Greek government made it difficult for them to bring out their families if they joined Macedonian Orthodox communities. Alignment with the Greek community meant that Macedonians were able to keep bringing relatives out unhindered, 'preserve them from harsh treatment' in Aegean Macedonia and lighten their economic difficulties back home. Once all their relatives were brought out, many reverted to religious and social life exclusively with the Macedonian community.[105]

In a study of Macedonians in Shepparton undertaken by James

Mapstone as part of a doctoral dissertation in the 1960s, he found that pro-Greek sentiments expressed by members of the Macedonian community 'may signify an expedient decision rather than total commitment to Greece'. Comments made by members of the Macedonian community which were drawn upon in the study to the effect that they took a pro-Greek stand 'because they feared that their relatives still in Greece would be shown discrimination if they did otherwise'. One respondent said that although he wanted to baptise his son in the Macedonian Orthodox Church, he went to the Syrian Orthodox Church because he 'did not want anything to happen to his family in Greece'. Another Macedonian stated that he wanted his daughter's marriage ceremony to be conducted by a Greek Orthodox priest due to fears for the welfare of his family in the village.[106] For many, attending a Greek church was in principle an unwanted experience, but one they felt pressured to do. One of many examples applies to John Nitson, a proud Macedonian from Lagen village (Lerin) who married in a Greek church in Melbourne in 1963 because his father was concerned about repercussions on family members should the wedding ceremony have taken place in a Macedonian church.

The experience of harsh oppression under Greek rule, which defined non-Greeks as inferior, had negative consequences for the self-perception of Macedonian identity for a section of the Macedonian population. In 'Assimilation and the Public and Private Identity of Macedonians: A Dialectical Expose', Pandora Petrovska examined the effects of assimilation on Macedonians from Aegean Macedonia under Greek rule, the socio-psychological consequences of the partitioning of Macedonia on the individual and the process that brought about ethnic change. Petrovska explained that fear induced by political, linguistic and cultural subjugation and the psychological effects of assimilation brought about a changeability in the ethnic self-identification of some Macedonians in Australia. A dual identity developed, where depending on the situation a Macedonian 'public' identity was suppressed, usually replaced with a pseudo- 'Greek Macedonian' identity, whilst at the same time maintaining a well-developed 'private' identity, sharing the same language and culture as other Macedonians regardless of what part of divided Macedonia they came from.[107] As such, some Macedonians privately have continued to maintain a strong connection to their language and culture; however, publicly they appear to have adopted the pseudo-'Greek Macedonian' identity and attendance of Greek churches.

Evidence of pressures applied to silence individuals has been evident through sudden and, at times, extreme changes in behaviours. For example, individuals who had been publicly outspoken and proud of their Macedonian identity suddenly withdrew from community life for no apparent reason; or, in a less subtle transformation, some individuals have been known to switch overnight into proud and outspoken Greeks. In such instances it is commonly accepted that the individual was threatened, either directly in Australia, or indirectly via close family members back in Aegean Macedonia. Threats to family members back in the villages typically included termination from employment, having land confiscated or ongoing harassment by the police and other authorities.

Greek priests have played a key role in the attack upon all things Macedonian. In Greek churches where Macedonians attended, they were told that baptisms, weddings and funerals conducted in Macedonian Churches were invalid, as the independence of the Macedonian church had not been recognised by the Greek, Serb and Bulgarian Orthodox Churches. At every opportunity, Greek priests in Australia have undermined the Macedonian church, and failed to embrace democracy, respect for diversity and multiculturalism, as well as displaying a lack of Christian principles in their denial and attacks against Macedonian identity.[108]

In 1965, the Greek Orthodox Church strategically purchased a church in Yann Street, Preston, among the large Macedonian community living in that suburb. It was planned that the new church would be specifically for Macedonians from Aegean Macedonia, that church services would be conducted in Greek and, although the church would come under the jurisdiction of the Greek Orthodox Church, it would be known in everyday language to the Macedonian adherents as the 'Macedonian Church'.[109] This deliberate strategy to attract Macedonians aimed to facilitate their 'Greekness' in Australia as they would conduct wedding ceremonies and christen their children in the Greek church.

A significant and paradoxical feature of the church was the name it was given, 'Sts Cyril and Methodius'. At the time, no other Greek Church in the world carried that name, as Sts Cyril and Methodius are Macedonian patron saints born in the Solun region of Macedonia and are saints to all the Slavic-speaking peoples of Eastern Europe. Ironically, elderly Macedonians tell stories how, in the past under Greek rule, Macedonians hid religious icons of Sts Cyril and Methodius, for fear that they would be criminally charged for possessing an anti-Greek religious symbol. Prior to the establishment of the Republic of Macedonia as an independent nation in 1991, the Greek state 'did not attribute any special honours to the two famous missionaries, even though they were born in Solun'.[110] Historically, such was the disdain for the apostles that during the Balkan Wars of 1912-1913, Greek soldiers burned images of Sts Cyril and Methodius and covered their ashes with dung.[111] Interestingly, in response to the emergence of independent Macedonia, the Greek state and church began to claim and celebrate Sts Cyril and Methodius exclusively as their own, manipulating and exploiting historical facts for political aims, and even constructed a new church in Solun to honour the 'exclusive Greek heritage' of the two saints.[112]

Strategically, the first Greek priests appointed to the Sveti Kiril i Metodi church in Preston were actually Macedonians, from the Lerin region villages of Kleshtina and Opsirina and, although services were conducted in Greek, the priests openly communicated with their congregation in Macedonian. The Church Committee was made up exclusively of Macedonians from the Lerin region; they conducted Committee meetings using their Macedonian mother tongue; and parishioners were drawn to the church due to commonalities of language, ethnic origin and an apprehensiveness about attending the Macedonian Orthodox Church due to concerns at being branded anti-Greek, there being repercussions for family members living under Greek rule. Former parishioners of the church believe that its Macedonian character and semi-independence endured for years until the loan for the church was paid. At this time, the Greek Orthodox

Church altered its concessional position, removed the Macedonian priests, and replaced them with a Greek priest who was vehemently anti-Macedonian and opposed to the Macedonian language being spoken in the church by parishioners or committee members.

The extent to which the Greek Government interfered in Macedonian community affairs and attempted to dissuade Macedonians from attending their own church and guiding them towards the Greek Church has been notoriously deceitful. A 1973 Australian Security Intelligence Organisation (ASIO) background brief on Greek government interest in the Greek community in Australia examined visits to Australia by officers of the Greek intelligence service and included intimidation of Macedonians (from Greece). Pavlos Tsamis, believed to be a high-ranking army officer specialising in Macedonian affairs arrived in Victoria intending to meet with leaders of the Macedonian Orthodox Community in an attempt to persuade them to renounce the Macedonian church and join with the Greek Orthodox community.[113]

Peter Pantopoulos was a Macedonian involved in setting up the Macedonian Orthodox Church in Queanbeyan and served as president of the church community in the early 1970s. He was approached several times by Pavlos Tsamis, and a well-known builder in the Canberra Greek community, and threatened that if he did not leave the Macedonian community and join the Greek organisation he could never return to his native homeland and the Greek government would seize all his property in Aegean Macedonia.[114] Pantopoulos made representation about his continued harassment to Members of Parliament, Mr Bob Whan (Eden-Monaro) and Stephen Mauger MLA (Monaro). Mr Mauger accompanied Pantopoulos to the Greek Embassy in Canberra to complain about the intimidation.[115]

In Perth, the Greek anti-Macedonian lobby spearheaded by the Greek consulate offered $25,000 towards the construction of the Macedonian Community Centre on condition that they terminated the scheduled building of the first Macedonian church. Macedonian activists were also directly approached and offered large sums of money for the church not to be built. However, while the Macedonian community successfully erected its church, Sveti Nikola, the

Greek bishop in Western Australia attempted to control and influence the new church by offering a Macedonian priest from the Lerin/Kostur district of Aegean Macedonia and proposing that he (the bishop) should consecrate the new church which would also save the Committee considerable funds as they would not have to bring out a Macedonian bishop or priest.[116] Similarly, it was common knowledge in the Melbourne Macedonian community that community leaders associated with Sveti Giorgi Macedonian Orthodox Church were enticed by Greek agents to adopt a pro-Greek orientation in return for substantial amounts of cash and other rewards, including preferential treatment for family members back in Aegean Macedonia and employment in the government service.

Those involved in the setting up of the first Macedonian Orthodox Church, Sveti Giorgi, in 1960, were openly Communist in their political leanings with strong links to the Australian Communist Party.[117] Their political affiliations were exploited in a time when being linked to Communist ideology was seen as being anti-Australian. Those opposed to the Macedonian community in Australia exploited Macedonian political affiliations by denouncing Macedonians in an attempt to hinder the establishment of the church which resulted in Macedonian activists subjected to monitoring by ASIO for many years. Discrediting the Macedonian community served the interests of the anti-Macedonian lobby and reinforced to Macedonians that the reach of the Greek government policy extended to their daily lives in Australia.[118]

There is evidence that Macedonian activists with Communist views were being monitored from as early as the 1930s. Kole (Nick) Karadzhov from Dambeni village (Kostur) arrived in Australia with his brother John in 1938, and was outspoken about Greek government genocide of Macedonians, and the Macedonian right for independence and statehood. Kole headed out into the Western Australian bush to clear farmland and cut timber and, within two weeks of his arrival, officers from the Attorney General's Department located and questioned him about his political beliefs, activities, and intentions.

Due to the ability to gather large numbers of people, Macedonian social organisations were especially targeted to accept Greek outward appearance which could be achieved by using imposed Greek place names in place of original Macedonian ones. In Melbourne during the early 1950s, a social organisation was established and held regular dances in the Fitzroy and Collingwood town halls. The founding members were from the Lerin region villages Klabuchishta, Sveta Petka, Opsirina and Negochani and, although they intended for the organisation to be social in character and non-political, cautious not to be seen as anti-Greek, they registered it as the 'Florina Organisation' using the Greek name for Lerin town. Although this ensured they would not be labelled anti-Greek, using the Greek name for Lerin was a point of contention for many, as the name Florina suggested a Greek social organisation, even though Greeks did not attend the events. A band played traditional Macedonian *oro*, which was very popular. However, it was played without the lyrics being sung, a compromise intended to avoid attention from the Greek consul and Greek media organisations which would regularly report on such things.[119]

The Florina organisation eventually folded in the early 1970s: no doubt its demise was impacted by external influences such as intensified politicisation by those seeking to promote Greek identity and undermine Macedonian identity. Regular dances were subsequently held by village organisations; however, members of the Greek consulate attempted to politicise village organisations by their adoption of the Greek name of the village and becoming members of 'Greek Macedonian' umbrella organisations.[120] When this occurred it brought disharmony and division of village communities, and these actions were deliberately intended to disrupt the cohesiveness of the Macedonian community and attack Macedonian identity. Australian-Greek ethnic media played their part in the anti-Macedonian campaign, reporting on village organisations that did not adopt a Greek name, labelling them Communists, Bulgarians or other anti-Greek synonyms. Similar intimidating tactics were used on individual Macedonians who were publicly accused of being anti-Greek because they were openly pro-Macedonian.

The ongoing anti-Macedonian activities of the Greek state were exposed in a 1982 confidential Greek government report compiled by the Security Branch of the Greek Police. The report detailed the campaign against Macedonians, in Aegean Macedonia and worldwide, detailing the gathering of information on the activities of Macedonian tourists entering Aegean Macedonia; the activities of Macedonian organisations in Germany, Canada, United States and Australia, including Macedonian church functions and the opening of a new Macedonian community centre in Melbourne; the activities of Macedonian human rights organisations both in Greece and abroad; and, finally, a list of strategies and recommendations on how the Greek authorities should deal with Macedonians.[121]

The Greek hand in Australia has been immensely strengthened by their community's organised political influence. Of the post-war migrant communities, the Greek community had been the most prominent from the 1960s onwards, and particularly under the left-dominated Victorian branch of the Australian Labor Party. The Australian Labor Party was particularly close to the Tito regime in Yugoslavia and both elements within the Labor Party shared a common hostility towards Macedonian nationalism. As Greek-Australians rose to prominence, mainly in the Labor Party, they openly supported Greek national interests in Australia and influenced government policies to the detriment of the Macedonian community.

An intense surge in anti-Macedonian activity at the beginning of the 1990s corresponded with the disintegration of Yugoslavia and the emergence of the Republic of Macedonia as an independent state. Whilst the Greek government attempted to prevent the international recognition of Macedonia, the attack upon Macedonian identity reached new and absurd levels. It is troubling that Greek-Australian Federal and State Members of Parliament, including Ministers, as well as some local Councillors supported, and continued to openly support, the Greek government's discriminatory position on Macedonia and Macedonian identity.

The powerful Greek lobby in solidarity with Greek-Australian politicians activated all their resources to attack Macedonian identity, with perhaps the most infamous example involving the 1994

Federal Government reclassification of Macedonians in Australia as 'Slav Macedonians'. This Directive applied to all people whose ancestry was linked to the Republic of Macedonia, while other Macedonians from under Greek, Bulgarian or Albanian rule were required by the Directive to be referred to as 'individuals associated with Slav-Macedonians'. The Federal Government Directive was deeply offensive to Macedonians and essentially took away their right to possess an ethnic identity. Based on the Federal Government Directive and, in a brazen rush for votes, the Jeff Kennett Liberal Government in Victoria renamed the Macedonian language (in the Language Directive) in the state of Victoria as 'Macedonian (Slavonic)'.

Professor Michael Clyne, Head of Linguistics at Monash University, described the move as 'disturbing and nonsensical', while Professor Chris Candlin from Macquarie University's School of Linguistics stated that 'the term Macedonian Slavonic is a political designation which has no basis as a linguistic description'. The Macedonian community was outraged at the discriminatory treatment it received and the Macedonian Teachers Association and the Australian Macedonian Human Rights Committee challenged the Directive through the Human Rights and Equal Opportunity Commission. They fought the matter through the Federal Court, Full Federal Court and the High Court of Australia before it was referred back to the Human Rights and Equal Opportunity Commission for further hearing. After a six-year campaign to remove the racist and discriminatory Directive, in September 2000, Commissioner Street handed down his determination against the respondent (Victorian Government):

> I declare that the respondent has engaged in conduct rendered unlawful by the section 9 (1) of the Racial Discrimination Act 1975 by the act of issuing the directive in terms of the memorandum dated 21 July 1994 which involved a distinction based on ethnic origin in re-naming the language Macedonian and had the effect of impairing the recognition on an equal footing of a human right in the cultural life of users of the Macedonian language and I declare that the respondent should not continue such unlawful conduct.[122]

Following a sustained lobbying campaign by the Australian

Macedonian Human Rights Committee, the racist and discriminatory 'Slav Macedonian' Directive was officially withdrawn from use by Federal Government Departments and agencies on 11 January 2012.[123]

Yugoslav influence

The occupation of north-western Macedonia by Serbia during the Balkan Wars (1912-1913) resulted in this part of Macedonia falling under direct Serbian rule until 1944 when the Republic of Macedonia was formed in the newly established Socialist People's Republic of Yugoslavia. The Republic of Macedonia was a great achievement for the Macedonian people, who had raised arms and fought for their national emancipation and, although they enjoyed freedoms in the spheres of language, education, and culture and had their own assembly, Serbian influence was felt at all levels of society through 'Yugoslavianisation' of Macedonia. Any display of Macedonian independence was strictly opposed by Belgrade and criticism towards Yugoslavia or Tito was considered a crime against the state. When Macedonians began to emigrate, they were expected to identify as Yugoslav in their new homelands and to join in with other 'Yugoslav communities' to form one group with Serbs, Croats, Slovenians, Bosnians and Montenegrins. This of course was unrealistic as each ethnic group had its own separate identity, history and traditions long before the creation of Federal Yugoslavia in 1944.

In Australia, the Yugoslav embassy in Canberra and its consulates attempted to influence and control Macedonian churches, cultural groups, social and sporting clubs and other organised associations with the aim that they come under the banner of Yugoslav clubs. A network of cronies and informers operated under the instruction of the embassy and consulates and these individuals strategically joined Macedonian organisations – in particular, churches – to influence their activities, drawing them towards a pro-Yugoslav orientation. This could involve celebrating Yugoslav national day (29 November), inviting representatives from the Yugoslav consulate, and generally advocating a friendly position towards Yugoslavia.

Promoting a positive relationship with the Yugoslav regime, and working in cooperation with the consulate, allowed individuals to financially benefit from that relationship as they were given preference in developing business ties with state-run companies in the Republic of Macedonia, or special endorsements were granted giving exclusive rights to bring musical artists from Macedonia for concert events or to bring out the latest films for screening in cinemas. These individuals also monitored and reported to the consulate on individuals who were seen to be behaving in an unfriendly manner towards Yugoslavia. The suspected presence of spies, infiltrators and informants had a considerable impact on large sections of the Macedonian community; people were intimidated, and this created mistrust and division in the community. Dr George Trajkovski was the Yugoslav Consul General in Melbourne from 1975 to 1979. He had a well-known reputation for interfering in Macedonian community affairs, threatening those who would dare criticise Yugoslavia and the Tito regime, or advocate independence for Macedonia. The consulate used people to infiltrate Macedonian community groups and it was reported that Dr Trajkovski expressed confidence that the 'consulate would succeed in consolidating a foothold in other Yugoslav community groups including the Macedonian Church organisation in Melbourne in which they had infiltrators'.[124]

The Sveti Giorgi Macedonian Church was formed in Australia prior to the emancipation of the Macedonian Church from the Serbian Orthodox Church in the Republic of Macedonia, as we have seen. As such, the Sveti Giorgi Church and a number of other Macedonian churches established in Australia during the 1960s and 1970s did not legally come under the jurisdiction of the Macedonian Orthodox Church (in the Republic of Macedonia), but, however, acknowledged a 'spiritual connection' to the mother church. Other Macedonian churches established at this time accepted the jurisdiction of the church in Macedonia. However, during the 1970s, a serious rift developed due to Yugoslav interference attempting to unite the church under one religious law. Article 23 of a newly designed constitution stipulated that one must be a citizen of the Republic of Macedonia to be eligible for appointment to a church committee. This law effectively discriminated against Macedonians from Aegean

Macedonia and confirmed that the Macedonian church was under considerable pressure to adopt the political ideology of the Yugoslav Communist regime. Article 23 was a hard pill to swallow for Macedonians from Aegean Macedonia as they were generally the ones behind the setting up of the first Macedonian churches in Australia and suddenly found themselves feeling excluded and relegated to second-class Macedonians. This policy deliberately fostered division between Macedonians from under Yugoslav and Greek rule.

When the first priests arrived from Macedonia, they were considerably more educated than the average Macedonian. Outside of their religious role, the practical benefit of priests to the community was that they could help people to manoeuvre through government department enquiries and provide administrative assistance. As such, Macedonian priests had important roles in the community and exerted significant influence; however, there was also a menacing side to their role in that priests were often handpicked and arrived as agents of the state, expected to work in collaboration with Yugoslav consular officials in Australia. The historian Janko Tomov explains that priests attended a 15-day Yugoslav State Security Service (UDBA) training course prior to taking up their appointments in Australia.[125]

The link between Church and Yugoslav politics was a cause of conflict for many Macedonians. Often, there was little attempt to conceal the relationship. For instance, during the opening of a Macedonian Orthodox Church in Melbourne in 1977, the Yugoslav Consul-General, George Trajkovski, was invited by the parish priest as a special guest and given the honour of addressing the 1,000 Macedonians who had gathered for the event. The Consul opened his speech with the words 'in the name of Yugoslavia, Tito and the Party'.[126] This infuriated many in the crowd who saw the Consul as openly attempting to politicise and control the Macedonian church. The Yugoslav Consulate also took particular interest in public broadcasting and media and sought to influence – and control – the voice of Macedonian radio programming. In 1975, Access Radio, a government-sponsored radio station that aimed at giving ethnic communities their own voice commenced operation. On the opening day of the launch of the Macedonian program, listeners were astounded to hear the Yugoslav Ambassador to Australia open the program 'in the name of Yugoslavia'.[127] It was generally accepted that certain radio announcers on important Macedonian radio programs had the explicit endorsement of the Yugoslav Consul. Sporting clubs were also not immune to meddling by the Yugoslav Consul. The Consul attempted to influence the principal Macedonian soccer club Preston Makedonia towards a pro-Yugoslav position, offering lucrative sponsorship deals with Yugoslav Airlines (JAT).[128]

It was not uncommon for the Yugoslav Consul to use open blackmail and intimidation against the Macedonian community. A well-known Yugoslav consulate staff member would visit Macedonian community events, especially where newly arrived Macedonians from the Republic of Macedonia gathered and would openly say 'anybody who refuses to identify himself or herself as a Yugoslav, or in any way is connected with "unfriendly" immigrants towards the Yugoslav government, sooner or later, when such persons return to visit the "homeland" will be dealt with accordingly'.[129] Threats of this nature caused concern to many people.

Macedonian folkloric dancing groups flourished in the 1970s and 1980s as young Macedonians joined to learn traditional dancing in a social and cultural setting. Dancing groups were established under the auspices of respective Macedonian churches and considered controversial when the first such groups were established independently of church communities. The United Macedonians was an independent dance group, established in the 1980s amongst the large Macedonian community in the northern suburbs of Melbourne. The committee resisted pressure to be associated with one of the leading churches in Melbourne that had close links to the Yugoslav consulate and was subsequently subjected to overt intimidation when a well-known pro-Yugoslav figure attended a general meeting, threatening parents that, if they did not withdraw their children from the 'anti-Yugoslav organisation', they would have 'problems with the authorities when they return to Yugoslavia'.[130] This same individual was known to openly intimidate people in the inner western suburbs of Melbourne with threats that they would be recorded in the 'black book' if they partook in anti-Yugoslav activities. People clearly understood this to mean that Yugoslav authorities would be alerted to their identity and they would be persecuted when they return to their homeland.

The Yugoslav Secret Police, the UDBA, maintained detailed files on Macedonians living abroad and organisations which were seen as unfriendly to the state. Family members in Macedonia were warned by UDBA when relatives in Australia were openly critical of the Yugoslav regime or agitated for independence of the Republic of Macedonia and were pressured to encourage relatives in the diaspora to withdraw from involvement in political activities. Macedonians living in Australia and other Western countries, including *pechalba* workers in Western Europe, upon their return were often pressured to provide information on individuals suspected of being involved in anti-Yugoslav activity.[131]

One of the most important organisations in Australia, and worldwide, was the *Dvizhejne za Osloboduvajne i Obidinuvajne na Makedonija* (Movement for the Liberation and Unification of Macedonia), known by its acronym, DOOM.[132] Established by Macedonian political émigrés living in Western Europe in the 1950s and 1960s, DOOM became a large-scale international organisation which led the struggle for the establishment of an independent Macedonia. Australia became an important base for DOOM activity with chapters established across all major centres where Macedonians resided. Macedonians from Australia were appointed to key positions in the movement. Organisational congresses held in Western Europe drew representatives from the Macedonian diaspora, including Australia. At the 1974 Congress in Munich West Germany, attended by 60 delegates, four Macedonians from Australia were elected to the Central Committee.[133]

DOOM did not specifically advocate violence as a means to achieve its aims; nevertheless, it was viewed as a hostile threat to the integrity of Yugoslavia. In response UDBA conducted a clandestine campaign in Europe, North America and Australia, to discredit and destroy the organisation. DOOM came under intense scrutiny as UDBA agents were sent to infiltrate its ranks, leading members threatened, distributors of the DOOM publication *Makedonska Nacija* intimidated and the Macedonian community discouraged from buying *Makedonska Nacija* as it was deemed to be 'anti-Yugoslav'. As the voice of DOOM and the worldwide Macedonian patriotic movement, *Makedonska Nacija* reported on the anti-Macedonian policies of the Greek, Yugoslav and Bulgarian governments and exposed the activities of their foreign diplomatic missions amongst Macedonian diaspora communities.[134] DOOM and *Makedonska Nacija* were demonised and branded as subversive and dangerous.

In Perth, during the 1970s, the committee of the Macedonian Community Centre, overwhelmingly made up of Macedonians from Aegean Macedonia, raised funds in support of DOOM and its publication *Makedonska Nacija*. This drew the ire of the Yugoslav Consul-General who openly declared that their activities jeopardised the security of Yugoslavia. The Consul threatened people that they would be prevented from returning to their place of birth (Republic of Macedonia). However, his threats were of no use when it came to Macedonians from Aegean Macedonia, as the Greek state was already preventing activists from returning to their place of birth there. The threats and activities of the Yugoslav Consul in Perth were seen to be creating fracture and division between Macedonians from Aegean Macedonia and those from the Republic of Macedonia.[135]

Key DOOM activists and authors of articles in *Makedonska Nacija* used pseudonyms to protect their identity and shield family members in Macedonia from attention of UDBA. For example, in 1974, Zvonomir Stankovski a resident of Skopje and the brother of the editor of *Makedonska Nacija* in Belgium, was closely scrutinised and his passport confiscated by UDBA to prevent him from migrating and joining his brother in Belgium where it was feared that he would also become a DOOM activist.[136] Supporters in Macedonia such as Konstantin Dinevski (Dinkata), Pande Eftimov and Giorgi Ordev were sentenced and imprisoned for co-operation with DOOM and promoting *Makedonska Nacija*.[137]

In its determination to destroy DOOM, the UDBA campaign turned violent with leading activists threatened, assaulted, and murdered by UDBA agents. In August 1974, shockwaves were sent

Македонска нација

Благој Шамбевски загина за Македонија. Слава му!

Photo 64: Blagoja Shambevski on the cover of *Makedonska Nacija*, 1974. Published in West Germany, *Makedonska Nacija* was the voice of the *Dvizhejne za Osloboduvajne and Obidinuvajne na Makedonija* (DOOM) and the worldwide patriotic movement and distributed throughout Macedonian communities in Australia.

throughout the organisation when UDBA agents in Munich, West Germany murdered Blagoja Shambevski, Secretary; in the United States, Josif (Jole) Jolevski, Secretary of DOOM (United States), was killed; and Ljube Filkovski, Vice President of the Central Committee, seriously assaulted, suffering life-threatening injuries.[138] DOOM was sent into further disarray in 1979 when the President and ideologue Dragan Bogdanovski was kidnapped by UDBA agents in France, drugged and conveyed in a Yugoslav diplomatic vehicle to Yugoslavia where he was put on trial in Skopje, Macedonia. According to official Yugoslav press reports of the trial, Bogdanovski was arrested after entering Yugoslavia illegally. His trial lasted two days in Skopje district court, where he was accused of 'association for the purpose of hostile activity against the state' from 1956 to 1979 while he was living in Western Europe.

According to the public prosecutor, Bogdanovski 'intended to undermine the social and political order of Yugoslavia, destroy the brotherhood and unity of the Yugoslav peoples and destroy the territorial integrity of Yugoslavia'.[139] The bogus trial found Bogdanovski guilty and sentenced him to 13 years jail. He served his sentence in the infamous political prison, Idrizovo, located outside Skopje, and was adopted as a prisoner of conscience by Amnesty International. Bogdanovski was released from prison in 1989 and, following the disintegration of the Yugoslav federation, he founded the political

Photo 65: Protest outside the former Yugoslav consulate in Melbourne organised by the United Macedonians of Victoria organisation demanding that Macedonians in Australia were afforded the right to participate in the first multiparty elections in the Republic of Macedonia, November 1990. (Source: Vangel Paterov).

party VMRO-Democratic Party for Macedonian National Unity (VMRO-DPMNE).[140] VMRO-DPMNE would become the most popular Macedonian political party in the diaspora with branches formed in almost all countries where there are sizable Macedonian communities, including Australia.

Intimidation and threats of DOOM activists, the high-profile murder of Shambevski and the kidnapping, trial and sentencing of Bogdanovski, reinforced the fearsome reputation of UDBA. Its reach beyond the borders of Yugoslavia created a real sense of fear and an atmosphere of suspicion amongst Macedonian Diaspora communities. Eventually, UDBA succeeded in its quest to destroy DOOM, usurping the organisation rather than wiping it out; however, small autonomous groups of loyal DOOM activists continued to operate for at least another decade, throughout the 1990s, passing the ideals of Ilinden on to the next generation and inspiring the establishment of new groups such as the United Macedonians.

Individuals with links to DOOM formed the United Macedonians organisation in Melbourne in the late 1980s, at a time when DOOM was in a state of decline. The United Macedonians would become one of the most important Macedonian political organisations in Australia in the late 1980s and early 1990s. It emerged at a crucial historical juncture as the Communist regimes in Europe began falling apart, leading to the disintegration of Yugoslavia. Unlike other prominent Macedonian organisations at that time which were generally positioned to the left and maintained friendly relations with the government of the Republic of Macedonia, the United Macedonians' leadership was rightist in orientation. It promoted secession of the Republic of Macedonia from Yugoslavia and the replacement of the socialist one-party system with a multi-party democracy. It openly opposed the influence of the Yugoslav consulate upon the Macedonian community and Macedonian Orthodox Church.

Endnotes

1 *Makedonska Iskra*, August 1950, p. 3.

2 Amongst the participants in the theatre production, *'Eden noyk pred Ilinden'*, were Trajan Damchev, Pando Kozarov, Dime Panoff, Sime Shapardanov, Giorgi Markovsky, Krume Filipov and Trajche Kolevsky. *Makedonska Iskra*, August 1954, p. 1.

3 A significant anniversary celebrated by Macedonians is 11 October (1941), which marks the date when Macedonians took up arms against occupying Nazi German and Bulgarian fascist forces during World War Two. The date was widely celebrated in Australia with large gatherings of Macedonians to honour the event; for example, in Sydney during the early 1980s, community celebrations were simultaneously held in Rockdale, Tempe, San Peters, Bass Hill, Villawood and other areas. In Bass Hill, the celebration was organised by the Yaguna Macedonian language school '11 October', the Makedonia soccer club from Yaguna and the Cultural Dance Group 'Makedonia' from Yaguna. I. Trpovski, '11-ti Oktomvri Svecheno Proslaven vo Sydney' [11 October Formally Celebrated in Sydney], pp. 20-21 in *Povod - Spisanie za Literatura, Kultura i Prosveta* [Povod - Periodical for Literature, Culture and Education], Drushtvo Grigor Prlichev, Sydney, November 1985.

4 *Makedonska Iskra*, August 1948, p.4 and August 1953, p. 3.

5 Done Dimov archival documents.

6 *Makedonska Iskra*, November 1950, p. 3.

7 *Makedonska Iskra*, June/July 1951, p. 3.

8 *Makedonska Iskra*, July 1949, p. 4. Veljan passed away in Sydney in June 1949, at 65 years of age.

9 Krsto Malikov died on 23 January 1952 as Chris Mallek, as he had Anglicised his name in Australia. He never returned to his homeland. After the Second World War the Republic of Macedonia fell under Communist Yugoslav rule and as Malikov was politically right-leaning he believed he would be unwelcomed by the authorities and likely face imprisonment. Giorgi Cekutkov, article titled 'Krsto Malikov', Makedonska Nacija website (www.makedonskanacija.mk), 15 April 2015.

10 *The Poverty Bay Herald*, 25 January 1905, p.4. Article titled 'Torrid Australia - Macedonians for the Northern Territory'.

11 *Makedonska Iskra*, September 1955, p. 1. Article titled 'Australian at Ilinden - A.G. Hales'.

12 *Border Watch* (Mt Gambier), 11 October 1930, p. 6.

13 M. Zekulich, *Costa's New World - The Life Story of Costa Kapinkoff*, Scott Print, Perth, 2007, pp. 15-16.

14 Mick Veloskey interview. Veloskey and Malco were soon followed into the air force by another Macedonian, George Pappas from Dambeni village (Kostur) who was also living in Perth at the time.

15 George Stefanoff and Margaret Ruhfus (nee Stefanoff) interview.

16 J. Factor, *Forgotten Soldiers: Aliens in the Australian Army's Employment Companies during World War II*, p. 2. http://www.yosselbirstein.org/pdf/eng/other/Forgotten_Soldiers.pdf

17 Ibid., pp. 5-6.

18 M. Trajcevski editor, *Kompas*, Vol 4, issue 1, number 13, p. 8.

19 John Karadjas interview.

20 *Sunday Times* (Perth), 31 August 1947, p. 4.

21 Connie Sideris interview transcript.

22 Founded in Fort Wayne, Indiana, it was originally established as the Macedonian Political Organisation before a name change to Macedonian Patriotic Organisation in 1952, but commonly known by its acronym, MPO. The organisations slogan has always been for a free and united Macedonia; however, it is also known for being pro-Bulgarian.

23 *Makedonska Iskra*, May 1948 issue, p. 3. Article titled 'Makedonsko Progresivno Dvizhenje vo Avstralia – Kako se organizira toa i koi se prvite initsiatori' [Macedonian Progressive Movement in Australia – How it was organised and who were the first initiators] by S. Sarbinov.

24 Attorney General's Department, Investigation Branch, Canberra, Memorandum for the Secretary of External Affairs, D/1054, dated 13 March 1935, National Archives of Australia.

25 V. Andonov, *Makedoncite vo Avstralija* [The Macedonians in Australia], Kultura, Skopje, 1973, p. 40.

26 *Makedonska Iskra*, May 1948, p. 3 and interview with Mick Veloskey. Edinstvo quickly grew and would also include Vasil Boskov, Todor Petroff, Boris Mano, Naum Mano, Lazo Mano, Kiro Angelkov, Stojan Sarbinov, Naum Kalchunov, Stoiche Stoichev and others.

27 Mick Veloskey interview.

28 *Makedonska Iskra*, May 1948, p. 3.

29 Mick Veloskey interview.

30 Commonwealth of Australia, Security Service, Document dated 23 October 1945, National Archives of Australia. The cablegram was signed by G. Mlantis, President and Boris Manoff, Secretary, Edinstvo.

31 Minutes from public meeting held by Edinstvo on 27 January 1946, Archive of the Macedonian Community of Western Australia.

32 S. Sarbinov, *Makedoncite vo Avstralija, 1940-1988* [The Macedonians in Australia 1940-1988], unpublished, p. 2, and Department of External Affairs, 'Yugoslavia – Yugoslav Immigrants' Association' (1947), National Archives of Australia.

33 S. Sarbinov, op. cit. p. 3.

34 *Makedonska Iskra*, November 1950, p. 3.

35 Financial statement of the Macedonian Hospital Committee dated 29 August 1947. Archives of the Macedonian Community of Western Australia.

36 Final financial statement of the Macedonian Australian Hospital Committee. Archives of the Macedonian Community of Western Australia.

37 V. Andonov, op. cit., p. 62.

38 Report of the Second Conference of the Macedonian Australian Peoples League, Western Australia, 31 August 1947 (Archives of Macedonian Community of Western Australia). Voting held by the branches included potential names for the hospital in Macedonia. Most voters selected Lazar Trpovski, a Macedonian national hero from Dambeni village (Kostur). Active in the liberation struggle in Aegean Macedonia he was imprisoned at Akronafplia from January 1939 to June 1941. Trpovski was eventually executed by the Greek government at Kozhani in 1943.

39 Ibid. A separate campaign to provide clothes for Macedonian refugees was organised in 1949 through the Red Cross.

40 Mick Veloskey interview.

41 Funds were raised by Macedonian communities in Australia and North America following the devastating earthquake in Skopje in 1963. Macedonians donated generously, with £3,500 collected in one evening at a public meeting in Melbourne. I. Chapovski, *The Macedonian Orthodox Church of St George*, York Press, Melbourne 1992, p. 45.

42 The women's committee was made up of G. Pappas, F. Dragun, K. Mias, P. Spiro, A. Pappas, A. Mladenis, N. Milias, L. Sincho and N. Karadzas. *Makedonska Avstralska Zhenska Seksia od Perth W.A. Minutna Kniga* 4 [Macedonian Australian Women's Section from Perth WA – Minutes Book 4], September 1948. Archives of the Macedonian Community of Western Australian.

43 Ibid.

44 Ibid.

45 *Army News* newspaper (Darwin), 5 May 1943, p. 3.

46 Mick Veloskey interview.

47 *Makedonska Iskra*, October 1946, p. 2.

48 *Makedonska Iskra*, September-October 1956, p. 5.

49 *Makedonska Iskra*, March 1948, p. 4; May 1948, p. 4; December 1946, p. 4.

50 *Makedonska Iskra*, October 1948, p. 1.

51 V. Andonov, op. cit., p. 144.

52 *The West Australian*, 15 April 1948, p. 21.

53 J. Shea, *Macedonia and Greece: The Struggle to define a new Balkan Nation*, McFarland, Jefferson, 1997, p. 172.

54 Ibid., p. 173.

55 P. Hill, *The Macedonians in Australia*, Hesperian Press, Perth, 1989, p. 86.

56 B. Bozinoski and V. Krstevski, *Chetvrta Generacija* [Fourth Generation], Macedonian Australian Association of Culture and Human Rights, Newcastle, 2012, pp. 367 (Riste Kulipach-Garabev interview).

57 T. A. Batrouney, *Cradle of Orthodoxy: St Nicholas Antiochian Orthodox Church Melbourne Victoria*, unpublished, 2001. The Lebanese St Nicholas Antiochian Orthodox Church was also known to the Macedonians as the Syrian Orthodox Church as many of the early Lebanese immigrants were known as Syrians.

58 C. A. Price, *Southern Europeans in Australia*, Melbourne University Press, Melbourne, 1963, p. 240.

59 B. Bozinoski and V. Krstevski, op. cit., p. 27.

60 Mick Veloskey interview. The Macedonians were grateful for the support they received from the Catholic and Anglican churches in Sydney but remained focused on establishing their own church. The committee sought to purchase an existing church, either in Newtown or Rockdale, amongst the Macedonian community; however, an Anglican church became available for purchase in nearby Roseberry. The purchase of this church in 1969, named Sveti Kiril i Metodi (St Cyril and Methodius), marks the beginning of Macedonian church life in New South Wales.

61 In a number of places around Australia prior to the establishment of their own church, in a sign of Christian brotherhood, Macedonians contributed towards the construction of other churches. For example, in Newcastle Phillip Pandel from Krpeshina village (Lerin) donated the roof tiles for the construction of the Russian Orthodox Church and provided an interest-free loan. B. Bozinoski and V. Krstevski, op. cit., p. 260.

62 L. Danforth, *The Macedonian Conflict: Ethnic Nationalism in a Transnational World*, Princeton University Press, Princeton, 1995, p. 213.

63 The following names appeared on the land title document for the site of the church at 82-92 Young Street Fitzroy, Paul Johnson (Pavle Janevski), Alekso Gjurovski, Done Opashinov, Tanas Rachkov, Krste Malinov, Tanas Naum Gazilajnov, John Milankov and Lazo Giamov. D. Merakovsky, *Istorija na Izma-*

meni Vernici [A History of Deceived Parishioners], Self-published, Melbourne, 2007, p. 15.

64 *The Age*, Melbourne, 3 August 1953, p. 2.

65 Kosta Kotchoff interview.

66 *Sydney Morning Herald*, 6 January 1954, p. 1.

67 D. Merakovsky, op. cit., p. 22

68 *Oro* is a traditional Macedonian folkdance where participants hold hands and dance in a circular motion.

69 Lazo Giamov interview.

70 Ibid.

71 T. Miovski, *Avstralija i Makedonskite Doselenici* [Australia and the Macedonian Immigrants], Misla, Skopje, 1971, p. 76.

72 Supreme Court of Victoria Judgement, April 1986, p. 7.

73 T. Miovski, 1971, op. cit., pp. 76-77. At around the same time (1967), the Macedonian Orthodox Church had broken free from its bondage under the Serbian Orthodox Church and re-established its independence two hundred years after its uncanonical abolition under Ottoman Turkish rule in 1767. The Sveti Giorgi Macedonian Orthodox Church in Young Street, Fitzroy was established in 1960.

74 Lazo Giamov stated that he worked as a real estate agent at the time and negotiated the sale with Archbishop Woods from the Anglican Church, who agreed to sell the property for a reasonable price on condition that it would continue to function as a church. Lazo Giamov interview.

75 D. Merakovsky, op. cit., p. 23.

76 Members of both church committees had strong links back in Macedonia with the struggle for independence from Greek rule, in particular during the recent Greek Civil War in the 1940s. Although there was a common sense of betrayal by the Greek Communist Party, members of the Sveti Giorgi committee were members of the Greek Communist Democritus League in Melbourne and this was an issue of contention between the two groups.

77 The Steering Committee was made up of three members, Risto Altin from Lagen village (Lerin), Stefo Alabakov from Neret village (Lerin) and Boris Vulkanov from Visheni village (Kostur). I. Chapovski, op. cit., p. 69.

78 Ibid., pp. 71-72

79 S. Sarbinov, op. cit., p. 6 and M. Clyne and S. Kipp, *Tiles in a multilingual mosaic - Macedonian, Filipino and Somali in Melbourne*, Australian National University, Pacific Linguistics, Canberra, 2006, p. 40.

80 S. Sarbinov, ibid., p. 6.

81 Appeal from the Macedonian Orthodox Community of Melbourne and Victoria to all Macedonian emigrants in Australia, 1960.

82 When the Macedonian Australian People's League ceased functioning, Edinstvo and other branches continued to work closely with the community and redirected their focus towards establishing churches.

83 Kosta Angelkov autobiography, unpublished, p. 116

84 Ibid., pp. 117-118

85 Ibid., p. 117

86 B. Bozinoski and V. Krstevski, op. cit., p. 262.

87 W. Lalich, 'Collective action of 'Others' in Sydney', *Journal of Multidisciplinary International Studies*, vol. 3, no. 1, January 2006, p. 16. (Lalich quotes the data from K. Cirevski, *Makedoncite vo Novata Tatkovina*, Sydney, 1999).

88 Macedonian (Self Independent) Eastern Orthodox Church, Receipts and Payments for the period ended 31 December 1967.

89 V. Bogdanovski, *Kratka Istorija za Prvite Makedonski Doselenici vo Kvinbejan* [A Short History of the Macedonian Immigrants in Queanbeyan], unpublished, 2009, and D. Dimov, *Staticheni vo Avstralija* [People from Statica in Australia], unpublished.

90 B. Bozinoski and V. Krstevski, op. cit., p. 365.

91 The Christmas-New Year period was the busiest on the Melbourne social calendar. During 1951-1952, a Christmas dance was held at the Oddfellows Hall on 25 December, a film screening event on 26 December, a community dance on 28 December, a New Year's Eve dance on 31 December and a New Year's Day dance at Oddfellows hall on 1 January.

92 P. Hill, op. cit., p. 71.

93 *Northern Star* newspaper, 15 April 1950, p. 8.

94 Ibid., p. 8.

95 Risto Vasilev was from Armensko village (Lerin) and Ana Vasileva from Egri-Dere village (Drama). Both families left their homes in Aegean Macedonia due to persecution by the Greek government and resettled in the Republic of Macedonia. Ana and Risto married in Skopje in 1955, at which time Risto worked as a musician and Ana worked in theatre. Upon their arrival in Melbourne in 1957 they initially lived in Fitzroy before making a permanent family home in nearby Carlton.

96 Velika Spirova interview.

97 B. Bozinoski and V. Krstevski, op. cit., p. 259. Interview with Gona Fotev-Murgev. Gona's father arrived in Australia in 1938.

98 S. Sarbinov, op. cit., p. 1.

99 Mick Veloskey interview, and 'A Life Macedonian Affairs – Interview with Mick Veloskey' from www.pollitecon.com

100 *Makedonska Iskra*, September-October 1956, p. 8.

101 Mitre refused to sign the oath and instead employed a solicitor to argue the case before the Greek authorities. However, following unsuccessful attempts at resolving the matter, his solicitor advised him to sign the oath and that, when he arrived in Australia, he could do as he pleased. Although in principle Mitre was opposed to the lawyer's suggestion, he finally agreed to the compromise which enabled him to leave and travel to Australia. Mitre Kircos (Kircov) interview.

102 Letter from Archbishop Ezekiel from the Greek Orthodox Archdiocese of Australia and New Zealand to the Honourable A.R. Downer, Minister for Immigration, dated 14 July 1960 (National Archives of Australia). It is interesting to note that the Minister's response was supportive of the Macedonian church and revealed government frustration with the demands of the Greek church.

103 Kosta Angelkov interview.

104 Vasil Rendev interview.

105 C.A. Price, op. cit., pp. 317-18.

106 J. Mapstone, *The Greek Macedonians of Shepparton: A study of immigrant assimilation in a rural area of Australia*, Australian National University, 1966, p. 47.

107 P. Petrovska, 'Assimilation and the Public and Private Identity of Macedonians: A Dialectical Expose', in Victor Bivell, ed., *Macedonian Agenda*, Pollitecon, Sydney, 1995, pp. 135-84.

108 There have been but a few rare examples of Greek priests displaying respect for Macedonian identity. Prior to the establishment of a Macedonian church in Newcastle, some in the Macedonian community attended the Saint Demetrius Greek Orthodox Church for their religious needs and found the priest, Father George, uncharacteristically non-political, welcoming, and respectful of Macedonians and their ethno-specificity. When the Sveta Bogorodica Macedonian Orthodox Church was established, and due to be blessed in 1969 by a Bishop from Macedonia, Father George approached the Macedonian Church Committee requesting permission to attend the blessing ceremony of the new Macedonian church and to meet with the bishop, to which the committee agreed and Father George subsequently attended the blessing ceremony. T. Miovski, 1971, op. cit., pp. 81-82 and B. Bozinoski and V. Krstevski, op. cit., p. 176 (interview with Kole Sazdanoff). See Miovski for further interesting detail regarding this story.

109 D. Merakovsky, op. cit., p. 43.

110 T. Passios, 'Greece Exploiting St. Cyril and Methodius for Political Aims', in *UMD Voice*, Vol VIII, Winter Edition, 2010, p. 12.

111 Carnegie Endowment for International Peace, *Report of the International Commission to Inquire into the Causes and Conduct of the Balkan Wars*, Published by the Endowment, Washington 1914, p. 199.

112 T. Passios, op. cit., p. 12.

113 Australian Security Intelligence Organisation, Background Brief, 'Greek government interest in the Greek community in Australia – visits to Australia by officers of the Greek Intelligence service', No 30/73, dated 12 December 1973, National Archives of Australia.

114 In July 1974, Pantopoulos also raised his concerns about harassment and intimidation by Greek spies and agents in a letter to the Prime Minister of Australia. A month before he sent the letter, his wife's parents were denied entry into Greece and Mr Pantopoulos stated that they were treated like criminals at Athens airport. Letter dated 23 July 1974, National Archives of Australia.

115 Australian Security Intelligence Organisation, Background Brief, dated 12 December 1973, op. cit. Stephen Mauger was the Liberal Member for Monaro in the New South Wales Legislative Assembly from 1965 to 1976, and was Minister for Youth, Ethnic and Community Affairs from 1975 to 1976.

116 T. Miovski *Makedoncite vo Zapadna Avstralija* [The Macedonians in Western Australia], Zdruzhenie na decata begalci od Egejskiot del na Makedonija, Skopje, 1999, pp. 93-94.

117 Many within the MAPL leadership maintained friendly relations with Communist Yugoslavia and the Communist parties of the Balkan States, including the Greek Communist Party. Senior MAPL activists were also members of the Australian Communist Party.

118 John Karajas interview.

119 Following Greek occupation, Macedonian music was not permitted as the Greek government attempted to completely wipe out any trace of Macedonian culture. However, in defiance Macedonians continued to play their music without the lyrics being sung.

120 When the United Villages Florina social organisation was formed in 1977, to placate elements that sought to politicise and create disharmony, committee members conducted all speeches in English, which also calmed those frightened of potential repercussions if seen to be linked to activities seen as 'too Macedonian'. Following the establishment of the Republic of Macedonia as an independent state, the United Villages Florina social organisation folded and was replaced by a new organisation, United Macedonian Villages, which explicitly presented itself as Macedonian, rejecting any Greek influences. Sadly, renegade individuals supporting Greek propaganda against Macedonian iden-

tity sought to establish politically motivated breakaway fringe 'Greek-Macedonia' social organisations. The highly politicised nature of these groups has accelerated their irrelevance to the community at large.

121 See C. Popov and M. Radin, *Contemporary Greek Government Policy on the Macedonian Issue and Discriminatory Practices in Breach of International Law*, Central Organisational Committee for Macedonian Human Rights, Australian Sub-Committee, Lakeside Press, Melbourne, 1989.

122 Human Rights and Equal Opportunity Commission (HREOC), Racial Discrimination Act 1975 (Cth) No: H97/189, Australian Macedonian Human Rights Committee (Inc) (Complainant) and State of Victoria (Respondent), p. 34.

123 For a summary of the lobbying campaign see 'Australian Government announces policy shift and recognises Macedonian community' in http://www.macedonianhr.org.au

124 Foreign Affairs document, File No 554/5/54, dated 2 November 1976, National Archives of Australia.

125 J. Tomov, *Mojot Pridones za Makedonija* [My Contribution for Macedonia], Brisbane, 2014, p. 123. The course was structured for selected individuals and priests migrating to Western countries and Australia. The State Security Service (*Sluzhba Drzhavna Bezbednost*) operated as the Yugoslav Secret Police but was known by the acronym UDBA referencing the original name of the organisation (*Uprava Drzhavna Bezbednost*).

126 Outraged at the remarks of the Consul, he was attacked by a group of parishioners and thrown to the ground. *Nova Hrvatska* (Sydney), No 4, 20 February 1977, p. 6.

127 *The Macedonian Migrants in Australia and Access Radio*, Central Committee of the Movement for Liberation and Unification of Macedonia, Melbourne, August 1975, p. 2.

128 The Consul, Trajkovski, had also attempted to infiltrate Croatian and Serbo-Yugoslav clubs in Melbourne and was engaged in planning the removal of the presidents of the two respective clubs. The president of the JUST soccer club, which was the principal 'Yugoslav' team in Melbourne, was seen as being too politically right-wing in outlook, and associated with the Chetnik Serbian nationalist movement during the Second World War, while a new president for the Essendon Croatia Soccer Club was perceived as someone who should be 'favourably disposed towards Yugoslavia'. The Consul intended to gain control of both soccer clubs, and they would then receive the support of the Consulate and a sponsorship deal with Yugoslav Airlines (JAT). ASIO intelligence report titled 'Yugoslav Consulate General, Melbourne – Interest in the JUST and Croatian Soccer teams', Document Number 994/79, Dated 20 June 1979, National Archives of Australia. It is noted that since the breakup of Yugoslavia, soccer clubs that previously identified as 'Yugoslav' transformed into Serbian clubs.

129 *The Macedonian Migrants in Australia and Access Radio*, Central Committee of the Macedonian Liberation and Unification of Macedonia, August 1975, p. 2.

130 Kiril Rizmanoski interview.

131 Up until the 1990 disintegration of Yugoslavia, Macedonians returning on holiday were required to land in Belgrade, Serbia, before boarding a connecting flight to Skopje or Ohrid airports in Macedonia. UDBA officers at Belgrade airport routinely questioned Macedonians from Australia (and other Western countries) about suspected anti-Yugoslav activities of individuals in the host country.

132 The organisation would undergo three name changes during its three-decade lifespan. Originally formed as 'Osloboditelen Komitet na Makedonija' (OKM) in Copenhagen Denmark in 1962, it underwent a name change to 'Dvizhenje za Obidinuvajne i Oslobiduvajne na Makedonija' (DOOM) in 1972, before a further name change in 1973 to 'Makedonskoto Nacionalnoto Osloboditelen Dvizhejne' (MNOD). Despite the name changes it was universally known to Macedonians as 'Dvizhenje za Obidinuvajne i Oslobiduvajne na Makedonija' or more commonly by its acronym, DOOM.

133 The following Macedonians from Australia were elected to the DOOM Central Committee in 1974, Riste Ristevski Secretary, Stanko Vasilev Political Secretary, and committee members Mihail Sharinovski and Trpe Tsalev. J. Tomov, op. cit., pp. 27-28.

134 It was common for authors of articles in *Makedonska Nacija* to use pseudonyms to protect their identity and shield family members in Macedonia from the retribution of UDBA.

135 Kosta Angelkov interview.

136 Internal communication from *'Republichki Sekretarijat za vnatreshni raboti, Sluzhba za drzhavna bezbednost, odelenie na grad Skopje'* 10 April 1975, [Republic Secretariat for internal affairs, state security service, division for Skopje, 10 April 1971], www.makedonskanacija.mk

137 J. Tomov, op. cit., p. 68.

138 *Makedonska Nacija*, Issue 23, p. 7.

139 Amnesty International, *Yugoslavia – Prisoners of Conscience*, Amnesty International Publications, London, 1985, pp. 41-42. The kidnapping of Bogadanovski was strategically timed immediately before the Fourth Annual DOOM Congress. His non-attendance at the Congress caused confusion among the delegates as his whereabouts were unknown. Shortly after the Congress, letters started appearing, purportedly from Bogdanovski, with contradictory statements designed to cause disarray in the ranks. Months passed before it was publicly revealed that Bogdanovski had been kidnapped.

140 Bogdanovski was appointed honorary president of VMRO-DPMNE before his death in 1998.

Part Six

Society and Culture Down Under

15

Picnics, Marriage and Music

Picnics

Traditionally, in Macedonian villages people gathered outdoors to celebrate village saints' days and other religious occasions. These events were held in the village square (*sred selo*) where people would eat, drink and dance to live music played by a band. In contrast, in Australia, most Macedonians arriving after the Second World War lived in cities, in a different physical environment from the villages in Macedonia. In Australian cities they lived in streets with houses arranged side by side, rather than in clusters as in the village (*maalo*), where everyone knew each other or were otherwise related, and ownership of homes was passed down from father to son.[1] In Australia you would live next door to whoever bought the house and there was no village square for neighbours to gather for festive occasions.[2] Back in the village they worked out in the open in their fields, whereas in Australia they worked long hours in factories. In the warmer months of the year it was popular for Australian Macedonians to come together as a community, gathering in parklands and bush settings which reminded them of the environment they left behind in the village, the green hills, forests, hills and valleys. It was a way to reconnect with the natural settings of their village homes.

The gathering of large numbers of Macedonians in parklands and bush settings in Australia became an important social tradition for the Macedonian community. Coming together for picnics provided them with an opportunity to gather in a 'spirit of community reunion, the chance to hear one's language and encounter one's own people *en masse*, [which] can be contrasted with day to day experiences when, as recent migrants, people so often felt their minority status'.[3] In market gardening and rural areas during the 1930s and 1940s, picnics were often held and rotated on farms belonging to Macedonians. In the 1930s, in Werribee South, one of the first community picnics was on the Goulopoulos family farm in O'Connor's Road; in Bridgetown, Western Australia, a picnic was held on the Surlev family farm, while in Wanneroo Macedonians initially gathered on farms before utilising the Wanneroo Showgrounds for regular community picnics. One of the first picnics held by the Newcastle Macedonian community was at the Kozari family farm in Medowie during the 1940s.[4] In Geraldton, picnics were held on Macedonian-owned farms until the community acquired its own land in the 1950s, which was then used as a dedicated picnic ground where Macedonians gathered every third week.

Community members took turns for the tasks in preparation for the gatherings, including food preparation, purchasing beer, and delivering supplies among other things. Co-operation was on such a scale that, according to Stan Milenko, 'it was as if we all had one father'.[5] In NSW in the 1940s and 1950s, Macedonian community picnics were held in Mona Vale, which was a Macedonian tomato-growing area; Nielsen Park on Sydney Harbour; Ashton Park at Mosman; and Picnic Point, Kiama and Royal National Park. The latter was well located between Sydney and Wollongong. Parkland in Raymond Terrace was a popular picnic destination for Newcastle Macedonians during the 1940s with buses arranged to convey community members. One of the early community picnics in Melbourne was organised by the Macedonian Patriotic Organisation in 1936. Community picnics were held at Mt Evelyn in the 1950s and from 1956, an annual picnic was held at Kalorama in the Dandenong Mountains for at least several years. Mt Evelyn and Kalorama were a considerable distance from Fitzroy, the heart of the Macedonian community in Melbourne at the time, and a large number were transported on buses from Fitzroy to the picnic grounds.

Macedonians developed emotional connections with certain bush settings where they gathered which reminded them of their homeland and Macedonian historical figures. Popular amongst Macedonians in Victoria was Mount Macedon, known for its extravagant homes and gardens and named after King Phillip II of the Kingdom of Macedonia; Mount Alexander named after Alexander the Great; and the Campaspe River named after a mistress of Alexander the Great's.[6]

Photo 66: One of the earliest Macedonian community picnics held by Macedonians in Melbourne, 1936. (Source: Margaret Ruhfus – née Stefanoff).

Because overwhelmingly Macedonians are of the Orthodox Christian faith, they celebrate Christmas on 7 January according to the Julian calendar. Since at least the early 1940s, December 25, which Macedonians refer to as 'Catholic Christmas', has been celebrated with a community picnic.[7] In Crabbes Creek during the 1940s

Photo 67: Macedonians from Newcastle, Sydney and Wollongong gathered at a community picnic in New South Wales, 1946. (Source: Kiril Murgev. Courtesy of Mendo Trajcevski).

Christmas day picnics were held on farms belonging to Naum Pavlovich and Stojan Milankoff. In Sydney, Macedonians gathered on 25 December at Royal National Park (Audley) while large numbers of the Melbourne community traditionally gathered at Eastern Beach in Geelong. One of the biggest events on the Melbourne Macedonian social calendar, the 'Geelong picnic' drew thousands of Macedonians and afterwards, the Melbourne Macedonians would visit relatives and friends in Geelong.[8]

From the 1970s, Macedonian churches began purchasing their own picnic grounds and constructing monasteries on these sites. The first Macedonian Orthodox monastery in Australia was Sveti Kliment Ohridiski (St Clement of Ohrid) at Macedonia Park in Kinglake, while other monasteries were constructed at Rocklyn (Sveti Naum Ohridski – St Naum of Ohrid), Donnybrook (Sveti Prohor Pchinski – St Prophet of Pchinja) and at Kembla Grange (Sveta Petka – St Parascheva) in New South Wales. Each monastery celebrated its patron saint with a service and a large community picnic, whilst the Sveti Prohor Pchinski monastery was the first Macedonian monastery in Australia to have a resident monk.

Photo 68: Macedonian community picnic, Macedonia Park, Kinglake (Melbourne), 1970s. Note the buses in the background that were used to transport people from Fitzroy. (Source: Peter Sarbinov).

Village associations were formed in Australia, enabling people to socialise in a familiar setting and keep alive their connection to their village. The village association represented a way of holding on to village life. Each village had its own patron saint, and an annual function was considered one of the most important village events of the year. Quite a few village associations purchased their own picnic grounds as a way of keeping the village community intact and recreating the Macedonian village landscape in a rural Australian setting. One of the first village associations formed in Melbourne in 1947 was the Buf Village Association which later purchased a 22-acre picnic ground in Lancefield, aptly named 'Boufski Park', where village members gathered for picnics.

Marriage

In traditional Macedonian culture it was not uncommon for a bride and groom to meet for the first time on their wedding day. In *Children of the Bird Goddess*, Kita Sapurma and Pandora Petrovska explored the lives of four generations of Macedonian women. Set in the late nineteenth century, two men from the villages of Rakovo and Bitusha, while on *pechalba* in Wallachia, struck up a friendship and decided that, as they each had a son and a daughter of marrying age, they should become in-laws. The two men wrote home to their families announcing that there would be a wedding when they returned home and gave instructions for the wedding preparations to commence. The day that the groom and his clan arrived in Bitusha at the home of the bride was the first time the bride and groom saw each other.[9]

Many *pechalbari* left young brides in Macedonia and brought them out after establishing themselves in Australia, whilst others having arrived as single men either returned to Macedonia for a bride or would seek out unmarried Macedonian girls in Australia. Due to a lack of unmarried Macedonian girls in Australia at that time, and parents being very strict, young single men would seek out unmarried girls, but had to approach their fathers to ask about their daughters. As Macedonians were dispersed around Australia, suitors would send letters to their potential bride's father and travelled considerable distances in search of a bride. In the 1930s Aleksandar Stefanoff travelled from Newcastle to Melbourne after hearing about a potential bride. The young women had to agree with the arrangement. Christine Trandos tells the story how, in the 1960s in Perth, suitors would come to her home and the expectation was that she would have to make a decision without knowing the boy, and that the older generation were 'impressed if a suitor came from a good family with money or property. But it was a difficult situation for the girl. Basically, she had to be betrothed to go out'.[10]

Other young men would return to the village in search of a potential bride. Suitable marriage partners were found through family networks and word of mouth, often through an intermediary known as a *stroinik* and arrangements could be finalised in a very brief timeframe, without any formal courtship taking place. A young man could write to his family expressing his intentions to find a marriage partner; arrangements were made for an exchange of pictures; and if both parties agreed, and with the endorsement from the two family patriarchs, a wedding would be organised. A potential bride could meet her future husband in Australia for the first time. Traditional methods for organising marriages still worked well in the first half of the twentieth century. When the time came for Kosta Pandov in Richmond, New South Wales, to seek a wife, his mother wrote to her cousin in Bistrica village (Bitola), sending a photograph of Kosta and requesting that he enquire about a potential bride for her son. Enquiries were made in the village through the parents of a potential bride, family reputations confirmed, photographs exchanged and the potential bride, Milica Kuzovska, agreed to the arrangement. Agreement on marriage was reached by both parties and documentation prepared to bring out the bride. Upon her arrival at Sydney airport in 1962, Milica and Kosta sought each other out with photographs in hand.

The practice of arranging marriages using no more than a photograph to confirm the appearance of a potential partner can have its drawbacks. In 1934, a Western Australian newspaper reported on the unusual events surrounding 'a marriage contract' in that a Macedonian resident of Wanneroo exchanged photographs with a girl in Macedonia and they agreed to get married. However, the photograph the suitor sent the girl was taken when he was much younger. When she arrived in Australia, she saw that he was considerably older than depicted in the photograph and decided not to go through with the

Photo 69: Celebration for Milica Kuzovska in Bistrica village (Bitola region) prior to leaving for Australia to marry Kostadin Pandov in Richmond, New South Wales, 1962. (Source: Kosta Pandov).

marriage. Within a couple of weeks, the young woman arranged to marry another Macedonian at Wanneroo. 'The new prospective bridegroom then arranged that the previous contract be annulled by the simple expedient of paying the first suitor £30 for the furniture which he had accumulated'.[11]

In the 1950s and 1960s, opportunities for young men and women to meet were at dances, picnics and other community gatherings. Wherever Macedonians formed communities, they came together socially to celebrate. Key dates revolved around religious days, particularly Easter and Christmas, Ilinden (St Elijah's day, which marks the beginning of the 1903 Ilinden Uprising); various saints' days such as Sts Cyril and Methodius; 'Miss Macedonia' competitions, various fundraising nights and village dances. Macedonian community life was vibrant. In Melbourne during the 1950s and 1960s, every Sunday night there was a community dance held in Fitzroy Town Hall, Collingwood Town Hall, or St Luke's Church Hall in North Fitzroy. A band performed traditional Macedonian music as well as modern English music. Entire families attended, often three generations of the one family. Everyone dressed in their best clothes. It was an opportunity to catch up with family and friends and dance to traditional Macedonian music which was very popular with young and old alike. Chairs positioned around the perimeter of the hall were reserved in the first instance for the old people as a mark of respect.

Macedonian community life was still quite conservative at that time. Community morals were conservative, and girls and boys stayed separated on opposite sides of the hall, with the girls under the watchful eyes of their parents. It was acceptable for a girl to dance with a boy once during the evening, but to have a second dance with the same boy indicated they were serious and gave the expectation that they would marry. It was normal during courting that the parents agreed that their son and daughter could go out and it was mandatory that they would be chaperoned. It was often up to the parents to agree on marriage arrangements.[12] This system of courtship and marriage in Australia largely ended in the 1960s.

Peter Mechkaroff, born in Neret village in 1934, tells how most marriages were arranged in the villages and that, even if a boy and girl liked each other, it was up to the parents to decide if it was a good match. Peter related the following story about a poor young man who could not find a suitable girl in his village and was told about a girl in a neighbouring village available for marriage. He went with his mother to meet the girl; however, her family considered – as she was a very plain girl – they were afraid she might be rejected. So, when the young man arrived, they organised for him to meet their daughter-in-law, who was agreed to be quite pretty. When the young man saw the girl, he was happy and agreed to the marriage. The families exchanged gifts, the engagement was formalised, and a wedding date was fixed for two weeks' time. On the day of the wedding, when the bride entered the church as the groom was standing at the altar, he muttered to his mother that it was not the same girl. However, as people put a premium on respect and shame and his mother did not want to cause embarrassment to the families, she said 'whether this is the girl or not, this is now your fate and you must marry her', and the marriage ceremony went ahead.

Photo 70: Cveta Trajkovska (left side) from Dolno Dupeni village (Prespa) disembarking from the Italian passenger ship *SS Galileo Galilei* at Port Melbourne in 1970. Cveta arrived in Melbourne to marry Vasil Kalcovski from Brajchino, a neighbouring village to her own. (Source: Gele Kalcovski).

During the 1950s and 1960s, throughout the year, but in particular, during the warmer months, the Exhibition Gardens in Carlton was a central meeting place for Macedonians living around Fitzroy. Young and old, families with children, and young single men were drawn there. People went there to find marriage partners and fathers went there to seek potential husbands for their daughters. Pavle Velov from Dolno Kotori (Lerin) village met his future wife there, Lena from Asanovo village (Lerin), and they married in 1961. Macedonian weddings were grand events traditionally celebrated over three days; weeks were spent preparing for the event and no expense was spared, with all extended family members, villagers and friends invited. There were elaborate wedding rituals, some of which have been brought to Australia, such as the mandatory shaving of the groom by the godfather on the day of the wedding. In the 1950s and 1960s, Macedonian weddings in Australia were held in civic town halls and were very different to the modern extravagant version held in reception centres today. Family and close friends were the first to be invited and arrived in the early evening to a sit-down dinner while a band played traditional Macedonian music. After dinner, tables were removed and chairs positioned alongside the walls to allow for an enlarged dance floor in preparation for the arrival of further guests, invited through a general invitation, to join in the celebration. Macedonians generally preferred that their children marry within their own culture and, in the past, studies have shown that Macedonians have maintained a high level of marriage within the group. A 1960s study by James Mapstone found that, of 92 marriages in the Shepparton Macedonian community, only two were outside the community. Other studies in the 1970s and 1980s revealed similar results. Anecdotal evidence suggests these statistics are changing in the twenty-first century.

Photo 71: Wedding photo of John and Kathy Kalcovski (from Brajchino village, Prespa and Armenoro village, Lerin, respectively) taken at Studio Nicolitch, operated by Pavle Nikolovski from Ohrid, on Gertrude Street, Fitzroy, 1964. (Source: John and Kathy Kalcovski).

Music

Traditional folk music, song and dance are integral parts of Macedonian culture. Songs reflect Macedonian life, and many are specific to particular occasions, such as when young men were preparing to leave their village to go on *pechalba*. *Pechalba* songs told stories of hardships that lay ahead, the isolation of working in foreign lands, and the pain of separation from loved ones. From their earliest arrival in Australia, Macedonian sleeper cutters, eucalyptus oil producers and other bush workers came together to share a drink, smoke, and sing songs expressing love for their families and homeland. It was typical that there was someone able to play a musical instrument during these times. Traditional Macedonian instruments were the flute (*shupelka* and *kaval*), large double reed horn (*zurla*), drum (*tapan*), bagpipe (*gajda*), three-string fiddle (*kemane*) and the accordion (*harmonika*). Each village had their own musicians to play at weddings and other village celebrations. Just as some villages were renowned for their men being linked to certain trades and occupations, there were also particular villages renowned for its musicians;

for example, in Trnava village, 'There was no shortage of musicians, all the men were musicians. It was like a tradition: everyone knew how to play an instrument'.[13] Prior to formal bands being established, anyone who could play an instrument provided the musical entertainment, and they were usually not very hard to find. In Wanneroo (Western Australia) in the early 1940s, families would often come together in an outdoor open space and a couple of men would play the banjo and trumpet for traditional Macedonian dancing.[14]

With the transition from an itinerant workforce to the establishment of communities in both regional areas and large urban centres, musical bands were formed in Macedonian communities and performed at weddings, christenings, dances, picnics and other celebrations. In Perth, a band of six musicians led by Jovan Peioff was formed in late 1946, which included Giorgi Gotcheff, Kosta Trpoff, Costa Kapinkoff, Stase Milentseff and Tony Veliovsky. Hristo Mechkaroff led a band in Manjimup, Western Australia, formed in 1942 and known as '*Makedonska banda*' with Risto Dimiroff, Petre Vlaoff and Sotir Koleff. In the 1940s, D. Velevich, a bagpipe player, led a band in Crabbes Creek, New South Wales; Alek Chadevich and Natso Trpcheff were popular musicians in Richmond, New South Wales, whilst Krste Kotevitch and Jone Belcheff were well known in the Rockdale area in Sydney. In Adelaide, three first cousins from German village (Lerin) formed a band made up of drummer Chris Kufalov, clarinettist Elia Kufalov and violinist Kole Mechkarovsky.

There were several bands in Melbourne during the 1940s and 1950s: Pavle from Neret village led a band and Pavle 'Matcheto' from Negochani village had a band. One of the most popular Macedonian bands in Melbourne during the 1950s and 1960s was the Lagen band ('*Lagenskata banda*'), led by George Hristov who played the piano accordion, along with four other band members. In Newcastle during the 1940s and 1950s, a band made up of Zhivko Kekev, Mile Todorovski, Riste Garabev, Johnny Fotev and Mijal Murgev performed at community events, while around the same time a band played at the South Werribee Macedonian monthly dance and the popular bagpipe player, Pavle Zhivanov from Sveta Petka village (Lerin), known as Pavle 'Gaidadzhijata' ('the bag piper') was from the local community. Pavle later moved to Shepparton where, together with his brother Krste, also a musician, they were very popular, playing at Macedonian celebrations and community functions. Musicians in constant demand would travel considerable distances for events. Petse Lazhenka from Sale, Victoria travelled to Sydney to sing (together with Georgi Zagroff from Sydney) at the MANS national conference gala dance in 1948; while in 1957, the Melbourne band 'Bilyana', led by Stefo Duketoff of Clifton Hill, travelled to Queanbeyan, NSW, to play at the wedding of the daughter of G. Douros.[15] Performing at Macedonian community functions and, in particular, weddings, provided musicians with surprisingly good income. In 1951, *The Argus* newspaper in Melbourne reported on the Macedonian wedding custom of guests sticking pound notes to the foreheads of musicians.[16]

Photo 72: Macedonian band performing in Sydney, circa 1960. (Source: Arthur Petrou).

Prior to the 1960s, Macedonian musicians in Australia predominantly came from Macedonia under Greek rule, due to most Macedonians being from Aegean Macedonia at that time. They were untrained and self-taught village musicians who preserved traditional Macedonian music even though it had been strictly forbidden by the Greek authorities. In contrast, since the end of the Second World War, apart from songs deemed too political, Macedonian music generally developed freely in the Republic of Macedonia. When Macedonians migrated to Australia in large numbers from the Republic of Macedonia in the 1960s and 1970s, among them were accomplished musicians, men who had formally studied Macedonian music and possessed a high standard of technical ability. In the 1970s there were approximately 20 trained musicians in Melbourne alone, with a similar number in Sydney. They brought a new standard of Macedonian music to the community and were regularly sought after to perform at weddings, christenings and other functions.

Photo 73: Farewell celebration with musicians in a Port Kembla backyard for Mitre Trajcevski's return to Macedonia, circa 1963. (Source: Mendo Trajcevski. Photograph by Dragan Grozdanovski).

The development of Macedonian musical bands in Australia was closely connected with the proliferation of dancing groups that were set up under the auspices of Macedonian Orthodox Churches. These cultural groups were very popular with young Macedonians: as a central cultural activity the groups became focal points within the community, and they made a significant contribution towards maintaining and promoting Macedonian identity with the young generation, many of whom were born and raised in Australia. Dancing groups sought out experienced choreographers to ensure that dancers performed to high artistic standards. In Sydney, during the 1960s and 1970s, the choreographer for the Ilinden Dance group (Sveta Petka church in Rockdale) acquired the services of a former dancer with the Macedonian National Dance Group, 'Tanec', in Skopje.[17] Dancing groups performed traditional Macedonian dances, often complex and technically challenging and each group had its own signature dance. Performers dressed in elaborate and colourful traditional costumes which were often manufactured in Macedonia specifically for the dance groups. Dancers performed in Macedonian community competitions between dancing groups at state and national level. They went on overseas tours to Macedonia, Europe and North America and took part in Australia Day celebrations, multicultural events and Moomba parades.

A band provided the music for each dancing group. Bands consisted of teenage boys, as young as 14 or 15, and usually not much older than 17, playing the piano accordion, drums, guitar and clarinet. Older established musicians provided tuition for the new generation of teenage boys playing Macedonian music in Australia and some young students travelled to Macedonia to train under the instruction of accomplished musicians. These musical bands played once or twice a week providing music for the folk dancing groups to train with. The bands trained all year round and performed before large audiences at the annual dancing group dinner dance. For many, this was the turning point where they came to the realisation how much Macedonians loved their traditional music, combined with the thrill of performing live. This inspired many young band members to further pursue music beyond the dancing group. These bands went on to perform at annual village association dinner dances and became available for weddings and christenings. Earnings could be very high for bands that were in demand, as one night's work could easily be the equivalent of the average weekly wage.

The number of musicians and musical groups peaked in the 1980s and 1990s, at which time the Melbourne Macedonian Musicians Association was formed, which advocated the promotion of Macedonian music and culture, fostered collaboration between musical bands and provided musicians with improved buying power, enabling instruments and equipment to be purchased at discounted prices. Large-scale Macedonian music festivals ran in Melbourne and Sydney where musicians, songwriters, composers and singers could express their artistic talent in front of audiences of over a thousand people. One of the largest festivals, the Macedonian Folk Festival was held in Melbourne from 1992 to 2001, and such was the status of the festival that Australian Macedonian singers, composers and musicians received international exposure. Some went on to successful careers in Macedonia and Australia.

16

Macedonians and Sport

The earliest Macedonian *pechalbari* in Australia worked hard and in their spare time socialised with one another, played cards, smoked tobacco, drank Turkish style coffee and the homemade alcoholic brew known as *rakija*. They were not known to engage in organised sporting activities before the Second World War. The first sporting activities were held in a social setting at Macedonian community picnics during the 1930s and 1940s and included physical and sporting competitions, such as wrestling and soccer matches. The sons of the first wave of *pechalbari* that arrived in the 1920s embraced the sporting culture of Australian society and partook in organised competitive team sports commencing from the 1940s, which included the establishment of Macedonian soccer, basketball and cricket teams, while others were involved in individual sports such as wrestling and boxing. Sport became one of the most rigorous areas of Macedonian community life and in time, particularly with second-generation Macedonians, sport became another way to nurture Macedonian identity in Australia.

Wrestling is perhaps the only sporting activity with which early twentieth century *pechalbari* in Australia had a traditional connection. Unofficial wrestling competitions and strong man events were a part of village life that Macedonian men brought with them to Australia. When Macedonian bush workers came together socially, they were known to demonstrate their manhood with physical displays of strength and friendly wrestling. Possibly the first Macedonian to enter the wrestling ring in Australia was the famous strongman, Todor Jurukot from Krstoar village (Bitola). Prior to arriving in Australia in the early 1920s, he had been to the United States on two occasions working in the railway and steelwork industries in Michigan and Iowa and, although not a trained wrestler, took part in a number of wrestling competitions against some of the most popular wrestlers of the time. Todor never lost a match and an American wrestling commentator famously crowned him 'the unofficial wrestling champion of the world'. Todor was in Australia on two occasions, for several years in the 1920s and then from 1938 to 1948. He only wrestled once in Australia, in the mid-1920s in Melbourne, where he defeated Billy Meeske, a three-time former Australian heavyweight-wrestling champion.[18]

In the 1940s, Nikola Sazdanoff from Capari village (Bitola) boxed in Wollongong and Chris (Riste) Vasileff, from Lagen village (Lerin), was a successful boxer in Perth. Wrestling, boxing and other combat sports continue to be popular with Macedonians. In the 1960s, Angelo Jovanovich was a heavyweight wrestler who competed against the cream of Australian wrestlers. During an international competition held in Queanbeyan, New South Wales, Jovanovich was promoted as the Macedonian champion.[19] Jim Demirov from Krpeshina village (Lerin) was a professional wrestler for more than 30 years and a multiple Victorian heavyweight champion. He was the Macedonian favourite in the heyday of Australian wrestling in the 1960s and 1970s when thousands attended Festival Hall in Melbourne every weekend and television coverage made household names of wrestlers. Demirov went on to become a successful wrestling promoter. Perhaps the most successful Macedonian wrestler was Lila Ristevska, a multiple Australian women's champion, fourteen times Oceania champion, who represented Australia for more than 15 years in Olympic wrestling and World Championships, also representing Macedonia at Olympic level. In 2019, mixed martial arts fighter and pride of Macedonians worldwide, Alexander 'The Great' Volkanovski, from Wollongong, became the Ultimate Fighting Championship (UFC) world featherweight champion.

A number of Macedonians have excelled playing Australian Rules football. Of note are Jim Marcou (Carlton), George Christie (East Fremantle), Paul Peos (West Coast Eagles), John Gastev (West Coast Eagles and Brisbane Bears), Mark Nicoski (West Coast Eagles) and Nick Malcheski (Sydney Swans). The most famous footballer of Macedonian descent, whose parents migrated from the village Banica (Lerin), was Peter Daicos, the 'Macedonian Marvel'. One of the greatest players in the history of the Australian Football League (AFL), he was inducted into the AFL Hall of Fame in 1999. One of the all-time Collingwood club 'greats', Daicos played 250 VFL/AFL games for the club from 1979 to 1993, spearheading the 1990 premiership win, and was twice club best and fairest and leading club goal kicker for five seasons. Daicos was renowned for his uncanny ability to score goals from almost impossible angles, bouncing the ball along the ground through the goals. His son, Josh, began playing for Collingwood's AFL team in 2017.

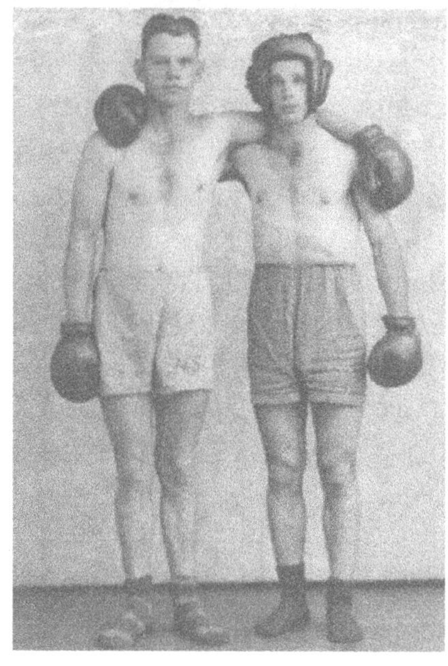

Photo 74: Nikola (Kole) Sazdanoff (on right) took up boxing in Port Kembla NSW, circa 1940. Macedonians were known to enjoy combat sports like wrestling and boxing (Source: Alex Sazdanoff. Courtesy of Mendo Trajcevski).

When the Edinstvo organisation was established in Perth in the 1940s, a sporting section was founded alongside cultural and educational branches. Initially a soccer team was formed, followed by a men's basketball team and significantly, in October 1948, a women's team, 'The Macedonians', was formed which competed in the West Australian Women's Basketball Association and marks the beginning of Macedonian women's involvement in organised sporting activity in Australia. Over the following decades the Perth community continued to lead in the field of organised sporting engagement. At its height in the 1960s, over a dozen Macedonian women's netball teams played in official competition, even though netball is a sport primarily played in Commonwealth countries with no links to the Balkans. Similarly, cricket is another sport with which Macedonians had no traditional connection, and only discovered after their arrival in Australia. The first Macedonian cricket team was formed in Perth in the 1940s competing under the name 'Macedonians'. Half a century later, in 1994, Macedonians in Newcastle NSW formed the 'Newcastle Macedonia Cricket Club' at District Park in Broadmeadow. Initiated by Chris Balalovski, who was also club president, he was joined by Tony Yoanou and Marjan Nastevski on the committee, and with 45 registered players and two senior teams, a district championship was won in the 1997/1998 season.[20]

Len Pascoe was a famous Australian cricketer with a reputation as a fearsome and aggressive right-hand fast bowler, regularly bowling at over 90 miles per hour. Born in 1950 in Bridgetown, Western Australia, his father migrated to Australia from the Bitola region village of Capari. Born Lenin Durtanovich, he took Len (Leonard) as his first name, Steven, his father's name as his middle name, and adopted an Anglicised version of his grandfather's Christian name Pasko, as his surname.[21] Pascoe's family moved to Bankstown, in Western Sydney and he attended Punchbowl Boys' High School. He represented NSW in Sheffield Shield cricket from 1974-75 until 1985. He made his test debut against England in 1977 and went on to play 14 Australian Test matches and 29 One Day Internationals. During the 1980 Centenary Test match against England, he took five wickets in the first innings (5 wickets for 59 runs). There is no doubt that he would have played more test matches for Australia had he not moved to World Series Cricket. A knee injury forced Pascoe into retirement in 1982 and he subsequently went on to coach the New South Wales state cricket team.

The most popular sport for young Macedonian men in Australia has, however, traditionally been soccer, and has attracted a wide range of ages to the game, as participating players and spectators. Soccer was first played socially in parks and at Macedonian community picnics in the 1940s and, that same decade, soccer teams were formed in Geraldton, Manjimup and Perth (Western Australia), Melbourne (Victoria), and Sydney and Richmond (New South Wales). The emergence of soccer teams was connected to youth and sporting branches of the Macedonian Australian Peoples League, which encouraged the involvement of young Macedonians in sporting activities. In 1947, it was reported in *Makedonska Iskra* that involvement in sporting activity was seen as an ideal way for Macedonians to engage more with the general Australian society. This was seen as a way to break down the anti-foreigner feeling which existed at that time.[22] Some of the most popular Macedonian clubs in Australia evolved from these early soccer enthusiasts. In Melbourne, from the Macedonian soccer team's humble beginnings in Fitzroy during the 1940s, they would grow into the most famous Macedonian soccer club in Australia, Preston Makedonia Soccer Club, with an international reputation in Macedonia and throughout the diaspora.[23]

The young men behind the formation of the Macedonian team in Melbourne were from the Lerin region who arrived in the 1930s to be reunited with their fathers who had settled in Fitzroy and surrounding suburbs. These young men had much in common – a proud Macedonian identity, a shared experience of oppressive Greek rule back home, and adjustment to a new life in Australia. They socialised and attended clubs and cafés together and although there had been talk during the early 1940s of getting together to start a Macedonian soccer team, the Second World War intervened. Its establishment was deferred until the end of the war when plans to set up a team recommenced with fervour. During 1946, young men gathered at the Dalmatian Club in Young Street, Fitzroy, and at Dane Trpkov's restaurant in Flinders Street Melbourne, where they discussed setting up a Macedonian soccer team.[24] Eighteen-year-old Lazo Giamov, together with friends, would meet at Dane Trpkov's restaurant, where Dane would talk to them about getting a Macedonian soccer team together and encouraged them to get involved and buy soccer boots. Similarly, 23-year-old Alex Theodorovsky would attend the Dalmatian Club with a group of friends and they keenly discussed setting up a Macedonian soccer team. The momentum was building for the team to come together.

In late 1946, young Macedonian men were coming together for their first training sessions at Gosch's Paddock (Yarra Park), on the corner of Punt Road and Swan Street (now Olympic Boulevard). The venue was chosen for its close proximity to the Macedonian community in Fitzroy, and there was no other suitable soccer ground situated near Gertrude Street where they could gather to train and play matches.[25] Gosch's Paddock would also become the match venue for the team and although there were no change room facilities, these were later provided by council. The two most instrumental people in the establishment of the team were Dane Trpkov, team manager, and Pando Daikoff from Banica village (Lerin). One of the most popular and motivated individuals involved in the establishment and history of the team, Pando was unanimously elected team captain and regularly played right back position.

After the first couple of training sessions, a meeting was held with all the players and the team manager where it was unanimously agreed to name the team Makedonia. According to Aleksandar Theodorovsky, one of the original team members, the name Makedonia was the natural choice as 'we were all Macedonians from Macedonia'.[26] At the time, the Macedonian Australian Peoples League and its newspaper *Makedonska Iskra* represented the voice of Macedonians in Australia and regularly reported on the injustices and persecutions of Macedonians in the Balkans. The players saw the team as connected to the MAPL and *Makedonska Iskra* and this gave them a sense that they were part of something bigger than just a soccer team and that, through their participation, they assisted in the struggle for the recognition of Macedonian identity. Match results and update reports on the progress of the team were regularly prepared by Pando Daikoff for *Makedonska Iskra*, and shortly after the establishment of the team, in the March 1947 edition, Daikoff proudly announced that 'a powerful football team has been organised' in Melbourne.[27]

Initially as a temporary measure, Pando Daikoff acquired Australian Rules football jumpers for the players to wear, while Dane Trpkov organised for player outfits to be manufactured and each player was required to pay for their own strip. When the player strips were completed for the 1948 season, the team wore red shirts, white shorts and red socks. The letters MSC, denoting 'Makedonia Soccer Club', were embroidered inside a yellow five-pointed star positioned on the left side of the front of the jersey. A large letter was added to the front of each jersey spelling Makedonia and, when the players walked out on to the pitch, they would stand in a line displaying the name Makedonia to their supporters who took great delight in the public show of their national name. Reflecting on what it meant to the players Aleksandar Theodorovsky stated that 'we may have not been great players but playing for Makedonia gave us great pride.' Similarly, Lazo Giamov stated that they played with passion for the name 'Macedonia'.

Photo 75: Lazo Giamov and Aleksandar Theodorovsky proudly representing the Macedonian soccer team in Melbourne, 1948. (Source: Aleksandar Theodorovsky).

At first, the team was not affiliated with the Victorian Soccer Federation; however, it was not difficult to organise friendly matches with established amateur clubs as well as other ethnic-based teams that were forming around that time. In 1947, Dane Trpkov, the team manager, organised regular matches with teams such as the Maltese George Cross team, the Jewish Hakoah team, a Serbian team, and others. Occasionally, when the team was short on players, Dane Trpkov would pull on a pair of boots and play. In 1948, the Macedonian team competed in the Victorian Amateur Football Association Third Division with the season opening on 17 April and running to late August. The first game was played in Newport against the newly formed Williamstown Soccer Club, resulting in a 4-0 victory over Macedonians.[28] However, at the return leg played in June at Yarra Park, Macedonians managed to score twice, but went down five goals to two. In the July 1948 issue of *Makedonska Iskra*, team captain Pando Daikoff reported 'We are not playing the best, but we are improving gradually', with the team having played seven games that year and four during the month of May, against George Cross, Olympic, University and Northern United. Macedonians also competed in round one of the Dockerty Cup competition on 19 June 1948, losing against Victorian Division One side, Yallourn.[29]

Reflecting on the progress of the team for the 1948 season, it was reported in *Iskra*, 'The Macedonian youth of Melbourne played in the league matches last season. This was done after a year of hard practice. The results were quite good, taking into consideration that this was their first season playing with more experienced and matured teams.'[30] At around this time (1948-1949) the team was strengthened with the arrival of player-coach Stefo Shusta/Shota from Lerin who brought his considerable experience, having played soccer in Lerin. He utilised his in-depth knowledge to develop the skills of the young enthusiastic Macedonian players.

From the outset the team attracted a dedicated following from the Macedonian community. Supporters eagerly made their way to the home games at Yarra Park, by foot or public transport, and although away games could be at considerable distances, the loyal supporters piled into the few cars that there were available or otherwise travelled on trains and buses, while the team travelled to away matches tightly squeezed into Dane Trpkov's car and Pando Daikoff's Austin truck.[31]

Keen support and an increasing number of inspired players resulted in the club fielding two teams in 1949, with Macedonians A team competing in the Third Division A competition and Macedonians B in the Third Division B competition. Macedonians A finished seventh from eleven teams, having played against strong opposition such as the Italian-backed Juventus and the Maltese George Cross who dominated the league. In August 1949, a local international series was held in Melbourne with proceeds to go to Prince Henry's Hospital. Due to there being a number of talented Southern European players, a trial match between Southern Europe A and Southern Europe B teams was played to assist selectors to choose the final team which would play against Australia in the next game. A player from the Macedonian team was selected to play on the outside right position for the Southern European B team.[32]

In 1949, team manager, Dane Trpkov, organised a one-off cup match with the principal Greek team in Melbourne with the winner to be presented a trophy. The game was played at Yarra Park and Macedonian supporters attended with high hopes of victory. A concerted effort saw the Macedonians win the match and to commemorate the occasion, a team photograph was taken in a local photographic studio (Allan Studio in Collingwood). It was a significant moment for the Macedonian players and their supporters who almost entirely originated from Aegean Macedonia.[33] Although the game was played in a sporting spirit, the win represented a symbolic victory over Greece and was a deeply satisfying achievement and a matter of national pride for the players and Macedonian supporters. In celebration of the victory, the players marched boisterously past the Greek Club in Lonsdale Street (Melbourne) with the trophy raised high. That evening celebrations for players and supporters went late into the night at the Macedonian Social Cub in Gertrude Street.

Photo 76: Following a triumphant victory over the Melbourne Greek team, the Macedonian team went to Allan photographic studio in Collingwood for a proud photo with the winning trophy, 1949. (Source: Aleksandar Theodorovsky. Photograph by Allan Studio).

Due to an increasing number of teams, in 1950, the Third Division was reformed into two competitions, north and south, with Macedonians competing in the south competition. It was expected that Macedonians would have a strong season with player reinforcements having come from the homeland; however, after 4 straight losses and 37 goals conceded, morale was low and the future of the team uncertain.[34] A Melbourne newspaper reported that in the next game against Flinders Naval Depot it was expected that 'Navy may make a 'cricket score' against Macedonians'.[35] Following the subsequent loss against Navy, Macedonians cancelled their remaining fixtures and withdrew from the competition.[36] Following the premature end to the 1950 season, Macedonians returned to field a team for the 1951 fixture in the Third Division Reserves league and were scheduled to play in the Dockerty Cup competition (the Reserve Cup) against Sunshine United on 11 August 1951. In 1952 efforts were made to restore the Macedonian A team with a recruitment drive of new players and although ten new players signed up for the team,[37] they did not take part in the formal fixture that season. However, the team continued to play friendly matches throughout 1952 and 1953. Over the next few years, there was no Macedonian soccer team competing in official competition in Victoria until a team representing Macedonia was entered in the inaugural Geelong-based World Cup in 1955. Macedonia took part in the knock-out competition, along with Holland, Italy, Hungary, Scotland, Croatia, Germany, England and Ukraine.[38]

Inspired by the soccer competition during the 1956 Olympic Games in Melbourne, Pando Daikoff, Dane Trpkov and Jani Pandzhari and others involved in the 1940s Macedonian team believed that the time was right for its re-formation and, on 30 March 1957, a general public meeting was held at 52-54 Young Street, Fitzroy. The meeting location in Young Street was the former Dalmatian Club, which had been purchased by the Macedonian community and was later demolished to enable the construction of the Sveti Giorgi church on the site. Over 200 people were in attendance supporting the re-establishment of the Macedonian soccer team. Steve Shota proposed that the team be named 'Makedonia' whilst John Ianopoulou suggested 'Alexander the Great'; however, it was unanimously decided that the name of the team would be 'Makedonia'. The name was adopted with enormous enthusiasm as described in a Macedonian newspaper report: 'The name of the Macedonian team has a long history, it has great significance for every one of US. It reminds us of our distant homeland. It reminds us of the names we called,

MOTHER and FATHER, that we saw the first light and took the first steps… MAKEDONIA, OUR MOTHER, OUR LAND, LIGHT'.[39]

Backed by the Sveti Giorgi Macedonian church community, the team initially operated as an unofficial branch under the auspices of the church which assisted with the purchase of player strips and other equipment, while social functions in support of the team were also held at the church. Training sessions were held at the original 1940s venue in Yarra Park (Gosch's Paddock), and enthusiastic young men arrived eager to start playing competitive matches. Application was made that year (1957) to register the club with the Victoria Soccer Federation and, although unsuccessful, the team played friendly matches before registering the team in the Sunday league competition, playing against mostly ethnic based Italian, Maltese, Serbian, Croatian and Greek teams. Official referees were not provided for Sunday league matches and Pando Daikoff, who had been such a driving force in the establishment of the team in the 1940s, again showed his commitment to Macedonian soccer and community by taking responsibility for refereeing all home matches at Yarra Park.[40]

Yarra Park was utilised for a short time before the soccer federation was approached, seeking a new home ground with improved facilities. Club administrators were pleased when a new ground was made available at Royal Park, opposite Melbourne Zoo. However, curiously, the club was not permitted to have soccer goal posts erected as a permanent fixture on the ground. The goal posts were kept at players' homes in Fitzroy and were taken to Royal Park on match days with a truck belonging to Todor Velov, the father of Pavle Velov, one of the players in the team.

Keen to compete in the official league, in 1958 an application was lodged but was unsuccessful due to the large number of applications from clubs.[41] The club continued to play in the Sunday league and its stature was growing in the Macedonian community. It became a focal point for the men and that year a reserve team was also formed. In 1959 Makedonia successfully affiliated with the Victoria Soccer Federation (VASFA) in the provisional league and the first match was played against North Richmond, ending in a 2–2 draw. The team now played in red and yellow colours with black shorts, which had been proudly donated by Pavle Kostov from Lagen village (Lerin); and ended the season in a respectable fourth position in the league with 10 wins, two draws and six loses.

In those early days, the players did not hesitate to use their own money in support of their team. Pavle Velov, former player from 1959 to 1964, and later a club administrator for many years, stated:

No one got paid back then, we loved playing for the team. We went to play in Bendigo, we only had three or four cars, yet 20 of us went in these cars. This was in the early days. We lost the game 2-1. We stopped in Harcourt on the way back to eat and have a drink. We were so happy we sang Macedonian songs. We were approached and asked what we were celebrating, they were surprised to hear that we had lost the match, but we were so happy. We had terrific spirit and it really meant something to have our own Macedonian team.[42]

With strong passionate support from the Macedonian community, the team had the most supporters whenever they played, both at home and away matches: in Seymour, Bendigo, Yallourn and other distant places the loyal supporters followed. Other clubs were astounded at the following the team had, and everywhere they went they had with them a joyful and positive atmosphere. Men would cram six to seven in each car and some would make their way to games using public transport. The underlying factor for the strong support was not so much an appreciation of the sport, 'they loved the fact that our team was called Makedonia'.[43]

Having arrived in Australia from the political states of Greece, Yugoslavia and Bulgaria, Macedonians were too often confused as being of those nationalities. The significance and sense of pride the team name (Makedonia) gave the Macedonian community cannot be understated. Regular reporting in the sports section in the Australian press on the results and developments of the team, always using the name Makedonia, was deeply satisfying to the Macedonian community and reinforced the freedoms Australia offered its citizens. A 1961 Macedonian newspaper report noted that 'The name Makedonia regularly appears in large and positive articles in the official newspaper of the football league in Melbourne *Soccer News*.

Regular articles reporting on the victories of Makedonia in the daily newspapers appeared in *The Sporting Globe*, *The Age*, *The Sun*, *The Herald*, and in other publications.[44]

In March 1961, the Club Committee held an extraordinary meeting announcing that after playing twelve rounds of the season and positioned on top of the second division the club aimed towards promotion into the first division for the 1962 season. The players were confident of success, there was a strong sense of brotherhood in the team and the club was experiencing significant growth with more players and supporters than ever before.[45] As anticipated, the club tasted success in Metropolitan League Two South in 1961, finishing first with 14 wins, two draws and two loses and, with a total of 30 points, two points ahead of second placed Oakleigh. Makedonia was promoted to Division One for the 1962 season.

Photo 77: Makedonia soccer team photographed at Royal Park in celebration of winning the Victorian second division title, 1961. (Source: Pavle Velov).

Self-belief and confidence at the club positively impacted the wider Macedonian community and inspired other Macedonian communities in Victoria to set up their own soccer teams in places like Shepparton and Geelong. In 1959, in Shepparton a group of young men, mostly from Bitusha village (Lerin) set up the Shepparton Makedonia soccer team, based at Shepparton East Primary School. The team was an immediate success, with hard-working farmers actively supporting the team and coming together in a vibrant atmosphere on match days. The club has enjoyed significant success over the years, notably in the 1980s, winning five consecutive grand finals.[46]

In Melbourne, the Macedonian club became the biggest institution in the Melbourne Macedonian community, rivalling the church. In fact, considerably larger numbers of people – overwhelmingly men – attended matches on Sundays, in comparison to those attending church. Sunday matches were the place where Macedonians could gather and speak their language, take their children along and immerse themselves in an atmosphere of Macedonian culture. The significance and role of the club expanded far beyond sport. People worked hard and gave their time generously to build the club. In the early 1960s the club moved from its ground at Royal Park to Merri Park on St George's Road in Northcote. At around this time Macedonians were moving into the inner northern suburbs of Northcote, Thornbury, Westgarth and Preston. Merri Park was used for one season before a longer-term home for the club was secured at T.A. Cochrane Reserve, Collier Street, Preston, behind the Preston and Northcote Community Hospital in 1963.

That year the club very nearly won the Federation Cup, after losing in a close encounter in the final against Coburg United. Cochrane Reserve was built over an old tip and, in preparation for the club's move to the site, the Council constructed player change rooms made from corrugated iron. A few years later council knocked the tin change rooms down and built new ones made of brick and included hot water. The move to Preston resulted in the name change to Preston Makedonia in 1964. Over two consecutive years, 1964 and 1965, the club finished a close second in Division One until the perseverance paid off in 1966 when Makedonia won the championship on one goal difference from second-placed St Albans, and gained promotion to the Victorian State League, the highest-level competition in the state.

Considerable success during the 1970s with championship seasons in 1974 and 1975 and State League Cup Winners in 1975 brought much happiness to the Macedonian community. The supporter base of the club swelled during this period as there were large numbers of Macedonians arriving from the Republic. After becoming Victorian champion in 1980, Preston Makedonia competed in a play-off against other state champions and, in 1981, they were promoted to the then National Soccer League (NSL) competition. At around this time the club would make its final move to BT Connor Reserve in the neighbouring suburb of Reservoir. Preston Makedonia competed successfully in the NSL for the next 13 years, achieving their best finish in 1987 as runner-up in the Southern Division Championship. Main rivalries were with the Serbo-Yugoslav Footscray JUST (Jugoslav United Soccer Team) and the Greek-backed South Melbourne. Victories over Footscray in the 1980 Victoria Cup Final, and the 1992 victory over South Melbourne in a thrilling penalty shootout for the prestigious Docherty Cup, are amongst the most beloved moments for the thousands of Makedonia fans.

Over the years the club has produced many champion players who have represented Australia at youth and senior level, notably including Sasha Ognenovski, FIFA Asian Footballer of the Year in 2010, the only Australian footballer to have received this award, and an Australian national team representative. With thousands of loyal supporters, the Preston Makedonia Soccer Club boasted one of the largest followings of any soccer club in Australia during its heyday of the 1970s and 1980s. In recent years the club has undergone a resurgence under the strong leadership of Zak Gruevski and a dedicated management team which has attracted a new generation of young Australian-Macedonians passionately supporting the club, and also drawn significant following from the wider community. With a vision and strategy for the future, the club and its strong supporter base is well positioned for continued growth and success, as a sporting club as well as a space of belonging and unity.

Endnotes

1 E. Stewart (nee Kolupacev), *Lexical Transference in the Speech of Macedonian English Bilingual Speakers in the Illawarra Region of NSW*, unpublished, MA thesis, Macquarie University, 1995, p. 125.

2 Ibid., p. 125.

3 M. Thomas, *A Multicultural Landscape, National Parks and the Macedonian Experience*, NSW National Parks and Wildlife Service and Pluto Press Australia, 2001, p. 44. A Macedonian interviewee, Mr Paul Stephen, described the significance of the picnics. 'People could expand their national feelings, gathering in their language. Because everybody worked in a fish and chip shop or a factory or something like that. So picnics were a tremendous outlet. People looked forward to this. They played a major part in or getting to know each other, and for people who would come from overseas it was an introduction to the people. They weren't alone. They could see there's other Macedonians here.' Ibid., p. 9.

4 The Kozari family from Aegean Macedonia were well known Macedonian activists and supporters of the Macedonian Orthodox Church. B. Bozinoski and V. Krstevski, *Chetvrta Generacija*, [Fourth Generation], Macedonian Australian Association of Culture and Human Rights, Newcastle, 2012, p. 45.

5 Stan Milenko interview.

6 S. Mooney, 'Naming Mount Alexander', *Victorian Historical Journal* Vol. 62, Nos. 3 & 4, Royal Historical Society of Victoria, December 1991/March 1992, pp. 131-36; p. 131. Mount Macedon, Mount Alexander and the Campaspe River were named in 1836 by Major Thomas Mitchell, explorer, and Surveyor General of New South Wales.

7 In Australia it is practice for Macedonians to exchange gifts on 25 December; however, 7 January is purely a religious celebration.

8 Since the 1990s an annual Christmas Day (25 December) community picnic also takes place at the Sveti Prohor Pchinski monastery grounds in Donnybrook, Victoria.

9 K. Sapurma and P. Petrovska, *Children of the Bird Goddess*, Pollitecon Publications, Sydney, 1997, p. 36.

10 B. Marwick, *Steve and Christine Trandos*, from *Stories of Old Wanneroo – As told to Bill Marwick*, Ultra Printing Services, Perth, 2002, p. 277.

11 *Western Argus* (Perth), 2 January 1934, p. 23.

12 Peter Mechkaroff autobiographical notes.

13 Lazo Giamov interview.

14 Anastas Vosnacos interview transcript dated December 2001, State Library of Western Australia.

15 *Makedonska Iskra*, April 1948, p. 4 and *Makedonska Iskra*, January 1957, p. 4.

16 The newspaper was reporting on the wedding of Victor Chapkoun and Joy Giouris. The ceremony was conducted at St Mark's Anglican Church in Fitzroy with the celebration at Richmond Town Hall. *Argus* (Melbourne), 7 May 1951, p. 20.

17 L. Mitreska, *The Macedonians in Rockdale – A Vivid Life*, unpublished, Sydney, 2015, p. 8.

18 V. Trajceski, *Najsilniot Makedonec – Todor Jurukot* [The Strongest Macedonian – Todor Jurukot], Self-published, Melbourne, 1995. Meeske was Australian Heavyweight Champion in 1915, 1918 and 1922. Todor Jurukot's feats of strength were legendary. In the 1930s, Jurukot worked at the Port Kembla steelworks with other Macedonians, including Todor Kasovski (Kasovich) from Bukovo. Kasovski recalled that it took four men to carry a pig iron mould, but Jurukot did it by himself, carrying one in each hand. M. Trajcevski, 'The First Pioneers' in *Informativen Vesnik* [Informative Newsletter], Macedonian Welfare Association Port Kembla, 2 December 1989, p. 10.

Krste Constantinou had been an amateur wrestler in Armensko village (Kostur) as a young man before he arrived in Australia during the 1950s. After working in the Gippsland bush, Krste set up a hamburger shop in Sale (Victoria). When a circus troupe arrived in Sale, challengers were given the opportunity to take on the resident circus wrestling champion. Krste volunteered to take on the circus wrestler and to everyone's surprise he defeated the champion. That evening it seemed as though everyone in Sale went to the hamburger shop to congratulate Krste. Nick Constantinou interview.

19 *The Canberra Times*, 16 October 1965, p. 20.

20 B. Bozinoski and V. Krstevski, op. cit., pp. 126-127. In 2014, Michael Spaseski, a talented cricketer of Macedonian heritage from Canberra was selected to represent the Prime Ministers XI against England.

21 P. Hill, *The Macedonians in Australia*, Hesperian Press, Perth, 1989, p. 132.

22 *Makedonska Iskra*, August-September 1947, p. 2.

23 Following the removal of ethnic names by the Victorian/Australian Football Federation, Preston Makedonia has become Preston Lions Football Club.

24 Dane Trpkov was from Nevoljani village (Lerin) and his restaurant was located on Flinders Street, next to Young and Jackson's Hotel (upstairs on the second level).

25 Aleksandar Theodorovsky interview.

26 Ibid.

27 *Makedonska Iskra*, March 1947, p. 2.

28 It was also a debut match for the newly formed Williamstown soccer club which played at Maddox Road, Newport.

29 The Dockerty Cup Competition is one of the oldest soccer cup competitions in Victoria. Teams from low leagues have the chance to play against teams from the premier league in the state in a knockout competition.

30 *Makedonska Iskra,* March 1949, p. 2.

31 Aleksandar Theodorovsky interview and Lazo Giamov interview.

32 *Soccer News*, (Victorian Amateur Soccer Football Association – Melbourne), 6 August 1949. The name of the Macedonian player was not mentioned in the article, whilst the winner of the match between Southern Europe and Australia was to go on and play against Great Britain.

33 During the 1940s all the players of the Macedonian team were from the Lerin region and, during this period, team members included Phillip Opashinov from Buf, Aleksandar Theodorovsky from Buf, Lazo Giamov from Trnava, Pando Daikoff from Banica, Greg (Gavro) Daikoff from Banica, Chris Pateras from Kabasnica, Neil (Naido) Johnson (Janevski) from Kalenik, Jim Johnson (Janevski) from Kalenik, Ziso Johnson (Janevski) from Kalenik, Jim Phillips from Lagen, Victor (Vasil) Chapkoun from Neret, Lazo Klapchev from Kalenik, Tom Klapchev from Kalenik, Risto Stanbanov (Chris Stanbanis) from Kalenik, Peter Psaltis (village unknown), Gregory Pavlidis (Pavlevski) from Banica, Chris Dellios from Lagen, George Taylor from Nevoljani and Michael Stovich (Serbian nationality). Key individuals closely aligned with the team but were not players included Kosta Taneff from Banica, Jani Pandzhari from Kotori and Dane Trpkov from Nevoljani (Team Manager).

34 'Clubs such as Juventus, George Cross, Macedonians, and Olympics, have received reinforcements from their homelands. They will give strong opposition to Australia's best clubs.' *Argus*, (Melbourne), Thursday 19 January 1950, p. 19.

35 *The Argus* (Melbourne), Saturday 22 April 1950, p. 45.

36 *Soccer News*, 29 April 1950 issue, p. 10.

37 *Makedonska Iskra* May-June 1952, p. 3.

38 R. Hay, 'Post war soccer in Geelong', pp. 1-12, from *Investigator*, Geelong Historical Society, June 1994.

39 *Makedonski Tsrkoven Vestnik* [Macedonian Church Newspaper], (Izdanie na Makedonskata Pravoslavna Opshtina Sv. Georgi) 6 August 1961, p. 4.

40 Pavle Velov interview.

41 *Makedonski Tsrkoven Vestnik*, 6 August 1961, op. cit., p. 4. Peter Daniels took over as the Secretary of the Club at this time.

42 Having played for the team to 1964, Pavle Velov later took up a role as a Committee member, and then as President of the Social Club from 1982 to 1984. Velov maintained a life-long association with the club.

43 Pavle Velov interview.

44 *Makedonski Tsrkoven Vestnik*, 6 August 1961, op. cit., p. 4.

45 Ibid., p. 4.

46 In 1972-73, Shepparton Makedonia underwent a name change to Lemnos Makedonia, taking on the name of the locality where it was based on the outskirts of Shepparton. In the 1980s, the club underwent a further name change to Shepparton Soccer Club. Competing in the North Eastern Soccer League (Goulburn North East Football Association as of 2009), it is the most successful senior club in the Goulburn district.

Afterword: 'Here to Stay'

Motivated by the political and economic turmoil that has characterised life in Macedonia in recent centuries, large numbers of Macedonian people have travelled abroad to seek work and improvements to their financial circumstances for at least the last 200 years. This book has provided a glimpse of what this process called *pechalba* has looked like in the context of Australia. The now thriving community of Macedonians living in Australia have established themselves economically, culturally, politically and in terms of their own religion in this young nation. The promise of return as laid out by the traditional terms of *pechalba* has predominantly been abandoned and Macedonians have made their home anew in Australia. Instead, the promise to their homeland comes in the form of nurturing and celebrating their cultural heritage as Macedonians in the place of settlement.

The first significant numbers of *pechalbari* arriving in Australia in the 1920s and 30s expected to earn income to send home to their families. However, as a result of tough economic times, their expectations around work and earnings did not materialise. Having undergone great personal sacrifice, they were unable to send desperately needed money back home to their families. With the passage of time, economic conditions changed, and their situation improved. With the skills and work ethic they cultivated in the village, they worked as market gardeners and farmers in rural areas, as labourers in factories and as enterprising business owners in the urban centres of Australia. When Macedonian women arrived to join their husbands, they immediately set out with the same unwavering work ethic as their male counterparts, jointly demonstrating the economic fruits of their labour and dedication.

They enjoyed living in close proximity to each other and developed rich community lives, enabling them to protect their culture, which they were not always able to freely express back home. In places like Fitzroy (Melbourne), Rockdale (Sydney) and North Perth, they could enjoy daily socialising with other Macedonians, gathering in local parks, attending weekend soccer matches, going to Macedonian churches and taking the family to a Saturday night dance – all within their suburb.

When they experienced racism or discrimination it was not because they were Macedonians, but rather simply because they were foreigners. Being Macedonian in Australia was not an impediment to succeeding; all they needed was an opportunity to advance. Their children were given educational opportunities that were completely out of reach for themselves in the homeland; as a result, successive generations of Macedonians have enjoyed significant accomplishments in professional fields and specialist employment.

When Australia found itself drawn into the Second World War, Macedonians voluntarily enlisted and many joined the Employment Companies/Civil Aliens Corps, carrying out important work for the war effort. The first national Macedonian organisation, the Macedonian Australian Peoples League, strongly supported the Australian war effort, and in a display of their Australian patriotism, keenly purchased war bonds. Subsequent generations look back proudly at their fathers' and grandfathers' service even though, disappointingly, the Returned Services League never accepted men from the Employment Companies/Civil Alien Corps as members because they were not on active service outside Australia.

Macedonian migrants in Australia gathered freely and celebrated openly, proudly asserting their unique culture which they considered their duty to pass on to their children. Unfortunately, as soon as they began to organise themselves in the new land, and in particular when the first churches were being established, propaganda activities directed by the Greek and Yugoslav embassies sought to influence the outward ethnic appearance of the Macedonian community, an experience all too familiar of their treatment back home.

Assimilatory pressures upon Macedonians in Australia are now associated with the dominant Anglo-Australian culture with language maintenance emerging as a major issue. However, anecdotal evidence suggests that the deteriorating use of the Macedonian language amongst young people has not fragmented the connection to their ethnic identity and Macedonian heritage. The basic foundation for Macedonians is their family which also provides the basis for maintenance of values, language, and religion. Whereas the Macedonian language was previously passed from parents to children, now it is an increasingly entrusted role of the grandparents (*dedo* and *baba*) in addition to sharing the duties of childcare to accommodate the demands of employment in contemporary Australian life. As such the roles of the *dedo* and *baba* have taken on an enhanced level of cultural importance, demonstrating that the Macedonian culture has not only survived in Australia, but that it is constantly evolving to meet the needs of modern life in a new setting.

The locus of the family has not been the only important site for cultural change among the Macedonians of Australia, for most aspects of modern life in a distant land have demanded frequent adaptation. Macedonian culture has found its place in Australia, with institutions like the Macedonian Orthodox Church catering to successive generations by conducting services in English, coupled with other initiatives for education in the Macedonian language. Over time, the spread of Macedonians throughout Australia has inevitably decentralised. New forms of cultural connectivity have emerged, such as online communities, social media pages, university clubs and live streamed events such as church services. These have accelerated in demand as a result of the COVID-19 pandemic of 2020.

An important factor in the drive to preserve their cultural legacy has been the ongoing struggle for Macedonian statehood. Despite attempts to foster a better mutual relationship with the independent Macedonian state since its independence in 1991, Macedonians in Australia have felt that they have not been able to rely on the republic for adequate support of its expatriates. Regardless, this has reinforced their resolve for self-sufficiency as well as a closer relationship with other organisations such as the Macedonian Orthodox Church in order to ensure the preservation and perpetuation of the Macedonian culture and identity in Australia.

Perhaps the greatest achievement of the Macedonians in Australia is not their inward-focused sentiments, but their successful integration into Australian society whilst maintaining their Macedonian roots. Previously, Macedonian picnics were held in bush settings outside metropolitan centres and were exclusively attended by Macedonians. Now, however, Macedonian food and cultural festivals are held as mainstream events in inner-city suburbs, providing greater accessibility for community members, as well as sharing Macedonian food, culture, song and dance to a much wider audience. Important pillars of Macedonian identity in Australia such as the Preston Lions Football Club, a leading sporting institution in Melbourne, has transformed from an almost exclusive Macedonian player base to an inclusive club for people of all backgrounds, all the while continuing to acknowledge and respect its Macedonian heritage.

Starting as *pechalba* Down Under, Macedonians have found a permanent place of home in Australia. Cities like Melbourne, Sydney, Wollongong and Perth boast significant numbers of Macedonian settlers and their cultural heritage lives on in their children, grandchildren, and great grandchildren. Macedonians left the homeland in pursuit of financial opportunities and instead found a new home Down Under. From prominent sportspeople, public figures, business owners and political activists, the breadth of contributions Macedonians have made to the very fabric of Australian society is immeasurable. This book does not hold the answers about what the future has in store for the Macedonians of Australia. What it demonstrates is that a Macedonian mark has been left on Australia, and it is here to stay.

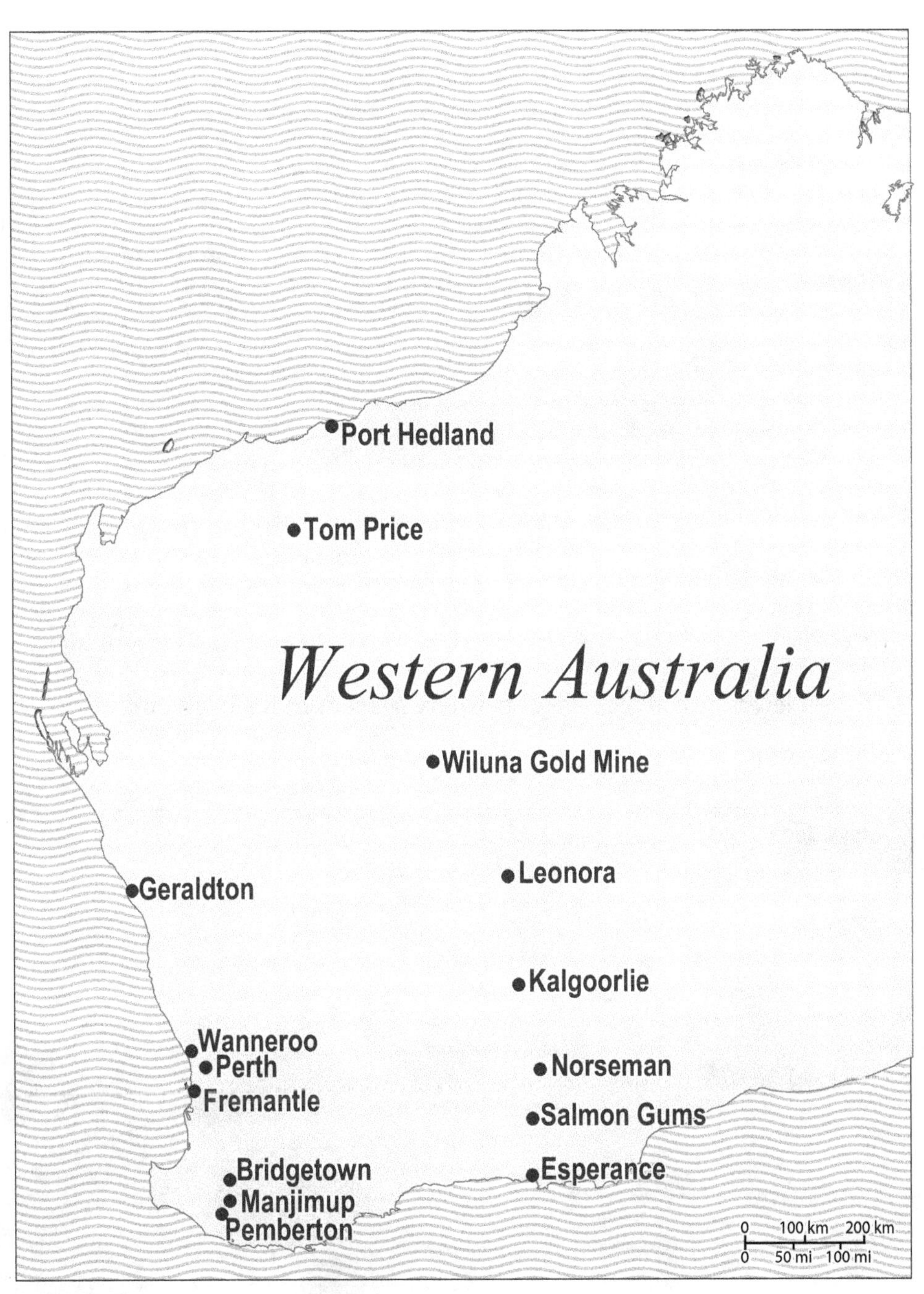

MAP 7 – Western Australia – places where Macedonians lived and worked.

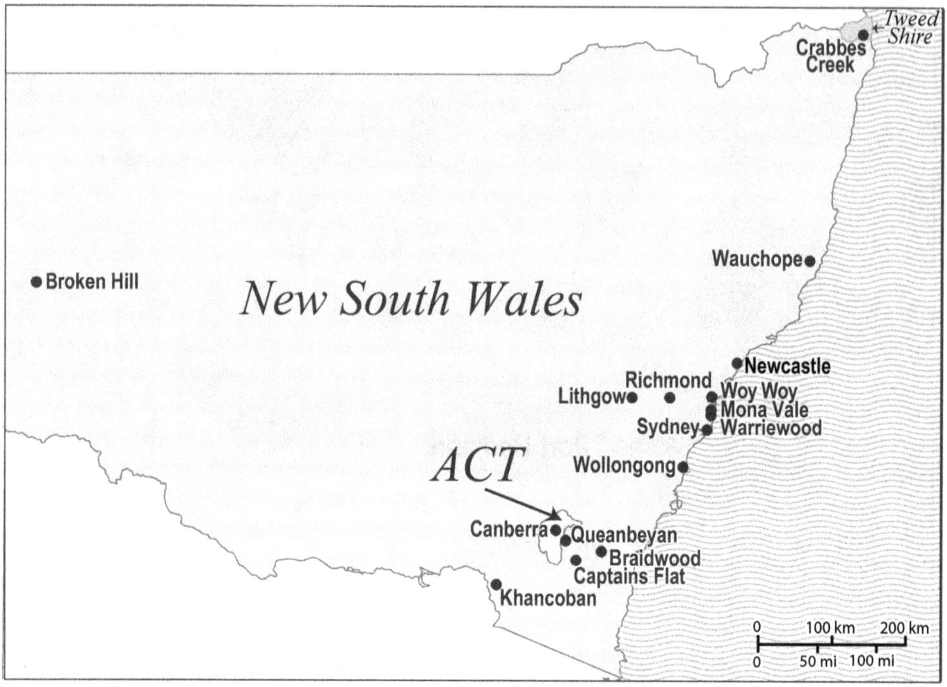

Tweed Shire
Crabbes Creek
Wauchope
Broken Hill
New South Wales
Newcastle
Richmond
Lithgow
Woy Woy
Mona Vale
Sydney
Warriewood
ACT
Wollongong
Canberra
Queanbeyan
Braidwood
Captains Flat
Khancoban
0
100 km
200 km
0
50 mi
100 mi

MAP 8 – New South Wales – places where Macedonians lived and worked.

Mildura
Kyabram
Tatura
Shepparton
Victoria
Omeo
Gippsland Region
Wairewa
Orbost
Nowa Nowa
Bairnsdale
Melbourne
Noojee
Werribee South
Maffra
Sale
Geelong
Camperdown
Carpendeit
Colac
Kernot
Leongatha
Yarram
0
100 km
0
50 mi

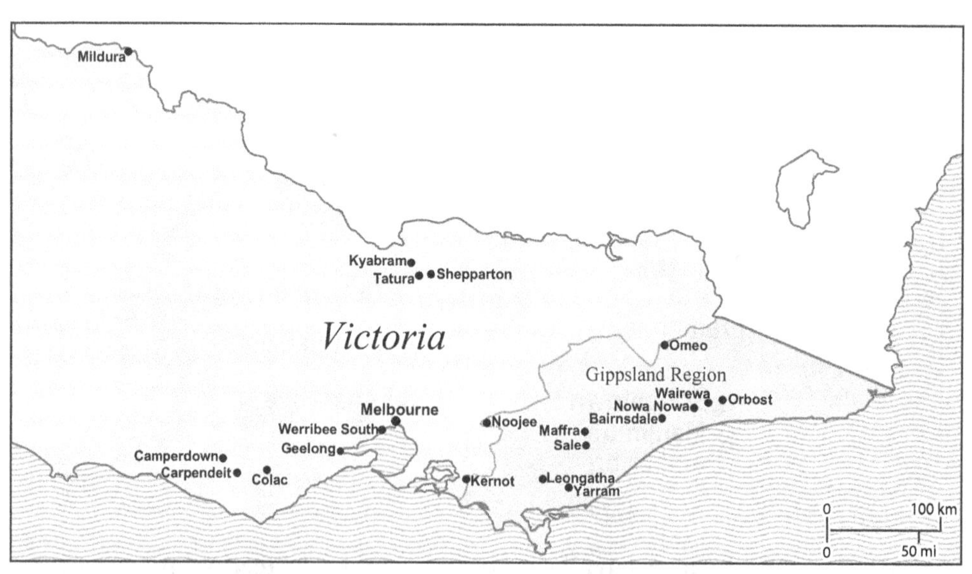

MAP 9 – Victoria – places where Macedonians lived and worked.

MAP 10 – Queensland – places where Macedonians lived and worked.

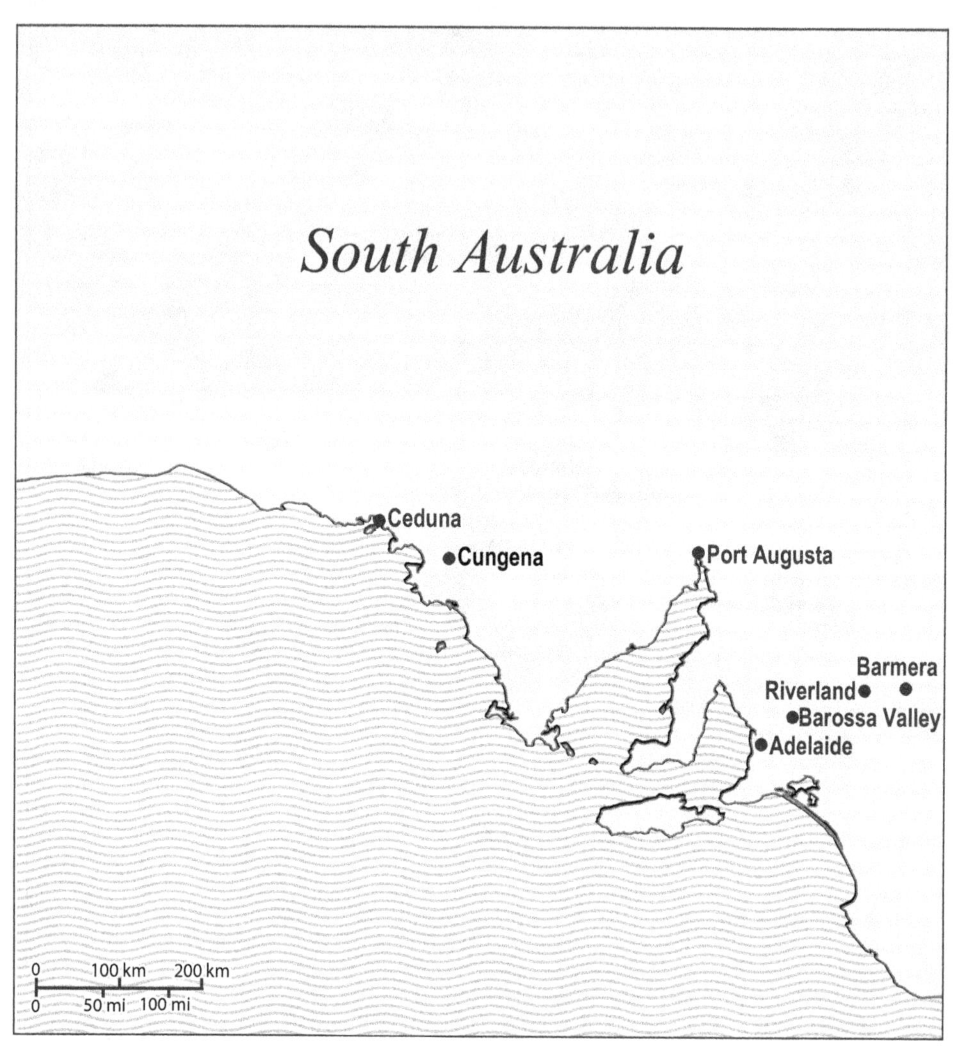

MAP 11 – South Australia – places where Macedonians lived and worked.

Glossary of Terms

Aegean Macedonia	That part of Macedonia that fell under the occupation of Greek rule following the Balkan wars of 1912-13. Also, can be referred to as Southern Macedonia or Macedonia under Greek rule/occupation.
Ohrid Archbishopric	The Archbishopric of Ohrid is the historical church of the Macedonian people and today known as the Macedonian Orthodox Church (Ohrid Archbishopric).
Baba	Grandmother.
Bafcha	Vegetable patch. In Australia, this term is used by Macedonians to describe a backyard vegetable patch.
Balkan States	Refers to Greece, Serbia and Bulgaria collectively.
Balkan Wars	The Balkan Wars of 1912-13 resulted in the territorial division of Macedonia between Greece, Serbia and Bulgaria.
Beg	Common term for Ottoman era feudal landlord.
Bozhik	Christmas. Macedonian Orthodox Christians celebrate Christmas on 7 January.
Cheta	A group of armed fighters. Common term when describing a unit of Macedonian revolutionaries, particularly from the Internal Macedonian Revolutionary Organisation (IMRO).
Chiflik	Ottoman era feudal estate operated by a *beg*.
Dedo	Grandfather.
Dekar	One thousand square metres of land.
DOOM	*Dvizhejne za Osloboduvajne i Obedinuvajne na Makedonija* (Movement for the Liberation and Unification for Macedonian).

Dzize	Ottoman personal tax.
Gajda	Bagpipe – musical instrument.
Ilinden rebellion	Famous 1903 rebellion against Ottoman Turkish subjugation for the freedom of the Macedonian people. The date of the revolt was on 2 August which marked the holy day of St Prophet Elijah on the Orthodox Christian calendar (Ilinden).
IMRO	Internal Macedonian Revolutionary Organisation (IMRO). Macedonian, see VMRO.
Komita	A Macedonian revolutionary freedom fighter. Typically relates to VMRO/IMRO fighters.
Korzo	Main Boulevard in Bitola town. Also known as Shirok sokak.
Lira	Ottoman Turkish currency.
Macedonia	Ethno-geographic Macedonia extends beyond the borders of the Republic of Macedonia and includes territories and Macedonian populations under the rule of Greece, Bulgaria and Albania. In Macedonian, the name is spelt as Makedonija, however there are variations, particularly in the diaspora which include Makedonia.
Makedonska Iskra	First Macedonian language newspaper in Australia published by the Macedonian Australian Peoples League – MAPL (*Makedonska Avstralijanska Naroden Soyuz – MANS*) from 1946 to 1957. English name, Macedonian Spark.
Makedonska Nacija	Publication of the DOOM organisation (*Dvizhenje za Osloboduvajne i Obidinuvajne na Makedonija*) and voice of the worldwide Macedonian patriotic movement during the 1970s and 1980s.
Maalo	A town or village quarter.
Mala Prespa	Part of Macedonia under occupation of Albanian rule following the Treaty of London, 1920.

MAPL	Macedonian Australian Peoples League. In Macedonian - *Makedonski Avstralski Naroden Soyuz (MANS).*
MPO	Formed in 1922 and based in the United States, the Macedonian Patriotic Organisation was established on the principles that it stood for a free independent and united Macedonia, however, is also known to promote Macedonia as ethnically Bulgarian. The MPO was previously known as Macedonian Political Organisation.
Napoljoni	French gold coins used in Macedonia during Ottoman rule and widely in Europe in the nineteenth and early twentieth centuries. The Ottoman Turks called them 'napoleondor'.
Oro	Macedonian traditional dance. Men and women dance whilst joined in a circle holding hands.
Panahida	Religious service for the dead.
Pechalba	Person who has gone to work away from his home, typically refers to those that have left to work abroad but includes those who left their homes to work in other parts of Macedonia.
Pechabar	Macedonian migratory worker. The plural version is *pechalbari.*
Pirin Macedonia	Part of Macedonia that fell under the occupation of Bulgarian rule following the Balkan wars of 1912-13. Also referred to as 'Macedonia under Bulgarian rule'.
Planina	Mountain.
Rakija	Homemade alcohol primarily made from the distillation of grapes leftover from wine production, however *rakija* can also be made from plums.
Soi	Extended family. The *soi* name can be different from the official family surname.

Stroinik	A middleman/go-between used by a bachelor who seeks a bride. Traditionally a *stroinik* is a male.
Tapan	Drum, musical instrument.
UDBA	The State Security Service (*Sluzhbaza Drzhavna Bezbednost*) operated as the Yugoslav Secret Police but was known by the acronym UDBA referencing the original name of the organisation *(Uprava Drzhavna Bezbednost).*
Valencija	Heavy woollen traditional handmade blanket/rug. Also, *valenci.*
Vardar Macedonia	Part of Macedonia that fell under the occupation of Serbian rule following the Balkan Wars of 1912-13. Later this part of Macedonia became one of six constituent republics of Yugoslavia and is also referred to as 'Macedonia under Serbo-Yugoslav rule'. Today this part is the independent and sovereign Republic of Macedonia.
Veligden	Easter.
VMRO	*Vnatreshna Makedonska Revolucionerna Organizacija* – see Internal Macedonian Revolutionary Organisation (VMRO).
Vodici	Epiphany – Christian celebration of when John the Baptist christened Jesus in the River Jordan. Macedonian Orthodox Christians celebrate *vodici* on 19 January.
Voivoda	Leader of a Macedonian revolutionary unit (cheta).

Bibliography

Primary Sources

Archives

Archives of the Macedonian Community of Western Australia (Perth)

Financial statement of the Macedonian Hospital Committee dated 29 August 1947.

Final financial statement of the Macedonian Australian Hospital Committee.

Makedonska Avstralska Zhenska Seksia od Perth W.A. Minutna Kniga 4, September 1948.

Report of the Second Conference of the Macedonian Australian Peoples League, Western Australia, dated 31 August 1947.

Doklad od vtorata konferencija na MANS za WA [Report from the second conference of MAPL in WA], 31 August 1947.

Archives from the Macedonian community New South Wales (Queanbeyan)

Receipts and Payments for the period ended 31st December 1967 from the Macedonian (Self Independent) Eastern Orthodox Church, Queanbeyan, New South Wales. (Note: Today this is the Macedonian Orthodox Church Sveti Prorok Ilija – St Prophet Elijah).

Archives from the Macedonian Orthodox Community of Melbourne and Victoria

Appeal from the Macedonian Orthodox Community of Melbourne and Victoria to all Macedonian emigrants in Australia, 1960.

Newspapers and magazines

Advertiser (Adelaide), 19 December 1950

Argus (Melbourne), 1927-1951

Army News (Darwin), 5 May 1943

Border Watch (Mt Gambier), 11 October 1930

Canberra Times, 27 April 1966

Dnevnik, (Skopje, Macedonia) 6 February 2015

Green Left Weekly (Sydney), 9 March 1994

Informativen Vesnik (Informative Newspaper), Macedonian Welfare Association of Port Kembla, 2 December 1989

The Janesville Daily Gazette, (Janesville, Wisconsin, USA), 10 November 1913

Kompas, Macedonian Welfare Association, (Port Kembla), 2005-2015

Makedonska Iskra, (Perth and Melbourne), 1946-1956

Makedonska Nacija, (Sweden), Issue 23

Makedonski Tsrkoven Vestnik (Izdanie na Makedonskata Pravoslavna Opshtina Sv. Giorgi), 6 August 1961

Northern Standard (Darwin) 21 June 1940

Nova Hrvatska (Sydney), No 4, 20 February 1977

Phoni tis Kastorias, (Kostur) 4 October 1959

Soccer News (Victorian Amateur Soccer Football Association – Melbourne), 1949-1950

Sydney Morning Herald, 6 January 1954

Sunday Times (Perth), 31 August 1947

Transpec Digest (Footscray), Spring 2012

Vesnik na Makedonskite Opshtini vo Avstralija (Perth), August 1982

Vesnik na Makedonskite Opshtini vo Avstralija (Perth), August 1983

Vjesti newspaper (Constantinople), 27 January 1910, Issue Number 61, Year XX,

The Canberra Times, 16 October 1965

The Poverty Bay Herald (New Zealand), 25 January 1905

The West Australian (Perth), 1931-1950

Western Argus (Perth), 2 January 1934

Interviews

Name	Year of birth	Place of birth	Place of interview	Date of interview
Ailakis, Peter	1960	Manjimup, Western Australia	Melbourne, Victoria	10 December 2014
Anastasovski, Mihailo	1934	Gorno Aglarci, Bitola, Macedonia (Republic)	Melbourne, Victoria	21 February 2015
Angelkov, Kosta	1934	Dambeni, Kostur, Macedonia (Aegean)	Perth, Western Australia	14 May 2015
Angelovic (Angelovski), Jim	1932	Dragosh, Bitola, Macedonia (Republic)	Geelong, Victoria	13 January 2014
Ashlakoff, Done	1940	Ofcharani, Lerin, Macedonia (Aegean)	Shepparton, Victoria	1 December 2013
Bogdanovski, Mitko	1907	Krivogashtani, Macedonia (Republic)	Melbourne, Victoria	27 January 2012
Bogdanovski, Viktor	1937	Lukovo, Struga, Macedonia (Republic)	Canberra, Australian Capital Territory	24 November 2013
Boskov, Peter	1935	Visheni, Kostur, Macedonia (Aegean)	Sydney, New South Wales	17 April 2014
Chulakovski, Sokrat	1950	Zgorzelec, Poland	Melbourne	22 April 2018
Constantinou, Nick	1959	Sale, Victoria	Melbourne, Victoria	8 December 2014
Damos, Alex	1945	Geraldton, Western Australia	Perth, Western Australia	12 May 2015
Damos, Victor	1960	Geraldton, Western Australia	Perth, Western Australia	16 May 2015
Dimov (nee Doikos Doikin), Cveta	1947	Statica, Kostur, Macedonia (Aegean)	Canberra, Australian Capital Territory	29 November 2013
Dimov, Done	1942	Statica, Kostur, Macedonia (Aegean)	Canberra, Australian Capital Territory	29 November 2013

Donelly (nee Ross), Shirley	1933	Casino, New South Wales	Crabbes Creek, New South Wales	13 November 2006
Eftimov, Kole	1924	Carev Dvor, Resen, Macedonia (Republic)	Bitola, Macedonia	20 March 2000
Georgopoulos, Victor	1967	Melbourne, Victoria	Melbourne, Victoria	10 December 2010
Giamov, Lazo	1928	Trnava, Lerin, Macedonia (Aegean)	Melbourne, Victoria	9 October 2009
Gochev, Risto	1932	Maala, Lerin, Macedonia (Aegean)	Melbourne, Victoria	30 June 2009
Goulopoulos (Gulev), Andrew	1940	Melbourne, Victoria	Melbourne, Victoria	8 May 2013
Kalcovski, Vancho	1942	Brajchino, Prespa, Macedonia (Republic)	Melbourne, Victoria	20 January 2017
Kalevich (Kalovski), Gogo	1930	Buenos Aeries, Argentina	Melbourne, Victoria	2 March 2013
Karajas (Karadzhov), John	1947	Perth, Western Australia	Perth, Western Australia	15 May 2015
Kirco (Kircov), Mitre	1920	Neret, Lerin, Macedonia (Aegean)	Sale, Victoria	7 June 2013
Mano, Manol	1962	Vrbnik, Korcha, Macedonia (Mala Prespa)	Melbourne, Victoria	4 October 2012
Kotchoff, Kosta	1927	Konomladi, Kostur, Macedonia (Aegean)	Melbourne, Victoria	8 April 2011 and 20 February 2016
Mechkaroff, Peter (Pandil)	1934	Kuchkoveni, Lerin, Macedonia (Aegean)	Shepparton, Victoria	12 December 2014
Milenko, Stan (Stavre)	1938	Dolno Kotori, Lerin, Macedonia (Aegean)	Perth, Western Australia	12 May 2015

Nitson, John	1940	Lagen, Lerin, Macedonia (Aegean)	Melbourne, Victoria	12 June 2013
Ognenov (Ognenis), Ilo (Lou)	1946	Bapchor, Kostur, Macedonia (Aegean)	Perth, Western Australia	15 May 2015
Pandov, Kosta	1932	Dolno Kotori, Lerin, Macedonia (Aegean)	Richmond, New South Wales	16 April 2014
Papas, Paul	1937	Lagen, Lerin, Macedonia (Aegean)	Melbourne, Victoria	31 October 2015
Paunovic (nee Sokleva), Katarina	1927	Klabuchishta, Lerin, Macedonia (Aegean)	Melbourne, Victoria	19 March 2019
Pavlevski, Bogdan	1934	Zheleznec, Demir Hisar, Macedonia (Republic)	Melbourne, Victoria	14 February 2015
Purcell (nee Turpin), Mary	1939	Perth, Western Australia	Perth, Western Australia	13 May 2015
Radevski, Cvetko	1928	Dragosh, Bitola, Macedonia (Republic)	Shepparton, Victoria	12 December 2014
Rendevski, Cane	1935	Dragosh, Bitola, Macedonia (Republic)	Geelong, Victoria	31 January 2013
Rendev, Vasil	1930	Dragosh, Bitola, Macedonia (Republic)	Shepparton, Victoria	12 December 2014
Rizmanovski, Kiril	1955	Ohrid, Macedonia (Republic)	Melbourne, Victoria	26 April 2013
Ruhfus (nee Stefanoff) Margaret	1951	Newcastle, New South Wales	Canberra, Australian Capital Territory	24 November 2013
Sarbinov (nee Spirova), Fania	1929	Neret, Lerin, Macedonia (Aegean)	Melbourne, Victoria	24 December 2006
Soklev, Chris	1944	Klabuchishta, Lerin, Macedonia (Aegean)	Melbourne, Victoria	25 May 2020
Spasevski, Stojan	1920	Graeshnica, Bitola, Macedonia (Republic)	Melbourne, Victoria	13 October 2006

Spirova, Velika	1911	Krpeshina, Lerin, Macedonia (Aegean)	Melbourne, Victoria	10 September 2008
Stefanoff, George	1938	Newcastle, New South Wales	Canberra, Australian Capital Territory	24 November 2013
Stergiou (nee Vosnacos/ Vosnacov), Christine	1931	Salmon Gums, Western Australia	Perth, Western Australia	14 May 2015
Stojanovski, Ilija	1923	Vrbeni, Lerin, Macedonia (Aegean)	Melbourne, Victoria	8 October 2008
Theodorovsky, Aleksandar	1923	Buf, Lerin, Macedonia (Aegean)	Melbourne, Victoria	20 June 2009
Tilev, Vasil	1954	Kradzhejevo, Gorna Dzhumaja Macedonia (Pirin)	Melbourne, Victoria	30 August 2012
Todevski, Riste	1957	Melbourne, Victoria	Melbourne, Victoria	2 March 2011
Trajcevski, Mendo	1953	Velushina, Bitola, Macedonia (Republic)	Wollongong, New South Wales	14 April 2014
Vasileva, Ana	1934	Egri-Dere, Drama, Macedonia (Aegean)	Melbourne, Victoria	12 February 2014
Veljanovski, Ilija	1936	Draslajca, Struga, Macedonia (Aegean)	Melbourne, Victoria	18 October 2009
Velov, Pavle	1939	Dolno Kotori, Lerin, Macedonia (Aegean)	Melbourne, Victoria	9 February 2009
Veloskey, Mick	1924	Gradche, Kostur, Macedonia (Aegean)	Sydney, New South Wales	15 April 2014

Unpublished materials

Angelkoff, Kosta, *Deinosta na edin emigrant* [Activities of an emigrant]

Angelkov, Kosta, Autobiography.

Batrouney, T.A., *Cradle of Orthodoxy: St Nicholas Antiochian Orthodox Church Melbourne Victoria*, unpublished paper, 2001.

Bogdanovski, Viktor, *Kratka Istorija za prvite Makedonski doselenici vo Kvinbejan* [A short history of the first Macedonian immigrants in Queanbeyan], 2009.

Delianov, Mitre,*Legendata na Selo Bapchor* [The Legend of Bapchor Village], Perth, 1976.

Dimov, Done, Autobiographical notes.

— *Staticheni vo Avstralija* [People from Statica in Australia].

Donnelly (nee Ross), Shirley, Autobiographical notes.

Factor, June, *Forgotten Soldiers: Aliens in the Australian Army's Employment Companies during World War II*, p. 2. http://www.yosselbirstein.org/pdf/eng/other/Forgotten_Soldiers.pdf

Glafchev, Alexander, *The Migrant Experience: From Village to Suburb*, University of South Australia, 1994. http://www.pollitecon.com/html/life/the_migrant_experience.htm

Jovanovski, Zoran,*The importance of cafes in Carlton and Fitzroy to settling migrants during the 1950s and 1960s was striking; in particular, the cultural significance of the Macedonian Social Club in Gertrude Street, Fitzroy, to Macedonian immigrants*, p. 6. (unpublished paper), www.unimelb.edu.au/infoserv/lee/htm/carlton_cafes.htm

Kapetanovski, John, Autobiographical notes (November 2011).

Kasovich (Kasovski), Ilo Untitled.

Kris, Betty, *A Study of the Slav-Macedonian Community in Adelaide*, South Australia, University of Adelaide, 1970, p. 9 (unpublished thesis).

Lazorov, Mara, *Life History of Kole Nedelkov Lazorov and his family*, Perth, Battye Library, Migrant Communities Archive.

Mapstone, James, *The Greek Macedonians of Shepparton: A study of immigrant assimilation in a rural area of Australia*, Australian National University, 1966.

Metkaroff, Peter (Pandil), Autobiographical notes.

Mitreska, Liljana, *The Macedonians in Rockdale - A Vivid Life*, Sydney, 2015.

Sarbinov, Stojan, Autobiographical data.

— Makedoncite vo Avstralija 1940-1988.

Sideris, Connie, Interview of Connie Sideris on 20 February 2007 for the Northbridge History Project.

Stewart (nee Kolupacev), Elizabeth, *Lexical Transference in the Speech of Macedonian English Bilingual Speakers in the Illawarra Region of NSW*, MA thesis, Macquarie University, 1995.

Vellios, Jim, Faded Memories - Life and Times of a Macedonian Villager, 2014. http://www.pollitecon.com/html/ebooks/Faded-Memories.pdf

Secondary Sources

Abadzhiev, G., editor, *Borbite vo Jugozapadna Makedonia pospomenite na Luka Dzherov i Lazar Dimitrov*, [Battles in south western Macedonia according to the memoirs of Luka Dzherov and Lazar Dimitrov], Drzhavno Knigoizdatelstvo na NR Makedonija, Skopje, 1952.

Achkoska, V., *Agrarno-Sopstvenickite odnoci, promeni i prosesi vo Makedonija 1944-1953*, [Agrarian Property Relations, Changes and Trends in Macedonia 1944-1953], Institut za Nacionalna Istorija, Skopje, 1998.

Allan Lovell and Associates Pty Ltd, *Fitzroy Urban Conservation Study Review*, Allan Lovell and Associates Pty Ltd, Melbourne, 1992.

Allbrook, M., editor, *Journeys of Hope (Six stories of family migration to western Australia 1937-1968)*, State Print, Perth, 1994.

Amnesty International, *Yugoslavia Prisoners of Conscience*, Amnesty International Publications, London, 1985.

Anastasovski, N., *The Contest for Macedonian Identity 1870-1912*, Pollitecon Publications, Sydney, 2008.

— 'The Arrival and Settlement of Macedonians in the Inner Western Suburbs of Melbourne', pp. 30-59, *Victorian Historical Journal*, Vol. 82 No.1 Royal Historical Society of Victoria, Melbourne, June 2011.

Andonov, V, *Makedoncite vo Avstralija* [The Macedonians in Australia], Kultura, Skopje, 1973.

Andonov-Poljanski, H.,*The Attitude of the USA Towards Macedonia*, Macedonian Review Editions, Skopje, 1983.

Andonov-Poljanski, H., editor, *Documents on the Struggle of the Macedonian People for Independence and a Nation-State*, Vol 11, University of 'Cyril and Methodius', Skopje, 1985.

Anon., *Na plovniot dzhin koj potonal so Titanik na 14 April godina imalo i Makedonci*, [There were also Macedonians that drowned with the sailing giant, the Titanic], www.makedonskanacija.mk, 24 May 2017.

Anon., *Dvajca Tresoncani zhrtvi na Titanik*, [Two people from Tresonche were sacrificed with the Titanic], www. makedonskanacija.mk, 8 February 2012.

Anon., *Galichki kashkaval na trpezata na brodot Titanik*, [Kashkaval from Galitchnik on the ship Titanic], www.makedonskanacija.mk, 27 January 2016.

Anon., *'Republichki Sekretarijat za vnatreshni raboti, Sluzhba za drzhavna bezbednost, odelenie na grad Skopje'* 10 April 1975, [Republic Secretariat for internal affairs, state security service, division for Skopje, 10 April 1971] www.makedonskanacija.mk

Association of Macedonians in Poland,*What Europe Has Forgotten: The Struggle of the Aegean Macedonians*, Report by the Association of Macedonians in Poland, Pollitecon Publications, 1992.

Birtles, B., *Exiles in the Aegean, A Personal Narrative of Greek Politics and Travel*, V. Gollancz, London, 1938.

Bivell, V., editor, *Macedonian Agenda*, Pollitecon Publications, Sydney, 1995.

Bistrichki, 'Why are we the Macedonians a separate nation', Fourth Congress of the Macedonian National Association of America, Detroit, 1934, pp. 74-82, *The Historical Truth (Documents, Studies, Resolutions, Appeals and Published Articles, 1896-1956*, Editors Pero Korobar and Orde Ivanovski, Kultura, Skopje, 1983.

Bozinoski, B. and Krstevski, V., *Chetvrta Generacija* [Fourth Generation], Macedonian Australian Association of Culture and Human Rights, Newcastle, 2012.

Brailsford, H.N., *Macedonia: Its Races and Their Future*, Methuen & Co, London, 1906.

Carnegie Endowment for International Peace, *Report of the International Commission to Inquire into the Causes and Conduct of the Balkan Wars*, Published by the Endowment, Washington, 1914.

Cekutkov, G., Article titled *Krsto Malikov* [Krsto Malikov], Makedonska Nacija website. www.makedonskanacija.mk, 15 April 2015.

Central Committee of the Movement for Liberation and Unification of Macedonia, *The Macedonian Migrants in Australia and Access Radio*, Melbourne, August 1975.

Chapovski, I.,*The Macedonian Orthodox Church of St. George*, York Press, Melbourne, 1992.

Christowe, S.,*This is my country*, Carrick & Evans, New York, 1938.

Clogg, R.A., *A Concise History of Greece*, Cambridge University Press, London, 1992.

Clyne, M. and Kipp, S., *Tiles in a multilingual mosaic – Macedonian, Filipino and Somali in Melbourne*, Australian National University, Pacific Linguistics, Canberra, 2006.

Cvetanoski, V., *Pechalbarstvoto Makedonska Sudbina* [Pechalba a Macedonian Fate], Iris, Struga, 2012.

Danforth, L.,*The Macedonian Conflict – Ethnic Nationalism in a Transnational World*, Princeton University Press, Princeton, 1995.

De Belle, E.B., *La Macedoine et les Macedoniens* [Macedonia and the Macedonians], Librairie Armand Colin, Paris, 1922.

Dimitrijevski, M., '*Makedonskoto iselenishtvo vo Amerika videno niz analiza na trudot na Gjorche Petrov: "Emigrantskoto dvizhenje za Amerika vo Makedonia"* [Macedonian emigres in America as analysed by Gjorche Petrov], pp. 289-297, from *Prv megunaroden nauchen sobir "iselenishtvoto od Makedonija od pojavata do denes"*, [First international gathering – emigration from Macedonia from its beginning] Agencija za Iselenistvoto na Republika Makedonija, Skopje, 2001.

Draganoff, P., *La Macedonie et les Macedoniens,* Paris, 1922.

Durham, M.,*The Burden of the Balkans*, Nelson, London, 1905.

Dzhambazovski, K., editor, *Gradja za istoriju Makedonskog naroda (iz arhiva Srbije)* [Material on the History of the Macedonian people (from the Serbian Archive)], Vol IV, Book III (1888-1889), Prosveta, Belgrade, 1987.

Dzhikov, S., *Progoneti* [Persecuted], Studentski Zbor, Skopje, 1991.

Eklund, E.K., *Steel Town: The Making and Breaking of Port Kembla*, Melbourne University Press, Melbourne, 2002.

Friedman, V., 'The Macedonian Dialects of Albania', *Slavic and East European Journal*, Vol. 55, n.4, American Association of Teachers of Slavic and East European Languages, 2011.

Gjorgiev, D., *Turski Dokumenti za Istorijata na Makedonija, Popisi od XIX vek* [Turkish Documents regarding the History of Macedonia, Census' in the 19th century], Book II, Arhiv na Makedonija - Matica Makedonska, Skopje, 1997.

— *Turski Dokumenti za Istorijata na Makedonija, Popisi od XIX vek* [Turkish Documents regarding the History of Macedonia, Census' in the 19th century], Book III, Arhiv na Makedonija - Matica Makedonska, Skopje, 1998.

Gorgiev, T., *Po Tragite Na Minatoto* [Tracing the past], Socialen Borec, Skopje, 1967.

Halpern, J., *The Pecalba Tradition in Macedonia: A Case Study*, University of Massachusetts, Anthropology Department Faculty Publication Series. Paper 58, Amherst, 1975.

Harper, J., 'The Pecalbars of Gippsland: Macedonian Farm Workers around Kernot in the 1930s', pp.2-9, *Gippsland Heritage Journal*, Number 28, Kapana Press, Briagolong, 2004.

Hay, R., 'Post war soccer in Geelong', pp. 1-12, *Investigator*, June 1994, (Geelong Historical Society).

Head, L., Muir, P. & Hampel, E., 'Australian Backyard Gardens and the Journey of Migration', pp. 326-347, *Geographical Review*, 2004.

Hill, P., *The Macedonians in Australia*, Hesperian Press, Perth, 1989.

— *Macedonians* from *The Australian People - An Encyclopaedia of the Nation, Its People and their Origins*, Jupp, J Ed. Angus and Robertson, 1988 (repr. 2001).

Jotevski, V., 'Preselbite na Makedoncite od Pirinskiot del na Makedonija 1948-1968' [Migrations of the Macedonians in the

Pirin part of Macedonia 1948-1968], pp. 145-153, *Iselenishtvoto od Makedonija od Pojavata do denes* [Emigres from Macedonia from emergence to today], Agencija za Iselenishtvoto na Republika Makedonija, Skopje 2004.

Karoski, S., *The Macedonian Community Profile*, for the Macedonian Australian Welfare Association of NSW, Ethnic Affairs Commission of NSW, 1983.

Karpat, K., 'The Ottoman Emigration to America 1860-1914', pp. 179-209, *International Journal of Middle East Studies*, Vol 17, Cambridge University Press, 1985.

Katardzhiev, I., *Makedonija i Makledoncite vo svetot* [Macedonia and the Macedonians around the world], Matica Makedonska, Skopje, 1996.

Katardzhiev, I., editor, *Spomeni - S.Arsov, P. Klashev, L. Dzherov, G.P. Hristov, A. Andreev, G. Papanchev, L. Dimitrov.* [Memoirs – S. Arson, P. Klashev, L. Dzherov, G.P. Hristov, A. Andreev, G. Papanchev, L. Dimitrov], Kultura, Skopje, 1997.

Konstantinov, D., *Pechalbarstvo* [Pechalba], Nauchno Drushtvo Bitola, Bitola, 1964.

Korobar, P. & Ivanovski, O., editors, *The Historical Truth (Documents, Studies, Resolutions, Appeals and Published Articles) 1896-1956*, Kultura, Skopje 1983.

Lalich, W., 'Collective action of 'Others' in Sydney', *Journal of Multidisciplinary International Studies*, Vol. 3, No. 1, UTSePress, University of Technology Sydney, January 2006.

Macedonian Welfare Workers Network of Victoria, *From War to Whittlesea – Oral Histories of Macedonian Child Refugees*, Pollitecon Publications, 1999.

Marwick, B., *Stories of Old Wanneroo - As told to Bill Marwick*, Ultra Printing Services, Perth, 2002.

— *The Times of Wanneroo - As told to Bill Marwick*, Wanneroo and Districts Historical Society, Perth, 2005.

Merakovsky, D., *Istorija na Izmameni Vernici* [A History of Deceived Parishioners], Self-published, Melbourne, 2007.

Miovski, T., 'Makedonsko Ognishtevo Manjimup' [Macedonian Hearth Manjimup], p. 84, *Makedonsko Iselenichki Almanac 1988*

[Macedonian Emigrants Almanac 1988], Matica na Iselenicite od Makedonija, Skopje, pp. 84-86.

— *Avstralija i Makedonskite Doselenici* [Australia and the Macedonian immigrants], Misla, Skopje, 1971.

— *Makedoncite vo Zapadna Avstralija* [The Macedonians in Western Australia], Zdruzenie na decata begalci od Egejskiot del na Makedonija, Skopje, 1999.

Mooney, S., 'Naming Mount Alexander', *Victorian Historical Journal* Vol. 62, Nos. 3 & 4. Royal Historical Society of Victoria, December 1991/March 1992.

Nedelkovski, B., 'Kumurdzhilnici vo seloto Virovo-Zheleznik' [Coal gatherers in the village Virovo-Zheleznik], pp.169-176, *Etnolog* [Ethnology], No 4-5, Skopje 1994 (Review of the Ethnological Association of Macedonia).

Obrebski, J., *Ritual and Social Structure on a Macedonian Village*, Research Report No. 16, Department of Anthropology, University of Massachusetts, Amherst, May 1977.

O'Brien, L., 'The Macedonian Community', pp.248-252, *Fitzroy, Melbourne's First Suburb*, Hyland House, Melbourne, 1989.

Ognenova-Michova, L. & Mitsou-Lazaridis, K., *A Girl from Neret*, Pollitecon Publications, 2006.

Ortakovski, V., *Minorities in the Balkans*, Transnational Publishers, New York, 2000.

Passios, T., 'Greece Exploiting St. Cyril and Methodius for Political Aims', *UMD Voice*, Vol VIII, Winter Edition, Washington, 2010.

Petrovska, P., 'Assimilation and the Public and Private Identity of Macedonians: A Dialectical Expose', pp. 135-84, in Victor Bivell, ed., *Macedonian Agenda*, Pollitecon Publications, 1995.

Popov, C. & Radin, M., *Contemporary Greek Government Policy on the Macedonian Issue and Discriminatory Practices in Breach of International Law*, Central Organisational Committee for Macedonian Human Rights, Australian Sub-Committee, Lakeside Press, Melbourne, 1989.

Price, C.A., *Southern Europeans in Australia*, Melbourne University Press, Melbourne, 1963.

Radev, S., *Rani Spomeni,* [Early Memories], Bulgarski Pisatel, Sofia, 1967.

Reed, J., *War in Eastern Europe – Travels through the Balkans in 1915*, Phoenix, London, (1916) 1994.

Rossos, A., 'Incompatible Allies: Greek Communism and Macedonian Nationalism in the Civil War in Greece, 1943-1949', pp. 42-76, *The Journal of Modern History*, Vol 69, No 1 (March 1997), The University of Chicago Press.

— *Macedonia and the Macedonians – A History*, Hoover Institution Press, Stanford, 2008.

Sapurma, K & Petrovska, P., *Children of the Bird Goddess*, Pollitecon Publications, 1997.

Seraphinoff, M. and Stefou, C., *This land we do not give – a history of Macedonian resistance to foreign occupation*, Nettle Hollow with the assistance of Aardvark Global, Shtip, 2008.

Shea, J., *Macedonia and Greece – the struggle to define a new Balkan nation*, McFarland, Jefferson, 1997.

Siljanovski, D., *Makedonija Kako Prirodna i Ekonomska Celina* [Macedonia as a Natural and Economic Unit], Makedonski Nauchen Institut, Sofia, 1945.

Simovski, T.H., *Atlas of the Inhabited Places of Aegean Macedonia*, Turk Tarih Kurumu Basimevi, Ankara, 1999.

Stefov, R., *Short History of the Macedonian People*, National Institution – Library "Grigor Prlichev", Ohrid, 2007.

Stojkov, S., 'Makedonskoto Malcinstvo vo Bugaria od priznavajne kon negirajne 1948-1989', [The Macedonian Minority in Bulgaria from recognition to negation 1948-1989], pp. 67-85, *Godishen Zbornik 2015/2016* [Annual Review 2015/2016], Universitet Goce Delchev, Shtip, Year 6, Vol VI.

Thom, L., *The Places Migrant Women Found Work in Wollongong 1943-1990*, Migration Heritage Project, Wollongong's Migration Heritage Thematic Study, 'Places Project'.

Thomas, M., *A Multicultural Landscape, National Parks and the Macedonian Experience*, NSW National Parks and Wildlife Service and Pluto Press Australia, Sydney, 2001

Todoroska, K., *Makedoncite vo Albania (1912-1991)*, [Macedonians in Albania (1912-1991)], Menora, Skopje, 2014. Todorovski,

G., *Malorekanskiot Predel* [The Mala Reka District], Institut za Nacionalna Istorija, Skopje, 1970.

Tomov. J., *Mojot Pridones za Makedonija (Preku aktivnostite vo DOOM, VMRO-DPMNE i AMKCP vo diasporata od 1970 - 2014)*, [My contribution for Macedonia (activities with DOOM, VMRO-DPMNE and AMKCP in the diaspora from 1970 to 2014)], Self-published, Brisbane, 2014.

Topuzoski, K., *Pitu Guli (1865-1903) Zhivot i Potoa* [Pitu Guli (1865-1903) Life and Beyond], Deset Dena Kushevska Republika, Krushevo, 1995.

Trajcevski, M., 'Macedonian Migration to the Illawara', pp 6-10, *Ties with Tradition*, Powerhouse Museum, Sydney, 2009.

Trajceski, V., *Najsilniot Makedonec - Todor Jurukot* [The Strongest Macedonian - Todor Jurukot], Self-published, Melbourne, 1995.

Trajkovska, I., *Vo Skopskoto selo Chucher, vo potraga na nesekojdnevna prikazna*, [In the Skopje village Chucher, in search of an unusual story]. The article was first published in the newspaper *Vecer*, but has been sourced from www.makedonskanacija.mk

Trenevski, M., *Nepoznata Juzhna Zemja* [Unknown Southern Land], Matica Makedonska, Skopje, 1992.

Trpovski, I., '11-ti Oktomvri Svecheno Proslaven vo Sydney' [11 October Formally Celebrated in Sydney], pp. 20-21, *Povod - Spisanie za literature, kultura i prosveta* [Povod - Periodical for literature, culture and education], Drushtvo Grigor Prlichev, Sydney, November 1985.

Zekulich, M., *Costa's New World - The Life story of Costa Kapinkoff*, Scott Print, Perth, 2007,

Zografski, D., editor, *Avstriski Dokumenti 1905-1906* [Austrian Documents 1905-1906], Vol I, Arhiv na Makedonija, Skopje, 1977.

Place Names

All Macedonian villages mentioned in this book that are under Greek rule are recorded by their original Macedonian names, which are the names used by Macedonians. The following list is of the original Macedonian village name and the Hellenised name, which was forced upon the Macedonians. The list also includes larger towns/cities, regions as well as some rivers.

Original Macedonian name	**Region**	**Hellenised version**
Armenoro	Lerin	Armenohori
Armensko	Lerin	Alonas
Asanovo	Lerin	Mesohori
Bapchor	Kostur	Pimenikon
Banica	Lerin	Vevi
Bistrica (River)		Haliacmon
Bitush	Lerin	Parorion
Brescheni	Kostur	Avgi
Breznitsa	Kostur	Vatohorion
Buf	Lerin	Akritas
Chetirok	Kostur	Mesopotamya
Dambeni	Kostur	Dendrohori
Dolno Kotori	Lerin	Kato Idrusa
Drenoveni	Kostur	Kranionas
Dzhupanishta	Kostur	Anolevki
Pazar/Enidzhe Vardar		Giannitsa
German	Lerin	Agios Germanos
Gabresh	Kostur	Gavros
Gorno Kleshtina	Lerin	Ano Kline
Grazhdeno	Kostur	Vronderon
Gradche	Kostur	Ftelia
Halkidik/a		Halkidiki
Kabasnica	Lerin	Proti

Kalenik	Lerin	Kaleniki
Klabuchishta	Lerin	Poliplatanos
Konomladi	Kostur	Makrohori
Kosinec	Kostur	Jeropigi
Kostur		Kastoria
Kozhani	Kozani	
Krpeshina	Lerin	Atrapos
Kuchkoveni	Lerin	Perasma
Kukush		Kilkis
Labanitsa	Kostur	Agios Dimitrios
Lagen	Lerin	Triandafilla
Lerin		Florina
Maala	Lerin	Tropeuhos
Mesta (River)		Nestos
Mokreni	Kostur	Variko
Negochani	Lerin	Niki
Neret	Lerin	Polipotamon/s
Nevoljani	Lerin	Skopija
Ofcharani	Lerin	Meliti
Orovo	Kostur	Piksos
Opsirina	Lerin	Etnikon
Oshchima	Kostur	Trigonon
Pilkati	Kostur	Monopilon
Pozdivishta	Kostur	Halara
Rudari	Kostur	Ekalitea
Rula	Lerin	Kotas/Katohori
Setoma	Kostur	Kefalarion/Kafalari
Shestevo	Kostur	Sidirohori
Smerdesh	Kostur	Krustalopigi
Solun		Salonika/Thessaloniki
Statica	Kostur	Melas
Struma (River)		Strymonas

Sveta Gora		Mount Athos
Sveta Petka	Lerin	Agia Paraskevi
Trebino	Kaljari	Kardia
Trcije	Lerin	Trivunon
Trnava	Lerin	Prasinon
Turije	Kostur	Korifi
Vardar River		Axios River
Visheni	Kostur	Vissinia
Voden		Edessa

Index of Names